Bronze sculpture, "El corazón del tiempo (The Heart of Time)" by Sergio Bustamante, greeting visitors at the entrance to the authors' home

Balloon vendors on the zócalo in Oaxaco

Pyramid of the Sun at Teotihuacán

On parade in Mexico City

White-washed stucco houses in Taxco

La Parroquia in San Miguel de Allende

Museum Gene Byron in Guanajuato

Lagunilla ("Thieves") Market in Mexico City   *Street vendors at the zócalo in Mexico Cit*

The many treasures found in shopping Mexico City's unique markets

Entrance to the Las Hadas Resort in Manzanillo

Latin American Tower in Mexico City   *West coast Mexico near Manzanillo*

Santa Prisca Parish Church in Taxco

Street scene in San Miguel de Allende

Street vendor in Tlaquapaque

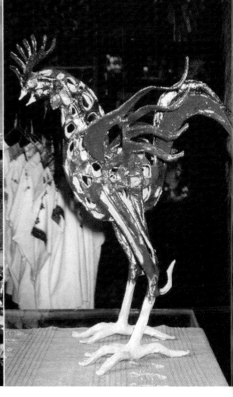

Wire & papier-mâché sculpture by Saulo Moren

Folk art at Galería Indigo in Oaxaca

Master coppersmith Margarito Garcia Nunez in
Santa Clara del Cobra, Michoacán

olk art at Vincente Hernandez Vasquez in
San Martin Tilcajete, Oaxaca

Folk art at Victor Artes Populares Mexicanos
in Mexico City

Master coppersmith Felipe Peréz Orneles at his workshop in Michoacán

Master ceramicist Luiz Manuel Morales Gámez in his workshop in Tzintzuntzan, Michoacán

Painting Abebrijes in Arrazolo, Oaxaco

Painted furniture production in Econgarícuraro, Michoacán

Praise for the Impact Guides

The World's Only Travel-Shopping Series

"YOU LEARN MORE ABOUT A PLACE you are visiting when Impact is pointing the way." – **The Washington Post**

"THE DEFINITIVE GUIDE to shopping in Asia." – **Arthur Frommer,** The Arthur Frommer Almanac of Travel

"THE BEST travel book I've ever read." – Kathy Osiro, **TravelAge West**

"AN EXCELLENT, EXHAUSTIVE, AND FASCINATING look at shopping in the East . . . it's difficult to imagine a shopping tour without this pocket-size book in hand." – **Travel & Leisure**

"BOOKS IN THE SERIES help travelers recognize quality and gain insight to local customs." – **Travel-Holiday**

"THE BEST GUIDE I've seen on shopping in Asia. If you enjoy the sport, you'll find it hard to put down . . . They tell you not only the where and what of shopping but the important how, and all in enormous but easy-to-read detail." – **Seattle Post-Intelligencer**

"ONE OF THE BEST GUIDEBOOKS of the season – not just shopping strategies, but a Baedeker to getting around . . . definitely a quality work. Highly recommended." – **Arkansas Democrat**

"WILL WANT TO LOOK INTO . . . has shopping strategies and travel tips about making the most of a visit to those areas. The book covers Asia's shopping centers, department stores, emporiums, factory outlets, markets and hotel shopping arcades where visitors can find jewelry, leather goods, woodcarvings, textiles, antiques, cameras, and primitive artifacts." – **Chicago Tribune**

"FULL OF SUGGESTIONS. The art of bartering, including everyday shopping basics are clearly defined, along with places to hang your hat or lift a fork." – **The Washington Post**

"A WONDERFUL GUIDE . . . filled with essential tips as well as a lot of background information . . . a welcome addition on your trip." – **Travel Book Tips**

"WELL ORGANIZED AND COMPREHENSIVE BOOK. A useful companion for anyone planning a shopping spree in Asia." – **International Living**

"*OFFERS SOME EXTREMELY VALUABLE INFORMATION* and *advice about what is all too often a spur-of-the-moment aspect of your overseas travel.*" – **Trip & Tour**

"*A MORE UNUSUAL, PRACTICAL GUIDE* than most and is no mere listing of convenience stores abroad . . . contains useful tips on bargaining in Asia . . . country-specific tips are some of the most valuable chapters of the guidebook, setting it apart from others which may generalize upon Asia as a whole, or focus upon the well-known Hong Kong shopping pleasures.*" – **The Midwest Book Review**

"*I LOVED THE BOOK!* Why didn't I have this book two months ago! . . A valuable guide . . . very helpful for the first time traveler in Asia . . . worth packing in the suitcase for a return visit.*" – Editor, **Unique & Exotic Travel Reporter**

"*VERY USEFUL, PERFECTLY ORGANIZED*. Finally a guide that combines Asian shopping opportunities with the tips and know-how to really get the best buys.*" – **National Motorist**

"*INFORMATION-PACKED PAGES* point out where the best shops are located, how to save time when shopping, and where and when to deal . . . You'll be a smarter travel shopper if you follow the advice of this new book.*" – **AAA World**

"*DETAILED, AND RELEVANT, EVEN ABSORBING* in places . . . the authors know their subject thoroughly, and the reader can benefit greatly from their advice and tips. They go a long way to removing any mystery or uneasiness about shopping in Asia by the neophyte.*" – **The Small Press Book Review**

WHAT SEASONED TRAVELERS SAY, INCLUDING STORIES THAT CHANGED LIVES

"*IMMENSELY USEFUL* . . . thanks for sharing the fruits of your incredibly thorough research. You saved me hours of time and put me in touch with the best.*" – **C.N.**, DeKalb, Illinois

"*FABULOUS!* I've just returned from my third shopping trip to Southeast Asia in three years. This book, which is now wrinkled, torn, and looking much abused, has been my bible for the past three years. All your suggestions (pre-trip) and information was so great. When I get ready to go again, my 'bible,' even though tattered and torn, will accompany me again! Thanks again for all your wonderful knowledge, and for sharing it!*" – **D.P., Havertown, Pennsylvania**

"*I LOVE IT*. I've read a lot of travel books, and of all the books of this nature, this is the best I've ever read. Especially for first timers, the how-to information is invaluable.*" – **A.K.**, Portland, Oregon

"*THE BEST TRAVEL BOOK I'VE EVER READ*. Believe me, I know my travel books!*" – **S.T.**, Washington, DC

"*MANY MANY THANKS for your wonderful, useful travel guide! You have done a tremendous job. It is so complete and precise and full of neat info.*" – **K.H.**, Seattle, Washington

"*FABULOUS BOOK! I just came back from Hong Kong, Thailand, and Singapore and found your book invaluable. Every place you recommended I found wonderful quality shopping. Send me another copy for my friend in Singapore who was fascinated with it.*" – **M.G.**, Escondido, California

"*THIS IS MY FIRST FAN LETTER TO A BOOK . . . you made our trip to Indonesia more special than I can ever say. I not only carried it in my backpack every day, I shared it with everyone I met, including a friend in Hong Kong, who liked it so much he kept it and I had to go out and buy another copy for myself when I got back stateside. The book taught us the customs, and through your teachings on how to bargain, I would even draw crowds to watch the Westerner bargain, and some wonderful chats after-wards, always starting off with 'You good bargainer. Where you from?' It was a wonderful trip and we credit your book for making it so. Thank you from my husband and myself, and everyone else we shared your book with.*" – **N.H.**, New York, New York

"*YOU SAVED ME . . . hurry up with the next book so I can find out what I did wrong in Burma!*" – **N.H.**, Chiang Mai, Thailand

"*I FURNISHED MY HOME IN FLORIDA using your wonderful books. What countries are you doing next?*" – **A.A.**, New York City

"*I WANT YOU TO KNOW HOW MUCH I ENJOYED YOUR BOOK. Like many people, I picked up a ton of guide books to China before we took off on our trip in May. However, yours was totally unique, and it was not until we had finished our trip that I fully appreciated everything you covered. It was also the only guidebook I took with us. Your book was the only one that mentioned the Painter's Village in Chongquing. When we arrived in Chongquing early in the morning, our guide told me the village was included in the tour, but several people wanted to skip it and go to the zoo. Fortunately, I was able to lobby the many art lovers on the tour by showing them what you had to say about the village and we did end up visiting it. It was a lovely day and the flowers were in bloom in the gardens surrounding the village. We were greeted warmly and enjoyed visiting some of the artists. I purchased two numbered prints and, although I did not meet the artist, I did get his business card. Once home, the prints were framed and I took a picture of them and wrote to the artist to see what he could tell me about them. Imagine my surprise when several weeks later I received an e-mail from him. His mother and father, both famous artists, lived in the village and his mother had forwarded my letter to their son who now lives in Tokyo. He is a well known illustrator . . . We have been corresponding by e-mail for nearly a year and I have been helping him with his English and in doing his website in English . . . We are looking forward to the day when we can have him visit us in California. Thank you for leading us to one of the highlights of Chongquing for without that experi-ence we would not have found a new and valued friend who has taught us much about China and life under Mao.*" – **C.S.**, California

"I'VE USED YOUR BOOKS FOR YEARS – earlier, the book on shopping in Thailand was wonderful and more recently your best of India has been very useful." – **S.M.**, Prince George, British Columbia

"I WOULD JUST LIKE TO SAY HOW MUCH I ENJOY YOUR SERIES. I have been an avid shopper and traveler for many years and it has often been difficult finding even a decent chapter on shopping, let alone an entire book. Your guides are a wonderful contribution to the industry." – **L.C.**, Honolulu, Hawaii

"GREAT! I followed your advice in Bangkok and Hong Kong and it was great. Thanks again." – **B.G.** , Los Angeles, California

"WE ADORE ASIA! We like it better than any other part of the world . . We have copies of your earlier editions and they are our 'Asian Bibles.' We also want to compliment you on doing such a masterful research job, especially on what to buy and where. Thanks to you we have some beautiful and treasured pieces from Asia. We could not have done it without your books." – **L.C.**, Palm Beach, Florida

"WE TOOK YOUR BOOK (to China) and had to concur with everything you said. We could hardly believe that 80-90% discounts were in order, but we soon found out that they were!! The Friendship Stores were everything you described. Many thanks for the book, it certainly was a help." – **L.G.**, Adelaide, Australia

"AFTER REVIEWING MANY TRAVEL GUIDES, I chose this book (China) to buy because it gave me not only insight to the same cities I am about to tour, but the how to's as well. With limited time in each city, I can go directly to the "best of the best" in accommodations, restaurants, sightseeing, entertaining, and shopping. It has also supplied me with advice on how to bargain!" – **an Amazon.com buyer**

"WE LOVED THE GUIDE. It's wonderful (Rio and São Paulo). We don't have anything like this in São Paulo." – **M.M**, São Paulo, Brazil

"LOVE YOUR GUIDE to India. Thanks so much." – **B.P.**, Minneapolis, Minnesota

"THANK YOU so much for the wonderful shopping recommendations on Johannesburg and Namibia. I did want to let you know how grateful we were to have your recommendations with us." – **M.S.**, Los Angeles

"I JUST WANTED TO THANK YOU for your shopping guide to Vietnam and Cambodia. We just spent our month-long honeymoon in Vietnam and it was very helpful to have read your book and to use it as a reference as we went along." – **H.F.**, San Francisco

"A MUST HAVE read for our travel group to Vietnam." – **S.B.**, Maryland

"YOU TWO ARE AMAZING! You have both added so much to our various travels by introducing us to places we would never see on our own. Thank you!" – **C.N.**, DeKalb, Illinois

The Treasures and
Pleasures of Mexico

By Ron & Caryl Krannich, Ph.Ds

TRAVEL AND INTERNATIONAL BOOKS

Best Resumes and CVs for International Jobs
The Complete Guide to International Jobs and Careers
Directory of Websites for International Jobs
International Jobs Directory
Jobs for Travel Lovers
Mayors and Managers in Thailand
Politics of Family Planning Policy in Thailand
Shopping and Traveling in Exotic Asia
Shopping in Exotic Places
Shopping in the Exotic South Pacific
Travel Planning on the Internet
Treasures and Pleasures of Australia
Treasures and Pleasures of China
Treasures and Pleasures of Egypt
Treasures and Pleasures of Hong Kong
Treasures and Pleasures of India
Treasures and Pleasures of Indonesia
Treasures and Pleasures of Italy
Treasures and Pleasures of Morocco and Tunisia
Treasures and Pleasures of Mexico
Treasures and Pleasures of Paris and the French Riviera
Treasures and Pleasures of Rio and São Paulo
Treasures and Pleasures of Santa Fe, Taos, and Albuquerque
Treasures and Pleasures of Singapore and Bali
Treasures and Pleasures of Singapore and Malaysia
Treasures and Pleasures of Southern Africa
Treasures and Pleasures of Thailand and Myanmar
Treasures and Pleasures of Turkey
Treasures and Pleasures of Vietnam and Cambodia

BUSINESS AND CAREER BOOKS AND SOFTWARE

101 Dynamite Answers to Interview Questions
101 Secrets of Highly Effective Speakers
201 Dynamite Job Search Letters
America's Top 100 Jobs for People Without a Four-Year Degree
America's Top Internet Job Sites
Best Jobs for the 21st Century
Change Your Job, Change Your Life
The Complete Guide to International Jobs and Careers
The Complete Guide to Public Employment
The Directory of Federal Jobs and Employers
Discover the Best Jobs for You!
Dynamite Cover Letters
Dynamite Networking for Dynamite Jobs
Dynamite Resumes
Dynamite Salary Negotiations
Dynamite Tele-Search
The Educator's Guide to Alternative Jobs and Careers
Find a Federal Job Fast!
From Air Force Blue to Corporate Gray
From Army Green to Corporate Gray
From Navy Blue to Corporate Gray
Get a Raise in 7 Days
High Impact Resumes and Letters
No One Will Hire Me!
Interview for Success
Job Hunting Guide
Job Interview Tips for People With Not-So-Hot Backgrounds
Job-Power Source and *Ultimate Job Source* (software)
Jobs and Careers With Nonprofit Organizations
Military Resumes and Cover Letters
Moving Out of Education
Moving Out of Government
Re-Careering in Turbulent Times
Resumes & Job Search Letters for Transitioning Military Personnel
Savvy Interviewing
Savvy Networker
Savvy Resume Writer

IMPACT GUIDES

THE TREASURES
AND PLEASURES OF

Mexico

BEST OF THE BEST IN
TRAVEL AND SHOPPING

RON AND CARYL KRANNICH, PH.DS

IMPACT PUBLICATIONS

MANASSAS PARK, VA

Photos: Cover photos by Ron and Caryl Krannich. Text photos taken by Ron and Caryl Krannich and Tom and Nancy Dungan.

Warning/Liability/Warranty: The authors and publisher have made every attempt to provide the reader with accurate, timely, and useful information. However, some information will inevitably change. The information presented here is for reference purposes only. The authors and publisher make no claims that using this information will guarantee the reader a trouble-free trip. The authors and publisher shall not be liable for any losses or damages incurred in the process of following the advice in this book. For more information on this issue, see the disclaimer on page xxii.

ISBN: 1 -57023-181-8

Library of Congress: 2003116093

Publisher: For information on Impact Publications, including current and forthcoming publications, authors, press kits, related websites, online bookstore, and submission requirements, visit the left navigation bar on the front page of www.impactpublica tions.com

Publicity/Rights: For information on publicity, author interviews, and subsidary rights, contact the Media Relations Department: Tel. 703-361-7300, Fax 703-335-9486, or email info@impactpublica tions.com.

Sales/Distribution: Bookstore sales are handled through Impact's trade distributor: National Book Network, 15200 NBN Way, Blue Ridge Summit, PA 17214, Tel. 1-800-462-6420. All other sales and distribution inquiries should be directed to the publisher: Sales Department, IMPACT PUBLICATIONS, 9104 Manassas Drive, Suite N, Manassas Park, VA 20111-5211, Tel. 703-361-7300, Fax 703-335-9486, or email: info@impactpublications.com.

Designed and formatted by Cortney Kreer.

Contents

Liabilities and Warranties

WHILE WE HAVE ATTEMPTED to provide accurate information, please keep in mind that names, addresses, phone and fax numbers, e-mails, and website URLs do change, and shops, restaurants, and hotels do move, go out of business, or change ownership and management. Such changes are constant facts of life in ever-changing Mexico. While we have included as much contact information as possible, e-mail addresses and websites are notoriously unreliable in Mexico since many individuals and companies fail to maintain such contact information from year to year. We regret any inconvenience such changes may cause to your travel and shopping plans.

Inclusion of shops, restaurants, hotels, and other hospitality providers in this book in no way implies guarantees nor endorsements by either the authors or the publisher. Recommendations are provided solely for your reference. The honesty and reliability of shops can best be ensured by **you**. It's okay to be a little paranoid when travel-shopping in Mexico. Indeed, always ask the right questions, request proper receipts and documents, use credit cards, take photos, and observe the 29 key shopping rules we outline in Chapter 3 (see pages 49-57) as well as on our companion website: www.ishoparoundtheworld.com.

The Treasures and Pleasures of Mexico provides numerous tips on how you can best experience a trouble-free adventure. As in any unfamiliar place or situation, and regardless of how trustworthy strangers may appear, the watchwords are always the same – *"watch your wallet!"* If it seems too good to be true, it probably is. Any *"unbelievable deals"* should be treated as such. In Mexico, as elsewhere in the world, there is no such thing as a free lunch. Everything has a cost. Just make sure you don't pay dearly by making unnecessary shopping mistakes!

Preface

WELCOME TO ANOTHER Impact Guide that explores the many unique treasures and pleasures of shopping and traveling in one of the most intriguing destinations in the Americas – Mexico. Join us as we explore this country's fascinating markets, shops, galleries, and artisan towns as well as visit its top restaurants, fine hotels, and other pleasures of travel. We'll put you in touch with the best of the best these places have to offer visitors. We'll take you to popular tourist destinations, but we won't linger long, since lifestyle shopping is our travel passion – combining great shopping with terrific dining, hotels, resorts, and sightseeing. If you follow us to the end, you'll discover a whole new dimension to both travel and shopping. If you join us in exploring our 13 travel-shopping destinations, you'll learn there is a lot more to Mexico, and travel in general, than taking tours, visiting popular sites, and acquiring an unwelcome weight gain attendant with new on-the-road dining habits.

Exciting Mexico offers wonderful experiences for those who know what to look for, where to go, and how to properly travel and shop major destinations in this fascinating country. While Mexico's travel image is most frequently associated with visiting museums, archaelogical sites, historic buildings, and beaches and participating in outdoor activities and festivals, for us Mexico is an important shopping destination with talented artists and craftspeople who produce unique art, jewelry, ceramics, textiles, folk art, leather goods, and handicrafts in the midst of excellent restaurants, hotels, and sightseeing. Mexico's people, products, sights, and sounds have truly enriched our lives.

If you are familiar with our other Impact Guides, you know this will not be another standard descriptive travel guide to history, culture, and sightseeing in Mexico. Our approach to travel is very different. As you will see in Chapters 2 and 3, this is a how-to book on travel and shopping. We operate from a particular people and product perspective, and we frequently show our attitude rather than just present you with the sterile "travel facts." While we seek good travel value, we're not budget travelers who will take you along the low road to Mexico. We've been there, done that at one stage in our lives, and found it to be an interesting learning experience. If that's the way you want to go, you'll find several guidebooks on budget travel to Mexico as well as a whole travel industry geared toward servicing budget travelers, backpackers, and campers with everything from cheap hostels to Internet cafés. At the same time, we're not obsessed with local history, culture, and sightseeing. We get just enough history and sightseeing to make our travels interesting rather than obsessive. Accordingly, we include very little on history and sightseeing, because they are not our main focus; we also assume you have that information covered from other resources. When we discuss history and sightseeing, we do so in abbreviated form, highlighting what we consider to be the essentials. As you'll quickly discover, we're very focused – we're in search of quality shopping and travel. Rather than spend eight hours a day sightseeing, we may only devote two hours to sightseeing and another six hours learning about the local shopping scene by visiting markets, factories, art galleries, studios, shops, and crafts towns. Through shopping, we meet many interesting and talented people and learn a great deal about their vibrant country.

> ❑ Our approach to travel is very different from most guidebooks – we offer a unique travel perspective and we frequently show our attitude.
>
> ❑ We're not obsessed with local history, culture, and sightseeing. We get enough history and sightseeing to make our travels interesting rather than obsessive.
>
> ❑ Through shopping, we meet many interesting and talented people and learn a great deal about their country.
>
> ❑ We're street people who love the "chase" and the serendipity that comes with our style of travel.

What we really enjoy doing, and think we do it well, is shop. For us, shopping makes for great travel adventure and contributes to local development. Indeed, we're street people who love the "chase" and the serendipity that comes with our style of travel. We especially enjoy discovering quality products, meeting local artists and craftspeople, getting good deals, unraveling new travel-shopping rules, forming friendships with local business people, staying in fine places, and dining in great restaurants where we often meet talented chefs and visit their fascinating kitchens. In many respects, Mexico is synonymous with fine art and craftsmanship. Accordingly, in Mexico we seek the best quality art, antiques, jewelry, textiles, folk art, home decorative items, and apparel as well as discover some of the best artists and craftspeople. In so doing, we learn a great deal about Mexico and its many talented and entrepreneurial people.

The chapters that follow represent a particular travel perspective on Mexico. We purposefully decided to write more than just another travel guide with a few pages on shopping. While some travel guides include a brief section on the "what's" and "where's" of shopping, we saw a need to also explain the "how-to's" of shopping in Mexico (Chapter 3). Such a book would both educate and guide you through this country's shopping mazes – from finding great art, jewelry, ceramics, antiques, and handicrafts and navigating numerous markets to getting the best deals and arranging for the shipping of large items – as well as put you in contact with the best of the best in restaurants, accommodations, and sightseeing. It would be a combination travel-shopping guide designed for people in search of quality travel experiences.

The perspective we develop throughout this book is based on our belief that traveling should be more than just another adventure in eating, sleeping, sightseeing, and taking pictures of unfamiliar places. Whenever possible, we attempt to bring to life the fact that Mexico has real people and interesting products that you, the visitor, will find exciting. This is a country with very talented artists, craftspeople, traders, and entrepreneurs. When you leave Mexico, you will take with you not only some unique experiences and memories but also quality products that you will certainly appreciate for years to come.

We have not hesitated to make qualitative judgments about the best of the best in Mexico. If we merely presented you with travel and shopping information, we would do you a disservice by not sharing our discoveries, both good and bad. While we know that our judgments may not be valid for everyone, we offer them as reference points from which you can make your own decisions. Our major emphasis is on quality shopping, dining, accommodations, sightseeing, and entertainment, and in that order. We look for shops which offer excellent quality and styles. If you share our concern for quality shopping, as well as fine restaurants and hotels, you will find many of our recommendations useful to planning and implementing your Mexican adventure. Best of all, you'll engage in what has become a favorite pastime for many of today's discerning travelers – lifestyle shopping!

Throughout this book we have included "tried and tested" shopping information. We make judgments based upon our experience – not on judgments or sales pitches from others. Our research method was quite simple: we did a great deal of shopping and we looked for quality products. We acquired some fabulous items and gained valuable knowledge in the process.

However, we could not make purchases in every shop, nor do we have any guarantee that your experiences will be the same as ours. Shops close, ownership or management changes, and the shop you visit may not be the same as the one we shopped. So use this information as a starting point, but ask questions and make your own judgments before you buy. For related information on shopping in Mexico, including many of our recommended shops, please visit our companion website: www. ishoparoundtheworld.com. For information on great travel deals, see our new travel discount website: www.travel-smarter.com.

Whatever you do, enjoy Mexico. While you need not "shop 'til you drop," at least shop it well and with the confidence that you are getting good quality and value. Don't just limit yourself to small items that will fit into your suitcase or pass up something you love because of shipping concerns. Consider acquiring larger items that can be safely and conveniently shipped back home. Indeed, shipping is something that needs to be **arranged** rather than lamented or avoided.

We wish to thank the many people who contributed to this book. They include shop owners, hotel personnel, tourism officials, and others who took time to educate us about the local shopping, hotel, dining, sightseeing, entertainment, and travel scenes. Special thanks go to Tom and Nancy Dungan who accompanied us on this adventure, shared several photos appearing in this book, and proved to be excellent shoppers, diners, golfers, and road warriors. They also frequently tested the local shopping, bargaining, and shipping scenes, often validating our observations on how rules and systems more or less work in Mexico.

We wish you well as you prepare for Mexico's many treasures and pleasures. The book is designed to be used on the streets of Mexico. If you plan your journey according to the first three chapters and navigate our major destinations based on the next 13 chapters, you should have an absolutely marvelous time. You'll discover some exciting places, acquire some choice items, and return home with many fond memories of a terrific adventure. If you put this book to use, it will indeed become your best friend – and passport – to the many unique treasures and pleasures of Mexico. Enjoy!

Ron and Caryl Krannich
krannich@impactpublications.com

The Treasures and
Pleasures of Mexico

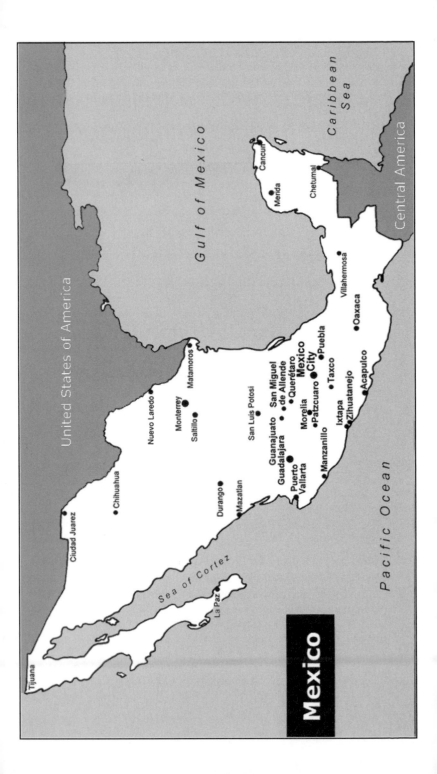

Welcome to Surprising and Seductive Mexico

WELCOME TO SURPRISING and seductive Mexico. You are about to discover one of the world's great travel-shopping destinations, a colorful and vibrant place that will initially enchant and enthrall you. And then it may subtly seduce you beyond your credit card and excess baggage limits! It may even change your life, especially if you decide to become a frequent visitor or settle in as a seasonal or permanent resident in one of Mexico's many select expatriate communities.

From ancient ruins, tropical rainforests, and gorgeous beaches to bustling markets, compelling art galleries, quaint colonial towns, colorful plazas, beautiful cathedrals, and scenic mountains, deserts, and canyons, Mexico seems to have it all. Join us on a unique travel-shopping adventure that may well change the way you travel, shop, and decorate your home!

Subtle Seduction

Representing the world's thirteenth largest country with a population of 104 million, Mexico is one of today's most popular tourist destinations that hosts over 20 million visitors a year. It's a big and inviting people-intensive country with all the chaos, color, and charm normally associated with Third World countries in transition. But Mexico is much more than just another Third World country. It's a lifestyle destination for thousands of visitors and expatriates who come here to discover the country's many exciting treasures and pleasures.

Mexico can be a wonderfully rewarding adventure for those who know the what, where, and how of navigating its fascinating landscape of people, places, and products. But this also can be a dangerous place for those who linger long: It may slowly enchant, seduce, and transform you. Indeed, thousands of visitors succumb to it each day. Some stay permanently – having discovered their special piece of paradise in San Miguel de Allende, Puerto Vallarta, Guadalajara, Cuernavaca, or Oaxaca – while others return as frequent and often frustrated visitors who can only temporarily enjoy Mexico's very pleasurable lifestyle.

The 6 C's of Many Mexicos

Mexico conjures up many different images, both positive and negative. If you are from the United States, Mexico is so near but often seems so far away. Crossing the border puts you into a very different country that both looks and feels unfamiliar. Language and culture, especially the way Mexicans organize and disorganize everything, from traffic and time to service and security, give this country an exotic feel to many outsiders who come from more orderly, managed, legalistic, and predictable societies. Mexico represents charming chaos and serendipity to many such visitors who also learn to enjoy the unpredictable. For example, fascinating central, colonial, and historical Mexico, including Mexico City, is very different from coastal, resort, and border town Mexico. The poorer rural and more traditional Indian south contrasts markedly with the richer and more industrialized and

> ❑ Mexico is the world's 13th largest country with a population of 104 million.
>
> ❑ For U.S. citizens, Mexico is so near but so far away because of differences in language, history, and culture.
>
> ❑ Mexico represents charming Third World chaos and serendipity to many visitors.
>
> ❑ Mexico is a country of great diversity, contrasts, and contradictions.
>
> ❑ Thousands of expatriates have settled in Guadalajara, San Miguel de Allende, Puerto Vallarta, and Oaxaca.

urbanized north. In fact, you'll encounter several Mexicos as you travel through the various states and regions. Discovering the right Mexico for you is one of the more enjoyable challenges of traveling to Mexico.

Mexico is many things to many different people. Accordingly, it offers numerous choices to discerning travelers in search of the best of the best in Mexico. It is those choices we wish to assist you with throughout this book. Above all, Mexico is a country of great diversity, contrasts, and contradictions. It exudes an intriguing history, colorful religion, surprising politics, attractive sights, delightful people, and compelling art, music, and entertainment. It's a complicated society that seems too easy to generalize about. It has a long Indian, Spanish, and mestizo history coupled with a Yankee imperialist tradition. Being colorful and chaotic is a function of several contrasts. It has great extremes of wealth and poverty, beauty and squalor, efficiency and inefficiency, quality and kitsch, and security and insecurity.

Just when you think you understand Mexico, it surprises you with additional complexity and contradictions. Despite initial impressions, this is not a simple country that lends itself to broad generalizations about the Mexicans. It deserves to be slowly savored and absorbed. With an open mind, sit back and enjoy what will become a very fascinating and rewarding show.

Geography, money, and history add to Mexico's diversity and complexity. Tourists and expatriates play an important role in Mexico's travel-shopping landscape. Jet into Mexico City, visit nearby Cuernavaca, Taxco, and Acapulco, and venture to the west coast to bustling and upscale Ixtapa, Zihuatanejo, Manzanillo, Puerto Vallarta, and Mazatlan and you're in several different resort worlds. Go inland to discover the history, culture, art, and architecture that accent the special colonial charms of Guadalajara, San Miguel de Allende, Guanajuato, Querétaro, Morelia, Patzcuaro, Puebla, and Oaxaca, or get decadent in party-throbbing Cancun and a few border towns, and you'll think you've just visited many different Mexicos. Along the way you'll meet many North American expatriates who have made Mexico their second home seasonally or full-time. These are all fascinating places that collectively make up Mexico. As the following chapters unfold, consider including several of these destinations in your travel plans. You won't be disappointed!

It's all here in what we call the 4 C's of Mexico – colorful, chaotic, charming, and compelling. Mexico also has been slowly adding two more C's – convenient and chic – as its tourist infrastructure continues to improve and entice visitors to further explore the many treasures and pleasures of this rewarding destination.

Something for Everyone

for a wide range of budgets and travel experiences. Focusing on everything from history, culture, ecotourism, education, sports, spas, and culinary adventures to shopping, crafts, and decadent beach, bar, and disco excesses, Mexico seems to offer something for everyone in search of a good time. It's a place where you can truly relax and enjoy a lifestyle devoid of the hustle and bustle of life back home. In addition, thousands of expat retirees, artists, writers, and musicians from the United States and Canada (www.mexpatriate.net and www.escapeartist.com) have settled here (especially in Guadalajara, San Miguel de Allende, Cuernavaca, Puerto Vallarta, and Oaxaca), and thousands of students annually flock to Mexico for "study light" experiences and for Spring Break blowouts in Cancun and Mazatlan. Indeed, several travel agencies specialize in "Spring Break and Grad Tours" (www.endlesssummertours.com, www.leisuretours.com, www.sts travel.com, and www.suncoastva cations.com) to ensure that students enjoy their annual Mexican beach, drinking, and mating rituals. Add to these many attractions a wonderful mix of restaurants, hotels, resorts, and shops and you have a potent formula for one very attractive destination, which many visitors return to again and again to sample its many additional charms.

> *Mexico seems to offer something for everyone in search of a good time – for all budgets and lifestyles.*

From upscale resorts, exclusive spas, and expensive golf courses to fine restaurants and designer jewelry, clothes, and accessories, Mexico also is taking its place among the elite destinations of the world. In a sense, there is a Mexico for every type of budget and style of travel. Like many other travelers, you should be able to quickly find the Mexico that best fits your travel interests, needs, and resources.

If this is your first trip to Mexico, chances are it will be the first of many more trips to come. If you are a repeat visitor, you know what we're talking about. Laid back and seldom boring, Mexico tends to grow on you after a few days. And if you are from the United States or Canada, Mexico is a convenient location for short weekend to 10-day trips. The only problem is that you may not want to leave, which many expatriates can testify is a problem they have learned to love, thank you!

Shopping Treasures

As you will quickly discover, this is a book about travel-shopping in Mexico. While Mexico has a great deal to offer all types of visitors, shopping ranks near the top as one of its major strengths and attractions. Shopping is everywhere, from colorful markets, street shops, sidewalk vendors, factories, pawnshops, handicraft emporiums, home production centers, and galleries to department stores, shopping malls, hotel shopping arcades, and chic boutiques. If you don't find it, chances are this ubiquitous phenomenon will find you! And it's often fun shopping as you uncover new places, discover unique treasures, and meet many interesting people, such as artists, craftspeople, merchants, and tourist personnel, and bargain for good prices. If you come with us, you'll also enjoy numerous auxiliary pleasures, such as wonderful restaurants, hotels, and sights, that go along in defining our "lifestyle shopping" in Mexico.

❑ Thousands of students annually flock to Mexico for "study light" experiences and for Spring Break blowouts, especially in Cancun and Mazatlan.

❑ Shopping is one of Mexico's major strengths and attractions. If you don't find it, chances are it will find you!

❑ Frequently referred to as "cha-cha shopping," kitsch is never far away wherever you shop in Mexico. It often qualifies as fun and serious folk art.

❑ Many visitors fall in love with the colorful folk art and become collectors of the works of famous Mexican folk artists.

Come with us as we take you on a very special adventure. For us, Mexico is a shopper's paradise for a variety of goods. It's also a lifestyle shopping destination where you can "shop 'til you drop" – but you can literally "drop into" some great places to cool your shopping heels!

From Kitsch to Quality

Before venturing any further into the travel-shopping delights of Mexico, let's talk seriously about a subject that you will most likely encounter sooner or later – Mexican kitsch. Some visitors to Mexico avoid shopping altogether because they consider local products too kitschy for their more sophisticated tastes. For many of them, Mexico seems to have lots of trash masquerading as treasures! There's some truth to this assessment, but the story of Mexico's shopping scene, especially for the ubiquitous arts and crafts, is much more complex, similar to Mexico itself. It extends into important areas of Mexican art, design, and color.

For travel-shoppers, Mexico is a shopper's paradise for everything from kitsch to quality – if you know what to look for and where to go. From indigenous folk art, handicrafts, and textiles to antiques, decorative items, jewelry, and imported designer clothes and accessories, Mexico has a great deal to offer inveterate treasure hunters and shopping sleuths in search of a very special travel-shopping experience.

Frequently referred to as "cha-cha shopping," kitsch is never far away wherever you shop in Mexico. Be forewarned that you will encounter a great deal of kitsch in the process of uncovering quality shopping. In fact, Mexico tends to be a very kitschy shopping center, more so than most countries we have visited. Much of the kitsch centers on what we might loosely call souvenirs, handicrafts, and folk art that come in many different mediums and forms: woodcarvings, masks, metal work, textiles, rugs, glass, clay figures, ceramics, stone sculptures, bronzes, painted furniture, jewelry, lacquerware, inlaid wood, copper, straw baskets, and papier-mâché figures. At times Mexico seems to be one huge workshop turning out an incredible volume of arts and crafts. Just explore a few crafts markets and emporiums and you may think you just descended into a great wasteland of artistically challenged craftspeople who lack a good sense of color and design. Much of what you see is truly kitschy – who in the world would ever buy, or much less produce, such poor quality and gaudy carvings, ceramics, and metal work? Is this child's play or the work of amateurs pretending to be engaged in a new form of artistic expression? Maybe it's best to call some of this kitsch "folk art" to give it greater credibility and value.

At the same time, some of the so-called kitsch qualifies as fun and serious folk art – complete with famous artists, award-winning craftspeople, and international dealers – that tends to blur the line between what is good art versus tourist handicrafts and tacky souvenirs. Visit the homes and workshops of Mexico's top folk artists, stay in such wonderful folk art decorated properties as Casa Viejo in Mexico City (www.casavieja.com) and Casa Luna B&B in San Miguel de Allende (www.casaluna.com), discover the fabulous private folk art collection of Dr. Lechuga (Museo Ruth D. Lechuga) in Mexico City, or venture into the La Mono Magica folk art shop in Oaxaca, and you'll surely acquire a new appreciation for what initially may have appeared to be Mexican kitsch. Delve further into the history of these art forms and the works of individual artists and you'll discover how important art is in the daily lives of Mexicans from all walks of life. This is the people's art. Like much of the country, folk art is very diverse, magical, and seductive. After a while, you get lost in a different world of color, design, and imaginative forms as you discover exciting art, artists, and craftspeople.

Like others, you may conclude that kitsch and folk art are in the eye of the beholder. Indeed, one of the great challenges of shopping in Mexico is to be able to separate the two. Assigning value to kitschy folk art is a recurring theme among travel-shoppers in Mexico. Many visitors fall in love with the colorful folk art and become collectors of the works of famous Mexican folk artists. They learn to quicky separate kitschy folk art from the truly quality end of the folk art spectrum. They aspire to acquire many of the fine works of top folk artists featured in the wonderful book *Great Masters of Mexican Folk Art* (Fomento Cultural Banamex, A.C. and Harry N. Abrams, Inc., 1998). For anyone interested in folk art, this is a "must read" book in preparation for a trip to Mexico. It may well become your folk art "bible" for shopping for the best of the best in Mexican folk art. You may even find a special place in your home to display the unique arts and crafts of Mexico that may have initially appeared to be kitschy. When that happens, you've finally discovered a very special aspect of Mexico and the Mexicans. Welcome to surprising and seductive Mexico!

A Cash-and-Carry Country

"So near but so far" is an apt description of Mexico when it comes time to ship your treasures home. Just because Mexico may appear close to home, don't assume it's easier and cheaper to ship from Mexico than from China or India. Indeed, we found it was cheaper and faster to ship from Cape Town in South Africa to Washington, DC than from anywhere in Mexico to Washington, DC. Shipping is notoriously unreliable and expensive in Mexico. Whenever possible, we recommend taking your goods with you from Mexico, especially if you are flying. It may cost you a little more in Excess Baggage charges, but it will be worth it in both the short and long run. If you drive to Mexico, plan to fill your vehicle with purchases.

An Exciting Destination

Mexico is a country of great history, beauty, charm, and exotic sights and sounds. From energetic, crowded, and architecturally impressive Mexico City to the colonial charms of Oaxaca, Mexico has a great deal to offer travel-shoppers. You can easily spend weeks treasure hunting for many unique products at bargain prices. Indeed, one of the most enjoyable ways to experience Mexico is to shop its many markets and shops. There you will discover some wonderful products, experience exotic sights and sounds, meet interesting people, and hopefully walk away with many unique treasures and good buys.

This book is about "lifestyle shopping" – combining shopping with great restaurants, hotels, and sightseeing.

But shopping can be a tricky business in Mexico, as is the case in most countries that boast colorful markets and shops that primarily cater to the tourist trade. Knowing where to go for good quality and prices is often a mystery, and especially if you are with a tour guide who leads you into "recommended" shops that invariably give them kickbacks (commissions) for steering clients to their shops.

As will soon become apparent, this book is especially designed for travel-shoppers who want to have a wonderful time discovering many of Mexico's unique treasures. We have attempted to cut through the shopping clutter to identify some of the best shops in several key destinations in Mexico. At the same time, we identify important aspects of the local shopping culture – from bargaining to "reading" shops – which should be useful when you make sojourns into markets and shops.

But this book is about more than just shopping. As travel-shoppers, we're into "lifestyle shopping," which means we enjoy combining shopping with great restaurants, hotels, and sightseeing. To just go shopping without taking in these other complementary aspects of travel to Mexico would be to miss the many joys of traveling through this delightful land.

Discovering Our Mexico

The chapters that follow take you on a well-worn path through the many highlight destinations of Mexico. Taken together, all of these places can be covered in a fast-paced four- to five-week trip. If you only have two weeks to spend in Mexico, we recommend focusing on four major destinations: Mexico City, Guadalajara, San Miguel de Allende, and Oaxaca. These are our top picks for enjoying the shopping highlights of Mexico.

Except in Mexico City, where we do a great deal of walking and occasionally hire a car and driver, we recommend driving to all of the other destinations. It's a convenient and fun way to enjoy Mexico's many cities, towns, and villages. Mexico's excellent toll roads, while expensive to navigate (but toll fees also include auto insurance!), are very safe, convenient, and fast. Indeed, Mexico is a very enjoyable place to drive – if you avoid many of the less than desirable back roads where driving can be slow, dangerous, and nerve-racking.

❏ If you have limited time, focus on these major destinations: Mexico City, Guadalajara, San Miguel de Allende, and Oaxaca.

❏ Mexico City has something for everyone. Spend a week there and you will only touch the surface of this great city.

❏ Taxco is one of the most picturesque and well main-tained cities in Mexico famous for its silver work.

❏ Acapulco has a few surprises for serious shoppers in search of good quality art.

❏ Puerto Vallarta remains popular with jet setters who now build mansions in the $5+ million range.

❏ Guadalajara offers some of Mexico's best lifestyle shopping opportunities.

We both begin and end our adventure in **Mexico City**. One of the world's largest cities with a population of over 25 million, Mexico City is where the action is. Like any big city, it can be intimidating at first. But after a couple of days, the city starts making great sense and is relatively easy and safe to get around in, despite its notorious congestion and high crime rate. The keys to navigating this place with ease and safety are to (1) select a centrally located hotel and (2) hire a car and driver – preferably a "rent-a-cop" – to get around to the many recommended places we outline in Chapter 4. From large handicraft emporiums, pawnshops, and weekend markets to chic boutiques and outstanding jewelry, art, antique, and home decorative shops, Mexico City has something for everyone. For history buffs and sightseers, Mexico City and its surrounding area have a treasure-trove of things to see and do. Its fine restaurants, hotels, and entertainment venues add to the many attractions of this world-class city. Spend a week here and you will only touch the surface of this intriguing city. Our recommendation: Spend the first four days and the last three days of your travel-shopping adventure in Mexico City – and do find a rent-a-cop to take you safely to all the great places!

Taxco seems to be everyone's favorite city for ambience and shopping despite its reputation for being a tourist trap – prices here can be higher than in Mexico City for the identical items! Only a one- to two-hour drive south of Mexico City, Taxco is one of the most picturesque and well maintained towns in Mexico. Its attractive white-washed adobe buildings, baroque churches, colorful plaza, and narrow and winding cobblestone streets arrayed against a spectacular hillside setting make Taxco a visual feast and a photographer's delight. Famous as a center for silver production, nearly 300 shops in this quaint town offer a wide range of silver jewelry, serving pieces, flatware, pots, and sculptures which are manufactured locally in small workshops. Many shops also offer gold jewelry and a wide range of handicrafts found in other communities of central Mexico. One to two days here should be plenty for covering shops and sites.

Acapulco lies about two hours south of Taxco along a beautiful bay that flows into the Pacific Ocean. A major cruise ship stop, Acapulco retains much of its long-deserved reputation as a romantic destination. Today it is anything but sedate. Acapulco remains a favorite destination for both Mexican and foreign tourists, many of whom are young party-goers who enjoy Acapulco's lively disco and nightclub scenes. During the high season Acapulco is wall-to-wall with people who head for the beaches and swimming pools during the day and then off to the bars, discos, and nightclubs until the early morning hours. Being a major cruise ship destination, Acapulco also has a certain honky-tonk element to it, complete with shops and emporiums that offer a wide range of overpriced goods (200 to 400 percent above retail!) to unwitting cruise ship passengers who are led into such shops by guides and other tourist personnel who rake off 20 to 30 percent commissions on everything they buy. Despite this type of shopping, which is largely confined to the shopping area near the cruise ship docks, Acapulco also has a few surprises for serious shoppers in search of good quality art. Spend a couple of days here to enjoy Acapulco's many fine hotels, restaurants, shops, sites, and entertainment venues.

Ixtapa and Zihuatanejo are located about three hours, or 150 miles, northwest of Acapulco, along Pacific coastal Route 200. New tourist destinations since the 1970s, these adjacent (10-minute drive) coastal communities have become very popular with upscale tourists and expats in search of either modern resort amenities or a small coastal village experience – or both. Zihuatanejo is an old fishing village which retains much of its Mexican character despite the influx of tourists to the neighboring resort of Ixtapa. Fine restaurants, boutique hotels, markets, and beautiful sunsets overlooking the picturesque harbor add to the appeal of this quaint town. Ixtapa is a relatively planned community complete with high-rise hotels, condominums, shopping plazas, two golf courses, a marina, and many well manicured lawns. While most tourists stay in Ixtapa's large properties, Zihuatanejo's small boutique hotels especially appeal to independent travelers. While shopping here is somewhat limited, nonetheless, you'll find a few very interesting shops offering many unique items not available elsewhere in Mexico. Taken together, Ixtapa and Zihuatanejo offer some wonderful opportunities to relax and enjoy the many treasures and pleasures of these two very complementary communities.

Manzanillo is located three hours south of Puerto Vallarta along the west coast and less than two hours from the inland state capital of Colima. Stretching along twin bays – Santiago and Manzanillo – this resort community is also a major industrial port and center for the Mexican navy. Once an "in" resort for jet setters – its best days were in the 1980s – today Manzanillo is a rather sleepy resort community boosting a few five-star hotels, some good restaurants, and golf courses that are especially popular with a community of condo-owning expats who enjoy the less touristy style of this place. There's not a great deal to see and do here, including shopping, but you may find Manzanillo to be a delightful place to visit, especially if you stay at the classic Las Hadas or the incredible Isla Navidad resort complex located about one hour north of Manzanillo and near the international airport. Many visitors only spend a day or two here on their way to Puerto Vallarta or Ixtapa-Zihuatanejo.

Puerto Vallarta remains one of Mexico's most popular resort destinations. Located only four hours west of Guadalajara by road, this once sleepy seaside village received instant international fame with the 1964 filming of Richard Burton and Elizabeth Taylor in John Huston's *Night of the Iguana*. Puerto Vallarta has continued to grow and grow into a world-class resort, complete with a six-lane boulevard, with all the amenities and costs such development implies. It remains a popular destination for jet setters and the rich and famous who now build mansions in the $5+ million range. It has everything – fabulous five-star hotels and resorts, outstanding restaurants, beaches, golf courses, water sports, shopping, entertainment, and sightseeing. At the same time, Old Vallarta is still a romantic and charming city with narrow cobblestone streets and lots of great shops and restaurants to explore. From fine art and jewelry to handicrafts and souvenirs, the quaint shops of Puerto Vallarta have a great deal to offer travel-shoppers in search of the best of the best. A two- to three-day stay here will be justly rewarded.

> ❑ Morelia is a great place from which to tour nearby arts and crafts communities where you can meet many talented artisans.
>
> ❑ Querétaro is one of Mexico's cleanest, tidiest, most charming, and architecturally appealing cities.
>
> ❑ San Miguel de Allende is everyone's favorite city – a shopper's paradise for fine arts and crafts and a well organized community of talented and quirky expats.
>
> ❑ Guanajuato is an unusual subterranean city noted for its hills, architecture, and attractive ceramics.
>
> ❑ Puebla, the "City of Tiles," offers wonderful colonial ambience as well as lots of interesting shopping.
>
> ❑ Oaxaca is Mexico's colonial jewel and one of its best kept shopping secrets – a place you are likely to fall in love with and acquire a new appreciation for folk art.

Guadalajara, along with its adjacent suburban community of Tlaquepaque, is Mexico's second largest city with a population of over 5 million. A major industrial center with a decided business emphasis, it also retains a great deal of sophisticated Old World colonial ambience. It has the look and feel of a modern yet cultured Mexican city that is not a product of mass tourism. In fact, unlike other major tourist destinations in Mexico, you'll seldom feel like a tourist in this charming city. Boasting a wonderful year-round climate and a lovely setting, this sprawling city has become very popular with American and Canadian expatriates as well as local and international artists and writers who have settled here permanently. A very modern city with five-star hotels, great restaurants, beautiful architecture, old churches, and wonderful shopping, Guadalajara may well become one of your favorite cities in Mexico. It's a big and bustling city, but it's also a very seductive city with many pleasant shopping areas. In fact, some of the

Mexico's best shopping for quality art, antiques, ceramics, glassware, metal work, furniture, handicrafts, lamps, candles, leather goods, and home decorative items can be found in downtown Guadalajara and in nearby Tlaquepaque and Tonalá. It's the perfect place to engage in lifestyle shopping. To shop and sightsee this city properly, plan at least three days here. One or two extra days here would most likely be justly rewarded.

Morelia and the nearby towns of **Pátzcuaro, Santa Clara, and Tzintzuntzan** are terrific places for sightseeing and shopping. The whole area is a virtual crafts center for producing a wide range of popular products – copper pots, ceramics, textiles, embroidery, pottery, stone carvings, jewelry, carved masks, and painted furniture. Indeed, this is a great place to take a crafts tour to nearby towns and villages where you will have an opportunity to visit artisans and craftspeople in their home-based workshops and buy directly from them. Morelia itself is a charming city of impressive colonial architecture, beautiful churches, and interesting museums that document the important role of Morelia in Mexico's march to independence. Combining shopping with sightseeing will easily require a two- to three-day stay in Morelia. We highly recommend making Morelia your base from which to visit the surrounding area. It's a lovely pedestrian-friendly city that invites visitors to sample its many charms both day and night.

> *We learned long ago that one of the best ways to meet the local people and experience another culture is to shop!*

Querétaro is located just over two hours by car northwest of Mexico City and within close proximity to San Miguel de Allende and Guanajuato. An important city in Mexico's drive to independence, today surprising Querétaro is one of the cleanest, tidiest, most charming, and architecturally appealing colonial cities in Mexico with a population of approximately 850,000. From beautiful plazas and baroque churches to museums, fountains, and shops, Querétaro is a delightful place to visit. It's a pedestrian-friendly city laid out for enjoying plazas, shops, and restaurants. Querétaro also is Mexico's gem-cutting center. You can easily spend a day or two exploring this city's many treasures and pleasures. Travel-shoppers will find at least a half day of worthwhile shopping along Querétaro's major streets and walkways and in museums and hotel shops. Staying one night here may be sufficient, especially if you plan to visit nearby San Miguel de Allende and Guanajuato.

San Miguel de Allende seems to be everyone's favorite city. Indeed, in the year 2000 *Condé Nast Traveler* named San Miguel de Allende one of the top 10 foreign cities for travelers. And for good reasons! Many repeat visitors to Mexico only go to San Miguel de Allende because of its wonderful ambience and attractions. Located within three hours driving distance northwest of Mexico City and nearly one hour northwest of Querétaro, this is a major center for American and Canadian expatriates who are drawn here year-round. Indeed, over 2,500 expatriates call San Miguel de Allende their home. Many of them are noted writers, artists, and musicians. This charming colonial city with cobblestone streets, picturesque doors, colorful buildings and fiestas, a landmark neo-Gothic church, quaint hotels and B&Bs, fine restaurants, and a plethora of cultural and education activities also is a shopper's paradise for fine art, ceramics, folk art, handicrafts, textiles, woodcarvings, furniture, glassware, metal work, jewelry, and home decorative items. Unlike most cities and towns in Mexico, this one is well organized with all kinds of activities going on, from city walks, yoga lessons, art classes, and literary readings to language institutes, jazz festivals, concerts, and social welfare projects. The talented and organizationally active expatriate community here is very proud of San Miguel de Allende and they show it through their many activities. There's always something interesting going on here that will tempt you to stay longer than you originally planned. For travel-shoppers, San Miguel de Allende is to Mexico what Santa Fe is to the United States – an important and fun art, culture, and educational center. Plan to spend at least two to three days here, although you may want to extend your stay to a week or 10 days.

Guanajuato is a very unique colonial city. Viewed from the hills, it's one of the loveliest cities in Mexico. Its hilly and winding cobblestone streets and underground passages can be very confusing for first-time visitors trying to navigate its intriguing web of streets and walkways. In fact, expect to get lost here several times during your stay. Don't worry, it happens all the time and you usually won't stay lost for more than 15 minutes. An extremely interesting city for its architecture and history, Guanajuato also is a vibrant university city. Its small landmark town square has a traditional bandstand and strolling musicians and minstrels who visit outdoor diners facing the square. It's a lively city especially in the evenings when the best show in town is in and around the square. This whole area is especially famous for its colorful ceramics, which are found in a few shops in Guanajuato as well as in nearby Santa Rosa and Dolores Hildalgo. Guanajuato is a good base from which to visit these places. A day or two here may be sufficient, especially if you also are staying in nearby San Miguel de Allende.

Puebla, Mexico's fourth largest city, is located only 80 miles east of Mexico City. A lovely old colonial city with strong Spanish and religious influences, Puebla is especially noted for its charming setting, expansive plaza, beautiful architecture, numerous churches and monasteries, and lovely ceramics. Known as the "City of Tiles," Puebla is the center for producing the world-famous hand-painted Talavera tiles. The tiles are displayed on numerous buildings throughout the city. But the city also offers good shopping opportunities for antiques, collectibles, religious art, folk art, jewelry, gift items, and sweets. A day or two here should be sufficient to cover the highlights of this attractive city. If you're visiting Puebla on a day trip from Mexico City, plan on a full day to cover its shopping and sightseeing. But it's most convenient to stay overnight in one of Puebla's small hotels.

Oaxaca is one of Mexico's colonial jewels and a travel-shopper's paradise. Wherever you plan to go in Mexico, be sure to include Oaxaca in your travel plans. Located 340 miles southeast of Mexico City, you can reach it by toll road within five hours. Capital of one of the poorest Indian states in the south, Oaxaca is rich in history, culture, architecture, and ambience. Easy-going and laid back, it's a lovely old colonial city offering a terrific range of sightseeing, dining, and shopping alternatives both within the city and in the outlying areas. For travel-shoppers, this pedestrian-friendly city of cobblestone streets and pleasant plazas yields some of the best shopping in Mexico for quality folk art, fine art, ceramics, distinctive black pottery, handicrafts, textiles, leather goods, and jewelry. The city boasts the second largest native crafts market in the country. In addition, Oaxaca offers several great restaurants and hotels. It is the perfect place to engage in lifestyle shopping. Nearby artisan towns and villages offer opportunities to meet artists and craftspeople and buy directly from their studios and workshops. The inspiring ancient Olmec ruins of Monte Alban, are located within six miles (a half hour drive) of the city. After a few days here, you'll most likely fall in love with this city and area. Plan a minimum of three days in Oaxaca; a week would be much better. Like many expatriates who have settled in this lovely place, Oaxaca may well become your favorite place in Mexico, comparable in many ways to attractive San Miguel de Allende and Guadalajara.

Taken together, our 13 destinations yield some of Mexico's greatest treasures and pleasures. While you may not have time to cover all of these places, at least sample those that appeal to your particular travel style. If you are a dedicated shopper, you'll definitely want to include Mexico City, Guadalajara, San Miguel de Allende, and Oaxaca in your travel plans – our four favorite lifestyle shopping destinations. You'll acquire some wonderful products, meet many delightful people, and enjoy some terrific hotels, restaurants, and sightseeing in the midst of great shopping. You'll also most likely encounter a shipping problem because you were successful in discovering so many quality treasures to grace your home and wardrobe!

A Special People Perspective

The pages that follow are not your typical treatment of travel in Mexico. While we recognize the importance of background information for developing a travel-friendly perspective, this book is not big on history, culture, and sightseeing. Indeed, there are numerous general guidebooks available on Mexico that basically focus on similar themes – history and culture – and we encourage you to acquire one or more of these guides as a companion to the focus in this book. Many of these books are heavy on history, monuments, and museums to the near exclusion of contemporary Mexico and its many talented people. Numerous budget guides, touting the oft repeated *"I'm a traveler, not a tourist"* philosophy, outline how to experience the cheap side of Mexico on your own. They provide a generous offering of inexpensive restaurants, hotels, and transportation for extremely budget-conscious travelers. If this is your primary interest and style of travel, you will find several guidebooks that offer this approach to Mexico.

Like other volumes in the Impact Guides series (see the order form at the end of this book and www.ishoparoundthe world.com), this book focuses on quality travel-shopping in Mexico. Yes, shopping. Contrary to what some travelers may think, shopping is not a sin. It can and does change lives for the better. We learned long ago that one of the most enjoyable aspects of travel – and one of the best ways to meet people, experience another culture, and contribute to local economies – is to seek out the best shops, markets, factories, and galleries – and shop! In so doing, we explore the fascinating worlds of artisans, craftspeople, and shopkeepers and discover quality products, outstanding buys, and talented, interesting, and friendly people. We also help support the continuing development of local arts and crafts. As many of our enthusiastic readers testify (see the introductory four pages of this book), our approach to travel changes lives. Our approach is all about talented people and what they have to offer discerning visitors in search of such talent.

A Travel-Shopping Emphasis

Much of *The Treasures and Pleasures of Mexico* is designed to provide you with the necessary knowledge and skills to become an effective travel-shopper. We especially created the book with three major considerations in mind:

- Focus on quality shopping.
- Emphasis on finding unique items.
- Inclusion of travel highlights, from top hotels and restaurants to major sightseeing attractions, that especially appeal to discerning travelers.

Throughout this book we attempt to identify the best quality shopping in Mexico. This does not mean we have discovered the cheapest shopping or best bargains, although we have attempted to do so when opportunities for comparative shopping arose within and between communities. Our focus is primarily on shopping for unique and quality items that will retain their value in the long run and can be appreciated for years to come. This means some of our recommended shops may initially appear expensive. But they offer top quality and value that you will not find in many other shops. For example, when we discover a unique piece of jewelry in Mexico City, we acknowledge the fact that the work is expensive, but it is very beautiful and special, so much so that you quickly forget the price after you acquire and continue to admire the workmanship. At the same time, we identify what we consider to be the best buys for various items, especially arts, crafts, ceramics, leather goods, and antiques.

We also include many of the top travel amenities and attractions in our selected cities. As with other volumes in the Impact Guides series, many of our readers appreciate quality travel. When they visit a country, they prefer discovering the best a country has to offer in accommodations, restaurants, sightseeing, and entertainment. While they expect good value for their travel dollar, they are not budget travelers in search of the cheapest hotels, restaurants, and transportation. With limited time, careful budgeting, and a good plan, they approach Mexico as a special travel experience – one that will yield fond memories for many years to come. By focusing on the best Mexico has to offer, we believe you will have a terrific time in this delightful country. You'll acquire some great products, meet many wonderful people, and return home with fond memories of an exciting travel-shopping adventure.

Approaching the Subject

The chapters that follow take you on a whirlwind travel-shopping adventure of Mexico with a decided emphasis on quality shopping, dining, accommodations, and sightseeing. We literally put a shopping face on this place – one we believe you will thoroughly enjoy as you explore Mexico's many other pleasures.

We've given a great deal of attention to constructing a completely user-friendly book that focuses on the shopping process, offers extensive details on the "how," "what," and "where" of shopping, and includes a sufficient level of redundancy to be informative, useful, and usable. The chapters, for example, are organized like one would organize and implement a travel and shopping adventure. Each chapter incorporates sufficient details, including names and addresses, to get you started in some of the best shopping areas and shops in each city.

> *As a travel-shopper, you are a very treasured guest rather than just another tourist or traveler.*

Indexes and table of contents are especially important to us and others who believe a travel book is first and foremost a guide to unfamiliar places. Therefore, our index includes both subjects and shops, with shops printed in bold for ease of reference; the table of contents is detailed so it, too, can be used as another handy reference index for subjects and products. If, for example, you are interested in "what to buy" or "where to shop" in Mexico City, the best reference will be the table of contents. If you are interested in folk art in Oaxaca, look under "Folk art" in the index. And if you are interested in learning where you can find good quality ceramics, then look under "Ceramics" in the index. By using the table of contents and index together, you can access most any information from this book.

The remainder of this book is divided into two parts and 15 additional chapters which look at both the process and content of traveling and shopping in Mexico. Part I – **"Smart Travel-Shopping"** – assists you in preparing for your adventure by focusing on the how-to's of traveling and shopping. Chapter 2, **"Best Kept Secrets of Savvy Travel-Shoppers,"** takes you through the basics of getting to and enjoying your stay in Mexico. It includes advice on when to go, what to pack, required documents, currency, business hours, transportation, tipping, tour groups, insurance, safety, and useful websites. Chapter 3 examines Mexico's major shopping strengths, from folk art and ceramics to jewelry and fine art. It also includes lots of advice on comparative shopping, shopping tips, bargaining rules, and shipping strategies for shopping at its very best.

The 13 chapters in Part II – **"Great Destinations"** – examine the how, what, and where of traveling and shopping in and around several of Mexico's major cities, towns, and villages. We start where most of the action is – Mexico City – and then travel south to Taxco and Acapulco. From there we head northwest along the Pacific coast to the attractive resort communities of Ixtapa-Zihuatanejo, Manzanillo, and Puerto Vallarta where shopping often takes a back seat to beaches, sports, and entertainment. From Puerto Vallarta we turn east and head inland to the wonderful colonial cities, towns, and nearby villages of Guadalajara, Morelia, Guanajuato, San Miguel de Allende, and Querétaro – one of the great travel areas of Mexico that is filled with some of Mexico's most fascinating history, culture, architecture, and shopping. We then head southeast through Puebla on our way to one of the great highlights of any trip to Mexico – the city and state of Oaxaca.

In each place we identify major shopping strengths; detail the how, what, and where of shopping; and share information on some of the best hotels, restaurants, and sightseeing for each community and surrounding area. If you decide to cover all of our destinations, you could easily do so in five well planned weeks by driving our circular route from Mexico City and back. But be sure to rent a car with a big trunk, or a van, since you'll most likely fill it up with many treasures you acquire along the way! As you'll quickly discover, this is a very fun and rewarding trip if you enjoy the adventure of driving in Mexico, which we highly recommend. There's no better way to really see the country, meet the people, and haul away your treasures than by car. While driving can be expensive, especially because of the high cost of toll roads, you can't beat the convenience of your own car.

Our Recommendations

We hesitate to recommend specific shops, restaurants, hotels, and sites since we know the pitfalls of doing so. Shops that offered excellent products and service during one of our visits, for example, may change ownership, personnel, and policies from one year to another, or they may suddenly move to another location or go out of business. In addition, our shopping preferences may not be the same as your preferences. The same is true for restaurants, hotels, and some tourist sites.

Since we put shopping up front in our travels to Mexico, our major concern is to outline your shopping options, show you where to locate the best shopping areas, and share some useful shopping strategies that you can use anywhere in Mexico, regardless of particular shops or markets we or others may recommend. Armed with this knowledge and some basic shopping skills, you will be better prepared to locate your own shops and determine which ones offer the best products and service in relation to your own shopping and travel goals.

However, we also recognize the "need to know" when shopping in unfamiliar places. Therefore, throughout this book we list the names and locations of various shops we have found to offer good quality products. In some cases we have purchased items in these shops and can also recommend them for service and reliability. But in most cases we surveyed shops to determine the quality of products offered without making purchases. To buy in every shop would be beyond our budget, as well as our home storage capabilities! Whatever you do, treat our names and addresses as orientation points from which to identify your own products and shops. If you rely solely on our listings, you will miss out on one of the great adventures in Mexico – discovering your own special shops that offer unique items and exceptional value and service.

The same holds true for our recommended hotels, restaurants, sites, and entertainment. We sought out the best of the best in these major "travel pleasure" areas. You should find most of our recommendations useful in organizing your own special Mexico adventures.

Should you encounter any problem with these recommendations, we would appreciate hearing about it. We also welcome recommendations and success stories! We can be contacted through the publisher:

Ron and Caryl Krannich
IMPACT PUBLICATIONS
9104 Manassas Drive, Suite N
Manassas Park, VA 20111-5211
Fax 703-335-9486
E-mail: krannich@impactpublications.com

While we cannot solve your problems, future editions of this book will reflect the experiences of our readers.

You also may want to stay in contact with the publisher's two travel websites:

www.ishoparoundtheworld.com
www.travel-smarter.com

The *i*ShopAroundTheWorld site is designed to complement the Impact Guides with numerous additional resources and advice. The site includes travel and shopping tips, updates, links to useful travel sites, recommended resources, and an online travel bookstore. If you have questions or comments, you may want to address them to us at this site.

The **Travel-Smarter** site includes some of the world's best deals on hotels, car rentals, travel insurance, cruises, airlines, travel packages, and golf tours around the world. Be sure to check out the "Hot Rates" and "Hot Deals" sections for many great online travel buys.

Expect a Rewarding Adventure

Whatever you do, enjoy your Mexico adventure as you open yourself to a fascinating world of travel-shopping. We're confident you'll discover some very special treasures and pleasures that will also make Mexico one of your favorite destinations.

So arrange your flights and accommodations, pack your credit cards and traveler's checks, and head for this delightful destination. Two to four weeks later you should return home with much more than a set of photos and travel brochures. You will have some wonderful purchases and travel tales that can be enjoyed and relived for a lifetime.

Shopping and traveling in Mexico only takes time, money, and a sense of adventure. Take the time, be willing to part with some of your money, and open yourself to a whole new world of travel. If you are like us, the treasures and pleasures outlined in this book will introduce you to an exciting world of quality products, friendly people, and interesting places that you might have otherwise missed had you just passed through these places to eat, sleep, see sites, and take pictures. When you travel our Mexico, you are not just another tourist or traveler. You are a special kind of visitor who discovers quality and learns about places through the people and products that continue to define their culture. Best of all, you support quality arts, crafts, and design as well as promote local talent, encourage entrepreneurism, and contribute to the development of local economies. As a travel-shopper, you are a very treasured guest rather than just another tourist or traveler. You'll leave Mexico with very special memories and quality products that will remind you of the wonderful time you had in a very special place called Mexico.

P A R T I

Smart Travel-Shopping

2

Know Before You Go

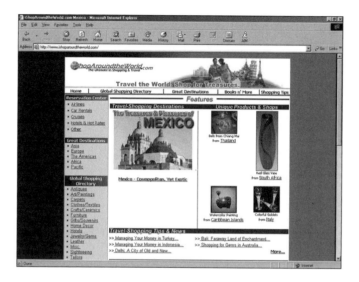

T HERE ARE A FEW THINGS you should know about Mexico before visiting this intriguing country. When, for example, is the best time of the year to visit? How should you pack? Are you likely to encounter many language problems? Should you join a tour group or travel on your own? Is it advisable to drive? What kind of documents do you need? How safe is the country? What can you legally take out of the country? Are there any particular websites that can help you plan your trip to Mexico?

Answers to these and many other basic travel questions can help you better prepare for your travel-shopping adventure.

Location and Geography

Occupying an area of nearly 2 million square kilometers and boasting a population of 104 million, Mexico is a relatively large country. In terms of geographic area, it's one-fifth the size of the United States, three times the size of Texas, or nearly the same size as Saudi Arabia, Indonesia, or Libya. It shares a 3,140-

kilometer (1,950-mile) border with the United States, a 962-kilometer border with Guatemala, and a 250-kilometer border with Belize. It boasts thousands of kilometers of coastline and beaches along the Atlantic and Pacific oceans.

Mexico is geographically a very diverse country of mountains, deserts, plains, wetlands, tropical rainforests, and beaches. Nearly two-thirds of the population resides in urban areas. Mexico City, with a population of over 25 million, dominates the country's political, economic, and cultural life. The second largest city is Guadalajara with a population of over 5 million. A few other cities have populations in excess of 1 million.

Mexico is best approached in terms of six distinct geographic, economic, and cultural regions:

- **Northern Mexico:** Includes the 3,140-kilometer border with the United States, the peninsula of Baja California, and the cities of Tijuana, Ciudad Juárez, Nuevo Laredo, Chihuahua, and Monterrey.

- **Central and Colonial Mexico:** Includes the west coast resorts of Mazatlán, Puerto Vallarta, and Manzanillo as well as the colonial cities of Colima, Guadalajara, Zacatecas, Morelia, Guanajuato, Querétaro, San Miguel de Allende, and San Luis Potosi.

- **Metropolitan Mexico City:** Mexico City, Pueblo, Cuernavaca, and Taxco.

- **Southern Mexico:** Acapulco, Ixtapa, Zihuatanejo, Oaxaca, and Tuxtla Gutierrez.

- **The Gulf Coast:** Xalapa and Veracruz.

- **The Yucatan Peninsula:** Campeche, Mérida, Cancún, and Cozumel.

Each of these regions and their related cities offers unique treasures and pleasures. Our focus on three of these regions – Central/Colonial, Metropolitan Mexico City, and Southern Mexico – will take you to several of Mexico's most exciting destinations.

Climate and When to Go

Depending on where you plan to visit, Mexico can be enjoyed year round. It has a varied climate influenced by its varied typography. It generally has two seasons – a rainy season from May to mid-October and a dry season from mid-October through April. The Yucatan Peninsula and southern Pacific coast also are affected by occasional hurricanes and tropical storms from June through October. Mexico City's high elevation gives it a pleasant climate during most of the year. During January and February, much of inland Colonial Mexico, especially Guadalajara, Guanajuato, Querétaro, and San Miguel de Allende, can become very cold at night.

Mexico's high season for tourists runs from mid-December until Easter. This also is the best time of year to visit in terms of climate, but prices are often higher at this time of the year for hotels and resorts. Most of our featured destinations have clear skies, sunny days, and temperatures in the 80s. The rainy months of June, July, and August can become very hot and humid. However, the coastal areas also can be very pleasant during this time of the year. The low season runs from the day after Easter to mid-December. Many hotels and resorts lower their prices by as much as 50 percent during the low season.

What to Pack and Wear

Light, cotton summer clothing is appropriate for most coastal areas. Since evenings can get cool in the interior, you may want to pack a light jacket for visits during December, January, and February.

You may want to pack formal attire (dress for women and a coat and tie for men) for dining in some of Mexico City's top restaurants. However, this formal attire rule is very relaxed. Indeed, on several occasions we encountered signs at top restaurants saying "Coat and tie required" but few diners actually observed the rule and the restaurant made no attempt to enforce their rule. In

fact, you may choose to forego packing such items since many of the best restaurants do not enforce dress, suit, coat, or tie rules. Smart casual is the best you'll ever have to dress. Resort wear is acceptable in the resort areas.

Sunglasses and sun hats come in handy during the dry season. Be sure to wear comfortable shoes since you will most likely walk a lot as you shop and explore archaeological sites.

We recommend carrying a small compass. It will come in handy since you may frequently become disoriented by streets, maps, and markets which often lack important details. Indeed, signage is a problem in Mexico. Our compass usually keeps us on track and helps us get into and out of our destinations.

Required Documents

Entry requirements for Mexico are relatively simple. You must provide proof of citizenship and country origin. The easiest way to do this is to present a valid passport. Alternatively, you can present a certified copy of your birth certificate (photocopies are not accepted), an official government document verifying citizenship, a certificate of citizenship, certificate of naturalization, or a consular report of your birth abroad and a photo ID, such as a driver's license (photo IDs are not accepted for minors up to 16 years of age). You will be issued a Mexican Tourist Permit (FMT), which is valid for stays of up to 180 days. There is no cost to you for this permit.

If you are driving into Mexico, you will need to present certain documents, pay a fee, and sign some paper work. You must present the following documents at the border:

1. Valid driver's license.

2. Original car registration and a copy of the car title.

3. Major credit card for paying a $16 car-importation fee. Without a credit card, you most post a bond equal to the value of the car.

4. Mexican Tourist Permit, which you were already issued at immigration.

5. A signed Carta Promesa de Retorno stating that you will return to the country you entered from. The document is available through AAA, Sanborn's, or Banco del Ejército (Banjercito) officials who are present at the Mexican Customs building.

6. A signed Temporary Importation Application stating that you are bringing the car into Mexico for personal use and will not sell it during your stay.

Put these documents in a safe place since you will need them again when you drive out of Mexico.

U.S. and Canadian visitors arriving by car also are well advised to purchase Mexican auto insurance policies since U.S. and Canadian auto insurance are not valid in Mexico. You can obtain this insurance at the border through several alternative insurance companies, such as Sanborn's Mexico Insurance (call 1-800-222-0158 to arrange this before you arrive at the border) or AAA auto club. In preparation for your trip, you may want to visit the Sanborn's Insurance and DriveMex.com websites to get free quotes on this insurance:

- **Sanborn's Insurance**   www.sanbornsinsurance.com
- **DriveMex**   www.drivemex.com

This insurance is sold on a daily or weekly basis, depending on the length of your stay. Don't be *"penny wise but pound foolish"* by not taking out such insurance. If you get into an accident in Mexico, it can become a very costly and time – consuming experience, including time in jail. At times you may have double insurance coverage because Mexico's high toll road fees include automatic auto insurance. Keep your receipt. Should you have an accident on a toll road, refer to your toll receipt for this insurance.

For more information on entry requirements to Mexico, visit the following websites:

- **U.S. State Department**   http://travel.state.gov/mexico.html
- **Travel Docs**   www.traveldocs.com/mx
- **Sanborn's Insurance**   www.sanbornsinsurance.com/mexcustoms.html
- **Guide2Mexico**   www.guide2mexico.com/content/mexdrive.htm
- **Mexico Travel Net**   www.mexicotravelnet.com/Travel_Tips/mexicoentry requirements.htm

Language

Mexico is a Spanish speaking country that also includes several indigenous Indian languages, which are widely spoken in southern Mexico. Many personnel in the tourism industry as well as in major shops speak some English. However, English is not as widely spoken in shops, restaurants, and tourist sites as one might expect. Few taxi drivers speak English. More and more tourist police, especially in Mexico City and Oaxaca, now speak basic English and can help visitors who  need assistance. If you don't speak Spanish, it's a good idea to learn a few Spanish words and phrases as well as carry a small

English-Spanish and Spanish-English dictionary to deal with some of the language challenges.

Time

Mexico is roughly in the same time zones as the United States and Canada. Mexico City is five hours behind Greenwich Mean Time (GMT). When it's 12noon, it's 7am in Mexico City. If you are in New York at 12noon, it will be 11am in Mexico City. If you have difficulty figuring out the time differences in reference to your time zone, you may want to visit these two websites:

www.timezoneconverter.com
www.worldtimeserver.com

Safety and Security

Most of Mexico is relatively safe to visit, assuming you take basic travel precautions such as always securing your valuables and being leery of strangers who approach you for anything. Use common sense wherever you travel in Mexico. Keep in mind that Mexico has a high unemployment rate, and drug use is a major problem related to crime.

While the crime situation in Mexico is often overstated, it's always best to error on the side of caution. Crime is on the rise in many places, and it is often violent crime – assaults, shootings, and rapes. Mexico City, as we will shortly see, has its own particular safety and security problems, especially taxi robberies, kidnappings, assaults, armed robberies, and muggings aimed at tourists. While local authorities have increased security in tourist areas, using special tourist police, you still need to be careful when choosing local transportation and watching out for pickpockets and purse-snatchers. The border cities of Tijuana, Ciudad Juarez, and Nuevo Laredo also report very high crime rates. Other cities report petty crimes, especially pickpockets and car break-ins.

If you are driving in Mexico, be very careful about stopping along highways to help people who appear to be in distress. Highway carjackings frequently occur in such situations. The toll roads tend to be safer. The government does have a fleet of green vehicles called the Green Angels that regularly patrol the major highways to help motorists in need of roadside assistance. If you do have a breakdown, hopefully a Green Angel will quickly find you.

The major safety hazard in Mexico is the traffic. If you drive, do so defensively and avoid driving at night. Assume drivers do not think about other drivers on the road. Indeed, many Mexican drivers fail to signal their intentions, drive very slowly, take unexpected actions, and may stop in the middle of the road to talk to someone. You should expect the unexpected. As a pedestrian, assume you have no rights since vehicles do not feel obliged to stop for you. Be careful when crossing streets.

Like anywhere else you travel, including New York City, you should take normal safety precautions by securing your valuables. It's okay to be somewhat paranoid about your possessions, especially your passport, money, and camera – and yourself. Be very cautious with your purse and wallet – hold them very close and with a firm grip. Keep your valuables, including your money and passport, in safe places, such as your hotel safe or in a money belt. If you must use an ATM, be aware that ATM users are often targeted by criminals; avoid using them at night. Also avoid wearing expensive looking jewelry and clothes that label you as wealthy. It's always a good idea to carry a photocopy of essential documents – front information in passport and Mexican Tourist Permit – as well as traveler's check receipts separate from the originals.

If you need reassurance about travel safety to Mexico, check out the U.S. State Department's online travel advisories and tips for Mexico:

http://travel.state.gov/mexico.html

You may also want to review the State Department's brochure, *A Safe Trip Abroad*, which is available online:

http://travel.state.gov/asafetripabroad.html

Also check out their special publication, *Tips for Travelers to Mexico*, which also is available online:

http://travel.state.gov/tips_mexico.html

This publication includes several useful safety tips, which many travelers often forget. They are well worth reviewing in preparation for your trip and before you pack your bags!

Getting There

Mexico is easily accessible by air, sea, rail, and land. If you are flying from the United States, several airlines fly nonstop from major cities in the United States to various cities in Mexico: American, United, Northwest, Southwest Airlines, U.S. Air, Mexicana, Aeromexico, Alaska Airlines, America West, Aerocalifornia, and Lacsa. To check on flight schedules and carriers, including airports, visit these websites:

- **AirWise**   www.airwise.com
- **OAG**   www.oag.com
- **SkyGuide**   www.sky-guide.com

Numerous cruise ships make regular stops at the Pacific coast resorts of Puerto Vallarta and Acapulco and at the Yucatan Peninsula resorts of Cancún, and Cozumel. Check out the cruise section on our discount travel website for information on cruises to Mexico, including specials:

www.travel-smarter.com

Explore Mexico specializes in cruise travel to Mexico:

www.explore-mex.com

If you plan to enter Mexico by car, see our earlier discussion on "Required Documents." Also check out Sanborn's useful website on entering Mexico by car and driving throughout the country:

www.sanbornsinsurance.com

Armed with insurance, a good map, a compass, a little paranoia, and a sense of adventure, driving is a wonderful way to experience the treasures and pleasures of Mexico. Best of all, having your own car is convenient for shopping, and especially for solving one of the major problems for U.S. and Canadian visitors to Mexico – shipping their treasures home. Just fill up your vehicle and head for the border!

International Tour Groups

Many visitors to Mexico come with an organized tour group. Several companies offer a wide variety of interesting package tours that may focus on a particular aspect of Mexico, from history, culture, religion, and textiles to bicycling, golfing, diving, or hiking. Many of these groups offer excellent value and good service. Best of all, they take out the hassles attendant with arranging your own travel details, especially local transportation, hotels, and guides. You'll find such tour groups through your local travel agent, or search for them online by using our favorite search engine for travel planning – google.com. Just enter the keywords "Travel Mexico" or "Tour Groups Mexico" and you'll pull up several relevant websites of groups specializing in travel to Mexico. You may want to check out the ads for Mexico in *International Travel News*. The names, addresses, and websites (hotlinks) of their advertisers are included in ITN's website: www.intltravelnews.com.

For information on tour operators specializing in Mexico, check out *Travel Weekly*'s annual reference guide to the top tour operators:

www.twcrossroads.com/twtouroponline/pages/carib.html

Also, survey the specialty tour operators for Mexico listed on FindTourOperators.com:

www.find-tour-operators.com/Mexico.php

Local Travel Assistance

If you arrive in Mexico as an independent traveler, you can easily find local travel agencies and tour operators that offer a variety of group and customized travel services: half- to full-day city tours, car and driver, English-speaking guide, hotel reservations, train and airline ticketing, cruises, and regional tours. Just check with your hotel or the local tourist office (operated by the Mexico Tourism Board or a state or city tourism office) for names, addresses, and phone numbers of reputable groups. Most cities have at least one tourist office that promotes tourism and provides assistance to visitors.

Online Travel Deals

If you use the Internet, you can easily make airline, hotel, and car rental reservations online for Mexico by using several online booking groups. For the best online travel deals, including hotel, airline, car rental, vacation packages, cruises, golf holidays, and travel insurance, see our special discount travel website, www.travel-smarter.com:

Pay particular attention to the "Hot Rates" and "Hot Deals" sections where you may be able to save up to 70 percent on hotels, cruises, and golf packages. The site is constantly evolving with many new and enhanced travel services, content, and tools (e-cards, city guides, currency converter, flight tracker), including super deals on vacation packages and last minute getaways.

When using the Internet to plan a trip, the best online deals relate to hotels. Travel-Smarter.com alone includes a worldwide inventory of over 60,000 discounted hotels. Last minute online cruise, golf, and vacation package deals also can be excellent travel buys. The good news is that many online deals relate to travel in Mexico. We recommend visiting www.travel-smarter.com before you finalize your plans for Mexico. You may be pleasantly surprised with its convenience and savings. You also can access the same travel reservation database through our travel-shopping website, www.ishoparoundtheworld.com. For related information on www.travel-smarter.com, see the full-page description for this site on the last page of this book.

Passing U.S. Customs

It's always good to know your country's Customs regulations before leaving home. If, for example, you are a U.S. citizen planning to travel abroad, the Department of Homeland Security's Customs and Border Protection (formerly the U.S. Customs Office) provides several helpful publications which are available through the agency's website: www.cpb.gov. Go to the "Travel" button at the top of the front page to access several useful online reports, including:

- *Know Before You Go! – Online Brochure*: Outlines facts about exemptions, mailing gifts, duty-free articles, as well as prohibited and restricted articles. Includes duty-free exemptions and duty rates.

- *International Mail Imports:* Answers many questions regarding mailing items from foreign countries back to the U.S. The U.S. Postal Service sends packages to Customs for examination and assessment of duty before they are delivered to the addressee. Some items are free of duty and some are dutiable. The rules have changed on mail imports, so do check on this before you leave the U.S.

U.S. citizens may bring into the U.S. $800 worth of goods free of U.S. taxes every 30 days; the next $1,000 is subject to a flat 3-percent tax (effective as of January 1, 2002). Goods beyond $1,400 are assessed duty at varying rates applied to different classes of goods. Since Mexico is a NAFTA (North American Free Trade Agreement) country, certain goods are eligible for free or reduced duty rates if they are grown, manufactured, or produced in Mexico.

Items mailed home are exempt from duty if the value is US$200 or less. Antiques that are 100 years old or more may enter duty-free, but folk art and handicrafts are dutiable.

Money Matters

The Mexican unit of currency is the peso ($). As we went to press at the end of 2003, the exchange rate between the U.S. dollar and the Mexican peso was US$1 to 11.161 pesos. To check on the latest exchange rates for various currencies relating to the Mexican peso, visit these currency converter websites:

www.oanda.com

www.xe.net/ucc

The Mexican peso is issued in paper notes of 20, 50, 100, 200, and 500 pesos. Coins are issued in denominations of 1, 2, 5, 10, and 20 pesos as well as 20 and 50 centavos (one peso equals 100 centavos). You should try to collect small change since many merchants do not have correct change. Getting small change seems to be a constant problem in Mexico.

Many shops, especially in tourist areas, will accept U.S. dollars in lieu of pesos. In fact, many shops in resort areas will quote prices in U.S. dollars rather than Mexican pesos.

Since airport exchange counters, hotels, and exchange houses (*casas de cambio*) do not give as good exchange rates as banks, you may want to exchange your money at banks (normally open Monday through Friday from 9am to 3pm).

ATMs are widely available in major cities and resort areas. Keep in mind that your bank will charge a transaction fee for using ATMs, but you'll usually get a better exchange rate when using an ATM.

Credit cards are widely accepted in Mexico. Most hotels, restaurants, and major shops prefer Visa or MasterCard. Many do not accept American Express because they must pay higher transaction fees and American Express does not pay them as quickly as the other companies do. Some places may want to add their transaction fee – 4 to 7 percent – on to your bill if you use a credit card.

Traveler's checks also are widely accepted in most tourist areas. Banks and shops tend to give a higher exchange rate to traveler's checks than to cash.

Tipping

Tips are expected by service personnel, who generally receive low wages. Consequently, you are well advised to carry lots of small bills for tips. Waiters in most major restaurants expect a 10- to 15-percent tip, if a service change is not added to your bill. Airport and hotel porters expect to receive US$.50 to US$1 per bag. Maids appreciate US$1 per day. Taxi drivers do not expect tips unless they help you with your luggage – US$.50 per bag. Parking attendants and gas station attendants expect tips – US$.25 to US$.50 is fine. Reward your tour guide with a US$2 to US$5 a day tip.

Taxes

Mexico's Value-Added Tax (VAT) is known as IVA. It runs 15 percent in most states (it's 10 percent in Cancún, Cozumel, and Los Cabos) and is included in the price of most goods and services. Consequently, the cost of your hotel room, meals, tours, transportation, and purchases will reflect this 15-percent hidden tax. Unlike VATs in some countries, Mexico's IVA is not refundable – you pay, it stays. However, you can avoid the IVA on goods shipped out of the country. Be sure to ask shops about waiving the IVA on such purchases. Some shops will automatically do this, whereas others don't seem to understand how the system operates.

Most states impose a 2-percent tax on accommodations, which normally goes to promoting tourism.

Foreigners are charged an airport departure tax of US$18. This tax is included in the airline ticket.

Electricity and Water

Mexico's electrical system operates the same as in the United States and Canada – 120 volts, 60 cycles.

Assume tap water and ice are not safe in Mexico. It's best to drink only bottled water, which is readily available in restaurants, hotels, grocery stores, and liquor stores. Canned, bottled, and packaged soft drinks, fruit juices, beers, and wines are good drinking alternatives.

Travel Insurance

You should consider taking out a special insurance policy when traveling, to cover situations not covered by your medical, home, auto, and personal insurance back home. For example, many insurance policies do not cover treatment for illnesses or accidents while traveling outside your home country. Check whether your medical insurance will cover treatment abroad, and consider acquiring evacuation insurance in case serious illness or injuries would require that you be evacuated for medical treatment in a nearby country or home through special transportation and health care arrangements. Many companies offer this insurance. One of the best kept travel secrets for acquiring inexpensive evacuation insurance is to join **DAN** (Divers Alert Network). In the U.S., call 1-800-446-2671 (The Peter B. Bennett Center, 6 West Colony Place, Durham, NC 27705; website: www.diversalertnetwork.org). Without evacuation insurance, special evacuation arrangements could cost from US$20,000 to US$50,000 or more! DAN's yearly rates are the best we have encountered. American Express has recently begun offering yearly insurance coverage at special rates as an option to its card holders. Whether or not you are into adventure travel and plan to engage in physically challenging and risky activities, health and evacuation insurance should be on your "must do" list before departing for your international adventure.

When considering special travel insurance, first check your current insurance policies to see if you have any coverage when traveling abroad. Also contact a travel agent to find out what he or she recommends for special coverage. The following websites will connect you to several companies that offer special insurance for travelers:

- **Travel-Smarter**   www.travel-smarter.com
- **World Travel Center**   www.worldtravelcenter.com
- **Travel Guard**   www.travelguard.com
- **World Travel Insurance**   www.globaltravelinsurance.com
- **Medexassist**   www.medexassist.com
- **Travelex**   www.travelex.com
- **Wallach**   www.wallach.com
- **QuoteTravelInsurance**   www.quotetravelinsurance.com
- **E Travel Protection**   www.etravelprotection.com
- **Travel Secure**   www.travelsecure.com
- **Travel Protect**   www.travelprotect.com
- **Global Cover**   www.globalcover.com

Business Hours

Most shops are open Monday through Saturday from 9 or 10am to 7pm or later. Many shops in towns and resorts close from 2 to 4pm and stay open until 9pm. Many shops are closed Saturday afternoon as well as all day Sunday, except in tourist resorts and shopping malls – good days to spend at markets, museums, and tourist sights. **Government offices** are open Monday through Friday from 8am to 3pm. **Banks** are open Monday through Friday from 9am to 3pm; some large banks may have branches open on Saturday (9am to 2:30pm) and Sunday (10am to 1:30pm). **Museums** are usually open Tuesday through Sunday from 9am to 5 or 6pm; Sunday is free admission day for museums throughout Mexico.

Useful Websites

Several websites provide useful information on Mexico. You should start exploring Mexico through these gateway websites:

- **Mexico Online**   www.mexonline.com
- **Mexico Connect**   http://mexconnect.com
- **Mexico Travel**   http://mexico-travel.com
- **Planeta**   www.planeta.com
- **Travelers Guide**   www.travelguidemexico.com
- **Visit Mexico**   www.visitmexico.com
- **Go2Mexico**   www.go2mexico.com
- **Know Mexico**   www.knowmexico.com
- **Si-Mexico**   www.si-mexico.com
- **Mexico Adventure**   www.mexicoadventure.com
- **Go Mexico**   http://gomexico.about.com
- **Mexico Channel**   www.mexicochannel.net
- **Advantage Mexico**   www.advantagemexico.com
- **Trip Advisor**   www.tripadvisor.com
- **Mexico Travel**   www.mexicotravel.com

We identify several other useful websites relating to the various cities and states we cover in the remaining chapters.

For useful online travel guidebook treatments of Mexico, visit the websites of Fodor's, Frommer's, and Lonely Planet:

- **Fodor's**   www.fodors.com
- **Frommer's**   www.frommers.com
- **Lonely Planet**   www.lonelyplanet.com

For travel-shopping information related to this guidebook as well as several other countries, visit our iShopAroundTheWorld website:

www.ishoparoundtheworld.com

Best Kept Secrets of Savvy Travel-Shoppers

W HILE SHOPPING IN MEXICO may initially appear familiar to you, there are certain things you need to know about acquiring treasures in Mexico that will make your shopping experience more rewarding. From meeting new people, discovering unique products, bargaining, and paying for items, to packing, shipping, and handling customs, you should find shopping to be one of the highlights of traveling in Mexico. You'll encounter an extremely enjoyable and rewarding shopping culture that will yield many cherished treasures to grace your home and wardrobe.

Discover Unique Treasures

Each destination we examine in subsequent chapters yields its own unique mix of products and shopping rules. In **Mexico City**, for example, you will be exposed to the full range of Mexican products, from arts, antiques, and jewelry to ceramics, leather goods, fashion, home furnishings, folk art, and souvenirs. As might be expected, the best shopping is found in cosmopolitan

Mexico City. By "best" we're referring to product selection, quality, and design as well as shopping venues – markets, shopping centers, boutiques, a huge government pawnshop, galleries, and museum shops. While prices in Mexico City may be higher, the selections and designs of most local products – as well as imported items – are the best in Mexico City. In fact, if you only have time to shop in one place in Mexico, make sure it's Mexico City.

❏ The best quality shopping in Mexico is found in cosmopolitan Mexico City.

❏ Mexico City offers the ultimate lifestyle travel-shopping adventure.

❏ Guadalajara is especially well known for its arts, antiques, furniture, leather goods, handicrafts, and home decorative items.

❏ San Miguel de Allende is noted for its fine art, ceramics, folk art, handicrafts, textiles, and jewelry.

❏ Oaxaca is a shopper's paradise for a wide range of intriguing folk art.

You also are well advised to start and end your Mexican sojourn in Mexico City. This city offers the ultimate lifestyle travel-shopping adventure, complete with fascinating markets and fine shops, hotels, restaurants, entertainment, and sightseeing. Visiting the many places in Chapter 4 will give you a good idea of what's available in Mexico City, including quality and prices, before venturing into other areas of the country. Indeed, many people mistakenly believe the best shopping can be found outside the major cities when, in fact, most of the "good stuff" has already found its way into discerning shops in the major cities. While buying at production sources in the countryside may seem to make good sense and result in interesting travel-shopping experiences, including meeting local artisans and visiting factories, it seldom results in the expected – good selection of inventory and better quality purchases and bargains than in the cities. After all, the city dealers have most likely already acquired the best products from the sources with whom they have long-term buying relationships. Consequently, many production sources have very little inventory on hand. And many local artisans set high prices because they know the market value of their treasures.

On the other hand, **Guadalajara**, **San Miguel de Allende**, and **Oaxaca** (Chapters 10, 13, and 16) offer many shopping surprises which are not readily found in Mexico City. These three cities deserve your special attention. Guadalajara, for example, is a major arts and crafts center noted for its arts, antiques, furniture, leather goods, handicrafts, and home decorative items. Many of Mexico's top artists and designers come from Guadalajara. San Miguel de Allende is a unique artist colony where shopping for fine art, handicrafts, folk art, textiles, and jewelry is a favorite pastime for visitors who quickly fall in love with this charming expat community. Intriguing, cultured, and colorful colonial Oaxaca is a shopper's paradise for a wide range of intriguing folk art not readily available in other parts of Mexico.

Best Buys

Mexico is by no means an inexpensive travel destination. Food is reasonable by most world standards. Indeed, dining out is often a real bargain. Shopping can be a bargain if you know where to go for good deals. Some shops primarily cater to tourists and their guides who receive anywhere from 10 to 30 percent commission on everything their clients purchase. If you shop in such places, expect to pay 10 to 30 percent above retail.

ART

Mexico has a long and vibrant creative art tradition which is well represented in its many museums, commercial galleries, and public spaces and manifested in its often bold and larger-than-life architecture. Indeed, art plays an important role in the history of Mexico (in Mexico City see the famous murals and paintings of Mexico's art icons Diego Rivera, Frida Kahlo, and Rufino Tamayo) as well as in the daily lives of Mexicans, more so than in most countries we visit. Numerous sophisticated galleries in Mexico City, Acapulco, Puerto Vallarta, Guadalajara, San Miguel de Allende, and Oaxaca offer fine collectible works of art by noted contemporary artists. Most galleries also hold special exhibitions. Representing both local and international artists and catering to international buyers and collectors, galleries often price their works for the international market which can be very high. In fact, good art and famous artists tend to command international prices since art in Mexico is very much an international business. For a good overview of Mexico's current art scene, as represented in its top museums and galleries, be sure to pick up a copy of the bilingual edition of *La Quía Artes de México Museos, Galerías y Otros Espacios del Arte (Artes de México Guide to Museums, Galleries, and Other Spaces of Art)*. This 400+ page paperback book annotates the major museums, galleries, and art spaces in Mexico City, Guadalajara, Monterrey, Puebla, Oaxaca, and San Miguel de Allende. It's available at several galleries and bookstores as well as through the publisher, Artes de México (www.artesdemexico.com, artesmex @internet.com.mx, Tel. 5525-4036, or Fax 5525-5925). It may very well become your shopping guide for quality art in Mexico. However, be sure to go beyond this guide as you discover your own galleries and artists in Mexico's many art centers. As we will see in the cases of Guadalajara, Puerto Vallarta, and Acapulco, three of Mexico's finest bronze sculptors – Sergio Bustamante, Ramiz Barquet, and Pal Kepenyes – should be at the top of your art browsing and shopping list.

CERAMICS AND POTTERY

Numerous communities and shops throughout Mexico offer a wide range of quality ceramics, pottery, and clay figurines. From the unique tableware of talented ceramicist Emilia Castillo in Taxco, beautifully executed majolica ceramics of Gorky González and Capelo in Guanajuato, and colorful glazed pottery produced in numerous factories in and around Dolores Hidalgo to the famous Talavera tiles and pottery in Puebla, glazed ceramic Katrinas of Juan Corres in Michoacán (Capula), and the communities of craftspeople making black and green-glazed pottery in Oaxaca, Mexico offers a dazzling array of artistic and functional ceramics, pottery, and figurines. Indeed, you could easily spend a month in Mexico searching for artisans engaged in the production of ceramics and pottery. Since much of this delicate work is fragile and shipping from Mexico is often unreliable, plan to take many of these purchases with you. If you fall in love with ceramic tableware you want to use for cooking or as serving pieces, make sure it's produced lead free. Most ceramics produced in Mexico have a high lead content, which is unsafe for everyday use.

FOLK ART

Mexico offers a treasure-trove of unique folk art that clearly reflects numerous indigenous artistic and religious traditions. From painted furniture, boxes, masks, and Day of the Dead figures to clay figurines, tin and copper art, papier-mâché figures, pottery, textiles, woven items, and imaginatively carved and colorfully painted animals known as Alebrijes, Mexico may dazzle you with its folk art. But be forewarned that much of Mexican folk art is an acquired taste. It often borders on being kitschy souvenirs and handicrafts found in abundance in various artisan markets. Really good quality folk art, produced by master craftsmen, is found in several top shops in Mexico City, Guadalajara, San Miguel de Allende, and Oaxaca. It's produced in abundance in many towns and villages of Oaxaca. Many visitors fall in love with Mexican folk art and become avid collectors. Indeed, it often becomes a passion or addiction among collectors who also transform their homes in Mexican folk art decorating style. An excellent introduction to Mexican folk art is found in the wonderful coffee table book entitled *Great Masters of Mexican Folk Art* (see our earlier discussion on kitsch and quality folk art on pages 5-8).

HANDICRAFTS

Mexican markets and shops are often jam-packed with a wide variety of colorful handicrafts. While some handicrafts are best classified as folk art, other items have an affinity with handicrafts found in many other countries. Artisan markets are usually the major centers for surveying and acquiring handicrafts. Look for stained glass, pots, masks, dolls, candles, glassware, metal figures, decorative mirrors, woven baskets, ceramic figures, carved boxes and animals, figurines, ceramic plates, leather goods, toys, papier-mâché figures, painted furniture, silver, and jewelry. Unfortunately, many places in Mexico give handicrafts a bad name. Indeed, handicrafts can range considerably in quality. For example, some of the best quality handicrafts are found at Fonart, a government-sponsored handicraft shop found in most major cities. The best Fonart shops are found in Mexico City. Artisan markets tend to stock a wide range of varying quality handicrafts and souvenirs, from treasures to truly tacky trash. Such places invariably become adventures in sorting through questionable quality handicrafts, many of which are best left behind. If you have little patience for such shopping, shop at Fonart for most of your handicraft needs. If you are into kitschy handicrafts, try the artisan markets as well as visit Centro Artesanal Buenavista in Mexico City, a true adventure in shopping for kitsch.

ANTIQUES AND COLLECTIBLES

Several shops and flea markets in Mexico are good places to shop for antiques and collectibles. However, be forewarned that any items that pre-date the colonial period (prior to 1520 A.D.) are prohibited from leaving Mexico. Several shops offer 17th and 18th century colonial furniture and accessories which can be very expensive. Flea markets are often great places to acquire a wide range of interesting collectibles – jewelry, furniture, porcelain, bronzes, masks, corkscrews, irons, bells, knives, lanterns, cameras, musical instruments, toys, coins, locks, and fixtures. Our favorite antique and collectible centers are found in Mexico City and Guadalajara. In Mexico City we especially enjoy browsing through the antique section of the National Pawn Shop, several high-end antique shops in the Zona Rosa area, and two delightful weekend flea markets, Bazar de Antiguedades (Plaza del Angel in the Zona Rosa area) and Lagunilla ("Thieves Market"). The flea markets tend to be fun places to discover unexpected treasures at bargain prices as well as practice your bargaining skills. Indeed, two of our most interesting purchases in Mexico – an old lantern for US$15 and an early Castillo silver pitcher for US$90 – were found in Mexico City's two weekend flea markets.

JEWELRY AND SILVER

Mexico offers a wide range of jewelry for both discerning and budget shoppers. It's especially noted for its silver jewelry, which is produced in abundance in Taxco and available in shops and markets throughout Mexico. Traditional gold jewelry can be found in many shops, but it's especially abundant at the National Pawn Shop and nearby Centro Joyero de Mexico in Mexico City. For fiery red and rock opals, amethysts, and other semiprecious stones, be sure to visit several jewelry shops in the charming city of Querétaro near San Miguel de Allende. The nearby city of Guanajuato is known for its turquoise inlaid gold jewelry. A few shops in Taxco also offer jewelry set with amethysts, garnets, topaz, agates, and opals. Several top jewelry shops, such as Tane, Astrid, Aplijsa, and Sergio Bustamante, have branch shops at major resorts in Mexico, especially in Acapulco, Ixtapa, and Puerto Vallarta, and in Guadalajara. In fact, outside of Mexico City and Taxco, major jewelers are usually found in the top hotels of Mexico's resorts. For unique and compelling jewelry designs in both gold and silver that especially appeal to visitors, be sure to visit two of our favorite jewelers whose designs are works of art: Tane (www.tane.com.mx) and Sergio Bustamante (http://sergiobustamante.com.mx). For a preview of their wonderful designs, collections, and selections, be sure to visit their websites before visiting their shops. You'll also find international jewelers, such as Tiffany's, Cartier, and Bulgari, well represented in the upscale Polanco section of Mexico City. Several local jewelry designers have factories and shops in Puerto Vallarta, Guadalajara, Querétaro, San Miguel de Allende, and Oaxaca. Puerto Vallarta also has a few international-oriented jewelry shops (see Viva) well worth visiting. For inexpensive jewelry, visit the various artisan markets that usually include vendors offering silver jewelry that invariably comes from Taxco's many silver factories.

LEATHER GOODS

You will find many types of inexpensive leather goods in Mexico, from shoes, wallets, belts, and handbags to jackets, hats, and luggage. Many markets are filled with inexpensive leather goods. But be careful in making such purchases. Leather quality is usually a tricky business. If you are particular about quality, you may want to pass on most locally produced leather goods, especially if the leather hides originated in Mexico. Most quality leather found throughout the world usually originates in Italy. Indeed, you may find a few shops in Mexico that offer excellent quality leather goods by local standards, but invariably the leather comes from Italy. In some cases the leather is imported from Italy and the products fabricated in Mexico. When you do encounter good quality Mexican leather goods, such as at Aries (in Zona Rosa) in Mexico City, prices tend to be comparable to imported name-brand Italian products.

CLOTHES AND ACCESSORIES

While Mexico is by no means a fashion center, it does offer some interesting clothes and accessories. Look for a variety of hand-made clothes (see next section on textiles), hats, handbags, and woven belts. T-shirts designed with local and international themes are ubiquitous in markets and shops. Resort communities have an abundance of locally produced and imported resort wear. Designer boutiques with the latest imported fashions can be found in Mexico City's upscale shopping areas and department stores and in resort communities such as Puerto Vallarta. Local fashion designers display their latest collections in the boutiques of Mexico City, Acapulco, Puerto Vallarta, and Guadalajara.

TEXTILES

Mexico has a strong textile and weaving tradition using both upright and back-strap looms. Look for colorful handmade rugs, blankets, bedspreads, cushions, doilies, napkins, table linens, shawls (rabozos), woven belts (fajas), and embroidered dresses, blouses, and children's clothes in several markets and handicraft shops throughout Mexico. Brocaded huipile blouses, woven from rough cotton, are found in Oaxaca's many markets and shops. The textile tradition is especially strong in Oaxaca where you can visit such popular weaving towns as Teotitlan del Valle, which produces rugs and wool sarapes. Many of the textiles have a decidedly ethnic look which may or may not integrate well with your wardrobe or home decor. But if you love to collect textiles as an art form, Mexico has a great deal to offer collectors. For an excellent introduction to quality textiles in Mexico, including featured artisans and photos of their exquisite products, see the extensive textile section in the book *Great Masters of Mexican Folk Art*.

FURNITURE AND HOME DECOR

Numerous shops offer a wide variety of wood and wrought iron furniture. Rustic and painted wood furniture is especially popular in the furniture shops of Mexico City, Guadalajara, Morelia, and San Miguel de Allende. Numerous shops also offer a wide range of attractive home decor items, including candles, candlesticks, lamps, metal sculptures, ceramic pots, mirrors, glassware, baskets, bird cages, and decorative animals. Several shops in cosmopolitan Mexico City, Puerto Vallarta, Guadalajara, and San Miguel de Allende – Mexico's four major furniture, home decor, and design centers – also import home decorative items from around the world. Don't be surprised to find Indian doors and chests, African stools, and Moroccan ceramics in such shops.

OTHER DISCOVERIES

You will discover many other appealing products during your travels in Mexico. Morelia, Pueblo, and Oaxaca, for example, are famous for their local sweets. Oaxaca is known for its local chocolate, coffee, and a powerful liquor known as Mezcal. Guadalajara is within 35 miles of the town of Tequila, which is famous for Mexico's most popular liquor. Many shops in Puerto Vallarta offer colorful beaded art works produced by the local Huichol Indians. Inexpensive, but potentially problematic, prescription drugs are hot items in many border cities as well as in pharmacies elsewhere in Mexico. Gifts and souvenirs abound throughout Mexico.

Take Key Shopping Information

Depending on what you plan to buy, you should take all the necessary information you need to make informed shopping decisions. Do your shopping research and documentation before you leave home. Shops in Mexico are not good places to get an expensive education, especially when it comes to purchasing ceramics, antiques, home decorative items, and jewelry. If you are looking for art, antiques, furniture, and accessories, include with your "wish list" room measurements to help you determine if particular items will fit into your home. Without floor and wall measurements, you may have to guess whether or not an interesting item will work in your home. Consider bringing along photographs of rooms you hope to furnish or add to.

If you plan to shop for clothes and accessories, your homework should include taking an inventory of your closets and identifying specific colors, fabrics, and designs you wish to acquire to complement and enlarge your present wardrobe. Be sure you know what colors work best for your wardrobe.

Do Comparative Shopping

You should do comparative shopping both at home and within Mexico in order to get a good idea of what is or is not a good buy. Our rule of thumb is that if a comparable item is available at home, and it is not at least 20 percent cheaper buying it abroad, it's probably not worth the effort of buying it abroad for such a small savings. After all, back home you most likely will have return privileges, and you may be protected by consumer protection regulations or you can take legal action should such items be misrepresented.

However, many items in Mexico are unique, especially jewelry, ceramics, antiques, folk art, leather goods, and handicrafts. These are the type of items one has to see, feel, and fall in love with – they must "speak" to you. Once in Mexico, we frequently found prices on identical ceramics and folk art could vary as much as 50 percent from one shop to another – which clearly justifies doing comparative shopping within Mexico.

The first step in doing comparative shopping starts at home. Determine exactly what you want and need.

> ❑ Take measurements and photographs of rooms that could become candidates for home decorative items.
>
> ❑ Be sure to take with you information on any clothes, accessories, or jewelry (sizes, colors, comparative prices) to look for in Mexico.
>
> ❑ Half the fun of shopping is the serendipity of discovering the unique and exotic.

Make lists. Spend some time "window shopping" on the Internet by examining the Mexican handcrafted items on sites such as www.novica.com and www.eziba.com.

Once you arrive in Mexico, your shopping plans will probably change considerably as you encounter many new items you had not planned to purchase but which attract your interest and buying attention. Indeed, half the fun of shopping while traveling in Mexico is the serendipity of discovering the unique and exotic – a beautiful copper pot, a gorgeous piece of jewelry, a nice ceramic dish, a fascinating papier-mâché Day of the Dead figure, a lovely carved and painted Alebrijes, or a compelling bronze sculpture or painting – things you could not have anticipated encountering but which you now see, feel, and judge as possible acquisitions for your home or office. These are the great shopping moments that require local knowledge about differences in quality and pricing. Many products, such as folk art, antiques, or paintings may be unique one-of-a-kind items that are difficult to compare. You must judge them in terms of their designs, colors, and intrinsic value. Other items, such as jewelry, ready-made clothing, and souvenir items, will beg comparative shopping because the same or similar quality items are widely available in numerous shops and markets.

You'll have plenty of opportunities to do comparison shopping in the shops and markets of the largest and most touristed cities – Mexico City, Acapulco, Puerto Vallarta, Guadalajara, San Miguel de Allende, and Oaxaca. Many of the shops in these cities offer similar items that beg to be compared for prices and quality. You are well advised to visit several shops soon after your arrival in these cities in order to get some sense of market prices for various items you are likely to frequently encounter.

At the same time, if you plan to visit artisan towns and villages in Morelia and Oaxaca, be sure to survey products and prices in the city shops and markets before venturing into the countryside. Don't assume prices will be cheaper outside the cities where labor and cost of living look cheaper. You may be unpleasantly surprised with the cost of your village purchase when you later visit a city shop or market and discover the same or similar item is cheaper there. After all, most locals know the market value of their products (they work with dealers and visit retail shops and markets in the cities), and you most likely will be viewed as a rich tourist visiting their ostensibly poor town or village. In some cases, you may find the same products in the city shops and markets to be cheaper than at the production source! But you'll only know this if you first survey products and prices in the cities before visiting the towns and villages.

Keep Track of Receipts

It's important to keep track of all of your purchases for making an accurate Customs declaration when you return home. Be sure to ask for receipts wherever you shop. If a shop doesn't issue receipts, ask them to create a receipt by writing the information on a piece of paper, include the shop's name and address, and sign it.

Since it's so easy to misplace receipts, you might want to organize your receipts using a form such as this:

CUSTOMS DECLARATION RECORD FORM

Receipt #	Item	Price (pesos)	Price (US$)
1. 2341	Earrings	5,000	$442.09
2. _____			
3. _____			
4. _____			

This can be especially useful when receipts are written in a language you cannot read. Staple a sheet or two of notebook or accountant's paper to the front of a large envelope and number down the left side of the page. Draw one or two vertical columns down the right side. Each evening, sort through that day's purchases, write a description of the purchase on the accompanying receipt, and enter that item on your receipt record. Record the receipt so later you'll know exactly which item belongs to the receipt. Put the receipts in the envelope and pack the purchases away. If you're missing a receipt, make a note beside the appropriate entry.

29 Shopping Rules for Success

Wherever you shop in Mexico, keep these basic shopping rules in mind. They may serve you well in identifying the best quality shops and in avoiding many mistakes frequently reported by visitors to Mexico:

1. **Don't expect great bargains and good value in Mexico.** Although this is ostensibly a Third World country that offers budget travel opportunities, many visitors find Mexico relatively expensive, especially for hotels, resorts, transportation, and shipping. Quality shopping also tends to be expensive. Indeed, for discerning travelers, Mexico is not an inexpensive destination and bargains are often difficult to find. The cost of staying in Mexico City, for example, can be very similar to New York City. Many goods may appear overpriced or prices may seem arbitrary – whatever the market will bear versus what something is truly worth. If you do comparative shopping, you'll often discover wide price fluctuations on similar items offered at different shops. The best bargains are found on items you can bargain for or which are found in government-operated shops, such as the network of Fonart shops for arts and crafts and the National Pawn Shop in Mexico City for jewelry and antiques.

2. **Expect to encounter lots of trash in the search for unique treasures.** Many visitors get turned off with shopping in Mexico, especially when encountering so many kitschy handicrafts, souvenirs, leather goods, and clothes in the markets and shopping centers. The real shopping challenge in Mexico is to cut through all the trash to find the "good stuff." If you visit many of our recommended shops, you'll quickly discover a different dimension to shopping in Mexico. You'll encounter outstanding quality products, meet talented artists and craftspeople, and acquire the very best Mexico has

to offer discerning shoppers. You'll also encounter some very high-end shopping for exclusive art, antiques, and jewelry – exquisite items that only very wealthy locals and international visitors can afford. Indeed, you may need to add a few zeros to your pricing expectations as $10 becomes $100 or $1,000!

3. **Prepare to shop in two very different shopping cultures which require different shopping skills.** The first world is the most familiar one for visitors – shopping centers, department stores, and hotel shopping arcades. Shops in this culture tend to have window displays, well organized interiors, and fixed prices which may or may not be all that fixed, depending on your ability to persuade shops to discount prices. The second shopping culture, consisting of traditional street shops, sidewalk vendors, market stalls, and touts, tends to be somewhat chaotic and involves price uncertainty and bargaining skills. You will most likely be able to directly transfer your shopping skills to the first culture, but you may have difficulty navigating in the second shopping culture which at times can be intimidating but often fun.

4. **Shop names may change because of tax issues.** If you can't find a recommended shop, it doesn't necessarily mean it moved or went out of business. Some shops change their names because of tax issues. Ask if the shop used to go under a different name.

5. **Plan your schedule around local shopping hours and traditions.** Many shops outside Mexico City and in resort areas close between 2pm and 4pm, a good time for a long lunch or to go sightseeing. Most shops open between 9am and 10am and close between 5pm and 8pm, depending on the city. However, even these hours can vary, depending on the shop. A shop that says it opens at 11am may not open until 1pm.

6. **Expect to find the best quality shopping at the best quality locations.** Quality shops tend to go where the money congregates. Therefore, it should come as no surprise that the best quality shopping is usually found in the shopping arcades of top quality hotels, which tend to screen the quality of shops that are allowed to rent their shop space, and in upscale neighborhoods. These shops tend to cater to the tastes of upper income visitors and wealthy local residents. Don't expect to do quality shopping in markets. These are fun and exotic places to acquire "bargains" and encounter a variety of interesting cultural experiences. When in doubt where to shop for quality items, head for the major hotels.

If the hotel does not have a shopping arcade, ask the concierge or front desk for shopping recommendations. They usually know the best places to shop based upon the experiences of their hotel guests.

7. **Focus your initial shopping on the major shopping areas.** Most shopping areas are very well defined – hotel shopping arcades, shopping centers, markets, factories, major streets, and vendor stalls at tourist sites.

8. **Remember to seek out the best shops by checking with people "in the know."** In addition to our "Best of the Best" shopping recommendations for each city, the concierges and front desk personnel in most five-star hotels know where the best shopping can be found. Knowledgeable about their community and frequently in communication with guests, shops, and fellow concierges, they usually have a good sense of the best shops to visit for quality, pricing, and reliability. They often know where their best guests shop for such popular items as jewelry, clothes, art, handicrafts, and antiques. They also know which shops generate complaints because of high prices, poor quality and service, and problems with shipping. Ask for their top three recommendations in different product categories. However, not all concierges are necessarily knowledgeable or objective about shopping. Some may get "kickbacks" for recommending you to particular shops. It depends on the hotel and the services it provides for its guests. Some concierges may essentially function as bell boys. In Mexico City, for example, concierges who really know the "ins" and "outs" of the city are found at the J. W. Marriott Hotel and Four Seasons Hotel. The worst people to ask for shopping recommendations are tour guides, drivers, touts, and general service personnel. They are either "on the take" or have no sense of quality shopping. You may pay dearly for their advice!

9. **Be sure to comparison shop for many items.** Many shops carry similar items, and prices can vary considerably from one shop to another on jewelry, clothes, leather goods, folk art, and handicrafts. Be sure to survey your shopping options by visiting various shops offering such products. You'll quickly get some idea as to how to best value these items.

10. **Bargain for most items you purchase in the markets.** Markets are fun places to practice your bargaining skills. Here, discounts can run from 20 to 70 percent, depending on the merchant and your haggling skills. Most will extend a discount if you ask the simple question, "*Is it possible to do any*

better on this price?" Doing better often means a 20-percent discount. If you do comparison shopping, spend some time with the merchant, and persist. Chances are you can get a 40- to 50-percent discount on many items in the markets. However, there are no hard and fast rules on bargaining – only whatever you can achieve with particular merchants.

11. **Don't assume you can bargain everywhere you shop in Mexico.** Bargaining is best done in markets, as well as with street vendors, where you are expected to haggle over prices. But once outside the markets, shops may give very little discounts on what they consider to be fixed prices. In fact, most shops don't discount, although some may extend a five- or 10-percent discount for cash. Just because you successfully bargain for discounts in the markets is no reason to assume that you can do the same elsewhere. When in doubt, probe for a discount by nicely asking our "possibility" question, *"Is it possible to do any better on this price?"* As you may quickly discover, life is full of possibilities in Mexico. Many merchants respond to this question with a discount, especially if you are purchasing expensive items in jewelry, art, or antique shops. The worst thing that can happen to you is to be told "no," but "maybe" or "yes" are likely outcomes.

12. **Get discounts by asking about IVA.** Many shops will arrange to take off the Value Added Tax (IVA) for shipping items outside the country. Since shops normally do not volunteer this information, or some shops still do not understand how the IVA works, you need to ask about an IVA discount. Some shops also are willing to take off the IVA even for items you take with you, although this is a questionable practice. Persistence over the IVA issue may pay off with a 10- to 15-percent discount on top of a five-percent cash discount.

13. **Be prepared for an archaic, inefficient, and time-consuming payment system.** Paying for items can be a laborious and irritating process. Many shops use an old check-and-balance payment system to prevent in-house fraud and errors. It basically works like this: You make your selections and give them to a clerk; the clerk adds everything up and gives you a receipt with the total cost and then keeps your purchases behind the counter until you return from your payment adventure; you then proceed to another section of the shop where you must stand in a payment line (it can get very long!) to purchase your goods; and with your receipt stamped or punched as "Paid," you return to the first clerk to

retrieve your purchases after showing your paid receipt. This whole payment process can take from 10 to 40 minutes to complete, depending on the length of the lines and the efficiency of the payment clerk, who may have difficulty counting money or may go on break!

14. **Expect to spend more time shopping than you initially planned.** Many of our recommended shopping areas, shops, and markets are delightful places to visit. Don't be surprised to find your shopping plans go awry as you take more time shopping in these places than you initially planned, especially if you encounter interesting merchants, dealers, and artisans whom you engage in conversations about their products.

15. **Ask for directions whenever you feel you need to do so.** Signage is often a problem when looking for particular streets and shops. At times, especially in markets, you may feel lost and have difficulty finding specific shops or products. Whenever this happens, just ask for assistance or wander around. Half of the fun of shopping in Mexico is discovering unexpected places.

16. **Be sure to check out all the rooms in a shop.** Some shops keep their best items in the back rooms or upstairs – for serious buyers and dealers. If a shop has a window display, don't assume what's on display represents the best inventory. If a shop catches your interest, go inside and check it out thoroughly. Ask about other rooms, especially what is upstairs and in the back or side rooms.

17. **When visiting art galleries, be sure to ask to see the gallery's complete inventory.** Most art galleries represent many different artists whose works are stored in back rooms or warehoused elsewhere. When you enter a gallery, you usually encounter the current exhibit, which is on display for only four to six weeks. Many galleries have catalogs or directories with photos of their complete inventory. Ask to see these books so you can get a better idea of their holdings. Chances are the current exhibit, which may be very disappointing, does not adequately represent the gallery and its many artists. Also ask about upcoming special events and exhibitions. If your timing is right, you may be invited to an opening or special exhibition where you will have a chance to meet artists.

18. **Ask for assistance and background information if necessary.** One of the great pleasures of shopping in Mexico is

learning about various products, artisans, and craftspeople. Since you may be unfamiliar with many local products, such as fine art, antiques, folk art, textiles, jewelry, leather goods, be sure to ask questions about the various selections. Shopkeepers tend to be very friendly and informative. They can quickly educate you about their products and artisans. In so doing, you will probably gain a new appreciation for "Made in Mexico" products as well as the history and culture of this fascinating country.

19. **Have fun visiting artisan towns and villages, but don't expect to find great selections and the best deals shopping at the source.** Most noted local artisans and craftspeople work with dealers in the cities who monopolize their inventory and select the best products. Many visitors, who drive miles to visit the local talent in their workshops and buy directly from them, are often disappointed to discover very little inventory is available and prices are not much different than in the top shops in the cities. Many of these people have already sold off their best inventory to top shops and dealers for cash. However, good prices and selections are often available through lesser-known artisans and craftspeople in the same communities. By all means plan to visit these production sources and meet noted artisans and craftspeople. But do so for the cultural experience rather than for a shopping advantage.

20. **Don't procrastinate when you fall in love with something while shopping.** If you see something you really love, buy it when you initially see it. This is especially true with one-of-a-kind items, such as fine art, folk art, and jewelry. If you decide to shop around and come back later, chances are the item will be gone, and you'll be disappointed for having procrastinated in expectation of getting a better deal elsewhere on something that was unique to begin with. Over the years, this has become one of our most important shopping rules that has frequently affected us and many other shoppers: Things you love and leave behind will invariably disappear by the time you return to buy them! In other words, if something initially "speaks to you," buy it because it will probably speak louder to the next individual who will immediately buy it.

21. **Watch where you walk.** Sidewalks and streets can be dangerous to pedestrians due to holes, trash, traffic, and overhanging window sills and wrought iron grates. It's relatively easy to twist an ankle, fall, or bang your head in such irregular street and sidewalk situations.

22. **Use your credit cards whenever possible.** Many shops accept major credit cards, especially Visa and MasterCard, although American Express is also accepted at many larger establishments. Many also will accept U.S. dollars. However, consider charging your purchase just in case you later have a problem with authenticity or shipping. While under no legal obligation to do so, your credit card company may be able to assist you in resolving such problems. Credit card purchases usually receive the best exchange rates.

23. **Collect receipts for everything you purchase.** You may need the receipt for Customs or as documentation for contacting the merchant. Make sure you have essential information on the receipt – shop name, address, and telephone and fax numbers as well as the salesperson you dealt with.

24. **Be suspicious of street touts and tour guides who want to take you shopping.** Beware of shopping in major tourist shops and factories frequented by tour buses and taxis. Like elsewhere in the world, these places tend to be patronized by clients of tour guides who get commissions – often in the 10- to 40-percent range – on everything their clients purchase. The quality of products in these places is usually mediocre and the prices are often high. Expect to pay a real premium for shopping in such places that are highly recommended by tour guides and drivers. Whatever you do, don't ask your tour guide or driver to help you bargain for an item – a frequent request of naive tourists. Your guide is not your friend in these places. He or she instead is the problem – leading you to the shopping slaughter where you are likely to pay 20 to 50 percent above retail! A percentage of what you pay for each item will go directly into the pocket of your guide or driver.

25. **Expect to encounter packing and shipping problems.** Packing and shipping can become a real challenge in Mexico, more so than in most countries we visit. Many shops are strictly "cash and carry" – they do not pack or ship. Some shops will only ship to the U.S. border – it's your problem to arrange to have it picked up and shipped beyond the border. Other shops have experience in packing and shipping since they regularly deal with international visitors and use DHL for air shipments. And still others use or recommend using PakMail. While reliable, such shipping services are usually very expensive. Indeed, we found it was much cheaper to ship comparable items from Cape Town, South Africa to Washington, DC than from Mexico City to

Washington, DC – a 10,000-mile difference! However, many other shops lack such packing and shipping experience. Don't assume a shop knows how to pack and ship. When in doubt, take items with you. If you decide to have items shipped, pay particular attention to the process. As you will quickly discover, the devil is in the details. Get a receipt describing the item and stating who is doing what and for how much. If an item is considered an antique or piece of art, the receipt should specify the age or state "original work of art" – important issues with U.S. Customs and its system of exemptions.

26. **In some cases, plan to do your own packing and re-packing.** Some small shops claim to do packing, but chances are you will not be happy with the result. Either closely supervise the packing process by instructing the shop how to pack things securely or do your own packing and re-packing by acquiring packing material, especially bubble wrap and cardboard. Don't trust even the best hotels to do an adequate packing job.

27. **Take photos of all your purchases, especially items being shipped.** We always take pictures of our shopping treasures just in case we have a shipment problem, which occasionally occurs. Better still, take a photo of the item with the merchant and/or shipper standing next to it or holding it. Such visual documentation may later come in handy and it's always a nice memorable photo of interesting people you met and did business with in Mexico. The photo also helps in later clearing Customs, especially if they are not sure how to classify and assess a particular item.

28. **Take items with you whenever possible.** While many shops can pack and ship, you may want to take smaller items with you. Don't just take a shop's word that they can ship with no problem. You may discover the cost of shipping a small item can be very expensive, especially when it arrives "collect" by international courier service!

29. **Take your purchases with you as part of your carry-on or check-through luggage.** Shipping from Mexico can be outrageously expensive unless you do your homework and seek out alternatives to standard approaches. We usually try to take our purchases with us whether they be small or large. In preparation, we usually limit ourselves to one check-through piece of luggage on our flight to Mexico. For the two of us, this allows us three more check-through pieces of luggage on our international flight back home. Our advice:

take very little luggage with you on your way to Mexico in anticipation of accumulating purchases along the way that you will want to take home with you. Alternatively, if two people are traveling together, take two pieces of luggage and fill the second one primarily with bubble wrap and packing materials. You still can have two boxes made for larger pieces and bring them home at no additional cost. You'll save a great deal of time and money by planning in this manner. If you purchase an item that can be checked through as luggage, such as a piece of pottery, ask the shop to pack the item well so it can be checked through with your airline as a piece of luggage. Be sure to check with your airline on the dimensions of allowable check-through items. Ascertain that the shop can do such packing or they can arrange for expert packing to protect delicate purchases. Even large pieces of pottery can be well packed (the packer builds a sturdy wood box) to be shipped through as an extra piece of luggage. But inquire thoroughly how they will do this. Don't assume anything. The best method is to pack delicate items well with sufficient bubble wrap or similar material in a sturdy cardboard box. Then pack the first box inside another sturdy cardboard or wood box with more packing material filling the space between the two boxes. Make sure the size of such boxes are within the dimensions allowed by the airline.

Bargaining Tips and Skills

If you're not used to bargaining when shopping, you will be at a price disadvantage in Mexico's many markets. If you consider yourself a good bargainer in other countries, you may quickly discover your bargaining skills may not work well in Mexico. This isn't China, Indonesia, India, Turkey, or Brazil.

FIXED PRICES AND NO BARGAINING IN MY SHOP!

Bargaining in Mexico primarily takes place in markets where vendors expect you to bargain. That's one reason why market prices may initially appear high. If you pay the first asking price, chances are you may over-pay by 20 to 50 percent because you failed to bargain. However, some market vendors will not negotiate much. At the same time, many shops have fixed prices. Some may feel personally insulted – and will actually tell you that you insulted them by asking for a discount – if you try to bargain. After all, they are not market vendors! Don't be intimidated by such false pride. Be nice but approach this as a business transaction – your money for the merchant's products. You may be able to chip away at the fixed retail price by employing some of our bargaining strategies, especially asking for cash discounts or waiving the IVAs on items shipped outside Mexico. We seldom pay full retail on big ticket items, whether purchasing at home or abroad. Don't worry about insulting some people in Mexico by asking for a discount. It's okay to be a bit culturally insensitive when it comes time to possibly saving US$100 or more! Again, this is business, and we're all part of the global economy.

BARGAINING AND PRICE UNCERTAINTY

Bargaining can be great fun and result in excellent buys. But for the uninitiated, bargaining can be very intimidating; it seems to be a waste of precious shopping and travel time. Individuals from fixed price cultures would rather see a price sticker and make a decision of whether or not to purchase without someone haggling with them over the price. But if everything were fixed prices, you would really miss out on an interesting cultural experience in Mexico. So let's take a look at some basic bargaining rules to put you on the road to shopper's heaven.

Not knowing the price of an item, many shoppers from fixed-price cultures face a problem. "What is the actual value of the item? How much should I pay? At what point do I know I'm getting a fair price?" After all, you don't want to be "taken" by an unscrupulous merchant who preys on naive tourists. Most of these questions can be quickly and accurately answered based on your comparative shopping experiences. Indeed, you should have some idea of the value of the item, if you've had a chance to do some comparative shopping. You have done comparative shopping among the various shops you've encountered in Mexico in order to establish a price range for positioning yourself in the bargaining process. You've visited shops in Mexico City's major shopping centers to research how much a similar item is selling for at a fixed price. You've checked with a shop in your hotel and compared prices there. In your hotel you might ask "How much is this item?" and then act a little surprised that it appears so expensive. Tell them that you are a hotel guest and thus you want their "very best price." At this point the price may decrease by 10 percent as you are told this is "our very special price for hotel guests" or you are told the price can be reduced if you pay in cash or have it shipped and thus avoid the IVA.

Once you initially receive a special price from your first price inquiry, you may get another 10 percent through further negotiation. But at this point do not negotiate any more, unless you are unwilling to take the chance this item may be gone if you later return for it. Take the shop's business card and record on the back the item, the original price, and the first discount price; thank the shopkeeper, and tell him or her that you may return. Repeat this same scenario in a few other shops. After doing three or four comparisons, you will establish a price range for particular items. This range will give you a fairly accurate idea of the going discount price. At this point you should be prepared to do some serious haggling, playing one shop off against another until you get the best price.

THE SAVVY SHOPPER

Savvy shoppers in Mexico quickly learn how to comparative shop and negotiate the best deal. In learning to be effective, you don't need to be timid, aggressive, or obnoxious – extreme behaviors frequently exhibited by first-time practitioners of the art of bargaining. Although you may feel bargaining is a defensive measure to avoid being ripped off by unscrupulous merchants, it is an acceptable way of doing business in many cultures. Merchants merely adjust their profit margins to the customer, depending on how they feel about the situation as well as their current cash flow needs. It is up to you to adapt to such a pricing culture.

Chances are you will deal with a merchant who is a seasoned business person. As soon as you walk through the door, most merchants will want to sell you items then and there.

The best deal you will get is when you have a personal relationship with the merchant. Contrary to what others may tell you about bargains for tourists, you often can get as good a deal – sometimes even better – than someone from the local community. It is simply a myth that tourists can't do as well on prices as the locals. Indeed, we often do better than the locals because we have done our comparative shopping and we know well the art of bargaining – something locals are often lax in doing. In addition, some merchants may give you a better price than the locals because you are "here today and gone tomorrow." After all, you won't be around to tell their regular customers about your very special price.

More often than not, the pricing system operates like this: If the shopkeeper likes you, you are a friend of a friend or relative, or he is in need of cash flow that day, you can expect to get a good price. Whenever possible, drop names of individuals who referred you to the shop; the shopkeeper may think you are a friend and thus you are entitled to a special discount. But if you do not have such a relationship and you present yourself as a typical tourist who is here today and gone tomorrow, you need to bargain hard. In fact, we encountered a silver and jewelry shop in Mexico City and a folk art shop in San Miguel de Allende that actually wrote personal notes on the back of their business cards so we could get 10 to 20 percent discounts from their friends or relatives who operated similar shops in Taxco and Oaxaca. When we arrived at these other shops, we showed the cards and were treated as very special shoppers.

PRACTICE 14 RULES OF EFFECTIVE BARGAINING

The art of bargaining in Mexico can take on several different forms. In general, you want to achieve two goals in this haggling process: establish the value of an item and get the best possible price. The following bargaining rules work well in most negotiable shopping situations.

1. **Do your research before talking about prices and initiating the bargaining process.**

    Compare the prices among various shops and market vendors, starting with fixed-price items in department stores and shops. Spot-check price ranges among shops in and around your hotel. Also, refer to your research done with catalogs and discount houses back home to determine if the discount is sufficient to warrant purchasing the item abroad.

2. **Determine the exact item you want to buy, but don't express excessive interest.**

    Select the particular item you want and then focus your bargaining around that one item without expressing excessive interest. Even though you may be excited by the item and want it very badly, once the merchant knows you are committed to buying it, you weaken your bargaining position. Express a passing interest; indicate through eye contact with other items in the shop that you are not necessarily committed to the one item. As you ask about the other items, you should get some sense concerning the willingness of the merchant to discount prices.

3. **Set a ceiling price you're willing to pay – and buy now!**

    Before engaging in serious negotiations, set in your mind the maximum amount you are willing to pay, which may be 20 percent more than you figured the item should sell for based on your research. However, if you find something you love that is really unique, be prepared to pay more if you can afford it. In many situations you will find unique items not available anywhere else. Consider buying now since the item may be gone when you return. Bargain as hard as you can and then pay what you have to – even though it may seem painful – for the privilege of owning a unique item. Remember, it's only money and it only hurts once. You can always make more money, and after returning home you will most likely enjoy your wonderful purchase and forget how painful it seemed at the time to buy it at less than your expected discount. Above all, do not pass up an item you really love just because the bargaining process does not fall in your favor. It is very easy to be *"penny wise but pound foolish"* in Mexico simply because the bargaining process is such an ego-involved activity. You may return home forever regretting that you didn't buy a lovely item just because you were too cheap to "give" on the last US$5 of US$50 of haggling. In the end, put your ego aside, give in, and buy what you really want. Only you and the merchant will know who really won this game, and once you return home the US$5 or US$50 will seem to be such an insignificant amount. Chances are you still got a good bargain compared to what you would pay elsewhere if, indeed, you could even find a similar item!

4. **Establish good will and a personal relationship.**

   A shrewd buyer is charming, polite, personable, and friendly. You should have a sense of humor, smile, and be light-hearted during the bargaining process. But be careful about eye contact, which can be threatening. Keep it to a minimum. Sellers prefer to establish a personal relationship so that the bargaining process can take place on a friendly, face-saving basis. In the end, both the buyer and seller should come out as winners. This cannot be done if you approach the buyer in very serious and harsh terms. You should start by exchanging pleasantries concerning the weather, your trip, the city, or the nice items in the shop. After exchanging business cards or determining your status, the shopkeeper will know what roles should be played in the coming transaction.

5. **Let the seller make the first offer.**

   If the merchant starts by asking you *"How much do you want to pay?,"* always avoid answering this rather dangerous set-up question. He who reveals his hand first is likely to lose in the end. Immediately turn the question around: *"How much are you asking?"* Remember, many merchants try to get you to pay as much as you are willing and able to pay – not what the value of the item is or what he or she is willing to take. You should never reveal your ability or willingness to pay a certain price. Keep the seller guessing, thinking that you may lose interest or not buy the item because it appears too expensive. Always get the merchant to initiate the bargaining process. In so doing, the merchant must take the defensive as you shift to the offensive.

6. **Take your time, being deliberately slow in order to get the merchant to invest his or her time in you.**

    The more you indicate that you are impatient and in a hurry, the more you are likely to pay. When negotiating a price, **time** is usually in your favor. Many shopkeepers also see time as a positive force in the bargaining process. Some try to keep you in their shop by serving you soft drinks, beer, or tequila while negotiating the price. Be careful; this nice little ritual may soften you somewhat on the bargaining process as you begin establishing a more personal relationship with the merchant. The longer you stay in control prolonging the negotiation, the better the price should be. Although some merchants may deserve it, never insult them. They need to "keep face" as much as you do in the process of giving and getting the very best price.

7. **Use odd numbers in offering the merchant 30 percent to 60 percent less than what he or she initially offers.**

    Avoid stating round numbers, such as 700, 1,800, or 1,000. Instead, offer 62, 173, or 817. Such numbers impress upon others that you may be a seasoned haggler who knows value and expects to do well in this negotiation. Your offer will probably be 20 percent less than the value you determined for the item. For example, if the merchant asks US$100, offer US$42, knowing the final price should probably be US$60. The merchant will probably counter with only a 20-percent discount – US$80. At this point you will need to go back and forth with another two or three offers and counter-offers. In some cases you want to initially offer 75 percent less than the asking price, depending on the item and seller.

8. **Appear a little disappointed and then take your time again.**

    Never appear upset or angry with the seller. Keep your cool at all times by slowly sitting down and carefully examining the item. Shake your head a little and say, *"Gee, that's too bad. That's much more than I had planned to spend. I like it, but I really can't go that high."* Appear to be a sympathetic listener as the seller attempts to explain why he or she cannot budge more on the price. Make sure you do not accuse the merchant of being a thief! Use a little charm, if you can, for the way you conduct the bargaining process will affect the final price. This should be a civil negotiation in which you nicely bring the price down, the seller "saves face," and everyone goes away feeling good about the deal.

9. Counter with a new offer at a 35-percent discount.

Punch several keys on your calculator, which indicates you are doing some serious thinking. Then say something like *"This is really the best I can do. It's a lovely item, but US$162 is really all I can pay."* At this point the merchant will most likely counter with a 20-percent discount – US$200. He may say that's the best he can do. But don't believe him. There's still more room to negotiate, if you become somewhat creative.

10. Be patient, persistent, and take your time again by carefully examining the item.

Respond by saying *"That's a little better, but it's still too much. I want to look around a little more."* Then start to get up and look toward the door. At this point the merchant has invested some time in this exchange, and he or she is getting close to a possible sale. The merchant will either let you walk out the door or try to stop you with another counter-offer. If you walk out the door, you can always return to get the US$200 price. But most likely, if there is still some bargaining room, the merchant will try to stop you. The merchant is likely to say: *"You don't want to waste your time looking elsewhere. I'll give you the best price anywhere – just for you. Okay, US$190. That's my final price."*

11. Be creative for the final negotiation.

You could try for US$180, but chances are US$190 will be the final price with this merchant. Yet, there may still be some room for negotiating "extras." At this point, get up and walk around the shop and examine other items; try to appear as if you are losing interest in the item you were bargaining for. While walking around, identify a US$10 item you like which might make a nice gift for a friend or relative, which you could possibly include in the final deal. Wander back to the US$10 item and look as if your interest is waning and perhaps you need to leave. Then start to probe the possibility of including extras while agreeing on the US$190: *"Okay, I might go US$190, if you include this with it."* The "this" is the US$10 item you eyed. You also might negotiate with your credit card.

Chances are the merchant is expecting cash on the US$190 discounted price and will add a 2- to 6-percent "commission" if you want to use your credit card. In this case, you might respond to the US$190 by saying, *"Okay, I'll go with the US$190, but only if I can use my credit card."* You may get your way, your bank will float you a loan in the meantime, and your credit card company may help you resolve the problem in case you later learn your purchase was misrepresented. Finally, you may want to negotiate packing and delivery processes. If it is a fragile item, insist that it be packed well so you can take it with you on the airplane or have it shipped. If your purchase is large, insist that the shop deliver it to your hotel or to your shipper. If the shop is shipping it by air or sea, try to get them to agree to absorb some of the freight and insurance costs.

This very slow, civil, methodical, and sometimes charming – but always focused – approach to bargaining works well in most market situations. It's less effective in the case of fixed-price shops that normally do not bargain and may initially reject any such efforts to bargain. However, Mexican merchants do differ in how they respond to situations, and many of them are unpredictable, depending on whether or not they like you. In some cases, your timing may be right: the merchant is in need of cash flow that day and thus he or she is willing to give you the price you want, with little or no bargaining. Others will not give more than a 10- to 20-percent discount unless you are a friend of a friend who is then eligible for the special "family discount." And others are not good businessmen, are unpredictable, lack motivation, take such initiatives as personal insults, or are just moody; they refuse to budge on their prices even though your offer is fair compared to the going prices in other shops. In these situations it is best to leave the shop and find one which is more receptive to the traditional haggling process.

This bargaining process often takes on additional drama in markets and with street vendors frequented by tourists. In some of these places you may encounter merchants who play "bait and switch": they urge you to come into their shop where you can buy a particular item for the cheap price of US$10, but once you enter the shop, the price mysteriously goes to US$50. His objective is to get you to come into his shop where he believes he will be in control of the negotiation process.

Over the years we've developed three additional rules for shopping in markets, with street vendors, and at tour bus stop shops:

12. **Observe the "8 Foot Rule" for negotiating your best deal:** Merchants maintain control by bringing customers into as well as keeping them in their shops. If you stand outside the shop to bargain (stay 8 feet from the merchant and his goods), you'll be in a much stronger bargaining position. However, if you're already in the shop, it may be time to make a "10 percent exit" – your exit could be worth another 10 percent discount! Do the following. Once you get near a final negotiated figure, walk 8 feet outside the shop. Yes, 8 feet and the price may drop again. Tell the merchant his final price is too much and that you need to think about it as well as look elsewhere. Say goodbye, turn around, and literally walk 8 feet from the entrance of the shop and stop. Turn around and look at the shop and merchant and then look up and down the street. Look as if you are trying to decide where to go next. Chances are your new friend will still be talking to you, trying to persuade you that he offered you an excellent price and asking you to please come back into the shop and talk. Shake your head and say *"It's too expensive. I really need to look some more."* Whatever you do, do not go back into the shop at this point; you'll be at a disadvantage if you do. You should now be in control of the situation. Make the merchant come to you in the street – that's your turf. Take your time and don't move from your position for at least three minutes. You can always pretend to look at your map. There's a high probability the merchant will come out and agree to give you the item at the final price you offered. For some unexplained reason, 8 feet seems to be the perfect distance for this final negotiation (we literally count our steps to make sure our final exit stops at 8 feet!); inside the shop the merchant may be within 6 inches of your face which may make you feel uncomfortable. By going into the street, you take final control of the negotiation. The merchant knows once you turn to leave, you'll probably be gone forever. The wise merchant knows it's better take less or lose out forever.

13. **If you're with a tour group, bargain hard on your own.** Do not ask your tour guide or driver to help you negotiate a price. Since most of these service personnel are being paid commissions on everything you buy at their recommended shop, don't expect them to be an enthusiastic participant in helping you bargain for a good deal which cuts into their commission! Many will tell you

the prices are fixed, which indeed they are . . . and you are the recipient of the "fix"!

14. **If you're visiting a bus stop shop or factory, don't buy where the crowds congregate, or at least try to be the last one out of the shop.** Remember, the herd never gets a good deal – it only gets taken to the slaughter. And he who buys early in the crowd tends to pay a high price. After all, the salesperson has no incentive to discount when he knows lots of naive tourists are willing to pay the full asking price. At this point, it's to your advantage to survey the competition next door or across the street. There are often similar shops nearby that do not have a busload of tourists shopping inside. If you visit these places, you may discover similar items are one-half to one-third the prices being asked at the other shop. If there are no comparable shops around, it's best to wait until everyone leaves the shop to get back on the bus. Being the last one out, chances are you can negotiate a good deal. After all, once you're gone, there will probably be little or no business until another bus comes. The one exception is if you find an item, one of a kind, that you absolutely must have. In this case, bargain as much as you can and then buy. If you walk out, you may return to find that someone from the bus has already purchased "your" item.

Whatever you do, have lots of fun bargaining for your loot. If you follow our rules, you'll approach such situations with confidence, and you'll walk away with a good deal. Some locals may even compliment you on your ability to bargain so well. Indeed, you'll probably be a much better bargainer than most locals!

Bargain for Needs, Not Greed

One word of caution for those who are just learning the fine art of bargaining. **Be sure you really want an item before you initiate the bargaining process.** Many tourists quickly learn to bargain effectively, and then get carried away with their new skill. Rather than use this skill to get what they want, they enjoy the process of bargaining so much that they buy many unnecessary items. After all, they got such "a good deal" and thus could not resist buying the item. Be very careful in getting carried away with your new-found competency. You do not need to fill your suitcases with junk in demonstrating this ego-gratifying skill. If used properly, your bargaining skills will lead to some excellent buys on items you really need and want.

Examine Your Goods Carefully

Before you commence the bargaining process, carefully examine the item, being sure that you understand the quality of the item for which you are negotiating. Then, after you settle on a final price, make sure you are getting the goods you agreed upon. At this point, do two things:

1. Take a photo of your purchase, ideally with the merchant posing with the item.

2. Ask for an official receipt that states what you bought, for how much, and when. Make sure the shop includes its name, address, phone, and/or fax and e-mail address.

You should carefully observe the handling of items, including the actual packing process. If you bought several items, make sure you count and recount exactly what you bought. It's often easy to get distracted at the end and forget to account for everything. Use your receipt as a final checklist before you leave the shop. If at all possible, take the items with you when you leave. If you later discover you were victimized by a switch or misrepresentation, contact the tourist authorities as well as your credit card company if you charged your purchase. You may be able to resolve the problem through these channels. However, the responsibility is on you, the buyer, to know what you are buying.

Beware of Possible Scams

Although one hopes this will never happen, you may encounter unscrupulous merchants who take advantage of you. The most frequent scams to watch out for include:

1. **Switching the goods.** You negotiate for a particular item, but in the process of packing it, the merchant substitutes an inferior product.

2. **Misrepresenting quality goods.** Be especially cautious in jewelry and antique shops. Silver and gold content may not be as pure as represented, and precious stones may not be as precious as they appear. The age and authenticity of antiques may be questionable.

3. **Goods not included in the package(s) you carry with you.** You purchase several items in one shop. The seller wraps them and presents them to you, but "forgets" to include one of the items you paid for.

4. **Goods not shipped.** The shop may agree to ship your goods home, but once you leave, they conveniently forget to do so. You wait and wait, write letters of inquiry, fax, make phone calls, and e-mail the shop; no one can give you a satisfactory response. Unless you have shipping and insurance documents, which is unlikely, and proper receipts, you may not receive your goods.

Your best line of defense against these and other possible scams is to be very careful wherever you go and whatever you do in relation to handling money. A few simple precautions will help avoid some of these problems:

1. **Do not trust anyone with your money** unless you have proper assurances they are giving you exactly what you agreed upon. Trust is something that should be earned – not automatically given to friendly strangers you may like.

2. **Do your homework** so you can determine quality and value as well as anticipate certain types of scams.

3. **Examine the goods carefully,** assuming something may be or will go wrong.

4. **Watch very carefully how the merchant handles items** from the moment they leave your hands until they get wrapped and into a bag.

5. **Request receipts** that list specific items and the prices you paid. Although most shops are willing to "give you a receipt" specifying whatever price you want them to write for purposes of deceiving Customs, be careful in doing so. While you may or may not deceive Customs, your custom-designed receipt may become a double-edged sword, especially if you later need a receipt with the real price to claim your goods or a refund. If the shop is to ship, be sure you have a shipping receipt which also includes insurance against both loss and damage.

6. **Take photos of your purchases.** We strongly recommend taking photos of your major purchases, especially anything that is being entrusted to someone else to be packed and shipped. Better still, take a photo of the seller holding the item, just in case you later need to identify the person with whom you dealt. This photo will give you a visual record of your purchase should you later have problems receiving your shipment, whether one of loss or damage. You'll also have a photo to show Customs should they have any questions about your shipment.

7. **Protect yourself against scams** by using credit cards for payment, especially for big ticket items which could present problems, even though using them may cost you a little more. Although your credit card company is not obligated to do so, most will ask the merchant for documentation, and if not satisfactorily received, will remove the charge from your bill.

If you are victimized, all is not necessarily lost. You should report the problem immediately to the local tourist office, the police, your credit card company, or your insurance company. While inconvenient and time consuming, nonetheless, in many cases you will eventually get satisfactory results.

Shipping Challenges

Shipping can be a problem in Mexico since many shops are not experienced with international shipping and international shippers can be very expensive. You should not pass up buying lovely items because you feel reluctant to ship them home. Indeed, some travelers only buy items that will fit into their suitcase because they are not sure how to ship larger items. We seldom let shipping considerations affect our buying decisions. For us, shipping is one of those things that must be arranged. You have numerous shipping alternatives, from hiring a professional shipping company to hand-carrying your goods on board the plane.

Before leaving home, you should identify the best point of entry for goods returning home by air or sea. Once abroad, you generally have five shipping alternatives:

1. Take everything with you.
2. Do your own packing and shipping through the local post office (for small packages only).
3. Have each shop ship your purchases.
4. Arrange to have one shop consolidate all of your purchases into a single shipment.
5. Hire a local shipper to make all arrangements.

Air Versus Sea Shipments

Taking everything with you is fine if you are from the U.S. or Canada and have your own car, van, or SUV to cart away your loot – the best shipping solution!

If you are flying out of Mexico, plan to take your purchases with you if you don't have much and if you don't mind absorbing excess baggage charges. If you are within your allowable baggage allowance, you can have large items packed to qualify as part of your luggage. If you have more items than what is allowable, ask about the difference between "Excess Baggage" and "Unaccompanied Baggage." Excess baggage is very expensive, while unaccompanied baggage is less expensive, although by no means cheap.

If items are small enough and we don't mind waiting six to eight weeks, we may send them through the local post office by parcel post.

Doing your own packing and shipping may be cheaper, but it is a pain and thus limited savings in the long run. You waste valuable time waiting in lines and trying to figure out the local rules and regulations concerning permits, packing, materials, sizes, and weights.

On the other hand, many shops, especially art galleries, can ship goods for customers. They often pack the items free and only charge for actual postage or freight. If you choose to have a shop ship for you, insist on a receipt specifying they will ship the item. Also, stress the importance of packing the item well to

avoid possible damage. If they cannot insure the item against breakage or loss, do not ship through them. Invariably a version of Murphy's Law operates when shipping: *"If it is not insured and has the potential to break or get lost, it will surely break or get lost!"* At this point, seek some alternative means of shipping. If you are shipping only one or two items, it is best to let a reputable shop take care of your shipping. Many shops in Mexico will ship using the air services of DHL, FedEx, or UPS. These are usually very expensive shipping services, especially for heavy items. In fact, the cost of shipping may exceed the cost of your purchases. Shops that don't pack and ship may recommend using PakMail. This is an excellent international franchise company that does extremely good packing (indeed, it often over-packs!) and can arrange for shipping. However, it's also a very expensive company for packing services. Be sure to check out their charges before arranging for packing and/or shipping. In Mexico City, contact PakMail in the Polanco district for packing and shipping services:

PakMail
Torcuato Tasso No. 325-B
Col. Chapultepec Morales
Mexico, D.F.C.F. 11570
Tel. 553-1613
Tel/Fax 5531-1604
E-mail: torcuatotasso@pakmail.com.mx

If you have several large purchases – at least one cubic meter – consider using a local shipping company, since it is cheaper and safer to consolidate many separate purchases into one shipment which is well packed and insured. Sea freight charges are usually figured by volume or the container. There is a minimum charge – usually you will pay for at least one cubic meter whether you are shipping that much or less. Air freight is calculated using both weight and volume, and usually there is no minimum. You pay only for the actual amount you ship. One normally does not air freight large, heavy items, but for a small light shipment, air freight could actually cost you less and you'll get your items much faster. However, many shops in Mexico prefer shipping everything by air freight rather than by sea freight or by crossing the border by road. Since this can be very expensive, make sure you understand the costs before deciding to purchase a large item. When using air freight, use an established and reliable airline, even though in the end you may not know who will actually transport your shipment. In the case of sea freight, choose a local company which has an excellent reputation among expatriates for shipping goods. Ask your hotel concierge or front desk personnel about reliable shippers. For small shipments, try to have charges computed both ways – for sea and for air freight. Sea shipments incur port charges that can further add to your costs. Port charges at the shipment's point of entry will not normally be included in the price quoted by the local shipping agent. They have no way of knowing what these charges will be. If you have figures for both means of shipping, you can make an informed choice.

CROSSING THE BORDER BY TRUCK

One might expect shipping by truck to the United States and Canada would be an even better and cheaper shipping alternative for those living in the U.S. or Canada. However, sending shipments to the U.S./Mexican border is often problematic. Some shops are experienced in running goods to the border and then arranging to have someone pick them up on the U.S. side and then shipping them on using domestic U.S. shipping services. In fact, several shops in Guadalajara and San Miguel de

Allende actually have "runners" who drive to the border within 24 hours to make such cross-border deliveries. If you have a very large shipment leaving Mexico, such as a half or full container, it will be worth your while to arrange your own cross-border shipping services. While a shop may arrange to have your goods trucked to the border and then off-loaded to be picked up by a U.S. shipper, this arrangement can be very costly if not fully understood and controlled. We recommend this less expensive alternative: Have the shop truck your goods to a border crossing, such as Laredo; you arrange to have a major U.S. trucking firm pick up your goods at the border. Yellow Freight is very experienced at doing such cross-border pick-ups, and they can be 30 to 50 percent cheaper than arranging the complete shipment in Mexico. If you have a large shipment leaving Mexico, it's worth having the shop hold your shipment until you work out the shipping details on the U.S. side. Let them ship to the border but you can easily arrange the remainder of the shipment.

We have tried all five shipping alternatives with various results. Indeed, we tend to use these alternatives in combination. For example, we take everything we can with us until we reach the point where the inconvenience and cost of excess baggage requires some other shipping arrangements. We consolidate our shipments with one key shop in a major city early in our trip and have shipments from other cities in that country sent to our shop for consolidation. We're also experienced with the cross-border trucking alternative using Yellow Freight.

When you use a shipper, be sure to examine alternative shipping arrangements and prices. The type of delivery you specify at your end can make a significant difference in the overall shipping price. If you don't specify the type of delivery you want, you may be charged the all-inclusive door-to-door rate. For example, if you choose door-to-door delivery with unpacking services, you will pay a premium to have your shipment clear Customs, moved through the port, transported to your door, and unpacked by local movers. On the other hand, it is cheaper for you to designate port-to-port. When the shipment arrives, you arrange for a broker to clear the shipment through Customs and trucked to your home. You do your own unpacking and dispose of the trash. If you live near a port of entry, you may clear the shipment at Customs and pick up the shipment yourself.

We simply cannot over-stress the importance of finding and establishing a personal relationship with a good local shipper, who will provide you with services which may go beyond your immediate shipping needs. A local shipping contact will enable you to continue shopping in Mexico even after returning home.

PART II

Great Destinations

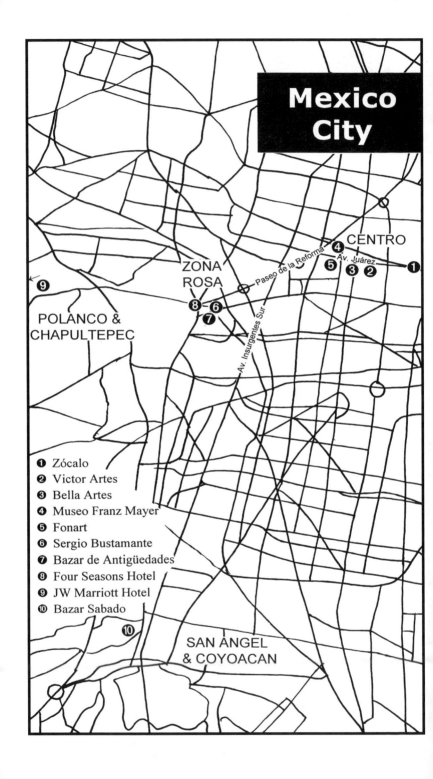

Mexico City

CENTRO

Paseo de la Reforma

Av. Juárez

ZONA
ROSA

Av. Insurgentes Sur

POLANCO &
CHAPULTEPEC

❶ Zócalo
❷ Victor Artes
❸ Bella Artes
❹ Museo Franz Mayer
❺ Fonart
❻ Sergio Bustamante
❼ Bazar de Antigüedades
❽ Four Seasons Hotel
❾ JW Marriott Hotel
❿ Bazar Sabado

SAN ANGEL
& COYOACAN

Mexico City

W ELCOME TO THE LARGEST, oldest, and possibly the most challenging city in North America. Boasting a population of over 25 million in a metropolitan area of 572 square miles, and at a height of 7,350 feet, today Mexico City is a sprawling and fascinating jumble of humanity. It's a grand city of compelling history, architecture, art, and culture which also is susceptible to deadly earthquakes, heavy air pollution, and high accident and crime rates. It's also a travel and shopping paradise for those who know how to navigate this intriguing place. It stimulates, captivates, and charms even the most jaded traveler.

Mexico City was once the capital of the Aztecs (founded around 1325 A.D.), which was then known as Tenochtitlán. Subsequently conquered by the genocidal Spanish conquistador Hernán Cortéz, who established it as the center of New Spain, Mexico City has had a long and fascinating Indian, Spanish, and Mexican history. This rich history is well preserved in the city's many ruins, monuments, and museums as well as depicted in its dramatic art that draws millions of visitors to this city each year. By North American standards, this is a very old and chaotic city that exudes a certain degree of crumbling Old World

75

elegance. It's full of interesting surprises for those who have the time and energy to explore its many unique treasures and pleasures.

An Exceptional City

Despite the many defects of big cities, we still love them after we get to know them. There are many exciting things about a community of 25 million people – especially the history, the talent, the businesses, the activities, and the opportunities to immerse yourself in a vibrant community. Mexico City is a grand and eclectic city that surprises visitors who learn to explore its unique treasures and pleasures. Above all, it's a city of exceptionally appealing art and culture. From the exclusive shops of Polanco and Zona Rosa to the trendy neighborhoods of Condesa, Roma, and Coyoacán and the historic center of the city (Centro Histórico), this is a fascinating city that both intimidates and seduces. It's old, it's new, it's polluted, it's sometimes dangerous, it's Third World, it's international, and it's chic and trendy – everything you ever wanted a city to be and not to be, and then some. It has its downsides, but they are minor in comparison to Mexico City's many positives. While this city can be challenging to the uninitiated, spend a week here and it will fall into place as you discover what this place is all about.

Mexico City is famous for many "firsts," "seconds," and "thirds," as well as for several major attractions:

1. It's the second largest city in the world.
2. It's the second highest city in North America.
3. It boasts the world's largest number of museums – 135 and still counting.
4. It is the oldest capital in the Western Hemisphere – founded in 1325.
5. It attracts over 14 million pilgrims who visit the Virgin of Guadalupe Sanctuary each year – making it the world's most visited Marian shrine.
6. It has the largest number of theaters (64) after New York, London, and Toronto.
7. Both the Historic Downtown (Centro Histórico) and Xochimilco are UNESCO World Heritage Sites.
8. It has 14 upscale shopping malls.
9. It is located within 45 minutes of the famous Pyramids of Teotihuacán.
10. It's one of the world's major art centers, especially for contemporary paintings and sculptures.

Getting to Know You

Despite its large size, ostensible chaos, and crime problems affecting tourists, Mexico City is a relatively easy and fun city to understand and get around in, especially for travel-shoppers who know what they want and plan accordingly. It's all here – thousands of hotel rooms, restaurants, and shops and many fine museums and entertainment venues. Once you know where you're going, expect to do a great deal of walking which at times can be exhausting. Armed with a good map, comfortable walking shoes, a car and driver, and a healthy sense of paranoia about personal safety, you should be well prepared to tackle this challenging city with ease and success.

While you can spend several weeks exploring this intriguing city, seven well planned days should be sufficient to cover all the sightseeing basics as well as shop and dine it well. Our recommendation: Start and end your travel-shopping adventure in Mexico City – four days at the beginning and three days at the end. Be sure to be there on at least one weekend so you can visit several interesting arts, crafts, and antique markets.

A Central City of Contrasts

Mexico City is the country's capital and thus the center for the federal government's politics and bureaucracy. Known as the Federal District (Distrito Federal or D.F.), the city also is Mexico's center for finance, commerce, transportation, communication, art, and education. It's a huge melting pot of many different peoples, cultures, and socioeconomic classes.

Like so many large cities in Third World countries, Mexico City is a magnetic urban center of many contrasts: great wealth and poverty, elegance and ugliness, noise and quiet, energy and slothfulness, greenery and asphalt, new and old. If it's Sunday, major areas of the city look abandoned, but it's a great day for exploring markets. If it's Mon-

day, the city seems immobilized by traffic and crowds. It's also a city many people come to both love and hate because of its combination of grand sites, friendly people, fascinating art and culture, fine restaurants and entertainment coupled with high costs, congested traffic, air pollution, poverty, crowds, filth, smells, and crime. In other words, Mexico City is a big city with many problems associated with big cities in general. For first-time visitors, this can be an overwhelming, frustrating, and expensive city that tries their sensibilities, patience, and pocketbook. Many of them can't wait to get out of this huge city to explore Mexico's many charming colonial towns and delightful resorts which seem more inviting and manageable.

For many seasoned and repeat visitors, Mexico City is a very stimulating place. It's one of the great cities of North America. Both modern and traditional, this energetic and stimulating city is full of wonderful surprises. It's a rapidly changing city undergoing a great deal of renewal, especially in the Centro Histórico (Historic Center) area. Hopefully, you too will discover the beauty in the beast of this city!

Getting Oriented

Mexico City is a huge urban conglomerate consisting of 16 districts (*delegaciones*) and nearly 400 neighborhoods (*colonias*). Many streets change names as they cut through different neighborhoods.

Most visitors focus on several key districts, neighborhoods, streets, and plazas in Mexico City. For the most part, these are walking areas which are best accessed by taxi or car:

❏ **Avenida Insurgentes and Paseo de la Reforma:** These are the city's two major intersecting streets from which most major areas of the city and suburbs can be accessed. They also are good orientation points for understanding the basic layout of this city. Running northeast to west, the wide, majestic, and statue- and fountain-adorned Paseo de la Reforma is the city's central strip for major hotels and shopping areas; it's Mexico City's version of Paris's Champs Élysées  with several traffic circles, mansions, and green areas. It also serves as the thoroughfare for linking the major districts of interest to visitors in search of Mexico City's most interesting treasures and pleasures – Alameda Central, Zona Rosa,

Condesa, Bosque de Chapultepec (Chapultepec Park), and Polanco. Running over 20 miles north to south, Avenida Insurgentes cuts through the popular southern districts of San Angel and Coyoacán and continues as a major exit to the city. If you orient yourself to these two intersecting streets, Mexico City begins to make better sense.

❑ **Centro Histórico:** Located east of Paseo de la Reforma via Avenida Juárez, this colorful and often chaotic 650-block area of crumbling elegance is centered along Francisco I. Madero Street and around the zócalo (Plaza de la Constitución), the city's oldest and largest square, and several adjacent streets. Covering an area of approximately four square miles, this is the oldest part of the city, where it all began nearly 650 years ago. Also referred to as "downtown," this area until recently has experienced a significant decline  in population attendant with a major earthquake in 1985 – from 600,000 people in 1985 to fewer than 180,000 residents today. A much neglected area in disrepair, today it is undergoing revitalization, with new hotels, restaurants, and refurbished buildings, to attract more tourists. It is one of the most heavily trafficked areas for tourists because of its high concentration of aging attractions. Here you'll find ancient ruins, museums, the Metropolitan Cathedral, the Presidential Palace, the National Pawn Shop, churches, street markets, gold and silver shops, restaurants, cafes, bars, hotels, and banks. It's a fascinating area for people-watching, especially from the restaurant on the top floor of the Majestic Hotel which overlooks the zócalo. This area begs to be extensively explored on foot, especially many of the side streets that connect to the zócalo or border the buildings facing the plaza. This whole area always seems to yield new discoveries and pleasant surprises the more you explore it. Indeed, the Centro Histórico is as much a cultural experience as an exercise in delightful sightseeing and shopping.

❑ **Alameda Central:** This popular area is located immediately west of the zócalo via Francisco I. Madero and Avenida Juárez (the same street with two different names that separate at

Lazaro Cardenas Street) and adjacent to Paseo de la Reforma. It includes several major museums, the Fine Arts Palace, the Latin American Tower, handicraft shops, and restaurants located next to or across the street from the large Alameda Park. The park is especially active on Sundays when crowds gather here to enjoy free outdoor entertainment.

❑ **Zona Rosa:** Located in a four-block area immediately south of Paseo de la Reforma (across from The Angel statue, Maria Isabel Sheraton Hotel, and U.S. Embassy) and west of Avenida Insurgentes, this area also is referred to as the "Pink Zone." Intersected by north-south Florencia, Amberes, Genova, and Niza streets and east-west Hamburgo, Londres, and Liverpool streets, this used to be the city's most upscale shopping and dining area until the Metro impacted on this neighborhood. It's still a center for some of the city's best antique stores (Connoisseur Art Gallery and the many elegant shops in the Bazar de Antigüedades), jewelry shops (Tane), boutiques, art galleries, a popular crafts market (Mercado Insurgentes), and some excellent restaurants, but it's also a very mixed area with numerous tacky souvenir shops, nightclubs, fast-food establishments, and clothing stores. Several sidewalk cafes and restaurants can be found along the pedestrian-only Copenhague and Genova streets. Despite its mixed nature, Zona Rosa still offers some of the best lifestyle shopping in Mexico City, especially along elegant Amberes Street. A very compact and intense area, Zona Rosa yields many surprising discoveries for dedicated shoppers. The whole area starts to come alive after 12noon.

❑ **Colonia Condesa:** Located immediately south of Zona Rosa and on the southeastern edge of Chapultepec Park, this once exclusive neighborhood in the early 1900s endured decades of decline until recently. Today it's an up and coming trendy area known for its Art Decor buildings and an energetic community of young artists, bohemians. entrepreneurs, and expatriates – Mexico City's version of New York City's SoHo area – who are transforming it with many small art galleries, boutiques, restaurants, and outdoor cafes. Much of this emerging activity is centered around Michoacán Street.

❑ **Bosque de Chapultepec:** Known as Chapultepec Park, this is the city's leisure and culture center because of its many outdoor activities along with a unique collection of fabulous museums. Consisting of an expansive 2,100-acre park of trees, lakes, botanical gardens, a zoo, a children's museum, playgrounds, jogging paths, and marble statues, the park also is home to the famous Chapultepec Castle/National Museum of History, National Museum of Anthropology, Museum of Modern Art, and Rufino Tamayo Museum. The park links the once upscale Zona Rosa area to the very upscale Polanco area.

❑ **Polanco:** This is Mexico City's most elegant lifestyle shopping, dining, and accommodations area. The center for Mexico's influential Jewish and Lebanese communities, Polanco's pleasant tree-lined streets of mansions, exclusive shops, and fine restaurants give this whole area a special ambience not found elsewhere in Mexico City. This is an area of great wealth and increasingly conspicuous consumption. Anchored by some of the city's top hotels – JW Marriott, Presidente Inter-Continental, Nikko, Camino Real, Casa Vieja, and Habita – this is Mexico's premier shopping center with Presidente Masaryk Street being its version of Rodeo Drive. Here you'll find the city's most exclusive jewelry shops, boutiques, and art galleries interspersed with fine restaurants, cafes, beauty shops, and shopping centers. This is where the rich and famous as well as many wannabees hang out. Not surprisingly, it's also where you will find some of the city's best shops for both imported and locally produced goods. Spend a few hours here and your whole image of Mexico and Mexico City will change. Viewed from the shops, restaurants, and hotels of Polanco, Mexico City is a very upscale and sophisticated place!

❑ **San Ángel and Coyoacán:** Located about 30 minutes south of the Paseo de la Reforma area via Avenida Insurgentes, these two adjacent communities are noted for their weekend markets, shops, museums, cobblestone streets, beautiful churches, impressive colonial homes, and vibrant plazas. The highlight of this area is San Ángel's popular Saturday market, the Bazar del Sábado, which includes many excellent quality shops and vendor stalls selling everything from souvenirs and paintings to upscale arts, crafts, jewelry, and furniture. On Sunday Coyoacán becomes very active as many people visit this quaint community to shop, dine, and sightsee.

Mexico City also is a good base from which to explore the surrounding area on day trips. Five areas in particular are worth including during your stay in the city:

❑ **Xochimilco:** Located about one hour south of the city center, Xochimilco is famous for its floating gardens and the wonderful Dolores Olmedo Museum. While the gardens are interesting, the museum is one of those "must visit" places in

Mexico. It includes a fabulous collection of paintings by two of Mexico's most renowned artists (and a turbulent couple) who have recently achieved even greater international fame through the movie *Frida* – Diego Rivera and Frida Kahlo.

❑ **Teotihuacán:** Located about 40 minutes northeast of Mexico City, the 150+ feet tall pyramids of Teotihuacán (Sun and Moon) remain two of Mexico's most popular tourist sites. The first major city built in the Western Hemisphere, Teotihuacán developed between 250 and 600 A.D. This awe-inspiring complex of ancient monuments emphasizes Mexico's important pre-Hispanic period.

❑ **Puebla:** Located two hours east of Mexico City, this charming and seemingly affluent city is especially known for its colorful Talavera ceramic tiles and pottery and delightful Spanish colonial architecture.

❑ **Cuernavaca:** Located one and a half hours south of Mexico City is one of Mexico's major centers for expatriates. This delightful garden city is known for its mild climate, spa resorts, fine restaurants, historic churches, galleries, and the fabulous Robert Brady Museum. An interesting city to overnight in, or spend a few hours visiting, on your way to Taxco, Acapulco, and Ixtapa/Zihuatanejo and the west coast.

❑ **Tula and Tepotzotlan:** Located about two hours north of Mexico City, Tula was the ancient capital of the Toltec civilization which was founded around the year 1000 A.D. While less spectacular than Teotihuacan, its 15-foot stone warriors at the top of the Pyramid of the Morning Star make this a most intriguing site to visit. Nearby Tepotzotlan is known for its 16th-century colonial church of ornate Churrigueresque architecture.

Getting Centrally Located

So much of enjoying your stay in Mexico City depends on the right selection of accommodations. Convenience and safety – rather than price – should be your primary considerations when selecting a place to stay in this city. While Mexico City has many good hotels, you may want to find accommodations in and around one or two areas – Polanco and Zona Rosa. These are the city's most upscale and secure areas. They are adjacent to the best shopping areas which also are conveniently located for reaching other major areas of the city for shopping and sightseeing. Heavily patrolled by both the local police and Army personnel, these areas also are relatively safe places to walk around during the day. Near Zona Rosa and along Paseo de la Reforma, look for the Maria Isabel Sheraton, Marquis Reforma, and the Four Seasons hotels. In the Polanco area, the best hotels include JW Marriott, Presidente Inter-Continental, Nikko, Camino Real, Casa Vieja, Renaissance, and Habita. While the Centro Histórico has a few good hotels, including the new 5-star Sheraton Centro Histórico, properties in this area are older, less well located for shopping and dining, and the area is not as safe as along the well patrolled Paseo de la Reforma and Polanco. For personal recommendations on hotels, see our section on accommodations (pages 128-134).

Quick and Easy Mexico City

Any large metropolis can be confusing for first-time visitors who need to quickly get a visual fix on where to best focus their limited time and attention. While Mexico City may initially appear confusing, it's really not all that difficult to get oriented to its various sections. Armed with a good map and some sense of direction, you should be able to quickly make sense of how to navigate this colorful city.

Mexico City on the Web

In preparation for your Mexico City adventure, you may want to visit a few English language websites that provide information on the city:

- **Mexico City**   www.mexicocity.com.mx
- **The News Mexico**   www.thenewsmexico.com
- **Travelers Guide**   www.travelguidemexico.com
- **Mexico-City-Mexico**   www.mexico-city-mexico.com
- **Mexico City**   www.mexicocity.gob.mx
- **Mexico City**   www.mexicocity.com
- **MexicoCityNet**   www.mexicocitynet.com
- **All About Mexico City**   www.allaboutmexicocity.com
- **Go2 Mexico City**   www.go2mexicocity.com
- **Art Mexico**   www.arte-mexico.com
- **Mexico Connect**   www.mexconnect.com

Several of these sites also convert to Spanish. For a good listing of websites in Spanish, do a search for "Mexico City" on the search engine www.google.com.

Local Publications

Once you arrive in Mexico City, look for several books, maps, and city publications which should be available through your hotel concierge or front desk or through the local tourist office. Two of the best books and booklets on Mexico City are the annual publications of TGM (Travelers Guide to Mexico):

- *Travelers Guide to Mexico City*
- *Travelers Guide to Mexico*

Both publications can be ordered directly from the publisher by mail or online:

Traveler's Guide to Mexico
Apartado (Box) 6-1007
Mexico, C.F. 06600, Mexico
www.travelguidemexico.com

The following English-language publications should prove useful:

- *Pocket Map Mexico City*
- *Mapa De Galerías*
- *The News* (newspaper)
- *This Is Mexico Pocket Guide*
- *The Gazer El Miron*

The Basics

There are certain things you should know about Mexico City before you descend into its streets to travel and shop this city well.

GETTING THERE

Mexico City is Mexico's great center for transportation and communication. It is easily accessible by air and road from major cities in North, Central, and South America. Nearly 25 cities in the U.S. and Canada now have direct flights to Mexico City. Most international flights go directly into Mexico City, although more and more international flights now service Mexico's major tourist destinations – Cancun, Puerto Vallarta, and Acapulco. The city also is the country's transportation hub. Numerous domestic flights originate in Mexico City to service hundreds of cities and towns throughout the country. All major highways and toll roads are linked to the city.

ARRIVAL

If you arrive by air, you will come into the Benito Juárez International Airport (Aeropuerto Internacional Benito Juárez) which is located very close to the city center (approximately six kilometers from the zócalo). Expect your arrival to be very chaotic, from disembarking at the gate to retrieving your baggage and getting into an official airport taxi. Welcome to the Third World where organization and management are not great strengths and where people and chaos are the watchwords. Be forewarned that there are transportation scams operating here. You'll need to take a taxi or the Metro from the airport to your hotel. You are well advised to use official airport taxis. You will find a prepaid taxi stand in the terminal. Select the type of vehicle you will need and pay your taxi fare at the taxi service stand. Then take your receipt to the designated taxi pick-up area along the cur – just outside the door. Someone will help you get into the proper taxi. However, this whole official transportation process can be intimidating to first-time visitors who aren't sure what's really happening to them. These ostensibly official taxi stands, for example, often seem to be operated by gangs intent on fleecing unsuspecting tourists. Be careful when you pay your transportation fee at the taxi windows – they may try to put you in a much larger and more expensive taxi than you actually need. Also, expect to be "assisted" by several self-appointed porters who insist on tips. While they can be very intimidating, don't give in to this routine extortion. Tip only if you receive a special service, which usually is not the case here. Tell them thanks and goodbye, including your driver who may try to extort a tip from you once you arrive at your destination. Most of these people do not deserve a tip, so don't make it difficult for other travelers by yielding to their brazen demands. The trip from the airport to most major hotel areas should take 20-30 minutes.

THE TRANSPORTATION CHALLENGE

Mexico City has a well developed public transportation system consisting of buses, taxis, and the subway – the Metro. But you must be cautious in your transportation choices because of major safety and security problems related to tourists. You also need to understand the economics of local transportation alternatives, especially when it comes to hotel cars, taxis, and cars and drivers. Indeed, you may initially feel you are dealing with one of the most exploitative local transportation scenes found anywhere in the world!

Your transportation choices are somewhat daunting. Let's first of all dismiss buses. While cheap, they are uncomfortable and famous for pickpockets who prey on tourists. The collective taxis, peseros or combis, are inexpensive mini-buses that run along set routes. Use your own judgment – cheap, convenient, and with a group. The subway or Metro is cheap, clean, convenient, and fast – a good way to get from one major tourist area

to another, especially Centro Histórico, Zona Rosa, and Chapultepec Park.

As we note later in our discussion of safety and security, you are well advised to hire a car and driver or only use radio (*sitio*) cabs. Never flag down a cab along the street. While most cabs may look like legitimate operations, in reality many tourists have been mugged or kidnaped by outlaw cab drivers. You will pay two to three times more for a radio cab, but they are safe to use. Wherever you are – near a hotel, restaurant, shop, or museum – ask the personnel to call a radio cab.

TAXIS, CARS, AND FRIENDLY RENT-A-COPS

Transportation costs in Mexico City can be very high if you don't fully understand how the city's taxis and hotel cars operate. In fact, you may feel you are at the mercy of the local transportation mafia which seems to control the taxis and cars recommended for tourists. The costs can be very high, ranging from US$10 to US$20 per ride in a city where such costs should be under US$5 per ride. The people who manage the tourist transportation system, especially hotel personnel, play on the safety fears of tourists by giving them mixed messages – this is a very dangerous city for tourists using buses and regular taxis versus this city is just as safe as any other large city, similar to New York City. At the same time, they tell you never to flag down a taxi, use only hotel cars, and always call for a radio cab.

So what exactly is the message? The truth is somewhere in between the two. There is definitely a potential safety problem with transportation in Mexico City. And increasing your street safety can cost you a great deal, depending on your choice of alternatives.

Local information on taxis can be confusing and misleading. Hotels recommend for safety purposes that you only use a hotel car, which costs three to five times more than a regular or radio taxi. While they are partly accurate about the safety problem, their solution is usually disingenuous because they have a financial interest in getting you to rent their expensive fleet of large comfortable cars. While they may insist otherwise, it is not necessary for you to use a hotel car. These people also recommend that you never flag down a taxi, which is good advice.

All you need to do is to use one of two types of taxis: a sitio (flat rate, no meter) or a radio metered cab. Two companies operate radio taxis with meters: **TaxiMex** (Tel. 5519-7690 – flag drops at 20 pesos) and **Servitaxi** (Tel. 5516-6020). These taxis charge more than a regular taxi, but they are considered safe for tourists. The best way to call these taxis is to stop at a hotel and ask the front desk or concierge to call a radio taxi. You then usually wait from five to 10 minutes for the cab to arrive. You will be given a taxi number which will be painted on the side of the cab. Most of these taxis charge 80 to 100 pesos per ride, which is expensive by local standards. The same ride might cost 20 to 40 pesos if you used a regular taxi.

But the taxi picture may be less complicated and frightful if you understand the taxi situation by the color of the line at the bottom of the license plates. According to our policemen/ guides, most taxis are safe – perhaps only 1 percent operate illegally and prey on tourists, just like in other big cities around the world. Taxis with a meter (flag drops at 4.80 pesos) and photo identification card on windshield or hanging from the rearview mirror are okay. Taxis with two different colored lines at the bottom of their license plates are fine:

- **Orange line:** These are *sitios*, which may or may not look like taxis. They may be just regular cars but with the orange line at the bottom of their license plate. Some of these cars can be found outside hotels or at *sitio* stands. Ask at a hotel or restaurant where to find a sitio or ask them to call you one.

- **Green line:** These are roaming taxis with meters. Many are the small green and white Volkswagen Beetles with several numbers painted in black on the car. Make sure they both have and use their meters. These are relatively inexpensive taxis, with many rides costing less than 40 pesos, which might cost 80 pesos with a sitio or 200 pesos with a hotel car.

If you encounter a problem with a taxi driver – the meter doesn't work or he tries to overcharge – threaten to report him to the police. Penalties are heavy – 500-peso fines.

Don't be overly influenced by hotel personnel who try to put you into their fleet of expensive hotel cars. Insist that they call a sitio or metered radio cab. Some will claim their hotel car is a sitio, which simply is not true and they know it's not true – they are just trying to get you to use their expensive hotel car. Save your money and use one of the radio taxis as outlined above.

If you are planning to stop at several places throughout the day, you may want to get a car and driver to take you around the city. Shoppers in particular will want to pursue this transportation option. In fact, in addition to being more convenient, it

may be cheaper to arrange for a car and driver. You can negotiate hourly or daily rates with them. You can arrange for such transportation through your hotel or a travel agency. Many hotel-sponsored drivers also freelance on the side as independent drivers and guides. Better still, make contact with the tourist police who patrol the major tourist areas, especially along Reforma near the

Angel monument and across the street from the Maria Isabel Sheraton Hotel. Engaged in both "moonlighting" and "daylighting," many of these tour-guides-turned-police-officers will serve as drivers during their day off. We have used them frequently and with great success. Not only do they speak excellent English and know where they are going, they provide the ultimate in security! While they do not carry a gun, they do have the presence of a cop which is very reassuring, especially when you explore some of the seedier sides of the city. For 80 to 100 pesos per hour (plus tip), you can have your personal driver and guide. Their initial asking price may be 120 pesos per hour, but you can bargain this down to 80 pesos per hour plus tip. As one of our jovial rent-a-cop drivers emphasized, he was *the best cop money can buy!* And, indeed, he was. This may be the smartest transportation decision you'll make in all of Mexico!

SAFETY AND SECURITY

Safety and security are big issues in Mexico City. In fact, in recent years Mexico City has received a bad reputation for safety and security among tourists. And for good reasons! Be very careful about pickpockets and thieves, especially on buses and the subway and in crowded markets. Secure your belongings, be a little paranoid, and watch where you walk both day and night. Most shopping areas outlined in this chapter are relatively safe. You may be pestered by freelance shoeshiners who want to clean and shine your shoes, an occasional tout who wants to help you with everything (need a taxi, go shopping, find something?), or beggars who are more pitiful than persistent. Several beggars are found in the historical downtown area, near the Zócalo, or in and around the Zona Rosa area. Smart in locating their street operations, they tend to hang out where the money is – near banks, exchange windows, hotels, and upscale restaurants. They are basically harmless – usually old women or young hard-living women (look older than their age) with small children and babies.

Visitors to Mexico City may feel safer and more secure than just a few years ago. Since this city had a soaring crime rate that had negatively affected tourism, it has taken this problem very seriously by doing certain things about it – from hiring former New York City Mayor Rudy Guiliani as an anti-crime consultant to creating specialized police units aimed at securing tourist areas against crime. The good news is that the government has started a new program of deploying dozens of special tourist police into the major tourist areas to make these areas more secure and give tourists more peace of mind. These are bilingual police who wear navy blue bullet-proof jackets with yellow police signs on them. They will eventually have 1,000 police in this program. Many are tour guides who serve as police officers in this special program. On their days off, they go back to their regular jobs as guides. They may have a seeming conflict of interest but this can work to your advantage. In some cases, their colleagues out of uniform may be in the area waiting to serve as guides to tourists on an hourly basis. Just approach one of these officers and ask them questions. They can be very helpful. You might ask them if they know of anyone who could serve as a driver and guide. Chances are they will recommend a colleague on his or her day off or volunteer themselves on their day off. They may also help you find a safe taxi. Since this is a new program heavily staffed with tour guides as police officers, feel free to approach these officers since they are on the street to help tourists.

Mexico City's new police chief, Marcelo Ebrard, who arrived in February 2001, has created five special police units:

- **Multi-lingual Tourist Police:** These police officers patrol in the Historic Center, along Reforma, and other high-trafficked tourist areas. They wear distinctive blue uniforms with bullet-proof vests with "Tourist Police" signs on their uniforms. Consisting of both male and female officers, they speak English and welcome questions from tourists. As noted in the previous discussion, some of these officers will function as freelance tour guides and drivers on their days off.

- **Horse-backed "Traditional Police" in mariachi hats and embroidered jackets:** These police officers patrol the famous Alameda Park area in the Centro Histórico district. They combine tourist entertainment with crime-fighting.

- **River Police:** These police patrol the canals of Xochimilco in the southern section of the city.

- **Robocops:** These are heavily armed police who patrol near street vendors.

- **Cargo Transport Police:** These police officers escort truck drivers through the city.

At the same time, but at a lower profile because of sensitive political issues, Mexican Army troops have been deployed to patrol the upscale Polanco area. You can't miss them in their distinctive gray uniforms and armed with heavy artillery. These well trained and disciplined crack troops are not to be messed with by anyone! Indeed, the well patrolled Polanco area feels like an oasis of safety in a city famous for its high crime rate.

In the end, Mexico City is like many other big cities when it comes to safety and security. Watch where and when you walk and be careful, especially with taxis and in markets and other crowded areas. Pickpockets are often active in these areas. Also, groups or gangs of three to six people may distract and rob you.

RENTING A CAR

Most major international car rental chains have offices near the Maria Isabel Sheraton Hotel on Reforma Avenue – Hertz, Avis, Thrifty, Europecar, Budget, and Alamo. All of these car rental firms have representatives at the airport. We found our best rate by reserving a car, prior to arrival in Mexico, on the Internet with Alamo (www.alamo.com). However, daily and weekly car rental rates are very high in Mexico – from US$50 to US$100 per day. Insurance is problematic, adding anywhere from US$5 to US$20 a day on your basic car rental rate. Before you leave home, be sure to check with your car insurance firm on coverage. Most U.S. policies will not cover you in Mexico. If you are an American Express credit card holder, American Express will automatically cover collision, theft, and comprehensive. However, you will need to take out a separate liability policy through the car rental firm for covering property damage and personal injury to the other party. This policy usually runs US$5 per day.

Driving In Mexico City

We don't recommend driving your own car in Mexico City. If you arrive in the city with your own car, park it in a safe place during your stay in the city. Traffic, parking, and security are major problems within the city. In addition, given costly daily car rental rates, you are probably better off hiring a car and driver for US$8 an hour than hassling with your own rental car. You'll not only have great security and a well informed guide, you'll most likely be touring the city with a very interesting personality who will enlighten you about his neighborhoods! Renting a car for traveling outside Mexico City makes good sense.

Water

The water in Mexico City, as well as elsewhere in the country, is not potable. With the exception of the JW Marriott Hotel, which has its own in-house water purification and treatment system, always use bottled water for drinking. Many hotels provide complimentary bottles of water in your room while others charge a standard mini-bar rate for drinking water. Be sure to ask upon arrival if the tap water is safe to drink and if bottled water is supplied on a complimentary basis for guests. If not, plan to find a nearby market for purchasing bottled water as well as any other drinks that should cost you one-fifth of what your hotel will charge for using your mini bar. These places can usually be found within a few blocks of your hotel. They sell large bottles of water for US$.60 to US$.70 per bottle – much cheaper than what hotels charge guests using the in-room mini bar.

Exchanging Money

You'll find numerous money changers in the many tourist areas. Shop around since the rates tend to be competitive. The money changers tend to give better exchange rates than the banks. Traveler's checks usually exchange at a lower rate, and some money changers do not want to cash them. We found our best rate at a money changer directly across the street from Sanborn's (House of Tiles) at Madero 4. The money changer gave us the same rate for traveler's checks as for cash (9.06). The rates at the airport also are good. While hotels generally give a lower exchange rate, some give nearly the same rate as banks and money changers – it depends on the hotel. The Four Seasons Hotel, for example, was giving 9.01, which was the same as most banks and money changers.

Shopping Mexico City

Mexico City is a shopper's paradise for a wide range of locally produced and imported goods.

TWO SHOPPING CULTURES AND STYLES

Expect to encounter two different shopping cultures which have their own particular shopping styles. The first shopping culture is that of the crowded indoor or outdoor market. Here goods tend to be crammed into small stalls or displayed on the ground. The ubiquitous shops fitting this description primarily offer souvenirs, handicrafts, jewelry, leather goods, and antiques. Here you'll encounter a combination of aggressive merchants who want to "make a deal" versus others who are

relatively lethargic. Most expect you to bargain and accordingly will accommodate offers. Expect discounts to run 10 to 20 percent, although some may go so far as give 30 to 40 percent discounts, depending on your bargaining skills and the vendor's cash flow needs at the moment. Many are fun places to shop. Some of the best markets in Mexico City are:

- Lagunilla Market ("Thieves Market")
- Bazar Sábado
- Centro "Informal Commerce" Street Market
- Centro Artesanal
- Mercado Insurgentes
- Mercado de Ciudadela
- Centro Artesanal de Buenavista

If you visit many of these shops and markets, you'll soon find your shopping day goes very slowly. But you will meet some very interesting people along the way, perhaps establish some long-term friendships, and find this to be a very rewarding shopping experience. You'll learn a great deal about products and the people behind them. This also is a culture of price indeterminacy and bargaining. While prices are seldom displayed on goods, once quoted, you are expected to bargain. However, the rules of bargaining are never quite clear. In some places you may end up with something at 40 to 50 percent of the initial asking price. In other places you may only receive a 10 or 20 percent discount, and some places may give no discount. This also is frequently a "cash and carry" culture – many merchants do not accept credit cards, nor do they pack to international standards. Expect to pay cash and take the item with you in a plastic bag or wrapped in a newspaper.

The second shopping culture is that of the boutique, department store, hotel shopping arcade, shopping mall, and pawn shop. Here goods tend to be nicely showcased in windows and display counters. Salespeople tend to keep their distance, letting customers browse on their own. Prices tend to be both displayed and fixed. While you may be able to negotiate some discounts, especially in street shops and jewelry stores with high ticket items, for the most part prices are inflexible, except during advertised sales periods. Most of these shops accept major credit cards and will pack and ship. This shopping culture also is very lifestyle-oriented, with many restaurants, cafes, and food courts to make shopping a very convenient social event.

Many visitors to Mexico City feel more comfortable with the second shopping culture, which is similar to shopping back home. They are often intimidated by the first shopping culture, especially when it comes time to "do a deal" – bargain over the price. Not knowing how to properly bargain, they often avoid these shops or pay the first asking price, which is usually too much. Savvy travel-shoppers in Mexico City learn how to handle both shopping cultures well.

TOUTS, GUIDES, AND THE COMMISSION GAME

Hovering over both shopping cultures are street touts, tour guides, and drivers who expect to receive commissions for bringing you to specific shops. They often claim to have a brother, cousin, or a friend who can give the visitor a very special price. This usually means they have prearranged deals with shops that give them 10 to 30 percent on everything their clients purchase. Invariably these are often mediocre tourist shops that depend on traffic being brought into their shops through sources who prey on tourists. Not surprisingly, if you buy in such shops, you end up indirectly paying the commissions through the shop's inflated prices. If you are being taken to a shop by a local, chances are you are indeed being taken! Many of the jewelry and handicraft shops in highly touristed areas fit this tour group pattern. In Acapulco, for example, you'll see groups of tourists, especially cruise ship passengers on a sponsored shopping adventure, being led inside these shops where their tour group leaders make a great deal of money from their mediocre purchases.

SHOPPING ON YOUR OWN

Shopping in Mexico City is easy, fun, and rewarding. You don't need, nor want, a guide to take you around to his recommended shops. All you need is a good map, this book, and a sense of adventure. In most cases, you can easily get around by Metro or radio taxis. However, you may find it more convenient to hire a car and driver if you're planning to cover a large area in a single day. If you practice the basic shopping rules for Mexico, which are outlined in Chapter 3, and visit many of our recommended shops in this chapter, you'll come in contact with the best of the best Mexico City has to offer. You'll operate effectively in both shopping cultures, meet some wonderful people, and leave Mexico City with several memorable treasures. If you are like many other visitors, you'll want to soon come back to experience more treasures and pleasures of Mexico City.

SHOPPING HOURS

Most shops open around 10 or 11am and close at 7 or 8pm, Monday through Friday. Many shops are open half a day (10am to 2pm) on Saturday and are closed all day Sunday. Several shopping centers and markets remain open on Sunday. Since most shops are closed on Sunday, this is usually a good day to visit museums, Sunday flea markets, and a few shopping centers that remain open.

DISCOUNTS AND BARGAINING

Most shops in Mexico City do very little discounting and are not interested in bargaining. But that does not mean you should always pay full retail. There are different ways to shave prices, depending on your bargaining skills and your understanding of credit card purchases and Mexico's slippery IVA system.

It never hurts to ask for a discount, even though you may have been told shops do not give discounts. If you don't ask, you won't know. After all, the worst thing that can happen is to receive a "No," which is where you began this process. However, if you ask for a discount, you may get a five to 10 percent discount. Some places may discount 20 percent or more. But most places, including market stalls, seem reluctant to bargain. On the other hand, expect to bargain a great deal at the weekend markets and flea markets. By bargaining, you may be able to get 40 to 50 percent discounts at these markets.

Many shops will automatically give you a 10 percent discount when paying with cash. Some also will waive the 15 percent IVA if you have your purchases shipped outside Mexico. Some may even give you a 15 percent "IVA discount" if you give them your mailing address but don't ship (this is probably illegal). However, this is a slippery area of discounting which is practiced differently by different merchants.

IVA SYSTEM

A 15 percent value-added tax (IVA) is added to all goods purchased in Mexico. But it's not really called a VAT in the sense of a European VAT. Expect to receive a 15 percent "discount" from some shops if you have your goods shipped outside Mexico. Be sure to ask for this discount. Some shops do not volunteer this information. Others say they can't do this – they still pay this tax. It's very confusing, varying from one shop to another. The bottom line is that shops must pay a 15 percent tax to the government for all retail sales. Wholesale purchases are exempt from this tax, but you must be a wholesaler and generate separate paperwork.

PACKING AND SHIPPING

Most shops will pack or will use a packing firm. Some will ship using DHL, FedEx, or some other well known express air service. Others will only pack – shipping will be your responsibility.

Unfortunately, shipping can be very expensive from Mexico City – a real shock to visitors from the United States who may think the costs will be minimal because of the close proximity of Mexico. It also can be very unreliable unless you use a well established, and expensive, international air service. In fact, we found it was much more expensive to ship items from Mexico City to Washington, DC than from Cape Town, South Africa to Washington, DC! Whenever possible, take things with you to avoid excessive shipping costs and the disappointment of lost goods.

If you encounter problems with packing and shipping, check with your hotel concierge, who may be able to arrange packing and recommend a reliable shipper. Also, check out **PakMail** (Tel. 5531-1613) at Torcuato Tasso 325-B, Polanco. While they are expensive, they will come to your hotel room and arrange everything. Very reliable, they pack well, using bubble wrap and cardboard, as well as provide complete documentation for airline and customs.

USING CREDIT CARDS AND CASH

Most large shops in Mexico City, including the National Pawn Shop, accept major credit cards. Many shops will automatically give you a 10 percent discount if you pay cash rather than use a credit card. Some will even take a personal check. Since many shops must pay very high commission rates to credit card companies, they prefer receiving cash and accordingly will pass on the savings to you.

What to Buy

Mexico City is a shopper's paradise for all types of locally produced items and imported goods. Expect to discover many of the following products during your stay in Mexico City.

CERAMICS

You'll find a wide variety of varying quality ceramics in the city's many shops and markets. Several handicraft shops, such as Fonart, carry good quality ceramic plates, bowls, and figurines from all over Mexico. The Puebla producer of the famous Talavera ceramics, **Uriarte Talavera**, has a well appointed showroom in the upscale Polanco area filled with attractive tableware, bowls, pots, trays, tiles, and bathroom items. Colorful blue and yellow ceramics from Puebla and Guanajuato are well represented at **Las Artesanias** in Polanco. But no one does ceramics with such artistic talent and imagination as the famous **Emilia Castillo** of Taxco who has one shop in Mexico City at the Camino Real Hotel displaying her wonderful collection of unique ceramics embossed with silver animal figures and designs. If you shop at Neiman Marcus in the United States, which is the exclusive U.S. representative for the Castillo line, you no doubt know her distinctive silver-on-ceramics work.

Keep in mind that many of the ceramics found in Mexico City have a high lead content and thus are best used as decorative pieces rather than usable dinnerware.

HANDICRAFTS

Handicrafts are ubiquitous throughout the shops and markets of Mexico City. From the truly tacky to the artistic, handicrafts come in many forms – wood carvings, glassware, candles, dolls, masks, pots, stained glass, metal figures, and decorative mirrors.

For top quality handicrafts, visit **Fonart**. For a sampling of a wide range of handicrafts, be sure to visit the expansive **Centro Artesanal Buenavista**, which we quickly nicknamed "Hog Heaven" because of its profusion of tacky arts and crafts. Several shops in the Zona Rosa area, such as **Flamma** and **Artesanos de Mexico**, offer a wide selection of locally produced candles, masks, dolls, pots, and ceramics. **La Primavera** in the Condesa area produces hand-blown glass.

FOLK ART

Many visitors to Mexico fall in love with its unique and colorful folk art. Indeed, if you visit the fascinating **Museo Ruth Lechuga** (Edificio Condesa B-6,2a. Calle de Pachuca, Condesa, Tel./Fax 5553-5538) or obtain a copy of *Great Masters of Mexican Folk Art*, you may acquire a new appreciation for this compelling Mexican art form. The real challenge is to find good quality folk art. While markets and handicraft shops abound with varying quality folk art, some of the best quality folk art in Mexico City can be found at **Victor Artes Populares Mexicanos** and **Fonart**. Several shops and vendors at the **Bazar Sábado** in San Ángel offer nice selections of folk art.

ART

Mexico City is well known as a center for art and artists. Indeed, you can easily spend several days just focusing on the city's many contemporary and avant-garde art galleries. This is serious art reflecting Mexico's strong artistic tradition in various art forms. The city abounds with galleries, antique shops, and markets offering a wide range of paintings and sculptures. However, don't judge an art gallery by its current exhibition. Many galleries change exhibits every one to three months. Be sure to ask to see a gallery's current inventory, which is often depicted in photo albums and kept in a back storage room. The largest concentration of fine art galleries can be found in the **Zona Rosa**, **Polanco**, and **Roma** areas. For fascinating, colorful, and whimsical anthropomorphic papier-mâché, bronze, and copper surrealistic sculptures – along with uniquely designed jewelry and furniture – be sure to visit the Mexico City gallery of one of Mexico's most talented and famous international artists and designers, **Sergio Bustamante**. Other tempting art galleries include **Connoisseur Art Gallery**, **Asian Art Gallery**, **Aura Galerias**, **Tere Haas Gallery**, and **Hevart's Galeria de Arte** in Zona Rosa. Numerous works of art can be found at several antique shops at **Bazar de Antiguedades** (Plaza del Angel) in Zona Rosa. **Galeria Schwarcstein**, **Galeria Oscar Roman**, **Galeria de Arte Misrachi**, **Galeria Alberto Misrachi**, **Galeria Lopez Quiroga**, and **Talento** in Polanco offer a wide selection of quality art. For relatively inexpensive art from lesser-known artists, visit the **Bazar Sábado** in San Ángel where you will find dozens of artists displaying their oil paintings and sculptures in the park area of Plaza San Jacinto. For a good overview of art in Mexico City, including artists, galleries, exhibitions, and even stolen paintings, be sure to visit this gateway art website: www.arte-mexico.com. You should also acquire a copy of the bilingual edition of *La Quía Artes de México* (see page 41) which is a comprehensive guide to the art scene in Mexico City, Guadalajara, Monterrey, Puebla, Oaxaca, and San Miguel de Allende. It's available at several galleries as well as in bookstores.

ANTIQUES AND COLLECTIBLES

Mexico City is a major center for serious antique dealers who primarily deal in European and colonial antiques. The largest collection of antique dealers under one roof is found at Bazar de Antigüedades (Plaza del Angel) in the Zona Rosa area. Very exclusive and expensive antique dealers include **Connoisseur Art Gallery**, **Rodrigo Rivero Lake**, and **Asian Art Gallery**. Be sure to check out a few noted weekend markets, especially **Lagunilla Market** ("Thieves Market") and **Bazar de Antigüedades**, which offer lots of interesting antiques and collectibles for treasure hunters. These are fun places to spend a Saturday (**Bazar de Antigüedades**) or Sunday morning (**Lagunilla Market**). Get there early so you become the proverbial *"early bird who gets the worm!"*

FURNITURE AND ACCESSORIES

While you'll find lots of interesting furniture and accessories in Mexico City's many antique shops, especially at **Bazar de Antigüedades** in Zona Rosa, a few shops offer uniquely designed new furniture and accessories. Some of the most interesting such shops, such as **El Patio** and **Adobe Disaño**, are found at the **Bazar Sábado** in San Ángel. For exclusive artistic furniture and accessories with the signature Sergio Bustamante look, be sure to visit the **Sergio Bustamante** gallery in Zona Rosa to inquire about their furniture line.

FASHION AND ACCESSORIES

Don't expect to find many locally designed and produced clothes and accessories that appeal to your sense of style, color, and quality. If you're in the market for the latest in European-styled clothes and accessories, however, look no further than the heart of the very fashionable Polanco area. Numerous shops along Presidente Masaryk Street will more than meet your needs. Here you'll find such famous brands as **Chanel**, **Emporio Armani**, **Hugo**, **Escada**, **Max Mara**, **Ermenegildo Zegna**, **Hermés**, **Versace**, and **Tommy Hilfiger**. Several shopping centers, such as Centro Santa Fe, Pabellon Polanco, and Plaza Moliere, carry international name brands such as **Benetton**, **Marina Rinaldi**, **Zara**, **Calvin Klein**, **Ungaro**, **Cerruti 1881**, **Façonnable**, **Nautica**, **Anne Klein**, and **Episode**. For nice quality Italian menswear, look for Scappino shops in a few shopping centers. Except for the El Palacio de Hierro department store at Plaza Moliere in Polano, don't expect to find much quality fashion and accessories in the city's department stories, which tend to be decidedly middle class.

JEWELRY AND SILVER

Many visitors to Mexico City discover some wonderful jewelry and silver that make a trip to this city especially worthwhile. The city has several excellent quality jewelry and silver shops that offer exclusive designs. Some of the silver shops are actually branches of shops headquartered in Taxco. Ironically, prices in some of these shops are cheaper in Mexico City than in their factory shop in Taxco – proving once again that "buying at the source" is not necessarily smart shopping! Taxco, the source in this case, is popular with tourists who don't know any better and thus often get gouged. Exclusive international jewelry is well represented at several shops in the Polanco area: **Tiffany's**, **Cartier**, **Bulgari**, **Berger**, and **Peyrelongue**. For locally produced and designed jewelry and silver, be sure to visit **Tane**, **Astrid**, **Aplijsa**, **Talleres de los Ballesteros**, **Izta**, and **D'Argenta**. Our favorite is **Tane**, which is by far one of Mexico's most exclusive and exciting jewelers. For both white and black pearls and pearl jewelry, be sure to visit **Ginza** (El Bazar del Centro) in the Centro Histórico. For Columbian jewelry with pre-Columbian designs, look for **L. A. Cano**. For locally produced designer jewelry, visit **Tanya Moss Designer Jewelry**. One of our very favorites is the multi-talented artist and designer **Sergio Bustamante** who now produces an exclusive line of beautiful gold and silver jewelry depicting his signature artistic designs. For unique ceramics incorporating silver embossed designs of animals and the cosmos, be sure to visit the **Emilia Castillo** shop at the Camino Real

Hotel before visiting the major factory shop in Taxco. For a very unique shopping experience for jewelry, including many bargains, visit the **National Pawn Shop**, which is located just opposite the Cathedral on the zócalo in Centro Histórico. Several gold shops, which make up what is collectively called the **Centro Joyero de Mexico**, also are found in the area adjacent to the National Pawn Shop, especially along Francisco I. Madera Street.

LEATHER

Many shops and markets in Mexico City offer a wide range of varying quality leather goods, from shoes, boots, and jackets to handbags, wallets, and luggage. However, don't expect to find very good quality locally produced leather goods. The exception to this rule is **Aries**, one of Mexico's premier leather designer shops (**Zona Rosa**, **Presidente Inter-Continental Hotel**, and **Camino Real Hotel**) with prices approaching those of the European designers. Not surprisingly, the best quality leather goods are imported from Europe, especially Italy. The best shops for quality leather goods are found in the exclusive Polanco area – **Louis Vuitton**, **Salvatore Ferragamo**, and **Fendi**.

PIRATED VIDEOS, CDS, AND DVDS

Several markets in Mexico City are centers for pirated videos and CDs. Prices usually run from US$1 to US$2 for a CD and US$3 for a video or DVD. The quality of these "illegal" products is generally good – better than in China, Vietnam, and Cambodia. You can easily find these pirated items at the Sunday Lagunilla ("Thieves") Market and the extensive informal street market immediately to the northeast and east of the zócalo in the Centro Histórico. Most vendors post signs stating their asking prices. Some may bargain if you buy in quantities. The best prices are found with vendors in the "informal commerce" street market that runs northeast and east of the zócalo.

Where to Shop

Shopping in Mexico City is concentrated in a few major sections of the city. From chic boutiques and exclusive galleries to street shops, shopping centers, department stores, and markets, Mexico City has a great deal to offer travel-shoppers.

Major Shopping Areas

Mexico City has five major shopping areas. Beginning with the most upscale, these shopping areas consist of:

Polanco

This is Mexico City's version of Rodeo Drive and Madison Avenue – the ultimate place to engage in lifestyle shopping. Located immediately to the north of Chapultepec Park, Polanco is the city's most upscale and affluent neighborhood noted for its many fine shops, art galleries, restaurants, and hotels that primarily cater to affluent residents. The main street – Presidente Masaryk – is this area's lifestyle shopping center. This four-lane tree-lined boulevard includes small shopping centers, boutiques, jewelry shops, and sidewalk cafes that give this section of the city a unique European ambience that especially appeals to the city's wealthy residents, many of whom live in the Polanco area. You'll recognize many of the international name brand boutiques that punctuate this street with exquisite attire, accessory, and jewelry offerings: **Alfred Dunhill, Burberry, Max Mara, Tommy Hilfiger, Escada, Hermes, Lowe, Emporio Armani, Cartier, Bulgari, Salvatore Ferragamo, Fendi, Louis Vuitton, Tiffany, Chanel, Ermenegildo Zegna**, and **Hugo**. Well known local names, many of whom offer quality international merchandise, include **Solito, Las Artesanius, Rubio, Scappino, Maria Isabel, Peyrelongue, Berger,** and **Marina Rinaldi**. Mexico's premier jeweler, **Tane,** has its headquarters shop here. Several of the side streets, such as **Julio Verne, Aristoteles, Campos Eliseos, Anatole France,** and **Alejandro Dumas**, house many fine art galleries, boutiques, and ceramic shops. The famous Talavera ceramics producer from Pueblo, **Uriarte,** has a well appointed gallery shop on Alejandro Dumas Street. The Polanco area also boasts a few shopping centers, such as **Pasaje Polanco, Plaza Mazarik, Plaza Zentro, Plaza Moliere**, and **Pabellon Polanco**. Both the Nikko and Presidente Inter-Continental hotels have several top quality shops such as **Galerie Alberto Misrachi (Nikko)** and **Aries, Tane, and D'Argenta** (Presidente Inter-Continental). Just outside these hotels are a few galleries, antique shops, silver shops, and gift shops well worth visiting: **Galeria Schwarcstein** (art), **Rodrigo Rivero Lake** (antiques), **Izta** (silver), and **Cabassi** (gifts). The nearby Camino Real Hotel has a small shopping arcade that includes the city's only branch of the famous Taxco-based silver ceramicist **Emilia Castillo** as well as branches of the city's major leather, silver, jewelry, and art galleries – **Aries, Tane, Astrid,** and **Sergio Bustamante**.

ZONA ROSA

Located just south of Paseo de la Reforma and immediately east of Chapultepec Park, this area consists of 12 square blocks of shops and restaurants. It's bounded by Reforma on the north, Niza on the east, Chapultepec on the south, and Florencia on the west. Once the city's most upscale shopping area, today this neighborhood is a mixed area of varying quality shops, galleries, markets, souvenir shops, restaurants, cafes, and money changers catering to a wide range of local residents and tourists. Densely packed Zona Rosa yields several shopping surprises, especially for jewelry, silver, art, antiques, and handicrafts. The area also is known for its trendy boutiques for young people. The major shopping section encompasses Hamburgo, Londres, Amberes, Florencia, and Estocolmo streets. The best quality shopping is found along Amberes Street. The Zona Rosa area includes the city's best antique center, **Bazar de Antigüedades** (Plaza del Angel), as well as two fine antique shops, **Connoisseur Art Gallery** and **Asian Art Gallery**. One of Mexico's top silver jewelers, **Tane**, has a shop here as does the noted Taxco silver maker **Talleres de los Ballesteros**. Handicrafts are well represented in the densely packed artisan market, **Mercado Insurgentes**. For jewelry, check out **Peyrelongue** and **Cartier**. For excellent locally produced leather goods, be sure to visit **Aries**. Unique candles can be found at **Flamma**. For an interesting collection of arts and crafts, visit **Artesanos de Mexico**. Good quality art galleries include **Aura Galerias**, **Tere Haas**, and **Hevart's Galeria de Arte** on Amberes Street. One of Mexico's most famous and inventive artists, **Sergio Bustamante**, has a shop here displaying his unique collection of papier-mâché, bronze, and silver creations. It's best to visit this area in the afternoon since many shops do not open until after 12noon. In the evening Zona Rosa becomes a popular area for dining, with such fine restaurants as **Tezka**, **Fonda**, and **Cicero**.

CENTRO HISTÓRICO

Located in the downtown area, which stretches from the zócalo, **Catedral Metropolitana** (Metropolitan Cathedral), Museo del Templo Mayor (Great Temple), and Palacio Nacional (National Palace) in the east to Alameda Park in the west, this is a rich and lively shopping area for a wide range of products and lots of local character. You may want to start exploring this area by having breakfast or lunch on the seventh floor of the **Majestic Hotel** which overlooks the zócalo. Visit the many small gold shops and the **National Pawn Shop** on the west side of the zócalo, explore the crowded streets behind the **Metropolitan Cathedral**, **Museo del Templo Mayor**, and **National Palace** for inexpensive street vendor goods (especially pirated videos, CDs,

and DVDs), or head up Francisco I. Madero where you will discover more gold shops and several specialty shops for wonderful folk art (**Victor Artes Populares Mexicanos**), jewelry (**Aplijsa
in El Bazar del Centro**), the House of Tiles (**Casa de los Azulejos**,
which also is a popular Sanborn's restaurant and department
store), and arts and crafts (**Fonart**). Spend some time exploring
the side streets near Santo Domingo Plaza to discover where
locals buy everything from engraved stationery to footwear.
This whole area, with its historic buildings, monuments, and
bustling streets, plazas, and parks, feels like you're in the real
Mexico City.

SAN ÁNGEL AND COYOACÁN

Located in the southern part of the city, these are two popular
weekend destinations for lifestyle shoppers. Once separate villages on the outskirts of the city, today these two neighborhoods with their cobblestone streets, old walled Spanish colonial
residences, and charming parks and plazas increasingly draw
visitors on the weekend to sample the area's many shops and
restaurants and visit the museum homes of such legendary figures as Leon Trotsky, Diego Rivera, and Frida Kahlo. Enjoy Saturday exploring the popular markets and shops at the Bazar
Sábado at San Ángel, a generic name for an area encompassing
several indoor and outdoor market activities. Here you'll discover artists and craftspeople selling their paintings and
handcrafted items in the parks, in a building called the Bazar
Sábado, and such fine adjacent shops as **Galeria San Jacinto**,
Galeria San Ángel, **Adobe Disaño**, and **Casa Azul**. Nearby
Coyoacán ("Place of the Coyotes"), a well known community of
artists, writers, and scholars, with its charming plazas (**Jardin del
Centenario** and **Jardin Hidalgo**) and lots of small shops and
restaurants becomes a very popular destination on Sundays   –
an enjoyable place to explore on foot and enjoy the many vendors, mimes, musicians, poets, artists, and clowns that congregate in and around the plazas.

COLONIA CONDESA AND ROMA

Located south of the Zona Rosa area, **Colonia Condesa** and
Roma are up and coming areas of small shops, art galleries,
restaurants, and sidewalk cafes – the city's trendy bohemian and
artistic area reminiscent of New York's Greenwich Village or
Paris's Marais district. **Casa Lamm**, a combination art gallery,
bookstore, and restaurant, serves as a center for this unique
community. **La Primavera** offers some lovely hand-blown glass
from its factory in Hidalgo. Several galleries in Colonia Roma
have organized the "Colonia Roma Cultural Corridor," an open

house that takes place one Wednesday each month (from 7 to 10pm). Call 5511-0899 for information on this event.

MARKETS

Mexico City has several markets well worth visiting for unique and inexpensive items. Some are weekend markets, whereas others are open all week long. The major markets include:

❑ **Bazar Sábado (Saturday Market):** *Col. San Ángel, Plaza de San Jacinto. Open Saturday, 9am to 6pm.* Located south of the city center – a 30-minute taxi ride from Paseo de la Reforma – this popular arts and crafts market is fully operational on Saturdays only. A good quality market, it's one of the best places in Mexico City to spend two or three hours on a Saturday morning or afternoon. Indeed, some visitors plan to be in Mexico City on a weekend just to come here. The market consists of several sections. The center of the market is the main park area in Plaza San Jacinto where dozens of vendors set up tables and easels to display their paintings and crafts. A disproportionate number of vendors are artists displaying oil paintings and sculptures; some actually paint while waiting for customers to come by to admire their works. Other vendors sell a wide range of handcrafted items, from ceramics, jewelry, and handbags to stuffed toys, masks, and bonsai trees. Adjacent to the park are three areas worth exploring. Facing the plaza and surrounding San Angel Church are several nice shops selling furniture, home decorative items, and arts and crafts. Look for **El Patio** (Plaza San Jacinto 15, Tel. 5616-1214 or Fax 5550-2488) for two expansive floors of rustic furniture and several rooms of attractive home decorative items, including paintings, candle holders, and masks, in a delightful hacienda-style setting. Next door is **Galeria San Jacinto** (Plaza San Jacinto 13, Tel. 5530-1959) for an interesting assortment of international arts and crafts. And just around the corner, along Av. Juárez, are two shops well worth visiting: **Galeria San Angel** (Av. Juárez 2A, Tel. 5550-2955 or Fax 5616-0644) for glass, candles, furniture, icons, paintings, silver trays, and numerous interesting home decorative items; and **Adobe Disaño** (Av. Juárez 2, Tel. 5550-6065 or Fax 5550-6399; www.adobedesign.com.mx) for many unique, and large, home decorative items – from huge metal roosters, pots, and cacti to candles, silver, lamps, metal art, and leather and wicker furniture from Mexico, Africa, India, and Indonesia. Directly across from these last two shops is an open air canvas-covered street market with numerous vendor stalls selling a vast array of arts, crafts, clothes, and souvenirs. But the major attraction in this area is the large red stucco exhibition hall directly across from the park which gives this area its name – **El Bazar Sábado**. This building is jam-packed with two floors of small shops offering attractive jewelry, arts, crafts, clothes, souvenirs, and home furnishings. The central courtyard includes a restaurant. Often very crowded, this popular center is well worth browsing for interesting items. As soon as you enter the building, turn to your left and follow the hallway past several shops and then turn right into the courtyard area. Just before entering the courtyard, you'll pass one of the most interesting and top quality home decorative shops – **Brondis** (Tel/Fax. 5391-6759) – with its attractive display of wrought iron lamps, tables, mirrors, and sculptures, including alabaster lamps and tables. Once inside the courtyard, look for jewelry stalls and a glass and ceramics shop on your left. Continuing around the courtyard, you'll come to an attractive arts and crafts shop near the entrance with a small shop next door offering attractive children's clothes – **Jeanne**. Near this shop is a stairway leading to the upstairs area which includes several small shops selling ceramics, jewelry, art, leather, and pillows. You exit the upstairs area via a restaurant stairway. There is also another stairway, near Brondis, that takes you to only one upstairs shop – **Mezzanine**. This shop offers some interesting textiles and arts and crafts from Oaxaca. After turning left as you leave this building, you may want to go next door to the **Del Risco House Isidro Fabela Cultural Center** or continue walking for nearly 200 meters until you come to a second park and plaza, which includes several vendors displaying their paintings, sculptures, and handicrafts. Facing this park is an old house which has been recently converted into an arts and crafts center while it continues under restoration – **Casa Azul** (Plaza del Carmen 25, Tel./Fax 5550-3223). This shop is jam-packed with quality arts and crafts from Mexico, Peru, Equador, and Colombia: jewelry, furniture, icons, candles, lamps, bird cages, ceramic jars, painted pot-

tery, rice paper, picture frames, plates, bowls, and metal art figures (giraffes, frogs, birds). **Casa Azul** plans to sponsor cultural performances in this grand old building. Indeed, the major purpose of this shop is to literally restore this building. Visitors to the Bazar Sábado should keep in mind that the whole area, including **Plaza del Carmen** and **Casa Azul**, is part of this market. While the street and park vendors primarily appear on Saturday, the most festive and crowded day, shops such as **Casa Azul**, **El Patio**, **Galeria San Ángel**, and **Adobe Disaño** are open throughout the week.

❑ **Lagunilla Market:** *3 blocks east of Plaza de Garibaldi. Open daily, 9am to 5pm.* For many visitors and locals, this is Mexico City's best market. While it is open daily, the best time to visit is on Sunday when it transforms itself into a big outdoor flea market. Also known as "Thieves Market," because of the many "hot" goods and pickpockets that prey on visitors, this is a fun Sunday market for browsing for antiques and collectibles and buying clothes, CDs, jewelry, stones, and brass items. But watch yourself here. Try to dress down for the occasion so you won't appear to be a rich target for pickpockets. The market is relatively safe if you take normal safety precautions. However, some guides may try to steer you away from this market by telling you it's an unsafe place to visit. Don't believe them since many of them wish to take their clients elsewhere – places that will give them commissions. A visit to this market is considered a waste of their time. Be sure to go on a Sunday. You won't be disappointed. The vendors tend to be very friendly and helpful. You can buy numerous items here at some very good prices, especially if you bargain. Many locals come here on Sunday to pick up bargains on clothes, footwear, perfumes, and food. In fact, a recent 20 percent government tax on perfumes was good for this market – you can easily purchase a US$100 bottle of department store perfume for only US$25 here. The market includes an excellent antique section that showcases an intriguing mix of merchandise: furniture, jewelry, porcelain, paintings, books, hats, bronze, Indian temple toys, copper pots, masks, cigarette lighters, police badges, pens, corkscrews, old irons, bells, knives, lanterns, bathtubs, telephones, cameras, rugs, binoculars, guitars, watches, trains, beds, and coins. Many of the antique dealers display their wares on the ground or operate from their vans and cars. Several of these ostensibly unassuming dealers also have large warehouses. If you find things you like, be sure to ask if the vendor also has additional items in a warehouse and try to determine if it's worthwhile to visit the warehouse during the week. This is one market you should not miss, even though some people may try to dissuade you for "safety and security" reasons. If you're concerned about safety, visit the market with a "rent a cop" (see page 88) as part of your Sunday touring activities.

❑ **Centro "Informal Commerce" Street Market:** This market actually has no name since it is both unofficial and spontaneous. It's where savvy local shoppers find great bargains. Located along five streets behind the Metropolitan Cathedral, Museo del Templo Mayor, and the National Palace northeast, east, and southeast of the zócalo – Justo Sierra, Seminario, Carmen, Correo Mayor, and Republica de Uruguay streets – this is an extremely colorful and congested street market that includes hundreds of sidewalk vendors selling a wide range

of inexpensive products. Snaking around vehicle- and pedestrian-clogged streets for nearly one kilometer, this spontaneous street market draws thousands of shoppers each day who snap up bargains and haggle for excellent prices on items normally found in street shops and department stores. If, for example, you are interested in purchasing pirated CDs, DVDs, and videos, you'll find dozens of vendors selling similar items at bargain basement prices: popular music CDs go for $8 to $10 (US$.90 to US$1.10) depending on whether you shop along Carmen Street ($8) or Seminario and Carmen streets ($10). DVDs and videos go for as little at $250 (US$2.70). Street vendors offer a dazzling array of inexpensive items piled high on tables, spread out on blankets, and emerging from car trunks: hats, caps, calculators, perfumes, artificial flowers, sunglasses, knock-off watches, wigs, toys, jeans, sweaters, T-shirts, shorts, underwear, towels, and kitchen items. Push carts, trolleys, trishaws, taxis, cars, vans, and buses compete for limited space with pedestrians and vendors who hawk their goods. Be sure to try your bargaining skills here. Very chaotic, this whole area offers some of the most interesting and energetic shopping in Mexico City. Take your camera since this area also offers some wonderful photo opportunities of fascinating street-level commerce. It's best to explore this whole area on foot.

❑ **Mercado Insurgentes:** *On Londres between Florencia and Amberes, Zona Rosa. Open Monday to Saturday, 9am to 5:30pm.* Located in the heart of the Zona Rosa area, this densely packed crafts market is filled with vendors offering a wide range of silver products, clothes, ceramics, paintings, boxes, and leather goods. Silver products, from serving pieces to jewelry, tend to be a major specialty here, especially at Plateria. Look for Castillo-style silver serving pieces (most have distinctive lapis lazuli or malachite parrots attached to tops and handles), but don't expect to find comparable quality to the real thing found at the Emilio Castillo shop at the Camino Real Hotel, even though a shop may claim the same artisan that does Castillo's pieces also produces their selections – a most unlikely claim. The merchants here tend to be very aggressive. Be sure to bargain hard – expect the first asking price on many items to be double what you should eventually pay. A 50 percent discount should be in order, especially from many of the silver vendors. Look for a nice silver and turquoise jewelry shop at the entrance to this market – **Art en Plata**.

❑ **Merced Market:** *Circunvalación between General Anaya and Adolfo Gurrión. Open Monday through Friday, 8am to 4pm, and Saturday, 8am to 2pm.* This is the city's largest market of primary interest to local residents who shop here for fruits, vegetables, packaged foods, and household goods. Some visitors who have never visited such a market may find it interesting as a cultural experience.

❑ **Nacional Monte de Piedad (National Pawn Shop):** *Located on the corner of Monte de Piedad and Cinco de Mayo, across from the Cathedral on the northwest side of the zócalo, Centro Histórico. Open Monday through Friday, 9:30am to 6pm, and Saturday, 8:30am to 3pm.* This is one of Mexico's most interesting shopping centers and experiences, a fun place to spend an hour browsing for unexpected treasures. It consists of several large rooms with vendor stalls and locked display cases offering a combination of used (pawned) and new gold jewelry at fixed prices. Many of the items have been pawned in the building next door (look for long lines of residents waiting to pawn their jewelry in the building on the north). To shop this area well, we recommend spending at least a half hour surveying the many jewelry offerings. Much of the pawned jewelry has a distinctive local look and thus may not appeal to your sense of design and style. The small gold earrings are a good buy (around US$32) and make nice gifts. These are new items which are found in several display cases (ask a nearby vendor to unlock the case so you can examine the offerings). Also, be sure to check out the combination antique and flea market shop across the walkway on the north side of this complex. In addition to some unique jewelry pieces, it offers many non-jewelry pawned items, such as lamps, silverware, icons, clocks, old toys, sculptures, paintings, and even pianos! The payment system here may at first be confusing to the uninitiated. If you find an item you wish to purchase, the vendor will give you a receipt. You must take this receipt to a payment window – Caja – where you complete the transaction. At times the lines here can be very long, taking up to 30 minutes to pay. Most people pay in cash, although you can use American Express on all purchases over 200 pesos. After you pay, take your stamped receipt back to the vendor who will give you your goods in exchange for the paid receipt. Since the National Pawn Shop is located adjacent to numerous small gold shops facing the zócalo, you may want to do comparative shopping at these shops before making purchases at the National Pawn Shop, and vice versa.

❏ **Bazar de Antigüedades:** *Plaza del Angelo, between Hamburgo and Londres streets in Zona Rosa.* Don't miss this one if you enjoy browsing for antiques and collectibles. This popular upscale antiques mall becomes a lively combination flea market and bazaar on Saturdays with vendors displaying their treasures on the ground throughout the passageways of this complex. This is a fun place to browse for unique treasures at bargain prices. Since everything is negotiable, be sure to bargain hard for everything.

❏ **Mercado de Ciudadela:** *Corner of Balderas and Ayuntamiento, four blocks south of Av. Juarez in the historical downtown area (Centro Histórico).* Also known as the Artesanias Ciudadela (Artisan's Market), this semi-covered outdoor handicraft market, surrounded by yellow walls, is jam-packed with over 200 vendor stalls and shops selling a wide range of arts, crafts, and souvenirs from all over Mexico. Most of what you find here is pure tourist kitsch – more trash than treasures. This can be a fun place to shop if you're not looking for anything special nor seeking quality items. The colorful array of products includes ceramics, glassware, clothes, sombreros, jewelry, hammocks, lamps, wrought iron decorative pieces, painted boxes and trays, placemats, pictures, and silver items. You can try to bargain, but don't expect much discounting since vendors seem reluctant to give more than a 10 or 20 percent discount. If you're in a real kitschy mood, this is the place to shop!

❏ **Centro Artesanal de Buenavista:** *Aldama 187, Col. Guerrero. Open daily 9am - 6pm, Sundays until 2pm.* If you're looking for a one-stop shop for all your handicraft needs, this is the place to visit. It's a huge emporium of handicrafts and furniture. From the moment you enter the door of this expansive warehouse and pass by the paintings, bronzes, and furniture on your left until you exit past the jewelry, clothes, and leather goods on your right, you may be overwhelmed by what you see. The product mix here goes on and on – tables, chairs, altars, wrought iron, decorative ceramics, pots, metal figures, luggage, sombreros, tin mirrors, cement garden pieces, glassware, ceramic dishes (be sure to check on lead content), leather coats and handbags, dolls, and boxes. The upstairs is primarily devoted to rustic furniture in need of more design talent. This is the ultimate shopping center for Mexican kitsch. While you may find a few appealing items here, most of this vast collection is tasteless and the quality is marginal. Indeed, you'll find very few treasures here. As one of our travel companions summed it up, *"Wow, this is hog heaven!"* Nonetheless, you may find some souvenir items here. If nothing else, visit this place just to get an idea of what you are likely to encounter elsewhere in Mexico. You'll probably quickly decide what you do and do not like – or perhaps discover you have been here too long to remember what quality really looks like!

❑ **Centro Artesanal (Mercado de Curiosidades):** *Corner of Ayuntamiento and Dolores, Reforma North. Open Monday through Saturday, 10am to 5:30pm.* This two-story building includes several vendor stalls offering a wide range of arts and crafts, from silver jewelry to ceramic tiles. Be sure to bargain hard.

SHOPPING CENTERS

More and more shopping centers are appearing throughout Mexico City. Popular with middle class families and young people, most of these places are air conditioned shopping malls offering a wide range of shops and restaurants. They are especially active on weekends. The major shopping centers are found in these areas:

POLANCO

❑ **Pasaje Polanco:** *Oscar Wilde 29.* This small shopping center is found in a courtyard of stucco buildings just off the main street, Presidente Masaryk. The most interesting shop here is **Las Artesanias** with its colorful ceramic bowls, plates, boxes, and ceramic tiles from Puebla and Guanajuato, and jewelry and tin mirrors on the first floor; and glassware, plates, shawls, and bronze bells on the second floor. **Artemis** includes contemporary furniture and home decorative items of primary interest to local residents.

❑ **Plaza Mazarik:** *Presidente Masaryk.* This two-story shopping mall includes several exclusive boutiques. Look for **Campanile** for men's Italian shoes, **Flavio Gatto** for women's Italian shoes, **Rubio** for jewelry, **Furla** for leather purses, **Scappino** for men's Italian clothes, and **Maria Isabel** for a nice selection of women's clothes and accessories.

❑ **Plaza Zentro:** *Presidente Masaryk*. A small and quiet shopping mall with exclusive name brands such as **Fendi** and **Louis Vuitton**.

❑ **Plaza Moliere:** *Corner of Horacio and Moliere streets*. This relatively new and upscale two-level shopping center with an attractive fountain in front includes nearly 100 shops offering a good selection of clothes, accessories, and home decorative items. Anchored by the popular department store **El Palacio de Hierro** with its many name brand goods. Look for such popular shops as **Zara**, **Dockers**, **Levis**, **Scappino**, **Maria Isabel**, **Den-Tro**, and **Versace Classic V2**. Includes a food court.

❑ **Pabellon Polanco:** *Corner of Hamero and Vazquez de Melia streets*. This somewhat aging three-level shopping center includes 114 shops and restaurants offering a relatively undistinguished collection of boutiques, shoe stores, jewelry shops, toy stores, and bedding shops. Anchored by Sears department store. Includes a food court with a McDonald's. Some of the best shops here includes **Tanya Moss** for designer jewelry, **Medialuz** for an interesting collection of colorful candles, and **Scappino** for Italian menswear.

SANTA FE

❑ **Centro Santa Fe:** *Av. Vasco de Quiroga 3800, Ciudad Santa Fe, Tel. 5259-4500*. Located southwest of Chapultepec Park, next to Sheraton Suites, in the city's rapidly developing new business center. This is the ultimate shopping center experience in Mexico. Indeed, Santa Fe is considered by many seasoned shopping observers to be the most exclusive shopping center in Latin America. It includes more than 300 leading shops and boutiques, restaurants, and movie theaters. It's especially noted for its popular amusement center for children.

Other major shopping centers include **Centro Coyoacán**, **Plaza Satellite**, **Perisur**, and **Pabellon Altavista**.

DEPARTMENT STORES

Mexico City has a few well known department stores that offer a good range of local and international products. However, few of these places are of interest to international visitors who may have similar, if not better, places back home. The major department stores include:

❑ **Palacio de Hierro:** *20 de Noviembre and the zócalo; Plaza Moliere; Centra Santa Fe; and four other locations.* This is the city's most upscale department store offering many name brands, such as **Long Champ**, **Salvatore Ferragamo**, **Cartier**, **Tiffany**, **Zegna**, **Hilfiger**, **Calvin Klein**, **Ungaro**, **Amni**, **Cerruti 1881**, **Boss**, **Façonnable**, **Nautica**, **Anne Klein**, and **Episode**. However, for some visitors who are used to **Saks Fifth Avenue**, **Neiman Marcus**, and **Nordstrom** as upscale department stores in the United States, Palacio de Hierro pales in comparison. Palacio de Hierro is more in line with an upscale Penney's or Sears punctuated with a few famous international name brands.

❑ **Liverpool:** *20 de Noviembre and the zócalo; Horacio and Mariano Excobedo; Centro Santa Fe; and four other locations.* This long established (since 1847) department store offers a wide range of products, from clothes to plants and pets. Includes interesting specialty sections showcasing Mexican designers, handicrafts, and sweets.

❑ **Sanborn's:** This popular combination department store and restaurant is found in several locations throughout the city. The most unique and popular Sanborn's – a major tourist attraction – is found in the House of Tiles at Francisco I. Madero 4 in the Centro Histórico. This also is great place for breakfast or lunch. The small department or convenience store side of Sanborn's includes everything from personal hygiene items to handicrafts, audiotapes, and CDs.

❑ **Sears Roebuck:** Found in eight locations throughout the city, this is a very popular department store for locals.

Best of the Best

Mexico City boasts many fine shops for discerning shoppers. We especially recommend the following shops for quality and value.

CERAMICS

❑ **Emilia Castillo:** *Camino Real Hotel, Leibinitz 100, Local 1-3, Col. Nueva Anzures. Tel. 5531-8873. Website: www.emiliacastillo.com.* Located just outside the Camino Real Hotel, this is one of Mexico's premier ceramics shops and one of our very favorite silver and ceramics designers in the world. It's a real class operation with gorgeous products created by true artists and craftsmen. Emilia Castillo works in ceramics, alabaster, sterling silver, and onyx as well as in other materials and natural stones. The main factory and shop are located in Taxco where the Castillo family has played a major role in developing Taxco's commercial silver trade. This shop offers a wonderful collection of gilded silver designs and figures on a distinctive line of tableware available in five colors: black, white, cobalt blue, green, and camel. If you're looking for something very special and distinctive to grace your dining table, you can acquire a complete dinner service with silver moon and star or fish designs. Look for plates, cups, saucers, bowls, flower vases, water pitchers, trays, napkin rings, and candle holders made with this unique silver treatment. Many of the pieces are literally works of art which also have functional use. The shop also includes bowls and candlesticks made of alabaster and onyx and embossed with silver figures. The silver designs include jaguars, dragonflies, toucans, and parrots. The shop also carries Castillo's signature silver trays, bowls, and serving pieces which include parrots inlaid with malachite. Neiman Marcus in the United States is the exclusive representative for the Castillo line of ceramics and silver. While you may find several silver shops imitating the Castillo designs, none compare favorably with the real thing found here. For a quick survey of Emilia Castillo's current collections, including her jewelry line, be sure to visit her website: www.emiliacastillo. com.

❑ **Uriarte Talavera:** *Alejandro Dumas 77, Polanco, Tel. 5282-2849 or Fax 5281-1788. E-mail: polanco@uriartetalavera.com.mx*. Open Monday through Friday, 10am to 7pm and Saturday and Sunday from 10am to 4pm. This is a great shop for products but a big service and shipping disappointment. If you visit only one ceramics shop in Mexico City, make sure it's Uriarte Talavera. Representing one of Puebla's most famous makers of Talavera pottery, this well appointed two-story shop is filled with some of the best quality ceramics you'll find anywhere in Mexico. The first floor includes many large blue and white jars and pots, serving dishes, place settings, bowls, trays, tiles, and bathroom items, including decorative sinks. You'll also find some award-winning signed ceramic figures created by some of Mexico's leading ceramic artists. During the Christmas season the shop offers an attractive selection of ceramic tree ornaments. The second floor includes more place settings as well as an attractive selection of plates, bowls, pots, and trays which are copies of famous ceramic pieces found in museums and private collections. Items here tend to be on the expensive side, but the quality is first rate. In fact, you may want to visit the shop early on in your visit to Mexico just to see what good quality ceramics look and feel like. Look for sale items in the outdoor courtyard. Also, be sure to check on the lead content of individual pieces – insist on lead-free dishes. The manager, Victoria, is very helpful and speaks excellent English. The shop claimed to be experienced in packing and shipping, and ostensibly ships by air using DHL. However, we did not find this to be true. Indeed, just the opposite, even after dealing directly with the owner of the shop. We cannot recommend them for shipping since they failed to ship a large prepaid order of a fellow traveler, even after eight months of repeated phone calls, faxes, and reports to the credit card company. In the end, the credit card company had to intervene in order to credit the customer's account. Since shipping with Uriarte Talavera appears to be a big problem, we can only recommend a "cash and carry" arrangement with this shop – take everything you buy with you rather than pay for your purchases and rely on this shop to pack and ship. If not, you, too, may be disappointed with their abysmal shipping service, and you'll feel you've been scammed by this operation. If you don't heed our advice, at least charge your purchases so you have some recourse if you do not receive your goods. If you plan to visit Puebla (4 Poniente 991, Tel. 2232-1598), be sure to visit their factory and shop. Factory tours are given Monday through Friday from 10am to 5pm.

❑ **Las Artesanias:** *Oscar Wilde 29, in Pasaje Polanco. Open Monday to Saturday, 10am to 8pm, and Sunday from 12noon to 6pm. Tel. 5280-9515 or Fax 5281-3218.* This two-level shop offers a large selection of colorful blue and yellow ceramics from Puebla and Guanajuato. Includes large ceramic jars and pots, small ceramic pieces (bowls, plates, boxes, ashtrays, picture frames), tin mirrors, Day of the Dead miniature figures, drinking glasses, ceramic tiles, shawls, bronze bells, and a jewelry section. A separate section on the ground floor includes large planters and pots. For some shoppers, many of the colors and designs may be over the top – an acquired taste bordering on the tacky.

A few selective handicraft shops, such as **Fonart** (Av. Juarez 89 and Patriotismo 691), carry good quality ceramics from all over Mexico.

HANDICRAFTS

❑ **Victor Artes Populares Mexicanos:** *Francisco I. Madero 10, Suite 305, 2nd Floor. Open Monday to Friday, 12:30pm to 7pm and Saturday by appointment only. Tel. 5512-1263.* Somewhat difficult to find because of its second-floor location in a rather dingy building just three doors east of Sanborn's (House of Tiles), this densely packed shop tends to yield some of the best quality folk arts and crafts in Mexico City. If you love Mexican folk art, you'll find this shop to be one of your best sources for acquiring excellent quality folk art. Representing many noted folk artists, the shop is a very reputable family business operated by two sisters and their partner. The father, who was a collector of folk art, started the business in 1952. The shop consists of three rooms, similar to offices, which are filled with a wide range of arts, crafts, and antiques. If after visiting the main shop you wish to see additional items, ask to be taken to the other two rooms which are usually locked. There's something for everyone here: masks, rugs, jewelry, silver, dolls, small figurines, paper cuts, clothes, lacquer boxes, ceramics, and papier-mâché figures. You may end up coming back to shop two or three times during your stay in the city. The prices here are both fixed and reasonable with items ranging from US$2 to US$5,000 or more. The distinctive wired painted animal figures by noted Michoacán artist Saulo Moreno sell for around 2,400 pesos here but go for 6,000 pesos in shops elsewhere, especially in San Miguel de Allende. The shop can arrange shipping. Very limited English spoken.

❑ **Fonart:** *Juarez 89 (corner of Balderas, across from Alameda Park), Centro Histórico. Open daily, 10am to 7pm. Tel. 5521-0171. Also has a branch shop at Londres 136A, Zona Rosa, Tel. 5598-5552, and a section within the Tourist Office at Presidente Masaryk 172. Open Monday to Saturday, 10am to 7pm.* This network of government-operated handicraft shops (Fonda Nacional para el Fomento de las Artes – FONART) is the retail operation of a program designed to promote Mexican arts and crafts. The good news is that Fonart displays some of the very best works in their shops. The largest, best, and most interesting Fonart shop is located at Juarez 89 – in an attractive old building with an enclosed central courtyard. Look for a nice selection of tempting pottery, copper pots, ceramics, jewelry, folk art, painted chairs, baskets, masks, knives, shawls, black pottery, terra cotta figures, candles, glassware, lacquer boxes and trays, stone garden pieces, furniture, rugs, and embroidered clothes. A great place for acquiring top quality and reasonably priced arts, crafts, and souvenirs. Prices here are fixed. Fonart is experienced in packing and shipping.

❑ **Casa Azul:** *Plaza del Carmen 25, Col. San Angel, Tel/Fax 5550-3223. E-mail: lepatmx@yahoo.com. Open daily, 10:30am to 7:00pm.* Located just around the corner from the Bazar Sábado and rising above a park that fills with artists on Saturdays, several rooms in this old restored house display a large assortment of quality arts and crafts from Mexico, Peru, Equador, and Colombia. Look for large metal figures – giraffe, frogs, birds

– outside in front of the entrance. Inside you'll find furniture, icon paintings, candles, lamps, bird cages, ceramic jars, silver, Santa Clara copper, blown glass, plates, bowls, painted pottery, picture frames, rice paper, and many unique items. The shop also puts on cultural performances for tour groups.

❑ **Centro Artesanal Buenavista:** *Aldama 187 Col. Guerrero, Tel. 5529-1254. Open daily, 9am to 6pm.* Welcome to Hog Heaven! Known as the Central Crafts Market, this is one huge handicraft and furniture emporium that seems to go on and on and on. Indeed, it claims to be the largest such market in the country – 200,000 Mexican articles displayed in 21,000 square meters of exhibition space. While this place may assault your sense of good taste, it does put under one roof the widest selection of tacky to okay arts and crafts anywhere in Mexico. You have to see this place to believe it. Don't expect great quality in a place where quantity seems to be the basic selection and organizing principle. It displays just about every conceivable local product, including paintings, large bronzes, wood and wrought iron furniture, ceramics, pots, metal figures, luggage, leather coats, handbags, copper and brass items, malachite stones, onyx, cement garden sculptures, blown glass, paper flowers, dolls, boxes, sombreros, silver mirrors, clothes, shoes, CDs, and tapes. Upstairs you'll find rustic furniture – tables, chairs, and beds. The shop will pack but not ship. Unless you're really into this stuff, you don't need to spend a great deal of time here, although walking the many aisles can be time consuming. Given the sheer volume of products, you may find a few interesting and inexpensive gift items here. However, don't make this one of your first shopping stops in Mexico City. Visit some of the quality places first, such as Fonart, so you'll have an idea of what you're dealing with at Centro Artesanal Buenavista in comparison to the really "good stuff" produced by Mexico's many talented artists and craftspeople.

❑ **Flamma:** *Hamburgo 167 or Florencia 22, Zona Rosa, Tel. 5511-8499.* Located on the corner of Hamburgo and Florencia streets, you can smell this shop as you pass by. It includes an attractive selection of handmade candles in all shapes and sizes. During the Christmas season, the shop is filled with lovely holiday candles. Includes many animal figures which make excellent collector's items – too cute to burn. The shop claims to offer the largest variety of candles and accessories in Mexico. Also includes a shop at the Bazar Sábado (Plaza San Jacinto No. 11, San Ángel).

❑ **Artesanos de Mexico:** *Londres 117, Col. Juarez, Zona Rosa, Tel. 5525-6235 or Fax 5514-7455. Open Monday to Friday, 11am to*

7pm. You walk up a stairway flanked with black pots functioning as a cascading waterfall in expectation of something very special. This rather unusual shop includes four rooms of furniture, masks, dolls, paintings, pots, ceramics, doll houses, and other items. It has a rather strange assortment of arts and crafts produced by a variety of Mexican artisans. An interesting shop for browsing.

❑ **Bazar Sábado:** *Plaza de San Jacinto 11, San Ángel, Tel. 5616-0082. Open Saturday, 10am to 7pm.* Housed in a red stucco 17th century mansion, this two-level arts and crafts building hosts the popular Saturday market, which draws thousands of visitors in search of quality jewelry, ceramics, textiles, stained glass, wrought iron lamps, tables, mirrors, sculptures, leather goods, and clothes available in numerous vendor stalls. Look for **Brondis** for nice glass and wrought iron creations and **Jeanne** for cute children's clothes. Nearby shops, such as **Galeria San Angel**, **Adobe Disaño**, and **Casa Azul**, offer excellent quality arts and crafts. Many of these shops are open seven days a week but are especially crowded on Saturday. See the "Market" section for more information on this popular weekend market.

❑ **La Primavera:** *Chihuahua 66, Colonia Roma. Tel./Fax 5584-4568.* This two-story factory outlet shop offers a good selection of hand-blown glass, both clear and colored, produced in its factory in Hidalgo. It includes many large vases, bowls, pitchers, candle holders, and decorative glass objects in blue, red, green, and yellow. Since this is a very small factory outlet shop, it does not display its inventory well. You'll have to carefully go over the rather disorganized and cluttered shelves. Be sure to pick up a copy of their catalog/brochure and price list.

❑ **Carretones:** *Carretones 5, near La Merced market. Open Monday to Friday, 10am to 2pm and 3-5pm; Saturday to 2pm. Tel. 5522-5311.* This factory shop produces colorful blown glass, including made-to-order items. Much of the product looks handmade and rustic – not particularly attractive designs. During the week you can observe the glass production process. The showroom displays a wide range of colored and clear glass. Located across from a local market, Carretones is somewhat difficult to find.

❑ **Tamacani:** *Insurgentes Sur 1748-B. Tel. 5662-4616. Fax 5662-7133. E-mail: tamacaniventas@hotmail.com.* If you're in the market for handmade wool rugs, this shop may be able to meet your needs. It offers 100% wood rugs and wall hangings as well as fabrics, cushions, and bedspreads. The showroom includes samples of several rugs they produce using their own designs inspired by Mexican motifs. All rugs are produced with a latex or rubberized backing. Tamacani also will make rugs to a customer's specifications. If you have particular colors and designs, bring them with you to this shop. They normally take six weeks to complete a customized rug. All rugs and fabrics are produced in its factory in Cuernavaca.

❏ **Arte Popular en Miniatura:** *Hamburgo 85, Col. Juarez, Tel. 5525-8145.* This very small shop sells tiny items – dollhouse furniture, lead soldiers, and miniature Nativity scenes. Very popular with collectors of miniatures.

ART GALLERIES

Mexico City has a thriving art community with numerous galleries representing some of Mexico's finest artists. The following galleries represent some of our favorites. They are very different from one another.

❏ **Sergio Bustamante:** *Amberes 13, Zona Rosa, Tel. 5525-9059. E-mail: mail@sergiobustamante.zzn.com. Website: http://sergiobustamante.com.mx. Also has galleries at the Hotel Nikko (Tel. 5282-2638) and Hotel Camino Real (Tel. 5254-7372).* Even if you're not an art connoisseur, you should at least visit this magical and compelling gallery. Indeed, after years of resistence, this has now become our favorite contemporary Mexican artist with a decided surrealistic style who works in a variety of mediums – papier-mâché, ceramics, bronze, silver, gold, canvas, paper, and wood. He's also an acquired taste. As soon as you walk into his gallery, you know you've encountered a very creative and prolific artist and designer. His colorful, imaginative, and whimsical anthropomorphic papier-mâché, bronze, and copper surrealistic sculptures transport you to a whole new world of art and fantasy. While you may become affixed to his unusual papier-mâché and ceramic figures, be sure to check out his jewelry and furniture lines – both wonderful additions to his artistic repertoire that also have established him as a major designer. The jewelry line is especially popular with visitors. The website (http://sergiobustamante.com.mx) showcases many of his major creations – ceramics, bronzes, papier-mâché, oil paintings, etchings, drawings, furniture, and jewelry. Sergio Bustamante's main gallery is found in Tlaquepaque, a major shopping suburb of Guadalajara in the state of Jalisco. The shop is experienced in packing and shipping – mainly uses DHL's air service which takes about one week for delivery.

❑ **Connoisseur Art Gallery:** *Intersection of Amberes and Hamburgo streets, Zona Rosa. Tel. 5208-6454, or Fax 5208-3780.* While more an exclusive antique shop (see "Antiques") than an art gallery, nonetheless, this shop is noted for its religious art, especially icons and paintings. It actually views itself as a combination gallery and museum. It also operates the nearby **Asian Art Gallery** (Amberes 11, Tel. 5525-3484) which includes gallery space on the second floor as well as an art gallery in Coyoacán, **El Círculo Azul** (Francisco Sosa 363, Tel. 5554-7665). The personnel here are well known art consultants and very responsive to art inquiries. So if you have a particular art need, they will try to fill it. Prices here run from US$2,000 to US$1 million.

❑ **Aura Galerias:** *Amberes 38, Zona Rosa, Tel. 5208-9679 or Fax 5533-2025. E-mail: aura@mail.internet.com.mx. Open Monday to Friday, 10:30am to 2:30pm and 4pm to 8pm, and Saturday by appointment.* This well appointed gallery in the heart of Zona Rosa's upscale shopping street includes an excellent collection of contemporary paintings and sculptures. Representing 30 artists, the gallery primarily deals with well known Mexican artists. It regularly exhibits works of top artists. The owners also function as art consultants. Their primary market deals with art in the US$1,000 to US$25,000 range. Their secondary art consulting market focuses on art in the US$10,000 to US$1 million range.

❑ **Galeria de Arte Misrachi:** *Lafontaine 243, at the corner of Homero, Polanco, Tel. 5250-4105 or Fax 5254-4902.* For years this has been one of Mexico's most important art galleries. It has been at the forefront of promoting many of Mexico's major artists, including Diego Rivera, Frida Kahlo, David Alfaro Siqueiros, and Francisco Zúñiga. It's also famous for its many major art publications. If you're looking for investment quality paintings, prints, and sculptures by many of Mexico's top modern artists, this gallery is well worth visiting. It represents 20 to 30 artists and hosts exhibitions every two months. The owner, Carlos Beraha Cohen, knows Mexican art very well and is an extremely engaging storyteller.

❑ **Galeria Alberto Misrachi:** *Presidente Masaryk 83, esq. Taine, Polanco, Tel. 5531-6439 or Fax 5531-8084. E-mail: misrachi@prodigy.net.mx. Also has a gallery in the Nikko Hotel, Campos Eliseos 204, Polanco, Tel. 5280-3866 or Fax 5281-4495.* Offers an excellent collection of contemporary paintings produced by some of Mexico's leading artists as well as several new and promising artists. Currently operated by the two sisters of the late Alberto Misrachi.

❏ **Talento:** *Anatole France 82, Polanco, Tel. 5148-5110 or Fax 5280-9039. E-mail: raguijarro@maxcom.net.mx. Website: www.talentoarte.com.* This attractive gallery represents 15 contemporary artists, both established and up and coming young artists. Includes both painting and sculptures, including the unique bronze works of Pal Kepenyes (see section on Acapulco, pages 169-170). The gallery changes its exhibits frequently, and thus what you see at any given time does not really represent well the gallery's current inventory. Ask to see their catalog of artists.

❏ **Galeria Lopez Quiroga:** *Aristóteles 169, Chapultepec Morales Polanco, Tel. 5280-1247 or Fax 5280-3960. E-mail: galoqui@infosel.net.mx.* Offers an excellent selection of contemporary Mexican art in a very attractive gallery space. One of the best organized art galleries, with books filled with photos of paintings that can be pulled from inventory. Represents nearly 15 artists. Occasionally has exhibitions. Includes a very large art library on the second floor. Look for sculptures in the outdoor exhibition area.

❏ **Galeria Oscar Roman:** *Julio Verne 14, Polanco, Tel. 5280-0436 or Fax 5280-1594. E-mail: romanos@prodigy.net.mx. Website: www.arte-mexico.com/romanosc. Open Monday to Friday, 10:30am-3pm and 5pm to 7:30pm, and Saturday, 11am to 2:30pm.* This is a very different art gallery with often eclectic and mild avant-garde collections that are both amusing and compelling. Specializing in contemporary paintings and metal sculptures, the gallery represents several international artists. Its very contemporary art focus also includes an attractive contemporary-style art space where exhibits normally change monthly.

❏ **Galeria OMR:** *Plaza Rio de Janeiro 54, Roma, Tel. 5207-1080 or Fax 5533-4244. E-mail: mailomr@webtelmex.net.mx. Website: www.galeriaomr.com. Open Monday to Friday, 10am to 3pm and 4pm to 7pm, and Saturday, 10am to 2pm.* Housed in a rambling two-story early 20th century house in the heart of the Roma district, this contemporary art gallery represents a varied group of Mexican and international painters, sculptors, and photographers. It also represents both established artists and talented young creators. Primarily working with museums and collectors, the gallery includes a large collection of art which can be viewed in several large inventory/photo albums in the office area.

❏ **Tere Haas:** *Amberes No. 12-B, Zona Rosa. Tel. 5511-6134.* Represents 10 contemporary artists from Mexico, the Philippines, Costa Rica, and the United States. Includes numerous paintings as well as bronze and stone sculptures. Very little English spoken here.

❑ **Hevart's Galeria de Arte:** *Hotel Krystal Rosa, Liverpool No. 155, Zona Rosa, Tel. 5228-9928, Ext. 471.* Relatively new, this small but interesting gallery represents noted contemporary and classic Mexican artists. It currently represents 10 painters and 8 sculpturers who work in bronze, black marble, white marble, and onyx. Paintings run in the range of US$200 to US$10,000+. Sculptures go for US$288 to US$23,000+. All prices include shipping. The gallery occasionally sponsors exhibitions at the Nikko Hotel.

❑ **Galeria Schwarcstein:** *Campos Eliseos 194, Polanco, Tel./Fax 5282-1278.* Located just a few doors east of the Nikko Hotel, this small but exclusive gallery offers an excellent selection of Mexican contemporary art and selective handicrafts. Very friendly and helpful.

❑ **El Jardin del Arte (The Art Garden):** *San Ángel and San Rafael. Open on Saturdays and Sundays.* If you enjoy shopping for art outside galleries and meeting directly with artists, then plan to participate in this weekend art market. Every weekend more than 700 local artists who belong to the Art Garden Association gather in four parks and plazas where they exhibit their works and sell directly to the public: Plaza San Jacinto and Plaza del Carmen in San Ángel on Saturdays (open 10am to 5pm); and Sullivan Park (behind the Monument of the Mother in the San Rafael district, three blocks northwest of the Insurgentes Norte and Paseo de la Reforma intersection, open 10am to 3pm) and Plaza del Carmen on Sundays. Some observers claim this is the largest outdoor gallery in the world!

ANTIQUES

❑ **Rodrigo Rivero Lake:** *Campos Eliseos 199 P.H., Polanco. Tel. 5281-5505, Fax 5281-5377. E-mail: rodrigo@rlake.com.mx. Website: www.rlake.com.mx.* By appointment only. There are antiques and then there are Rodrigo Rivero Lake's antiques – numerous cuts above everything else you will see in Mexico. This is not just a collection of antiques. It's an important statement  about quality art and antiques in Mexico. You have to see it to believe it. This is a stunning antique emporium for serious antique collectors who are interested in acquiring museum-quality treasures. The owner is one of those rare breeds of global collectors who has an eye for sourcing the very best and rare pieces available. Many of his antiques are currently on loan with major museums in Mexico and he regularly supplies museums around the world. His gallery is jam-packed with an awesome combination of fully restored rare chests, screens, paintings, furniture, religious figures, silver, pillars, crucifixes, carvings, and even stone fireplaces dating from the 16th century. The international mix of antiques is fascinating as you transport yourself into previous centuries where top artists and artisans produced treasures that grace fine museums and homes of the rich and famous. In addition to a very large collection of Mexican antiques, many pieces come from Spain, the Philippines, Colombia, Bolivia, and India. Given the quality of this collection, individual pieces tend to be very expensive. Indeed, a gorgeous rare 17th century carved and painted 10-panel screen of Mexico City goes for US$1.2 million. However, you also can find some items for under US$1,000. The extremely affable and compelling owner also will do reproductions of any pieces, including those on loan with museums. Serious buyers may be invited to tour his extensive warehouse, which is located about 15 minutes from the main gallery, or view his home, which is adjacent to this 10th story gallery. The warehouse includes an impressive collection of stone carvings, columns, furniture, art, and decorative pieces from Mexico, Spain, China, Indonesia, and India. The Indian collection is massive. Indeed, this is the closest you'll get to India in Mexico! Here you'll find a fascinating collection of stone and wood columns, huge doors (tallest is 27 feet), furniture, carvings, stone arches, and carved figures. Be sure to carefully survey the walls and ceilings of the covered warehouse, which include many unique antiques.

❑ **Connoisseur Art Gallery:** *Intersection of Amberes and Hamburgo streets, Zona Rosa. Tel. 5208-6454, Fax 5208-3780.* You'll immediately recognize the concept as soon as you walk through the door – this is a unique gallery-museum. Specializing in religious and colonial art and antiques from the 13th century on, this beautiful gallery displays rare pieces discovered in Mexico, the Philippines, and other places around the world. Look for carved religious figures, large crucifixes, chests, tapestries, tables, chairs, desks, icons, and paintings. All are collector's items ranging from US$2,000 to US$1 million. The enthusiastic and extremely knowledgeable director, Diana Arizcorreta B., lovingly explains each piece as if you were on a very special museum tour with your private docent. The owners also operate three other galleries, including the nearby **Asian Art Gallery** at Amberes 11.

❑ **Mejico Antiguo:** *Estocolmo 17, Zona Rosa, Tel. 5525-6177.* This shop specializes in old architectural pieces, furniture, religious art, paintings, masks, candle holders, and pots. An eclectic collection of quality items.

❑ **Bazar de Antigüedades:** *Plaza del Angel. Between Hamburgo and Londres, across from Insurgentes Market, in Zona Rosa.* If you want to get a quick overview of the type and quality of antiques available in Mexico City, be sure to visit this antique center. Consisting of more than 30 antique shops, this is a one-stop center for antique lovers in search of good quality antiques with a European flair, especially French, Italian, and Spanish themes. Individual shops offer a combination of paintings, bronze statues, furniture, lamps, ceramics, pottery, religious figures, clocks, glassware, icons, chandeliers, mirrors, toys, jewelry, rugs, and bric-a-brac. Most shops are located on the first level, although you will find a few shops on the second level – check the separate side staircases. On Saturdays numerous vendors display antiques and collectibles along walkways and halls on the first level.

JEWELRY AND SILVER

Many of Mexico City's jewelry shops also offer a variety of silver products, from serving pieces to decorative art. At the same time, many silver shops also offer a line of both silver and silver-plated jewelry. A few high-end jewelry shops primarily offer uniquely designed jewelry along with imported watches.

❑ **Tane:** *Presidente Masaryk 430, Polanco, Tel. 5281-4299 or Fax 5281-5876; and Amberes 70, Zona Rosa, Tel. 5207-3802 or Fax 5511-8783. Website: www.tane.com.mx.* Tane is synonymous with quality silver in Mexico. Indeed, this is Mexico's premier silver designer and fabricator who works with four product lines: serving pieces, flatware, artistic figures, and  jewelry. You know this is a very special store as you enter a security vault at the main store in Polanco. The designs and selections here are stunning – from beautifully designed silver serving pieces, flatware, and trays to artistic figures and jewelry in both silver and gold. The Zona Rosa store also offers an excellent range of products.

❑ **Sergio Bustamante:** *Amberes 13, Zona Rosa, Tel. 5525-9059. E-mail: mail@sergiobustamante.zzn.com. Website: http://sergiobustamante.com.mx.* Also has galleries at the Hotel Nikko (Tel. 5282-2638) and Hotel Camino Real (Tel. 5254-7372). In addition to the intriguing art (see the "Art Gallery" section above), this shop includes Sergio Bustamante's distinctive silver and gold jewelry collection. Look for his playful animal, blazing sun, and half moon figures fashioned into beautifully executed necklaces, bracelets, earrings, and pendants. This is the closest you'll get to "wearable art" with this master artist and designer.

❑ **D'Argenta:** *Hotel Presidente Inter-Continental. Tel. 5281-3056 or Fax 5359-1125. E-mail: info@dargenta.com. Website: www. dargenta.com.* This shop, which is part of the Fonart Company, offers excellent quality gold and silver plated copper serving pieces, sculptures, decorative art, and jewelry in its D'Argenta Collection. While the silver jewelry is supplied by their partner, Taxco-based **Talleres de los Ballesteros**, all other silver items are produced in D'Argenta's Mexico City factory. Several of their more than 250 designs have won international prizes for excellence. The shop offers an intriguing collection of large sculpted silver jaguars, tigers, horses, giraffes, swans, and female figures, which make wonderful decorative art pieces and gift items. They also commission limited editions developed by some of Mexico's leading artists who create both pre-Hispanic archaeological and contemporary designs. They regularly exhibit their unique works at major international trade fairs. D'Argenta offers one of the nicest collections of quality silver pieces that also represent a good variety of themes and motifs that go far beyond much of the standard Taxco look-alike silver products.

❑ **Talleres de los Ballesteros:** *Amberes 24, Zona Rosa, Tel./Fax 5511-8281; Presidente Masarik 126, Polanco, Tel. 5545-4109 or Fax 5545-4976. Website: www.ballesteros.net.* Also includes four shops in Taxco, as well as shops at the airport and in Cancun, Spain, San Francisco, and San Antonio. Based in Taxco, this is one of Mexico's most famous silver shops which has a major presence in Mexico City. In fact, prices in its Mexico City shops are often better than at the manufacturing source in Taxco, a well trafficked tourist center that commands higher prices. Its largest shop is in Polanco, although the Zona Rosa shop includes a very large selection of silver products. Includes a wide selection of sterling silver and silver-plated serving pieces, figures, and jewelry. The brightly lighted shops display well the work of this noted manufacturer.

❑ **Izta:** *Alejandro Dumas 7-A, Polanco, Tel. 5282-0024 or Fax 5281-5197. E-mail: info@izta.com.mx. Website: www.izta.com.mx.* This small but long-established silver shop produces beautifully crafted silver pieces, from bowls to silverware, in its Mexico City workshop. Excellent workmanship and lovely designs. Gives special discounts on shipments to addresses outside Mexico.

❑ **Berger:** *Presidente Masaryk 438, Polanco. Tel. 5281-4122, Fax 5281-5803. E-mail: berjoy@mail.internet.com.mx. Website: www. bergerjoyeros.com.mx. Also at Centro Comercial X-0, Altavista 206, Local 2, San Angel, Tel. 5616-1594 and Fax 5616-5869; and two locations in Cancun.* This is one of Mexico's finest jewelers that more than holds its own against its big name international neighbors in Polanco – **Cartier**, **Bulgari**, and **Tiffany's**. In operation for over 50 years, Berger produces outstanding jewelry designs for a large range of very tasteful gold and silver jewelry that also incorporates precious stones and pearls. The main store in Polanco includes three floors of quality jewelry. The ground floor is largely devoted to more than 30 top brands of watches, including **Patek Philippe**, **Cartier**, **Bulgari**, **Ebel**, **Chopard**, **Piaget**, **Rolex**, **Omega**, **Corum**, **Tagheuer**, **Gucci**, **Breitling**, and **Montblanc** – one of the largest selections found anywhere. The first and second floors include showcase after showcase of stunning jewelry. Our advice: Before making any substantial jewelry or watch purchases in Mexico City, be sure to visit Berger first. Berger also owns the **Bulgari** shop, which is located directly across the street from its main shop in Polanco.

❑ **Peyrelongue:** *Presidente Masaryk 440, Polanco. Tel. 5281-3992 and Fax 5511-5817. E-mail: ventas@chronos.com.mx. Website: www.chronos.com.mx. Also at Amberes 5 and 14, Col. Juárez, Zona Rosa.* This long-established French-owned jewelry stone includes an excellent range of gold and silver jewelry using precious stones and black pearls. The ground floor includes several showcases of fine jewelry. The first floor is devoted to a large range of top name Swiss watches.

❑ **Aplijsa:** *El Bazar del Centro, Isabel La Catolica 30-104. Tel. 5510-1840 or Fax 5521-1007. E-mail: info@aplijsa.com.mx. Website: www.aplijsa.com.mex.* Also operates four shops in Guadalajara. Housed in a lovely old mansion called El Bazar del Centro, which is operated by Aplijsa, the shop extends throughout both levels of the building. Look for black and white pearls, colored stones, coral, and semi-precious stones (black sapphire, emerald, amethyst, tiger eye, lapis, carnelian, malachite, peridot, and turquoise) made into lovely jewelry pieces, especially necklaces.

❑ **Ginza:** *El Bazar del Centro, Isabel La Catolica 30-108. Tel. 5518-6543.* Offers an excellent selection of white and black pearls in the lovely El Bazar del Centro setting.

❑ **L.A.Cano:** *Plaza Moliere, C-29, Polanco, Tel. 5280-7938. Also has shops at Centro Santa Fe (J-46), Perisur (H-50), and the airport (B-44).* This exclusive shop offers very nice gold reproduction jewelry with pre-Columbian designs based on archaeological pieces found in Mexico and Colombia. You'll also find their pieces in the Four Seasons Hotel's boutique.

❑ **Emilia Castillo:** *Camino Real Hotel, Leibinitz 100, Local 1-3, Col. Nueva Anzures. Tel. 5531-8873. Website: www.emiliacastillo.com.* While primarily a talented ceramicist who produces uniquely designed tableware, Emilia Castillo (see "Ceramics" above) also produces an attractive 18k gold and sterling silver jewelry collection of bracelets, necklaces, and earrings with animal (alligators and turtles) motifs. For examples of her jewelry work, visit her website.

❑ **Tanya Moss Designer Jewelry:** *Presidente Masaryk 360 (at Pasaje Polanco), Tel. 5281-0697. Also at the Pabellon Polanco Shopping Center; Av. de la Pax 57, San Ángel; Mundo E Mall; Parque Duraznos; and Interlomas.* This creative jewelry designer produces a wide range of attractive gold and sterling silver jewelry using pearls, amber, and precious and semi-precious stones. Many of her designs reflect Mexican themes and have a very petite look to them.

❑ **Astrid Joyeros:** *Camino Real Hotel, Mariano Escobedo 700, Polanco, Tel. 5203-2121; and Westin Galeria Plaza Hotel, Zona Rosa, Tel. 5211-0014.* Offers a good selection of silver and gold jewelry, silver animal figures (elephants and jaguars), and white and black pearls. Also has shops in Acapulco, Ixtapa, and Puerto Vallarta.

❑ **Nacional Monte de Piedad (National Pawn Shop):** *Located on the corner of Monte de Piedad and Cinco de Mayo, across from the Cathedral on the northwest side of the zócalo, Centro Histórico. Open Monday through Friday, 9:30am to 6pm, and Saturday, 8:30am to 3pm.* This is one of the most unique jewelry markets in Mexico – where you can purchase the pawned gold jewelry of the locals. See our previous discussion of this jewelry center on page 108.

❑ **Centro Joyero de Mexico:** *Located on the west side of the zócalo, along Monte de Piedad and one block west along Francisco I Madero, Centro Histórico. Most shops are open Monday through Friday, 9:30am to 6pm, and Saturday, 8:30am to 3pm.* Located in and around the National Pawn Shop and the Majestic Hotel, dozens of small gold and jewelry shops and stalls line these two streets as well as occupy interior spaces of this large shopping center. Most of these places offer similar items – rings, bracelets, gold chains, pendants, and watches. A good place to do comparative shopping and acquire some nice gift items at reasonable prices.

LEATHER

❑ **Aries:** *Florencia 14, Zona Rosa, Tel. 5533-2509. Also has shoes at Plaza Polanco, Perisur, Presidente Inter-Continental Hotel, and Camino Real Hotel.* This is one of Mexico's premier leather designer shops. It offers top quality leather items, from handbags and briefcases to wallets and desktop organizers. The designer bag for carrying a rolled up blanket is especially clever. Well displayed in beautifully designed shops, the leather items are Mexico's answer to Louis Vuitton and Gucci. The boutique at Florencia 14 is the main shop with the largest selection of leather items.

❑ **Louis Vuitton:** *Plaza Zentro, Polanco. Tel. 5282-2005.* Offers excellent quality French leather luggage, bags, and travel accessories.

❑ **Salvatore Ferragamo:** *Presidente Masaryk 440, Polanco, Tel. 5281-4333. Also has shops at Plaza Moliere, Perisur, and Central Santa Fe.* High fashion Italian leather shoes and accessories. Also includes silk shawls and clothing.

❑ **Regina Romero:** *Alejandro Dumas 107, Polanco. Tel. 5181-0461.* Offers a nice collection of elegant leather shoes and boots.

GIFTS

❑ **Cabassi:** *Campos Eliseos 199, Polanco, Tel. 5281-1611 or Fax 5281-1509. E-mail: aleredo@hotmail.com.* Located across from the Nikko Hotel, this shop includes a nice collection of ceramics, candles, pillows, copper pots, boxes, shawls, trays, glasses, and jewelry.

❑ **Four Seasons Boutique:** *Four Seasons Hotel, Paseo de la Reforma 500, Zona Rosa/Colonia Júarez, Tel. 5230-1818.* This is one of the nicest hotel shops we encountered. The focus here is on quality selections. Look for excellent folk art, pre-Columbian jewelry (from L.A. Cano), silver jewelry (from Tane), books, and clothes.

BOOKS

❏ **Librería Pegaso at Casa Lamm:** *Álvaro Obregón 99, Local A, Roma. Tel. 5208-0171 or Fax 5511-1471.* Attached to a popular art gallery and restaurant, this large bookstore offers a huge selection of books with special emphasis on the arts. Includes an English section and children's book section along with travel books, jewelry, and production ceramic figures. Very crowded on weekends.

❏ **Palacio de Bellas Artes (Palace of Fine Arts):** *Eje Central Lázaro Cárdenas and Av. Juárez.* Includes a nice gift shop and bookstore with a good range of art books, CDs, and postcards. While there is an entrance fee to tour the building, you can go directly to the bookstore free of charge.

Accommodations

Mexico City offers a good range of accommodations for all types of budgets, from five-star luxury and boutique hotels that go for US$200 to US$400 a night to inexpensive budget arrangements that cost US$20 to US$50 a night. However, the price ranges for five-star properties may be much lower if you book your reservations online. For example, some US$300 a night properties may offer $99/night specials if you book through their website. Indeed, we've often found the top hotels to be the best buys when examining their special rates. Indeed, they discount much more than less expensive properties. The least expensive hotels will be found in the downtown Centro Histórico area. The most expensive properties tend to be concentrated in the major business and shopping areas – Polanco and Zona Rosa. If you're concerned about safety and convenience, which you should be, you are well advised to upgrade your accommodations and stay at properties in the Polanco and Zona Rosa areas. Most of these properties cater to business people and upscale travelers who are very safety and convenience conscious. Several of them also have small shopping arcades with some of the city's most exclusive art, jewelry, and fashion shops. The areas around the hotels in these areas are well patrolled by both the police and military, and the hotels make special efforts to look after their guests. The concierge services tend to be excellent and the hotels maintain their own fleets of cars and drivers. While you will pay more for such properties, in the end the extra safety and convenience may be well worth it. Best of all, these are very fine properties.

Most major hotels offer special packages or discounted rates when making reservations online. Be sure to check out the hotel website for special deals as well as examine several other websites that offer special online and competitive rates. We often find the hotel's website offers the best value. For example, in a recent spot check of the Hotel Presidente Inter-Continental, we found a special US$99.95 rate by going to the hotel site (www.intercontinental.com). A so-called 35 percent discounted rate through an online hotel wholesaler, www.mexicohotels.com, was US$179.95. As you will quickly discover, it pays to shop around for special rates on four- and five-star hotels. In fact, you may end up getting a better rate on such properties than you would on so-called budget hotels that only offer full-rack rates.

The following properties represent the best of the best in Mexico City.

❑ **JW Marriott Hotel:** *Andrés Bello 29 (also has a Campos Elíseos street entrance), Polanco, Mexico, D.F. 11560, Tel. (52-55) 5999-0000 or Fax (52-55) 5999-0001. Toll-free from the US & Canada 800-228-9290. Website: www.marriotthotels.com.* Located in the exclusive Polanco district, overlooking the greenery of Chapultepec Park and next to the Museum of Contemporary Art, the 311-room JW Marriott Hotel Mexico City is considered one of Mexico City's finest. It also is the recipient of many awards including being rated as 2nd Best Hotel in Latin America and rated 4th in the world on its guestrooms by readers of *Condé Nast Traveler* magazine. Only a handful of the Marriott hotels worldwide are designated as JW Marriotts – a distinction that puts them in an elite group. A unique feature of this hotel is its outer entryway which gives access from the streets on both sides of the hotel. This first public space encompasses a large area with a high ceiling and lots of glass, three massive copper-clad columns – each different from the others – and lots of granite. This impressive outer entrance gives way to a second entrance through a gorgeous antique tall double door of heavily carved wood and brass from India. This is the entrance to the warmth and luxury of this Marriott. The lobby and lounge areas are beautifully appointed with warm wood, tapestries, and Oriental carpets – all softened with lots of greenery, and in the case of our Christmas-time visit with a profusion of red poinsettias along with a beautifully decorated tree gracing the lobby.

The 311 guestrooms, which include stunning suites and duplex apartments, are spacious and nicely appointed with a large armoire that houses the television and mini bar, a working sized desk, and artwork. There are just enough touches of Mexico to give a sense of place, but without being overdone. The bathrooms are clad in travertine and marble, well lighted, and offer expected amenities – hair dryer, magnifying mirror, scale, and terry robe. Executive Floors offer an exclusive lounge where breakfast is served every morning and cocktails and hors d'oeuvres are served in the evening. We found the service to be first rate and the concierge service ranked with the best. The *JW Grill* restaurant features international cuisine in a fine dining atmosphere. *Café Pergamino* offers casual dining and a choice of either a la carte or buffet. The breakfast buffet was one of the best we have experienced – anywhere! On sunny days guests can enjoy meals on the terrace. The *Thai House* restaurant has its own separate entrance across the outer entryway from the reception area. A 24-hour Business Center offers full secretarial services including translation services. The 7th floor Health Club, with views of Chapultepec Park, offers cardiovascular and weight resistance equipment, steam room, sauna, and whirlpool. Even in January it was comfortable on the outdoor sundeck by the heated pool. Conference/Banquet Facilities. Includes a delightful small but densely displayed art shop offering bronze cast figures and paintings. It's located just outside the Campos Elíseos street entrance – **Castellanos** (Andrés Bello 29 Local 2, Tel. 5282-8888, ext. 6603).

❑ **Four Seasons Hotel:** *Paseo de la Reforma 500, Zona Rosa/Colonia Júarez, Mexico, D.F., 06600, Tel. (52-55) 5230-1818, Fax (52-55) 5230-1808. Toll-free from US & Canada 800-332-3442. Website: www.fshr.com.* The Four Seasons is located on the historic Paseo de la Reforma near the shopping and entertainment venues of the Zona Rosa and Chapultepec Park. Combining Spanish Colonial styles and French influences, the hotel presents an elegant facade to both the street entrance and the interior courtyard. Most of the 240 guestrooms look out onto the center courtyard. The spacious and well appointed rooms offer all the amenities expected from the Four Seasons/Regent Hotels – the hotel chain earning top rankings in myriad surveys. The ample marble bathrooms have a tub and separate shower enclosure as well as a lighted make-up mirror, bathrobes and hairdryer. *El Restaurante* culinary specialties from both the old and the new world are beautifully presented and served in elegant surroundings. The AAA Five-Diamond restaurant has also been named the best hotel restaurant in Latin America by *Condé Nast Traveler* Readers' Choice Awards. *Café Four Seasons* serves international and local specialties in a relaxed atmosphere. *El Bar* decorated with an English decor depicting a library offers a wide selection of tequilas, mezcal from Oaxaca, and sophisticated beverages. The multilingual concierge service is helpful with questions regarding the hotel facilities or cultural, entertainment, dining or shopping interests the guests may pose. Business Center; Health/Fitness

Center; Conference/Banquet Facilities. Includes a small but excellent boutique shop, the **Four Seasons Boutique**, with a fine collection of folk art and jewelry (from L.A. Cano).

❑ **Sheraton Maria Isabel Hotel & Towers:** *Paseo de la Reforma 325, Mexico D.F., 06500, Tel. (52-55) 5242-5555 or Fax (52-55) 5207-0684, Toll-free from the US & Canada 800-903-2500. Website: www.sheraton.com.* Located on the Paseo de la Reforma, overlooking the Zona Rosa business and shopping district and facing the Angel of Independence Monument, the Sheraton Maria Isabel's 755 guestrooms – including 67 suites and 5 penthouse suites – have all been recently renovated. The elegant decor in neutral tones as well as the sound-proof guestrooms promote a peaceful rest. The Towers features VIP services and amenities. *The Towers Lounge* on the 18th floor, offers very nice continental breakfast and afternoon cocktails. Veranda features Mexican and Continental cuisine; *Café Pavillion* serves buffets in a atmosphere reminiscent of colonial times; *Cardinale* features homemade pastas and Italian specialties. *Jorongo* is a traditional Mexican bar with entertainment and beverages. Business Center; International Fitness Center; Conference/Banquet Facilities.

❑ **Hotel Presidente Inter-Continental:** *Campos Elíseos 218, Polanco, Delegación Miguel Hidalgo, Mexico D.F. 11560, Tel (52-55) 5327-7700 or Fax (52-55) 3276-7737. Toll-free from the US & Canada 800-447-6147. E-mail: intercontinental.com/comments.shtml. Website: www.intercontinental.com/comments.shtml.* Enter the open and spacious lobby with its colorful decor and feel of Mexico and visit the group of small, but exclusive shops off to the right of the entrance via the very wide staircase. The 659 guestrooms and suites offer a choice of business rooms, deluxe rooms, ladies' rooms (specially guarded by security officials at night), non-smoking rooms, as well as rooms for handicapped guests. Rooms are decorated with tasteful touches of Mexican handicrafts. Club Floor rooms offer extra services and amenities. *Frutas y Flores* coffee shop serves daily buffet breakfast and lunch Monday through Friday, and is open 24 hours. La Chimena serves Mexican and international cuisine. At *Alfredo Di Roma* Italian cuisine is the specialty. *Balmoral* is a tea house with a simple menu. *Au pied de Cochon* is famous for its Parisian bistro serving excellent, reasonably priced food. *Palm Restaurant's* specialties are fine meat cuts and American style lobster. Business Center; Fitness Center; Conference/Banquet Facilities. Offers an excellent selection of shops in its two-level shopping arcade to the right of the reception area, including the exclusive **Tane**, **D'Argenta**, and **Aries**.

❏ **Camino Real Mexico City:** *Mariano Escobedo 700, Polanco, Mexico D.F. 11590, Tel. (52-55) 5263-8888 or Fax (52-55) 5263-8898. Toll-free from U.S. and Canada 800-722-6466. Website: www. caminoreal.com/mexico.* Situated on eight and a half acres, a member of The Leading Hotels of the World, the Camino Real is the only resort hotel in Mexico City. Its central location allows easy access to museums as well as business and shopping districts. Only five levels high, the Camino Real sprawls horizontally rather than rising vertically. Its bright pink and yellow facade and minimalist design provides the backdrop for an amazing collection of art by contemporary Mexican artists. The 714 guestrooms and suites feature deluxe amenities expected in a luxury hotel. Camino Real Club Floors offer additional amenities. The airy *Azulejos Restaurant* serves international and Mexican cuisine. *La Huerta*, an informal coffee shop, provides a variety of homemade pastries as does *Café Tamayo* – along with other specialties. *La Cirque* opens soon. Business Center; Fitness Center; Conference/Banquet Facilities. Includes both indoor and outdoor shopping areas with such exclusive shops as **Emilia Castillo**, **Sergio Bustamante**, **Tane**, **Aries**, **Astrid**, and **Castellanos**.

❏ **Hotel Nikko Mexico**: *Campos Eliseos 204, Polanco, Mexico D.F. 11560, Tel. (52-55) 5280-1111 or Fax (52-55) 5280-9191. Toll-free from the US & Canada 800-908-8800. E-mail: nikko@nikko.com.mx. Website: www.nikkohotels.com.* The second largest hotel in Mexico City, this modern high-rise offers views as well as easy access to Chapultepec Park and the Museum of Anthropology. Its 744 guestrooms offer the expected amenities. Standard rooms can be a bit cramped; the rooms on the Executive Floors offer more space and amenities. *The Teppan Grill* and Benkay both offer Japanese specialties; *Les Célébrités* offers Mediterranean cuisine; and *El Jardín* serves Mexican and international cuisine. Business Center; Fitness Center; Conference/Banquet Facilities. Includes a small shopping arcade with two fine art shops – **Galerie Alberto Misrachi** and **Sergio Bustamante**. Also, look for art exhibitions at this hotel.

❏ **Hotel Marquis Reforma:** *Paseo de la Reforma 465, Cuauhtemoc, Mexico D.F. 06500, Tel. (52-55) 5229-1200 or Fax (52-55) 5229-1212. Toll-free from the US & Canada 800-235-2387. E-mail: marquis@ri.redint.com.* A member of The Small Luxury Hotels of the World, located on the Paseo de la Reforma near shopping and business districts, the Hotel Marquis Reforma merges Art-Deco decor with 21st century technology in its 208 (includes 84 suites) guestrooms. Three Executive Floors offer additional amenities. *Café Royal* on the lobby level offers casual dining overlooking Reforma Avenue. *Restaurant La Jolla* serves international specialties with a Mexican touch. The outdoor *La Plaza*, located in the interior courtyard is especially popular for Sunday brunch. Business Center; Fitness Center; Conference/Banquet Facilities.

❑ **Casa Vieja:** *Eugenio Sue 45, Polanco, Mexico, DF 11560, Tel. (52-55) 5282-0067 or Fax (52-55) 5281-3780. E-mail: casavieja@mexico boutiquehotels.com.* Situated in a quiet residential area in the upscale Polanco district, this rambling house has been lovingly restored and transformed into a colorful and charming all-suite boutique hotel. Near the Museum of Anthropology and Chapultepec Park, the neighborhood is a lovely place just to take a walk, admire the architecture of nearby homes, or sit on a park bench overlooking a small water basin and watch the birds or the children playing. Every corner of Casa Vieja is decorated with folk art selected by the owner (a famous TV personality) from the various regions of Mexico. Paintings by noted artists decorate the refrigerator doors. Each of the 10 suites (either one or two bedrooms) is different from the others and named after a famous Mexican intellectual. The Mexican architecture features outdoor terraces – many of them actually covered from above with glass for a large greenhouse effect – with colorful bougainvillea cascading from the balconies. A picture window overlooking an inside garden is a feature in each suite. Each suite has a full kitchen, hydromassage bathtub, audiovisual system including CD and videocassette player. The hotel's Mexican rooftop garden restaurant, *Arbol de la Vida*, is named after its floor-to-ceiling Tree of Life sculpture. The menu changes daily. Breakfast is included. Meeting room available.

❑ **Airport Marriott Hotel Mexico City:** *Puerto Mexico 80, Mexico D.F. 15520, Tel. (52-55) 5133-0033 or Fax (52-55) 5133-0030. Toll-free from the US & Canada 800-228-9290. Website: www.marriott hotels.com.* If you arrive in Mexico City on a late evening flight, have an overnight layover before a morning onward flight, or have an early departure, the Airport Marriott Hotel offers a convenient, comfortable alternative to a downtown hotel. The Airport Marriott is conveniently connected to the Mexico City International Airport by a covered pedestrian skybridge. Its 600 guestrooms, which include 17 suites, offer attractive and comfortable surroundings with two telephones with data ports, in-room safe, mini bar, hair dryer, iron and ironing board. Executive Level rooms and lounge provide additional amenities. Five restaurants satisfy cravings for American or international cuisine. Specialty coffees and breads are available at *The Gourmet Bean*. Or dig into a piping hot pizza from *Pizza Hut*. For more leisurely dining, savor the a la carte selections for breakfast, lunch, or dinner at *Las Flores*. For an authentic taste of Mexico, *Cualli* offers all-day dining. The *Lobby Lounge* is a relaxing retreat after a day of meetings or sightseeing. 24-Hour Business Center; Rooftop Health Club; Meeting/Banquet Facilities.

Restaurants

Mexico City is a gourmet's delight for local and international cuisine. It's also a city where people love late night dining. Restaurants abound throughout the city, but especially in our major shopping areas of Polanco, Zona Rosa, Centro Histórico, and Roma. Many of the best restaurants are found outside hotels, although hotels such as the Camino Real, Nikko, Presidente Inter-Continental, and Four Seasons boast several fine restaurants. Most restaurants add a service charge of about 14 pesos per person. Hotel restaurants do not charge extra taxes. Waiters expect a 10-15% tip. Locals tend to dine late – after 1pm for lunch and after 9pm for dinner. Be sure to make reservations for most major restaurants or plan to arrive early. Expect formal attire requirements for many top restaurants – coat and tie for men, although you can often get in with less. In fact, many restaurants that say they require a coat and tie really don't. But the rule is there if they wish to enforce it and they may if you dress too casually or don't look appropriate for their establishment. Casual attire is acceptable at most restaurants.

Major non-hotel restaurants are usually closed for dinner on Sundays. Be sure to check on hours of restaurants before planning a Sunday dinner. In fact, Sunday is a good time to sample some great hotel restaurants.

The city also has lots of standard international fast-food restaurants – McDonald's, Burger King, Subway, Pizza Hut, Denny's, VIPS, and KFC. **Sanborn's** is a local favorite with many branches throughout the city. The most interesting Sanborn's restaurant and department store is housed in the old **Casa de Azulejos** (House of Tiles) at Madero 4 (Tel. 5518-6676) – a good place for a Mexican lunch when visiting the Centro Histórico area.

Look for a wide range of cuisines in this international city: Mexican, Argentine, Spanish, Italian, French, Greek, Chinese, Japanese, and Thai. Since you're in Mexico, you should try many of the city's fine Mexican restaurants, which produce a surprising array of inventive dishes that go far beyond the stereotypical fare you might associate with Mexican cuisine. Indeed, Mexican cuisine ranks at the top of our restaurant recommendations –

many wonderful settings, inventive chefs, and outstanding dishes to make Mexico City a gourmet's delight.

Some of the best restaurants in Mexico City include the following:

Mexican

❏ **La Hacienda de Los Moreles:** *Vázquez de Mella 525, Col. del Bosque, Tel. 5096-3054 or 5096-3055 or Fax 5096-3056.* Reputed to be Mexico City's best Mexican restaurant, this one does not disappoint. Indeed, it often surprises. From the moment you arrive at the grand cobblestone entrance, with flames leaping from impressive torches, until you are seated in the charming dining room of this expansive and well appointed hacienda, you know you've come to a very special place. The service is exceptionally friendly and impeccable, with only an occasional glitch. The extensive menu includes featured specials, daily specials, and a wide selection of tempting appetizers, soups, entrees, and desserts. The tortilla soup and fish dishes are especially outstanding. The creme brulee, which is not on the dessert trolley, is excellent. Includes live mariachi music. Formal attire required, although many patrons get in without the obligatory coat and tie. Reservations are a must for this popular restaurant. Considered by many people to be expensive, although surprisingly less expensive than other major restaurants. Actually, considering the setting, service, and quality of food, this is a good value restaurant.

❏ **Cicero Centenario:** *Londres 195, Col. Juárez, Zona Rosa, Tel. 5525-6530 or 5525-6130.* As soon as you walk into this delightful restaurant, you sense it's a very special place. Beautifully laid out with tall ceilings, bamboo trees, and ambient light, you feel you're dining in an outdoor courtyard which is enclosed as a tastefully decorated dining room. Attentive service, great atmosphere, and live music make for a memorable dining experience. In addition to the wonderful setting, the kitchen here really shines. Everything on the menu seems to get rave reviews. We especially enjoyed the Don Porfirio's soup (dry tortilla soup traditional style) and the squash-flower soup. Also, try the stuffed chicken breast with huitlacoche, chicken breast old style grilled, fish filet wrapped in banana tree leaf, sea-bass filet in pepper sauce, or "Arrachera Centenario" ("The Best" beef). This is the type of restaurant you'll want to return to again and again.

❏ **Fonda El Refugio:** *Liverpool 166, Col. Juárez, Zona Rosa, Tel. 5207-2732 or 5525-8128.* Located near the American Embassy, this very popular and long-standing Mexican eatery is found in a charming old house. It's a favorite of many expatriates.

The energetic staff delivers excellent service along with some of the largest portions of any restaurant. The dishes here are delicious, especially the moles and combination plates. Try the mushroom soup, chile rellenos, quesadillas, enchiladas, or the plato surtido con chile relleno. The desserts unexpectedly arrive at your table in their original dishes! The rice pudding and Mexican creme brulee are especially noteworthy. Reservations are essential since seating space is very limited in this crowded restaurant.

❑ **San Angel Inn:** *Calle Diego Rivera 50, at Altavista, San Gnel, Tel. 5616-0537.* Housed in a charming old hacienda and ex-convent, this popular restaurant produces many wonderful dishes, from chile rellenos and classic huitlacoche in crepes to poblano chicken breast and tortilla soup. For dessert, try the "floating island" (meringue with fresh strawberries or raspberries) and cream pastries.

❑ **Café de Tacuba:** *Tacuba 28, Centro, Tel. 5518-4950.* This popular café in the heart of the old city is a good choice for breakfast, lunch, or dinner. Great colonial atmosphere. Especially noted for its mole poblano, tamales, enchiladas, chile rellenos, and pastries. Unique evening entertainment from Thursday to Sunday.

❑ **Isadora:** *Moliere 50, Polanco, Tel. 5280-1586. Closed Sunday.* The changing menu of this wonderful restaurant draws a dedicated group of diners. Offers many inventive dishes with an emphasis on seafood. Noted for its cooking festivals.

❑ **T Cla:** *Moliere 56, Polanco, Tel. 5282-0010. Closed for dinner on Sunday.* This relatively new and trendy restaurant serves many fine dishes, including its signature beef dish, filete T Cla, and a crab-stuffed chile relleno.

FUSION/ECLECTIC

❑ **MP Café Bistro:** *Andrés Bello 10, Polanco, Tel. 5280-2506.* This relatively new and trendy Asian-Mexican fusion restaurant, operated by noted chef-owner Monica Patiño (also owns Taberna del León), produces some wonderfully creative dishes. For an appetizer, try the tasty roasted duck tacos. For entrees, sample the roasted sea bass or sweet and sour chicken breast. For a delightful dessert that will get your attention, try the tempura "cheesecake" with salsa. Excellent wine selection.

ARGENTINE

❏ **Cambalache:** *Arquimides 85, Polanco, Tel. 5280-2080.* Considered by many beef lovers to be Mexico's top Argentine restaurant. Famous for its huge steaks, beef cuts, and chicken.

FRENCH

❏ **Fouquet's de Paris:** *Hotel Camino Real, Mariano Escobedo 700, Polanco, Tel. 5203-2121. Closed Sunday.* One of the city's finest restaurants. Famous for its pâtés, lamb chops, and desserts.

❏ **Champs Élysées:** *Paseo de la Reforma 316, Zona Rosa, Tel. 5525-7259. Closed Sunday.* Very popular with businessmen at lunch, this restaurant serves outstanding French cuisine. Try the sea bass, red snapper, pepper steak, or roast duck.

INTERNATIONAL

❏ **La Galvia:** *Campos Eliseos 247, Polanco, Tel. 5281-2310 or 5281-0560.* Conveniently located near three of the city's top hotels – JW Marriott, Presidente Inter-Continental, and Nikko – this fine restaurant has it all, with great music, ambience, and art gracing the walls (it's for sale). For appetizers, try the tostada with crab meat. Some of the best entries include sea bass in three-chili sauce over sliced potatoes, mixiote with seafood and black beans, curry shrimp and spinach, salmon with soy sauce and tepanyaki vegetables, and roasted duck in pineapple sauce. Excellent service.

❏ **Tezka:** *Corner of Amberes and Liverpool, Col. Juárez, Zona Rosa. Tel. 5228-9918.* Serving inventive Basque-French cuisine in a charming setting, this small restaurant produces excellent Spanish dishes. Try the sea bass with mango ravioli, roast lamb with melon ravioli, venison with leaven sauce, gilled squids with corn oil, or sea bass with leek ashes.

Seeing the Sites

Being the oldest city in the Western Hemisphere, boasting the largest number of museums (100+) in the world, and hosting a very vibrant art community, Mexico City has many things to see and do. You can easily spend a week visiting the city's many appealing sites.

PLAN FOR DIFFERENT AREAS

Most of the major museums and buildings of interest to visitors are disproportionately found in and around Chapultepec Park (between Polanco and Zona Rosa areas) and the Centro Histórico. These are two very different sightseeing experiences – a peaceful park versus a very vibrant commercial center. During the week, you may want to start your sightseeing at the huge plaza (Zócalo) in the Centro Histórico. This is a great place to combine sightseeing, people-watching, shopping, and dining. Work your way around the Zócalo (Metropolitan Cathedral, Templo Mayor, National Palace, National Pawn Shop, Jewelry Center, and Majestic Hotel) and then venture west along Francisco I. Madera, and explore a few side streets, as you head for the House of Tiles, Palace of Fine Arts, Alameda Park, and Franz Mayer Museum before reaching the city's main thoroughfare, Paseo de la Reforma. Although often crowded with both local and international tourists, this is still one of the most rewarding areas to explore in Mexico City. Sightseeing within Chapultepec Park is very different – primarily stand-alone museums in a huge park. There's very little nearby shopping and dining. In fact, you may want to visit this area on Sunday – when shops and restaurants are closed anyway and when admission to museums is free.

Keep in mind that most museums are closed on Mondays. Since many shops and restaurants are closed on Sunday and most museums offer free admission on that day, you may want to schedule several museum visits on Sundays. However, be forewarned that this "free admission" day also results in larger crowds on Sundays.

MUSEUMS AND BUILDINGS

CHAPULTEPEC PARK

❑ **Museo Nacional de Antropologia (National Museum of Anthropology):** *Chapultepec Park, Tel. 5553-6381. Website: www.sunsite.unam.mx/antropol. Admission $2.50. Open Tuesday to Saturday, 9am to 7pm, and Sunday (free), 10am to 6pm.* This is simply a stunning museum, especially for those who love archaeology and the history and culture of the Aztecs and Spanish in Mexico. It also includes an impressive collection of artifacts showcasing the lifestyles of Mexico's indigenous groups. You can easily get carried away with all of the wonderful displays and spend a whole day here. Its two floors of nearly 100,000 square feet of display space cover the history of every Mexican state with numerous impressive artifacts, photos, and descriptions. The huge carved Olmec heads from Veracruz are especially impressive. This is one of the finest museums we have encountered anywhere in the world.

❑ **Museo Rufino Tamayo (Rufino Tamayo Museum):** *Paseo de la Reforma at Calle Gandhi, Section 1 of Bosque de Chapultepec, Tel. 5286-6519. Admission $1.50. Open Tuesday to Sunday, 10am to 6pm.* This modernistic museum houses many paintings by one of Mexico's famous muralists, Tamayo.

❑ **Castillo de Chapultepec (Chapultepec Castle):** *Section 1 of Bosque de Chapultepec. Tel. 553-6224. Open Tuesday to Sunday, 9am to 5pm.* Lots of fascinating history has passed through this hilltop castle, from Emperor Maximilian to several Mexican presidents. Initially constructed in 1795 for the viceroys of Spain, it was converted into a museum (National Museum of History) in 1940. Offers many interesting displays, including 55,000 relics, depicting various phases of Mexican history, both pre- and post-revolution. Includes murals by Orozco and David Alfaro Siqueros.

❑ **Museo de Arte Moderno (Museum of Modern Art):** *Paseo de la Reforma and Calle Gandhi, Section 1 of Bosque de Chapultepec. Tel. 5553-6313. Open Tuesday to Sunday, 10am to 6pm.* Includes a rich collection of art produced by noted contemporary Mexican artists as well as changing exhibits of international painters, sculptors, lithographers, and photographers.

CENTRO HISTÓRICO

❑ **Cathedral Metropolitana (Metropolitan Cathedral):** *Zócalo, Centro Histórico.* Located on the north side of the zócalo, this is Mexico's most famous cathedral as well as the oldest (begun in 1573) and largest one in Latin America. The impressive baroque structure includes five altars and 14 chapels. Constantly under repair and uneven because of its sinking foundation, the cathedral is a "must see" for anyone visiting this section of the city.

❑ **Palacio Nacional (National Palace):** *Zócalo, Centro Histórico. Open daily, 9am to 5pm.* Located on the east side of the zócalo, this long three-story government building is where the president of Mexico conducts business. For visitors, the highlight attraction is the huge Diego Rivera mural on the second floor which depicts the history of Mexico with powerful socialistic themes.

❑ **Templo Mayor and Museo del Templo Mayor (Great Temple):** *Near the northeast corner of the zócalo, Centro Histórico. Open Tuesday to Sunday, 9am to 5pm.* Located just off the east side of the Metropolitan Cathedral, this is the archaeological site of the Great Temple (Pyramid of Huitzilopochtli) of the Aztecs, the most important religious center at the time of the Spanish conquest of the Aztec capital of Tenochtitlan in 1531. Visitors walk on an elevated walkway from which they can view the ruins below. The museum building on this site includes a wonderful collection of Aztec artifacts – tools, masks, jewelry, and figurines. The whole area around this site is filled with street performers and vendors selling a variety of goods, especially pirated videos, CDs, and DVDs at excellent prices.

❑ **Museo Nacional de Arte (National Museum of Art):** *Calle Tacuba 8, Tel. 5512-3224. Open Tuesday to Sunday, 10am to 5:30pm.* Recently renovated, this opulent 100-year-old structure houses an impressive collection of Mexican art from colonial times to the mid-20th century. Features such famous artists as Jose Maria Velasco, Juan Correa, Diego Rivera, and Jose de Ibarra.

❑ **Palacio de Bellas Artes (Fine Arts Palace):** *Eje Central Lázaro Cárdenas and Av. Juárez. Tel. 5512-3633. Open Tuesday to Sunday, 10am to 9pm.* This impressive white-marble opera house is the venue for the popular Ballet Folklórico de México as well as other excellent national and international performances. The building is an architectural marvel which includes a Tiffany stained-glass curtain and murals by Rivera, Orozco, and Siqueiros. Includes a nice gift shop stocked with lots of books and CDs.

VERY SPECIAL "MUST-SEE" MUSEUMS

The following places offer extensive private collections that have been turned into museums. They are great places for learning about Mexico's rich history of fine arts, antiques, folk art, and crafts. Serious shoppers will appreciate the educational value of these special museums.

❑ **Museo Dolores Olmedo Patino:** *Av. México 5843, Col. La Noria, Xochimilco. Tel. 5555-1016 or Fax 5555-1642. E-mail: dificult@mdop. org.mx. Website: www.art-history.mx/mdop. Open Tuesday through Sunday, 10am to 6pm. Admission $25.* Located south of Mexico City at Xochimilco – a 45-minute drive from Zona Rosa – this is the museum and home of noted art collector and philanthropist Dolores Olmedo who still resides on the beautiful grounds of the Hacienda La Noria. This is a relatively new museum opened to the public in 1995. Nicely manicured lawns peppered with peacocks, turkeys, and ducks give visitors the sense that they are entering palace grounds. Instead, they are treated to a unique collection of art and artifacts acquired by Dolores Olmedo: paintings, drawings, pre-Columbian art, folk art, and ceramics. Nearly 200 paintings and drawings are from her famous artist friends Diego Rivera, Angelina Beloff (Diego's first wife), and Frida Kahlo (Diego's second wife). Beautifully displayed in several well appointed rooms, and interspersed with displays of pre-Columbian pottery and ceramic figures (the wall of Colima dogs is especially fascinating), this is a very special place to become acquainted with the works of Diego Rivera and the artistic achievements of two important and talented women in his life. A separate gallery displays several important works by Frida Kahlo. A building near the cafeteria also displays an excellent collection of folk art, from Day of the Dead figures, ceramics, and trees of life to black pottery, green ceramic figures, masks, and paper cutouts. A gift shop at the entrance offers a good collection of art books and handicrafts. What's especially compelling about this unique museum is its wonderful combination of beautiful grounds, gardens, animals, and architecture. Be sure to take your camera for outdoor photos – especially the gardens and peacocks on the lawns and in the trees. You also may encounter the owner's friendly charcoal Mexican dogs.

❑ **Museo de Frida Kahlo:** *Londres 247, at Allende, Coyoacan. Tel. 5554-4999. Open Tuesday to Sunday, 10am to 6pm.* This is the colorful and intriguing home museum of famous artist and cult figure Frida Kahlo and her husband Diego Rivera. Displays many pre-Columbian and folk art objects collected by the couple and a few paintings. Includes a shop with a good collection of Kahlo and Rivera books and memorabilia.

❑ **Museo Franz Mayer:** *On the north side of Alameda Park at Av. Hidalgo 45. Tel. 5518-2267. Open Tuesday to Sunday, 10am to 5pm. Free admission on Tuesday.* Beautifully laid out over two expansive floors, this museum showcases an exceptional private collection (German immigrant Franz Mayer) of over 10,000 antiques consisting of paintings, inlaid chests, doors, sculptures, clocks, watches, tapestries, textiles, lacquerware, glassware, and ceramics primarily from the 16th to 19th centuries. You can easily spend half a day exploring this intriguing museum. Includes a lovely courtyard with a cafeteria, an interesting bookstore, and two old churches flanking the building, one of which is sinking badly.

❑ **Museo Ruth Lechuga:** *Edificio Condesa – 6, 2a Calle de Pachuca, Col. Condesa. Tel./Fax 5553-5538. By appointment only. Admission $15.* This is a very special treat for anyone interested in Mexican folk art. Dr. Ruth Lechuga, an Austrian Jew who at the age of 19 faced persecution in the days before World War II, emigrated to Mexico in 1939 and fell in love with her adopted country and its folk art traditions. Over the year she has amassed an awesome collection of folk art from every state in Mexico. The collection is lovingly displayed in her three adjoining apartments that are filled from floor to ceiling with one of the most impressive indigenous ceremonial mask collections available anywhere. The masks, which now number over 12,000, are organized by both state and function. In contrast to today's commercial masks, these are genuine items produced and used for Indian and mestizo ceremonies. Several rooms also include displays of pottery, lacquer boxes, baskets, ceramic figures, miniatures, textiles, cutouts, books, beaded art, musical instruments, paintings, piñatas, toys, and Day of the Dead figures. The real highlight of this museum is Dr. Lechuga, who accompanies guests from room to room explaining her collection. Expect to spend at least an hour here. You'll most likely walk away with a renewed appreciation for Mexican folk art. Indeed, Mexican folk art will never look the same after visiting this unique museum.

OTHER INTERESTING HIGHLIGHTS

❑ **Basílica de Nuestra Señora de Guadalupe (Basilica of Guadalupe):** *Villa de Guadalupe, Tel. 5557-6022. Open Tuesday to Sunday, 10am to 6pm.* Located in the northern part of the city, this is Mexico's most revered shrine to its patron saint and an important religious center in Latin America. Constructed in 1974, it's located where the Virgin of Guadalupe miraculously appeared before Indian Juan Diego in 1531 and subsequently resulted in uniting Indian mysticism with Catholicism. Expect to encounter crowds here.

❑ **La Torre Latinoamericana (Latin American Tower):** *Madero and Lázaro Cárdenas, Centro Histórico, Tel. 5521-0844. Open daily, 9:30am to 11pm.* Take the elevator to the 37th floor and then take another elevator to the 42nd floor observation deck. Offers one of the best panoramic views of the city.

Entertainment and Nightlife

Mexico City offers a very lively and sophisticated range of entertainment and nightlife matched only by Rio de Janeiro in Latin America. From the famous Ballet Folklorica to traditional mariachi bands, opera, theater, dance clubs, jazz bars, and cultural festivals, Mexico City seems to have something to offer everyone in the entertainment department.

Since roaming the city at night can be dangerous (see our previous discussion on crime and safety, pages 88-90), be sure to take special precautions when venturing out in the evening. It's best to take a hotel car or a radio (*sitio*) taxi to and from your destination. By all means avoid walking the city at night.

To find out what's currently going on in Mexico City, check with your hotel concierge as well as survey the Friday edition of the English-language newspaper *The News* and the Sunday edition of the *Times*. Tickets to various events can be acquired through TicketMaster (Tel. 5325-9000).

THE PERFORMING ARTS

❑ **Ballet Folklórica de México:** *Palacio de Bellas Artes (Palace of Fine Arts), Juárez at Eje Central Lázaro. Secure tickets through the* *box office (Tel. 5512-3633), Ticketmaster (Tel. 5325-9000), or hotels and travel agents. Performances on Wednesday, 8:30pm, and Sunday, 9:30am and 8:30pm.* If you attend only one cultural performance in Mexico, make sure it's the world famous Ballet Folklórica. This colorful and stylized production takes place in the lovely Palace of Fine Arts, one of the city's architectural masterpieces which also includes an excellent bookstore just off the lobby area. After the Tiffany-glass curtain rises, the show awes its audience with a series of dances from pre-Hispanic times to the present day, including Aztec ritual dances and a wedding celebration, all performed with an exciting mix of musicians, dancers, and singers. Since this is a very popular show with visitors, be sure to reserve tickets well in advance. The box office is open Monday through Saturday, 11am to 7pm, and Sunday, 9:30am and 8:30pm. Do check on performance times and locations since the show venue sometimes changes (moves to the National Auditorium at Chapultepec Park), and the Ballet Folklórica performers may be on an international tour.

❑ **Musical performances:** The Palace of Fine Arts is the center for major classical musical productions, including the **National Opera** (two seasons run from January to March and August to October) and the **National Symphony Orchestra**. Check with your hotel or the box office at the Palace of Fine Arts for current performances and times. The city's major concert hall, which is home to the **Mexico City Philharmonic**, is the **Ollin Yolitzli** (Periféricio Sur 5141, Tel. 5606-7573). Look for contemporary and pop musical performances at the **Auditorio Nacional** (Paseo de la Reforma 50, Tel. 5280-9234), **Teatro Metropolitano**, Independencia, Tel. 5510-1035, and **Palacio de los Deportes** (Av. Rio Churubusco and Calle Añil, Tel. 5237-9999, ext. 4264).

❑ **Theatrical productions:** While some theatrical performances are in English, most are in Spanish. For a listing of current English-language productions, survey what's going on in *The News*. Theaters tend to be spread throughout the city.

NIGHTLIFE

Mexico City parties very late at night and into the early morning hours. Cocktails start around 7pm or 8pm, and dinner takes place from 9pm to 11pm. Nightclubs and discos tend to get started around 11pm, peak around 2am, and start quieting down at 3am. Be careful if you consume much alcohol. The city's high altitude will most likely affect your performance after a couple of drinks.

Much of the city's nightlife for both visitors and locals is centered around the upscale bars and discos of major hotels, especially the lobby bars at the Maria Isabel Sheraton, Presidente Inter-Continental, Camino Real, and Galería Plaza hotels and the roof-top bar at Habita Hotel in Polanco. Zona Rosa, especially Niza and Florencia streets, is filled with lively bars, discos, and nightclubs. This is an especially attractive area for visitors since it also includes many of the city's best restaurants, and the well patrolled streets are relatively safe at night. A great deal of nightlife also is centered in Condesa, Roma and Centro Histórico and along Paseo de la Reforma and Avenida Insurgentes Sur. Some of the most popular nightspots include:

BARS

❑ **Area:** *Habita Hotel, Polanco, Tel. 5282-3100. Open Thursday to Saturday at 9pm.* This trendy terrace bar overlooking the city is popular with young business people.

❑ **Bar León:** *Republica de Brasil 5, adjacent to the zócalo in Col. Centro, Tel. 5510-2979. Open Wednesday to Saturday, 9pm to 3am. Free salsa classes on Saturday, 5 to 7pm.* This small but popular salsa bar is a fun place to check out the local music and dance scenes.

❑ **Mama Rumba:** *Queretaro and Medellin, Colonia Roma. Live music Thursday to Saturday (starting at 11pm), Tel. 5564-6920. Also has a branch in San Angel (Tel. 5550-8099).* This popular Cuban restaurant-bar offers great music and a large dance floor.

❑ **El Nivel:** *Moneda 2, just off the zócalo, Col. Centro, Tel. 5522-9755. Open from noon, Monday to Saturday.* The city's oldest (1855) and most traditional cantina. Serves inexpensive drinks and offers free appetizers.

❑ **Bar Milán:** *Milan 18, Col. Juárez, near Zona Rosa, Tel. 5592-0031. Open Tuesday to Sunday, 9pm to 2am.* A local institution noted for its eclectic and loud music. Exchange your pesos at the entrance for "Milan money" to purchase drinks. Draws a young crowd.

❑ **La Bodeguita del Medio:** *Cozumel 37, Col. Florida, Tel. 5661-4400. Opens at 2pm.* Decorated with photos of celebrities and reminiscent of Ernest Hemingway's popular Havana nightclub, this place serves inexpensive Cuban dishes and lots of drinks. A Cuban band entertains in the afternoon and evening.

DISCOS

❑ **Arcanto:** *Chapultepec Park, El Lago Restaurant, Tel. 5272-2061. Open Thursday to Saturday, 10pm.* One of the city's most exclusive discos overlooking a lake and fountain.

❑ **La Boom:** *Rodolfo Gaona 3, Tel. 5580-6473. Open Wednesday, Friday, and Saturday, 9pm.* One of the city's largest and most lively discos. Especially popular with young people.

❑ **Pervert Lounge:** *Uruguay 70, Col. Centro, Tel. 5510-4454. Open Wednesday to Saturday, 10:30pm.* Popular with young crowds, this funky and psychedelic disco has a decidedly retro '60s theme.

Nightclubs

❑ **Adonis:** *Homero 424, Polanco, Tel. 5250-2064. Open Thursday to Saturday, 10pm.* Reservations recommended. A combination Lebanese restaurant (downstairs) and nightclub (upstairs) complete with live Middle Eastern music and belly dancers. Popular with the local Lebanese community.

❑ **El Habito:** *Madrid 13, Coyoacán, Tel. 5659-1139. Shows Friday and Saturday, 10:30pm.* Reservations essential. Offers a wide variety of musical and political satire shows. Best appreciated if you understand Spanish.

❑ **Jorongo Bar:** *Sheraton Maria Isabel Hotel, adjacent to Zona Rosa, Tel. 5242-5555. Open 7pm to 3am.* This long-established bar and nightclub offers outstanding mariachi bands and romantic trios. The perfect place to enjoy such music in a relaxing setting.

Mariachi Music

In addition to the excellent mariachi bands at the **Jorongo Bar** and a few top restaurants, such as **La Hacienda de los Morales and Café Tacuba**, the center for mariachi music at night is **Plaza Garibaldi** (5 blocks north of the Palace of Fine Arts, between República de Honduras and República de Perú, Col. Cuauhtémoc). Here numerous strolling musicians gather in the plaza to play for fun, tips, and requests (US$3-5 per song or US$10 for 3 songs). If you decide to visit this plaza at night, be very careful as you walk around this area. Follow our previous advice on safety and security (on pages 88-90), especially in reference to using taxis and walking in areas not well patrolled by police and security personnel.

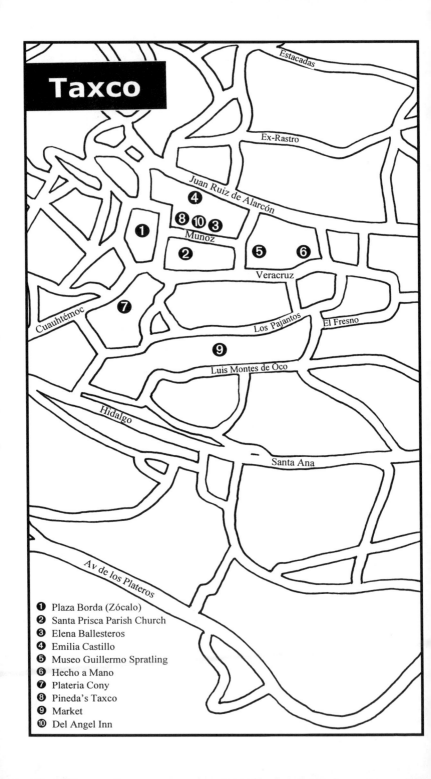

Taxco

- Estacadas
- Ex-Rastro
- Juan Ruiz de Alarcón
- Munoz
- Veracruz
- Cuauhtémoc
- Los Pajantos
- El Fresno
- Luis Montes de Oco
- Hidalgo
- Santa Ana
- Av de los Plateros

1. Plaza Borda (Zócalo)
2. Santa Prisca Parish Church
3. Elena Ballesteros
4. Emilia Castillo
5. Museo Guillermo Spratling
6. Hecho a Mano
7. Plateria Cony
8. Pineda's Taxco
9. Market
10. Del Angel Inn

Taxco

T AXCO IS TO MEXICO what Bali is to Indonesia – it's an artisan and shopping center but with architectural standards and zoning! Beautifully sited on the side of a steep hill, with densely packed red-roofed, whitewashed stucco buildings, a labyrinth of narrow and winding cobblestone streets, picturesque churches, and a lovely plaza, this is one of Mexico's most attractive cities for lifestyle shoppers and visitors of all types. A jewel of a city, Taxco also is a visual feast and a photographer's delight. One senses you can point a camera in any direction and get a great photo.

Declared a national historical monument in 1928, which requires owners to restore and maintain old buildings as well as construct new buildings in conformity with the old ones, Taxco is well maintained with an almost picture-postcard quality. Indeed, starting at the center with the stately Santa Prisca y San Sebastian Church on the small Plaza Borda, the city quickly unfolds in splendid architectural harmony. Often crowded with busloads of tourists and day-trippers, Taxco also can be a tourist trap for the uninitiated. But approached properly, this city can be a wonderful travel-shopping adventure for at least a day or two. Our advice: Head for Plaza Borda and just have fun exploring the surrounding shops and restaurants that converge on the plaza as well as line several side streets. Wear a good pair of walking shoes since this is a walking city where navigating over irregular cobblestones and steep streets can sometimes be difficult.

Blessed with Luck and Talent

Located about 100 miles southwest of Mexico City (two hours by toll road) and 170 miles north of Acapulco, this city of approximately 50,000 people is the perfect stop for travel-shoppers on

their way to Acapulco and the nearby attractive Pacific coast towns of Ixtapa and Zihuatanejo.

Taxco is a well-preserved colonial city that has witnessed lots of intriguing history since Hernán Cortés and his troops discovered the city's silver mines in 1522. Taxco's central plaza, Borda, takes its name from the famous Frenchman who developed the area's silver industry during the 18th century and thus made both himself and the city very wealthy as well as financed the construction of the impressive Mexican baroque church facing the plaza, Santa Prisca y San Sebastian (Santa Prisca Parish Church). After a lengthy period of decline, by the mid-20th century the city had transformed itself into a world-famous center for silver jewelry and artisans. This came about by the singular efforts of talented American architect-designer-writer William Spratling, who began training hundreds of silver artisans in the 1930s to produce attractive silver jewelry designs, many with pre-Hispanic themes. Spratling's work resulted in developing Taxco into a center famous for silver jewelry and silver artisans. In fact, many of the major silver artisans and shops today trace their origins to family members who apprenticed under Spratling many decades ago. Two of his most famous apprentices, the Castillo brothers, went on to develop some of Mexico's finest silver work and literally put Taxco on the international silver map. Their descendants still operate one of the finest silver and porcelain workshops and shops in Taxco and Mexico City, **Emilia Castillo.**

The Silver Shopping City

Nicknamed the "Silver Capital of the World," Taxco is all about silver and shopping. Boasting more than 100 silver shops and workshops, Taxco's many talented artisans produce an incredible amount of silver jewelry, table accessories, and art pieces to overwhelm most any visitor. While much of the production ends up in shops in Mexico City and abroad, a good sampling of this city's wholesale silver production remains in Taxco's many look-alike shops. Each day hundreds of day-trippers from Mexico City and Acapulco descend on this quaint community to explore its interesting streets, browse its many silver shops, or simply enjoy the ambience of this unique community from the vantage point of a restaurant or café facing the central plaza. Time permitting, they may visit a few sightseeing attractions, dine in a charming restaurant with a view, or just have fun getting lost along the city's many winding and hilly streets. Except for the crowds of tourists and some high prices, there's not much to dislike about this place. But there's not much to keep one here beyond a one- or two-day visit.

Getting to Know You

Once you get yourself centrally located and oriented, Taxco is a relatively easy place to explore. In fact, when it comes to shopping, dining, and sightseeing, the city seems much smaller than it looks from a distance. Indeed, you may quickly discover you can do everything you want to do within four or five hours – just like many of the day-trippers you'll encounter. But if you're driving from Mexico City on your way to Acapulco, it's a good idea to overnight in Taxco. In so doing, you'll also be able to enjoy the city at night.

Many visitors initially become disoriented with Taxco's geography. Here are some of the basics for getting oriented to Taxco:

1. Enter the city from the main highway, just before the Posada Hotel.

2. Expect to navigate lots of narrow one-way streets and occasionally get lost for the lack of signage.

3. Be prepared for winding and steep cobblestone streets.

4. Park your car around Plaza Borda – it costs 5 pesos per hour (pay the parking attendant).

Once you reach Plaza Borda, you're ready to explore the city. Most shops and restaurants are found around the plaza and along a few adjacent streets that connect to the plaza – Juan Ruiz de Alarcon, Calle Celso Muñoz, Cuauhtemoc, and Calle de la Veracruz. Around the plaza, look for the church, silver shops (many are family-related shops), and a museum.

Shopping Taxco

The **first** rule of shopping in Taxco is **buyer beware** – prices are not necessarily cheaper at the source! In fact, you may find prices on Taxco silver in Mexico City to be cheaper than in Taxco. This is not surprising since Taxco is a big tourist center where tourists don't know any better. Most think prices are cheaper at the production source which, in this case, is Taxco. Shops understand tourist shopping behavior (often naive) and price their products according to what the traffic will bear.

The **second** shopping rule is to **shop around**. Ideally, you should have shopped around in Mexico City and thus have a good sense of what silver should cost there. If not, you'll have to do your comparative shopping here. Given the numerous shops in Taxco that sell similar items, you should be able to quickly compare prices on similar products. Visit three or four shops and you'll get a good idea of the "going rate" on similar products.

The **third** shopping rule is to **bargain** or at least ask for the **wholesale price**. Since you can assume prices here are somewhat inflated because of the tourist traffic, try to at least get a 15 percent discount on your purchases. One way to get this discount is to buy "wholesale." Shops that sell to you as a retail customer must pay a 15 percent tax to the government. But if they sell to you "wholesale," they do not have to pay this tax. Whether you are classified as "retail" or "wholesale" is really up to the discretion of the shop. When it comes time to buy something in a shop, just tell the shop personnel that you are buying "wholesale." In many cases the shop will automatically discount 15 percent with no questions asked. If they ask questions about your wholesale status, indicate that you are purchasing "samples" for back home. Another way to get a 15 percent discount is to have your purchases shipped to your home outside Mexico. Some shops will do this whereas others don't seem to understand how this system works (see our discussion for Mexico City on pages 93-94).

The **final** shopping rule in Taxco is to just wander the main streets. Half the fun of shopping in Taxco is discovering shops that offer unique products. Many shops have their own silver designs, offer copies of Spratling's designs, and carry a wide range of products, from jewelry to sculptures.

Most shops are within five minutes walking distance from Plaza Borda. Start by circling the plaza. Here you'll discover such shops as **Plateria Linda**, **Plateria Perlita**, **Sabastian**, and **Pineda's Taxco**. Some of the best silver shops are found on side streets. Taxco's premier artisan and silver shop is **Emilia Castillo** (Juan Ruize de Alarcon, No. 7, Tel./Fax 622-3471) located immediately south of Plaza Borda. Other top shops include: **Plateria Corny** (Cuauhtemac No. 8, Tel./Fax 622-0179); **Elena Ballesteros** (Calle Celso Muñoz No. 4, Tel. 622-3767); and **Hecho a Mano** (Calle de la Veracruz No. 4, Tel./Fax 627-1851).

Best of the Best

While there are hundreds of silver shops in Taxco offering a wide range of silver goods, the following shops represent the best of the best Taxco has to offer.

❑ **Emilia Castillo:** *Juan Ruiz de Alarcon 7, Tel./Fax 622-3471. Website: www.emiliacastillo.com.* Located near the plaza, just off the main road entrance, this is Taxco's most famous and exclusive silver shop which has created a unique marriage between

silver craftsmanship and porcelain tableware. It's also one of our very favorite shops in all of Mexico. This shop alone is worth stopping in Taxco. If you visited the Emilia Castillo shop at the Camino Real Hotel in Mexico City, you're probably already familiar with some of the products you'll encounter in this attractive showroom. Most items found here are designed for gracing dining rooms. It includes Emilia Castillo's trademark silver pots and serving pieces combined with malachite and lapis lazuli figures. They are produced in both pure silver and plated silver. Other silver items are combined with onyx and alabaster. The distinctive ceramic dinner plates and bowls, embossed with unique silver designs and available in black, cobalt blue, green, white, and camel colors, set this shop apart from any other in Mexico. Indeed, this is where the rich and famous shop, where politicians and corporate executives purchase gifts for special guests, and where countless visitors have left Taxco with some really unique and special treasures that speak well of quality design and craftsmanship in Mexico. You may be able to visit their workshop (around 100 artisans) by appointment. Neiman Marcus is the exclusive representative for Emilia Castillo's products in the U.S. Many of the items destined for Neiman Marcus can be purchased here for 20 percent less – even larger savings if shipped directly to your home address (do not have to pay 15 percent tax). For more information, see our description of the Emilio Castillo shop in Mexico City on page 126.

❑ **Elena Ballesteros:** *Calle Celso Muñoz 4, Tel. 622-3767 or Fax 622-3907.* This is one of Taxco's top silver and gold jewelry shops for exclusive designs and quality products. Located just off the plaza, next door to the Del Angel Inn Restaurant and to the left of the church, this well appointed shop displays its treasures well. Its gold jewelry line includes necklaces and rings set with sapphires and opals. The shop also offers some tableware. From award-winning designs and exclusive jewelry and silver art pieces, this shop stands out as one of Taxco's best quality establishments.

❑ **Talleres de los Ballesteros:** *Florida 14, Tel. 622-1076. Website: www.ballesteros.net.* Operating since 1937, this is one of Taxco's most noted family-operated silver businesses. Includes many lovely silver serving pieces. Also has shops in the Zona Rosa and Polanco areas of Mexico City.

❑ **Hecho a Mano:** *Calle de la Veracruz 4, Tel./Fax 627-1851.* Located behind and to the left of the church, this silver shop offers some of the most unique silver designs in Taxco. Indeed, after visiting several of Taxco's look-alike silver shops, the designs here should catch your eye. The owner and manager, Manuel Porcayo Figueroa, makes many of the designs. Some of the silver designs are copies of old designs, and nearly 50 percent of the pieces are one of a kind – necklaces, bracelets, rings, and earrings. The shop also includes Spratling designs. Just outside the inside entrance to this shop are two small silver and handicraft

shops operated by Manuel's brother and father-in-law. These shops offer inexpensive items.

❑ **Plateria Cony:** *Cuauhtemoc 8, Tel./Fax 622-0179. E-mail: brilanti@silver.net.mx*. Located directly east of Plaza Borda, this combination silver jewelry and art shop offers many unique silver designs of the owner's famous grandmother, Anita Brilanti. Look for attractive silver necklaces, bracelets, and earrings. The shop also includes some paintings and bronze sculptures. The shop displays the grandmother's designs along with a book that features her work.

❑ **Pineda's Taxco:** *Plaza Borda 1, Tel. 622-3233 or Fax 622-4150*. Located on the corner of Calle Celso Muñoz and Plaza Borda – just to the left of the church – this expansive silver and art shop offers a wide selection of good quality silver jewelry, and sculptured black obsidian stone art pieces, bronze sculptures, silver masks, and large metal balloons, owls, and octopuses. You're bound to find something here.

Accommodations

Perhaps because Taxco has been viewed as a stop-over on the route between Mexico City and Acapulco, rather than as a destination in itself, there are no five-star properties here. But the two described below are worth considering when planning your accommodations in this city.

❑ **Posada de la Misión:** *Apdo. 88, Cerro de la Misión 32, 40230 Taxco, Mexico, Tel. (52-762) 622-0063, Fax (52-762) 622-2198*. Considered the leading hotel in Taxco, the Posada de la Misión is close in, within walking distance to the town center. 120 guestrooms and 30 suites range from standard doubles to two-bedroom suites with kitchenettes and fireplaces. Guestrooms have terraces, many of which have a lovely view of the town with buildings gracefully cascading down the hillside and magenta colored bougainvillea in lush profusion. Guestrooms are distributed in clusters giving the vast property the feel of a small, intimate hotel. Artist Juan O'Gorman had a favorite room here, and a mosaic mural of his, paying tribute to the Aztec emperor Cuauhtemoc, overlooks the pool area. Expected amenities, but fairly basic decor. Restaurant; Pool and Recreation Facilities; Meeting Rooms.

❑ **Monte Taxco:** *Apdo. 84, Lomas de Taxco, 40210 Taxco, Mexico, Tel. (52-762) 622-1300, Fax (52-762) 622-1428*. Located high on a hill at the edge of town, guests staying at Monte Taxco need a car or to hire taxis to get back and forth from the town center to the hotel. Alternatively, guests can take a cable car from the hotel to the town. The 153 guestrooms, 6 suites and 32 villas provide expected amenities, but fairly basic decor. Given its elevated location, the views of the city domes and spires are splendid. Three Restaurants; Pool and Recreation Facilities; Disco.

Restaurants

❑ **Del Angel Inn Restaurant:** *Celso Muñoz 4, Tel. 622-5525 or Fax 622-3318.* Located to the left of the church, this restaurant offers the perfect combination – great view, great service, and great food. From the third floor outdoor dining area, with its green plastic chairs and tables, you have a wonderful view of Taxco as well as the upper one-third of the church next door. However, the second floor dining area is more comfortable and intimate. Try the fajitas (three kinds), tortilla soup, or enchiladas with cheese. Portions tend to be large.

Seeing the Sites

Just seeing this picturesque city, with its white-washed buildings and cobblestone streets, is probably the major attraction. Many visitors simply enjoy hanging out at the lovely Plaza Borda and engage in people-watching. They can also do this by finding a table with a good view at one of the many second floor restaurants on the plaza. The major sites include:

❑ **Santa Prisca Parish Church:** *Located on the Plaza Borda, Open 5am to 9pm.* Constructed between 1751 and 1758, this is one of Taxco's major symbols. This beautiful Mexican baroque (Churrigueresque style) church includes 12 gilded carved altars and an interesting portrait gallery.

❑ **Museo Guillermo Spratling:** *Porfirio Delgado l. Tel. 622-1660. Admission $3. Open Tuesday to Saturday, 9am to 6pm; Sunday, 9am to 3pm.* Located near the north rear of the Santa Prisca Parish Church, this museum showcases the private art collection of William Spratling. Includes many pre-Hispanic artifacts. This is the former home of Taxco's famous resident that has been converted to a museum.

❑ **Casa Humbolt:** *Calle Juan Ruiz de Alarcón 6. Tel. 622-5501. Admission $2.25. Open Tuesday to Saturday, 10am to 5pm; Sunday, 10am to 3pm.* Displays an interesting collection of colonial art, much of which comes from Santa Prisca.

❑ **Spratling Ranch:** *Taxco Viejo. Tel. 622-6108. Open Monday to Saturday, 8am to 1pm and 2pm to 5pm.* Located 15 minutes from Taxco, this is the factory that continues to produce famous Spratling silver products from the original molds. Includes a shop.

❑ **Rancho la Cascada:** *Taxco Viejo. Tel. 622-1016. Open Monday to Saturday, by appointment.* Located 15 minutes from Taxco, this is the workshop of the famous Castillo silver family.

Entertainment

There's not much to do in Taxco in the evening other than go shopping or dining. The late night action is found in Acapulco, which is a 170-mile drive south of this city. Again, Taxco is all about shopping.

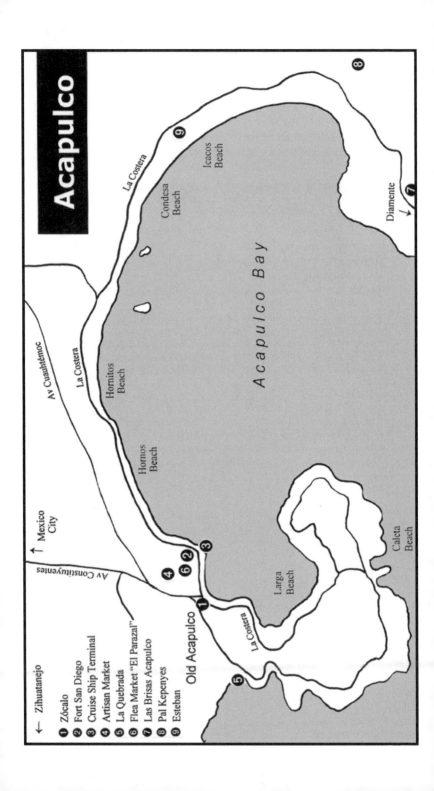

Acapulco

← Zihuatanejo

1. Zócalo
2. Fort San Diego
3. Cruise Ship Terminal
4. Artisan Market
5. La Quebrada
6. Flea Market "El Parazal"
7. Las Brisas Acapulco
8. Pal Kepenyes
9. Esteban

↑ Mexico City

Av Cuauhtémoc

Av Constituyentes

La Costera

Hornos Beach

Hornitos Beach

Condesa Beach

Icacos Beach

Diamente

Acapulco Bay

Larga Beach

Caleta Beach

La Costera

Old Acapulco

Acapulco

W ELCOME TO A GREAT LEGEND, both fabled and faded but now back in business in a very big and glitzy way. Blessed with a great climate, lovely beaches, gorgeous views, pristine lagoons, and lush vegetation, Acapulco was once Mexico's version of the French Riviera. Here international jet-setters, playboys, and the beautiful people of Hollywood used to party to the pleasure of the international celebrity media. Glamorous celebrities downing margaritas, cliff divers demonstrating their fearless talents at La Quebrada, picturesque bays and beaches, and Elvis Presley in the 1963 movie *Fun in Acapulco* all contributed to Acapulco's image as a fun and exotic resort destination with an incomparable nightlife.

While many of its old stars of the '40s, '50s, and '60s have faded, Acapulco has recently transformed itself into Mexico's most popular resort destination and one of its fastest growing communities for real estate investors and vacation home (condo and timeshare) owners. Variously referred to as the "Pearl of the Pacific," "Queen of Mexican Resorts," and "Disco Capital of the World," Acapulco is now the most visited tourist destination in all of Latin America. It remains a popular honeymoon destination, with the Las Brisas Hotel still offering wonderful wedding packages.

From the hills of the Sierra Madre Mountains overlooking Acapulco's compelling bay and golden beaches, this is truly a special place. It's understandably romantic when viewed from a distance and especially at night when the city lights sparkle over the shimmering waters of Acapulco Bay. At the street level, Acapulco is less appealing to the eye during the day – a cement jungle of unattractive buildings accented by high-rise hotels, lots of traffic congestion, and the chaos of crowds. But when night falls, the city transforms itself with its dazzling night clubs, loud discos, and packed restaurants. For many visitors, Acapulco is the ultimate vacation destination – relax, unwind, and indulge one's decadent side.

Everyone Is Invited, But...

Acapulco has become an attractive resort appealing to a wide range of visitors, many of whom come from Mexico City and several countries south of the border. While international and local celebrities still visit and many wealthy families maintain palatial villas in the hills and frequent the area's fine restaurants, Acapulco is a mass tourism destination for beaches, sports, dining, shopping, and entertainment. It draws singles, couples, families, gays, the rich, the middle class, and everyone in between. If you are looking for the peace, quiet, and tranquillity associated with such places as nearby Ixtapa and Zihuatanejo, Acapulco probably is not your type of resort. It's Mexico's biggest party city – a kind of mature west coast version of east coast Cancun, especially during the crowded months of January and February, when the beaches fill up during the day and the restaurants, bars, discos, and dance halls come alive at night.

- ❏ Acapulco is blessed with a great climate, lovely beaches, and a fabulous bay view.

- ❏ Acapulco is now the most visited tourist destination in all of Latin America.

- ❏ This is a crowded and noisy party city that appeals to a particular type of traveler.

- ❏ Less than four hours by road, Acapulco is the closest beach destination for Mexico City residents.

- ❏ The city comes alive at night when bars and discos entertain visitors who have largely whiled away the day on the beach.

Shoppers in Acapulco find a few interesting places to spend money. The shopping range here is great, from fine art and exquisite jewelry to tacky markets, jewelry of questionable value, and souvenir shops primarily catering to, as well as fleecing, cruise ship passengers and other unsuspecting tourists who think they are in the real Mexico. Serious shoppers focus on a few key art galleries that offer exceptional quality paintings and sculptures. Other shoppers simply have fun looking for typical resort wear, souvenirs, and tourist trinkets – a good leisure daytime activity for those who enjoy prowling the streets and visiting restaurants before or after their daily beach activities.

If you like beautiful views, beaches, crowds, and a very active nightlife and don't mind the noise and glitz, Acapulco may be the perfect destination for you. Indeed, the city has a particular character that appeals to travelers who love to party.

Mexico City's Playground

Boasting a gorgeous harbor accented with sleek cruise ships, the famous cliff divers at La Quebrada, and miles of beaches, resorts, condos, golf courses, lagoons, tropical jungles, restaurants, nightclubs, discos, and shops, Acapulco retains its legendary reputation as a hip place to relax and enjoy the many pleasures of a vibrant resort community. It's a go-go resort 24 hours a day. Indeed, today's Acapulco surprises many visitors who assume this place had faded away to newer and more popular resorts, such as Puerto Vallarta and Cancun. The truth is that Acapulco is an eternal survivor – it's just different as well as pleasantly decadent, dynamic, and decidedly upscale  Mexican. It seems to have something for everyone who enjoys the many pleasures of holiday travel.

While Acapulco no longer attracts the many international celebrities it was once noted for – Frank Sinatra, Errol Flynn, Johnny "Tarzan" Weismuller, John Wayne, Gary Cooper, Harry Belafonte, Dean Martin, Red Skelton, Hedy Lamarr, and Elizabeth Taylor – nonetheless, Acapulco still appeals to many less conspicuous rich and famous who often stay at the exclusive pink and white Las Brisas Hotel overlooking the city's spectacular harbor or they maintain expensive villas in the hills overlooking the city and ocean. Especially popular these days with Mexican tourists, Acapulco is still an attractive destination for many international visitors. Often crowded and noisy with local holiday makers and festive cruise ship passengers, this is a fun resort for most people who spend two to three days – or even a week or more – enjoying its many treasures and pleasures. For residents of Mexico City, who live 240 miles north of this city, Acapulco is their closest beach destination – a fact that ensures the continuing vitality of this city. Using the four-lane toll road, they can drive to Acapulco in less than four hours. Not surprisingly, Acapulco benefits tremendously from its close proximity to Mexico City.

Resilience and Transformation

Located in one of Mexico's poorest states, Guerrero, Acapulco is a resilient oasis of nearly 2 million people that attracts over 1.5 million visitors a year. The city has undergone numerous transformations. Indeed, it seems to have had many lives. It first served as Spain's major port connection between colonial Mexico and the Philippines from the 16th to the 18th century. For nearly 250 years Acapulco prospered as the key trading link between Mexico and Asia, complete with adventuresome stories about the fabled Manila Galleon and famous pirates such as Sir Frances Drake. With the defeat of the Spanish in the War of Independence (1818), trade between Mexico and Asia nearly disappeared and with it went Acapulco's prosperity and role as interpol. This once thriving port gradually reverted to its pre-16th century status as a small nondescript fishing village.

It wasn't until 1927 that the first road connecting Acapulco with Mexico City was completed – a five- to seven-day adventure via narrow winding roads. Thereafter Acapulco gradually developed from a sleepy village on a gorgeous horseshoe bay into a popular tourist destination. But the major stimulus came with World War II and the closing of Europe to U.S. travelers. Celebrities and jet-setters, who normally headed for Europe and the French Riviera, discovered Acapulco and made it their popular playground. From World War II through the 1960s, Acapulco became an "in" destination for the rich and famous. The decades of the '50s and '60s were especially good for Acapulco.

With direct international flights inaugurated in 1964, Acapulco opened up to mass tourism. Its beautiful curving bay surrounded by steep hills and expansive beaches provided a visual feast both day and night. Fabled hotels and resorts, such as the legendary Las Brisas, which now has a "Wall of Fame" of celebrity cement hand prints and signatures, added to the city's glamorous status. The list of celebrities, from Errol Flynn to John Wayne, continued to grow. It soon became a favorite wedding and honeymoon destination for thousands of people, including Elizabeth Taylor and Michael Todd, John and Jackie Kennedy, and Bill and Hilary Clinton. During the 1980s and 1990s Acapulco grew rapidly as a major tourist destination, with many new high-rise hotels, condominiums, restaurants, bars, and discos to service its growing number of visitors. Although Cancun and Puerta Vallarta became the new "in" destinations, Acapulco more than held its own – it stayed on top.

While the city lost much of its glamour and reputation as Mexico's French Riviera to more luxurious and exclusive upstart resort areas along the Pacific coast during the 1980s and 1990s, nonetheless, Acapulco has managed to transform itself even further to attract a steady stream of both local and international visitors who come here for conventions, honeymoons, package tours, spring break, or weekend escapes. Acapulco is especially popular with local tourists from Mexico City who also have invested heavily in the city's many condominiums, timeshare complexes, and other real estate offerings. Indeed, buying and selling real estate seems to be one of the major activities in this rapidly developing resort community.

If you are looking for a quiet and relaxing resort destination, Acapulco may not be the place to visit. This is one of the biggest, noisiest, and liveliest cities in Mexico, with lots of people, traffic, hotels, restaurants, markets, shops, and discos. Two to three cruise ships a week dislodge their passengers onto the city's streets for several hours to crowd its markets and restaurants. The city especially comes alive at night when nightclubs entertain visitors who have largely whiled away the day on the beach or along the main streets engaged in dining and shopping. Disco-hopping is a favorite nighttime activity.

Acapulco is a full-service resort community where you can also go deep sea fishing, scuba diving, parasailing, jet boating, and cruising as well as take a day trip to the famous silver and shopping city of Taxco. Acapulco seems to have something for everyone. For frequent visitors, Acapulco is simply paradise.

Acapulco on the Web

In preparation for visiting Acapulco, you may want to visit these and many other websites that provide useful information on the city:

- **All About Acapulco**   www.allaboutacapulco.com
- **Acapulco**   www.acapulco.com
- **Visit Mexico**   www.visitmexico.com

- **Access Mexico**   www.accessmexico.com
- **Trip Advisor**   www.tripadvisor.com

Some hotel websites, such as www.fairmont.com (go to the section on Acapulco), include useful content on the city. Several other websites, such as www.acapulco-villa.com, www.acapulco.gtahotels.com, and www.acapulco-now.net, primarily focus on discounted hotels for Acapulco.

Getting to Know You

Acapulco is a relatively easy city to understand and get around in. From the cruise ship dock and popular diving cliffs of La Quebrada in the west to the lush Diamante area and the airport in the east, Acapulco stretches for several miles around one of the world's most beautiful bays and continues on to a series of other attractive bays. High-rise beachfront hotels face the C-shaped Acapulco Bay where an occasional cruise ship accents its festive setting.

The city is perhaps best viewed as having three major sections that run from west to east:

1. **Old Acapulco** in the west with Fort San Diego, the zócalo, fishing pier, cathedral, flea market, central market, post office, and La Quebrada. Also known as the central downtown area, this is a very busy nondescript place with narrow streets and numerous shops catering to both locals and tourists. Visitors come here to see the divers of La Quebrada, view Fort San Diego, and explore the more than 400 shops that make up the popular Flea Market "El Parazal," which is the focus of many cruise ship passengers who disembark in this area.

2. **Costera Miguel Alemán**, the beachfront road, connects numerous hotels, restaurants, bars, discos, nightclubs, and shops from west to east. This is where the tourist action is centered. Frequently referred to as "Costera," this is where much of the city's very active daytime (beaches, restaurants, and shops) and nighttime (bars, discos, and nightclubs) life is centered for visitors. Recently transformed with attractive landscaping, this very busy tree-lined six-lane boulevard is the area of Los Hornos Beach, Condesa Beach (the city's most popular), and Icacos Beach. It includes such major hotels as Costa Club, Continental Plaza, Fiesta Americana Condesa, Villa Vera, Fiesta Inn, El Presidente, and Hyatt Regency. It also includes the Convention Cultural Center, municipal golf course, the CICI children's park, and numerous shops, restaurants, discos, and bars. The best quality shopping is found in this area. Dis-

count shoppers will even find a Wal-Mart and Sam's Club in this area.

3. **Eastern Acapulco**, which leads to the airport, includes the rapidly developing Diamante area (Punta Diamante, or Diamond Point) with its many huge luxury resorts and condominiums, golf courses, residential complexes, Puerto Marques, and Revolcadero Beach. Here you'll find such major hotels as Las Brisas, Camino Real, Quinta Real, Pierre Marques, Acapulco Princess, and Mayan Palace as well as the world-renowned Tes Vidas Golf Club. Punta Diamante is Acapulco's newest residential and tourist development area which includes 30 miles of beach and green areas. This is a much more expansive, upscale, and quieter area of Acapulco. Indeed, if you want to get away from the noise and crowds, and luxuriate in lush surroundings, go east of Acapulco Bay.

From Old Acapulco to the Diamante area, Acapulco stretches for more than 10 miles along the bay and beaches. The curved Acapulco Bay alone runs for seven miles. Getting from one section to another requires some form of transportation. If you have a car, it's relatively easy to drive from one area to another. If you must take taxis, which are plentiful, transportation can become costly, especially since many taxis overcharge visitors who fail to bargain. Indeed, you should always bargain for your taxi – offer half the amount requested before getting into the cab. You may settle for more, but start at half before reaching agreement. Buses also cover this area and are relatively inexpensive and convenient.

The Streets of Acapulco

If you're driving, the city is relatively easy to navigate as long as you stay on the main thoroughfare – Costera Miguel Alemán. This six- to eight-lane beachfront street snaking around Acapulco Bay – popularly known as the Costera – is often choked with buses, trucks, taxis, horse buggies, and cars that manage to reduce this crowded strip into a two-lane passable street. Watch for stopping buses and taxis, fast lane-changing trucks and cars, and jay-walking pedestrians. Numerous one-way streets in Old Acapulco can be confusing, especially since many lack good signage. Taxis can be expensive, especially if you are staying at a hotel or resort far from the city center and if you don't bargain properly. Having your own car in Acapulco is very convenient, although at times parking can be a real problem.

Shopping Acapulco

While shopping is often a favorite pastime activity for visitors in Acapulco, there's not a great deal of good quality shopping here to justify more than one day of street sleuthing. Indeed, serious shoppers miss the shopping delights of Mexico City and look forward to discovering the many treasures of Guadalajara, San Miguel de Allende, and Oaxaca. Some visitors can dispense with Acapulco's shopping in just a few hours. On the other hand, if you are into high-end art (famous painters and sculptors), you'll encounter a few interesting galleries in Acapulco. You'll even discover the fascinating bronze sculptures and jewelry of noted local artist **Pal Kepenyes**, who displays his works in his lovely home gallery overlooking the city. Art lovers often extend their one-day shopping adventure into two days or more, depending on what they find and whom they meet. Some shift their shopping focus to Taxco, a relatively quick 170-mile drive north of Acapulco, which makes for an interesting day trip for shopping and sightseeing.

RESORT-STYLE SHOPPING

Acapulco's shopping complex consists of two large handicraft and souvenir markets, a few shopping malls, and several hotel and street shops. Most items found in Acapulco come from other areas of Mexico – Taxco, Mexico City, Guadalajara, and Oaxaca – or are imported from abroad. After all, this is a resort community that caters to many visitors who arrive by plane or ship. As such, you'll find most of the shopping oriented to the beach resort crowd, with a disproportionate number of shops and market stalls offering resort clothes, jewelry, handicrafts, and souvenirs. Look for swimwear, T-shirts, silver and gold jewelry, and lots of kitschy handicrafts, from sombreros to painted ceramic figures. Nonetheless, you will find a few excellent quality shops that offer a good selection of art, jewelry, and designer clothes.

A FEW NEW RULES

As you shop the streets of Acapulco, keep these six observations and shopping rules in mind. They will help you save money, avoid scams, and identify the best quality shops:

1. **It can be expensive.** Since Acapulco is a big resort center catering to a monied crowd, expect prices to be higher here than elsewhere in Mexico. Art can be very expensive here. As a result, feel free to bargain harder in Acapulco than in other cities. A 10 to 20 percent discount in Mexico City, for ex-

ample, should translate into a 30 to 40 percent discount in Acapulco. On the other hand, the local Wal-Mart and Sam's Club keep many prices in line with local expectations.

2. **It's "buyer beware" in many places.** This is especially true near where cruise ships dock. Expect to get ripped off big time at shops that primarily cater to cruise ship passengers, such as the popular **Joyeria Margarita** (jewelry and souvenir emporium at I. de la Ilave 2) in Old Acapulco that has been putting the screws to tourists for nearly 30 years. Such tourist shops inflate prices by 200 to 300 percent, guides get kickbacks, street touts get their cards punched (they cash them in later), and the quality of jewelry and souvenirs is questionable. The naive shoppers pay dearly for the friendly customer service, including the famous complimentary margaritas and other drinks! If you shop here, 70 to 80 percent discounts would bring prices to acceptable retail levels. Even within the nearby Flea Market "El Parazal," it's buyer beware. As one of our friendly shopkeepers at **Jewelry By Gloria** volunteered in broken English, *"We don't screw nobody here!"* Well, maybe they don't, but there's a lot of screwing going on elsewhere. You'll need to get tough and bargain hard in Acapulco since there's a high probability you're being offered "tourist retail" prices – i.e, double what you should be paying.

3. **Beware of street touts who want to take you shopping:** Especially in Old Acapulco, near the zócalo, you may encounter friendly individuals who approach you with official-looking badges that hang on a chain around their necks. One of their standard approach lines is that they would like to help you or practice their English, supposedly because they are official guides who need the practice. These are the guys who will invariably take you to a shop that ostensibly will give you great prices (actually 200 to 300 percent above retail!) and punch their commission cards. Don't waste your time with these touts who know nothing about quality shopping. They are only after your time and money – both of which are better spent doing other things rather than meeting such a local.

4. **Some of the best quality shops are found in the major hotels.** While many of the major art galleries are found along the Costera, the best jewelry stores and boutiques can be found in the city's major hotels and resorts. Look for some of Mexico's major jewelers, such as **Tane** and **Astrid**, in Las Brisas, Hyatt Regency, and Fiesta Americana hotels.

5. **Shopping hours are usually 10am to 2pm and 5pm to 9pm.** While there are exceptions to this rule, in general most shops

are open eight hours a day, with a traditional 2pm to 5pm closing – a good time for the beach, late afternoon dining, or a siesta.

6. **You'll often get lost and frustrated with addresses, or the lack thereof.** Signage is a big problem in Acapulco. Shops may have an address, but you will probably have a devil of a time trying to find the place. Consequently, you may need to ask three, four, or five people where to find a shop, even in the major shopping areas. Chances are they won't know because they are from out of town or recent arrivals. In Old Acapulco, asking such questions will often result in adopting a street tout who wants to take you to a shop that will give him commissions or punch his card. If you find yourself wandering around aimlessly, don't worry; it happens to lots of visitors to Acapulco. Just remember where you parked your car!

SHOPPING AREAS

Major shopping in Acapulco is concentrated in two areas – along Costera Miguel Alemán and in the downtown area of Old Acapulco. A few upscale hotels, such as Las Brisas and the Hyatt Regency, offer some excellent shops, especially for art, jewelry, and gift items.

Costera Miguel Alemán is Acapulco's main shopping street. The best shopping is found at the eastern end of this boulevard, known as the Golden Zone (Zona Dorada). But this whole area is lined with many shops and shopping plazas offering clothes, beachwear, art, jewelry, handicrafts, and souvenirs. Close to the major beaches, hotels, restaurants, and entertainment centers, shops here cover an area of nearly four miles.

Shopping in the **downtown area of Old Acapulco** is more geared to locals and cruise ship passengers, with a heavy concentration of handicraft and souvenir market stalls and overpriced jewelry stores. There's very little quality shopping found in this area. In fact, if you skipped this area altogether, you wouldn't miss much other than a lot of street touts and cruise ship passengers.

MARKETS

Acapulco has two main markets of interest to visitors. Neither is worth special efforts to find unless you have a great deal of time to kill and are interested in seeing what people will actually buy in Acapulco. And even that's not so interesting.

❏ **Flea Market "El Parazal":** *Located in the heart of Old Acapulco, along Matamoros Street and next to Tepito Market, only a 10-minute walk from the cruise ship docks.* Also known as the Artesan Market, this is the better of the two handicraft markets. It consists of nearly 450 stands or stalls that offer similar items – clothes, jewelry, T-shirts, sombreros, masks, and blankets – just what every cruise ship passenger needs to decorate his or her ship cabin. The market comes alive when a cruise ship docks, which happens about every three days. Our favorite shop here is the very personable **Jewelry By Gloria** (Stand 169, Tel. 834-767), which includes a nice selection of silver jewelry with some of the better designs we encountered. This shop also offers a few souvenir items, such as rugs, hats, and onyx figures. If that's not enough, they also will rent or sell you a condo!

❑ **Mercado de Artesanias:** *Located across the street from the Plaza Bahia along the main boulevard, Costera Miguel Aleman*. This is a crowded flea market jam-packed with beachwear, T-shirts, jewelry, and the usual mix of handicrafts and tasteless souvenirs. There's not much here to recommend. Indeed, you've probably seen it all elsewhere in Mexico. If you collect T-shirts, you may want to browse-and-bargain through the many stalls of this market.

Shopping Centers

The city has three major shopping centers popular with visitors in search of souvenirs, beachwear, clothes, restaurants, and entertainment. Don't expect to find quality shops here – these are mainly mass-tourism areas:

❑ **La Gran Plaza:** *Costera Miguel Alemán 1632, Tel. 7486-6478. Open 9am to 9pm*. This is the city's largest shopping mall with 135 shops, a cinema, and a food court. Includes several clothing stores, a department store (Fabricas de Francia), Foot Locker, Radio Shack, and American Express.

❑ **Plaza Bahía:** *Costera Miguel Alemán 125, next to Costa Club Hotel, Tel. 7485-69-39*. Located in the heart of the beach and hotel area, this imposing four-level air-conditioned shopping center caters to shopping, dining, and entertainment needs with boutiques, clothing stores, a sporting goods shop, restaurants, a video arcade, a movie theater, and a bowling alley.

❑ **Artesanías Finas de Acapulco:** *La Costera and Ave Horatio Nelson, Tel. 7484-80-39*. Often referred to as AFA-ACA, this department store is filled with handicrafts and souvenirs – folk art, pottery, paintings, papier-mâché sculptures, onyx chessboards, wooden masks, silver jewelry, clothes, and furniture.

STREET SHOPS

Most street shops are found near the major hotels and beaches, along Costera Miguel Alemán, and on the streets leading to the zócalo near the Flea Market "El Parazal" in Old Acapulco, Along Costera Miguel Alemán, look for **Sergio Bustamante** (#120-9) for fascinating works of this famous artist as well as prints and frescos of other artists; **Esteban** (#2010) for quality paintings, sculptures, handicrafts, clothing, and accessories; **Galeria** (#112) for a nice selection of affordable art. Just off the main boulevard, near Hotel Acapulco Continental, is one of Acapulco's top art galleries for paintings and sculptures – **Galeria Rudic** (Vicente Yañez Pinzón 9).

HOTEL AND RESORT SHOPPING

Excellent quality shops can be found in the city's many major hotels and resorts:

❑ **Las Brisas Hotel and Resort:** Look for **Tane** and **Real** for jewelry, the **Art Gallery** for good quality paintings and sculptures; and the **Pink Shop** for crafts and logo items.

❑ **Hyatt Regency Hotel:** Look for **Armando's**, an attractive boutique for women, **Tane** for silver jewelry, and **Suzett's** for 14k and 18k gold jewelry and silver jewelry and gift items.

❑ **Fairmont Acapulco Princess Hotel:** Includes **Minett** for jewelry and gift items and **Aca Joe** for popular T-shirts and active wear for men.

❑ **Fiesta Americana Hotel:** Includes a branch of **Astrid**, one of Mexico's best jewelry shops found in many resort areas, and **St. German** for good quality swimwear.

CRUISE SHIP SHOPPERS

Shops for cruise ship passengers are a world unto their own – very focused on groups and individuals who have limited time to spend their money and who generally seek small items they can hand-carry to their ship. Like any cruise ship port city, Acapulco has many shops that primarily cater to cruise ship passengers. Located north of the pier, past Sanborn's and Woolworth's, many of these shops offer questionable quality products, often inflate their prices, and pay commissions to street touts and cruise ship personnel who steer tourists to their shops. The Flea Market "El Parazal" is especially popular with cruise ship passengers. As we noted earlier in our discussion of "A Few New Rules" and "Markets," it's buyer beware in this shopping area. If you arrive by ship in Acapulco and have some time to explore the city, you may want to skip this area and go directly to the main shopping area along Costera Miguel Alemán.

Best of the Best

Most of the best places to shop in Acapulco deal with art and jewelry. We especially recommend the following shops for quality and unique items.

ART

❑ **Rudic Art Gallery:** *Vicente Yañez Pinzón 9, Tel. 484-1004 or Fax 484-8344. E-mail: mirtille@acabtu.com.mx. Open 10am to 10pm.* Somewhat difficult to find along a side street off of the Costera (across from the Continental Hotel), this is the city's top gallery and also its most expensive. Represents some of Mexico's major contemporary painters and sculptors, including Armando Amaya, Leonardo Nierman, Casiano Garcia, and Trinidad Osorio, as well as some up and coming young artists. The same owner operates the art gallery shop at the Las Brisas Hotel and Resort. The restaurant next door, Le Jardin  de Artistes, is a good place to dine outdoors among large bronze sculptures after visiting this nice gallery.

❑ **Pal Kepenyes:** *Guitarrón 140, Tel. 484-3738. By appointment only (will probably need to be escorted since it's difficult to find for those unfamiliar with residential areas in the hills).* This unique gallery and artist are a treat for art lovers. A beautiful expansive home gallery in the hills overlooking Acapulco Bay, this is a very special place to visit. Pal Kepenyes, a Hungarian political prisoner and refugee who escaped to Paris in 1956 and came to

Mexico in 1960, is an extremely creative and prolific artist. He's primarily a metal sculptor who produces a dazzling array of welded figures and bronze castings as well as jewelry. The main gallery overlooking the city includes many of his largest sculptures. The side rooms include a wide range of figures, from fascinating bronze chickens to buffalos, female figures, flowers, and doors. The very personable and dynamic Pal is a delight to meet. Try to visit late in the day so you can also enjoy the sunset over drinks with Pal and his wife. If you visited the Talento art gallery in Mexico City, you probably encountered a few of Pal's metal sculptures.

❑ **Sergio Bustamante:** *Costera Miguel Alemán 120-9, Tel. 484-4992 or Fax 484-2251.* This gallery displays the colorful and whimsical papier mâché, ceramic, and bronze sculptures of Sergio Bustamante (see gallery descriptions for both Mexico City and Guadalajara). It includes selected pieces of Bustamante's unique jewelry collection. Unlike other Bustamante galleries, this one includes frescos and copies of prints depicting the Sistene Chapel from another artist.

❑ **Estaban Fine Art Gallery:** *Costera Miguel Alemán, Tel. 484-3084 or Fax 484-8452. E-mail: Esteban@aca.quik.com. Website: www.esteban-acapulco.com.* This is a combination art gallery, craft shop, boutique, coffee shop (Le Café), and real estate office – reflecting the fact that the owner has many different interests that he has turned into businesses. The Estaban Fine Art Gallery section, which is on the right side of this two-shop complex, includes a small but nice collection of original paintings, sculptures (bronze and ceramic), lithographs, and serigraphs produced by noted national and international artists. For online examples of their art, visit www.esteban-acapulco .com/gallery.htm.

❑ **Galeria 21:** *Costera Miguel Alemán 112, Tel. 484-1007 or Fax 484-3229. E-mail: luispeimbert@hotmail.com.* Located cross from the Twin Towers, Fiesta Inn, and President Hotel, this relatively new gallery includes a nice collection of affordable paintings and sculptures. Offers a few religious icons and lithographs. Represents many up and coming artists from Mexico, Guatemala, and Costa Rica.

JEWELRY

❑ **Tane:** *Las Brisas Hotel, Carretera Escénica 5255, Tel. 469-1234; and the Hyatt Regency Hotel, Costera Miguel Alemán 1, Tel. 469-6900.* These are branch shops of one of Mexico's top silver jewelers and producers of trays, candle holders, vases, tableware, and bowls. Offers exquisite designs and top quality.

❏ **Astrid:** *Fiesta Americana Hotel, Tel. 484-2828.* Carries an exclusive line of nicely designed 14k and 18k gold jewelry with precious and semi-precious stones as well as attractive silver jewelry and gift items from Taxco.

❏ **Minett:** *Acapulco Princess Hotel. Tel. 469-1000.* Offers a fine collection of uniquely designed gold jewelry incorporating both precious and semi-precious stones. Includes silver jewelry and gift items. Carries the unique silver and ceramic tableware of Emilia Castillo.

CLOTHES AND ACCESSORIES

❏ **Esteban:** *Costera Miguel Alemán, Tel. 484-3084 or Fax 484-8452. E-mail: Esteban@aca.quik.com. Website: www.esteban-acapulco.com.* This well known local designer, who has operated here for more than 35 years, offers an extensive collection of uniquely designed and trendy evening wear, casual clothes, swimwear, and accessories (handbags and hats) under the Esteban label. Men's clothes are found upstairs.

Accommodations

Acapulco boasts over 400 hotels with more than 20,000 rooms. You'll find a full range of accommodations here, from five-star to one-star hotels and guesthouses. Some of the best properties include the following.

❏ **Las Brisas Acapulco:** *Carretera Escenica 5255, Acapulco, Gro. 39868 Mexico, Tel. (52-744) 469-6900, Fax (52-744) 446-532. Toll-free from the US & Canada: 888-559-4329. E-mail: brisa@brisas.com.mx. Website: www.brisas.com.mx.* Set amidst 40 acres of lush hibiscus gardens on a hillside above Acapulco Bay, Las Brisas is known for its signature hibiscus flower, as well as the color pink which you will see everywhere – it even sets its pink and white jeeps apart from the rest. A village of 263 spacious casitas, built into the natural contours of the hillside, over 200 pools, and an attentive staff make a stay here special. Opened in 1957, Las Brisas has been well maintained, though the architectural styling of the initial casitas is suggestive of the period. A member of The Leading Hotels of the World and winner of many readers' award magazine polls, Las Brisas has gained a reputation as "the honeymooners paradise" – primarily because of the privacy the casitas provide to guests. The 263 casitas, most with a private pool, include 32 suites and junior suites. Marble floors, mahogany woodwork, and a view of the Pacific from wide private terraces are signatures of Las Brisas. Breakfast of coffee, fresh fruit, and sweet rolls is delivered each morning, without disturbing the guest, through a "magic box" that opens from the outside – for delivery, and from the inside the room – for retrieval. Fresh hibiscus flowers are everywhere: on room service trays, on the bathroom towel racks, on the pillows at turn-down time, and sprinkled in the swimming pools. The Brisas Beach Club is the premium category, pampering guests with upgraded accommodations, services, and amenities.

For fine dining, try *Bellevista Restaurant* for a dinner of international cuisine and a magnificent view of Acapulco Bay. Bellevista is also open for breakfast. *La Concha* is open for lunch and features seafood and grilled specialties. Visit the *Deli Shop* for salads, sandwiches, and cool drinks. The *Bellevista Bar* is a place to relax and enjoy the sunset while sipping your favorite drink. Business Center; Fitness Center – as well as water and recreational activities; Conference/Banquet Facilities.

❑ **Camino Real Acapulco Diamante:** *Carretera Escénica, Km 14, Calle Baja catita, Acapulco Diamante, 39867 Mexico. Tel. (52-744) 435-1010, Fax (52-744) 435-1020. Toll-free from U.S. or Canada 800-722-6466. Website: www.caminoreal.com/acapulco.* Enter the lobby on the hotel's upper level and enjoy the stunning view of the bay. The 157 guestrooms and suites are set into the terraced hillside and slope down towards the private beach. Rooms are decorated in cool pastels and have luxurious bathrooms. Eleven extra-spacious Club Rooms have their own concierge and provide additional amenities. *La Vela* offers international cuisine as well as dishes typical of Acapulco. *Cabo Diamante* is an informal open-air restaurant which offers an international menu. The pool restaurant and bar serves sandwiches and refreshing beverages. Fitness Facilities include three swimming pools on different levels with a waterfall, Jacuzzi, gym, spa services, beach club, tennis court, and access to golf. Conference/Banquet Facilities.

❑ **Fairmont Acapulco Princess:** *Playa Revolcadero, A.P. 1351, Revolcadero 39300, Tel. (52-744) 469-1000, Fax (52-744) 469-1016. Toll-free from U.S. & Canada 800-441-1414. Website: www.fairmont. com.* Located on a wide stretch of beach, this massive resort is comprised of three buildings, one shaped like a huge Aztec pyramid. With 927 recently renovated guestrooms and 92 suites, the spacious accommodations are light and airy with cane furniture, marble floors, and large closets. Spacious bathrooms have Jacuzzi tubs. Each guestroom or suite has a private terrace. Three restaurants offer a wide variety of cuisines. Fitness Facilities include 11 tennis courts, 5 pools, full spa, range of water activities, 18-hole golf course; Business Center; Conference/Banquet Facilities.

Restaurants

Acapulco has many wonderful restaurants that offer spectacular views and a wide range of fine international cuisines. Indeed, dining is one of the great highlights of visiting Acapulco. Be sure to make reservations at all major restaurants, and especially during the high season. With over 160 restaurants to choose from, the following represent some of the best of the best for dining.

❑ **Kookaburra:** *Carretera Escénica. Located near the Las Brisas Hotel and next to Spicey, Tel. 446-6039.* Put this one at the top of your "must dine" list. This very romantic open-air restaurant overlooks Acapulco Bay. Offers outstanding dishes such as shrimp with tamarind sauce and pineapple sauce.

❑ **El Tabachín:** *Fairmont Pierre Marques Hotel. Apdo. 1351, Playa Revolcadero, Revolcadero. Tel. 466-1000. Open 7pm to 11pm.* This outstanding French-Asian restaurant gets high marks for being one of Mexico's best restaurants. Inventive Chef Gino Guercio offers many wonderful dishes such as New Zealand lamb in roasted ginger and poached Dover sole fillet in lemongrass sauce. Includes a tequila bar.

❑ **Coyuca 22:** *Avenue Coyuca 22, Tel. 482-3468. Closed May through October.* This beautiful restaurant with ancient Greek decor is ideally sited with a panoramic view of the city. It's a great place for early diners to enjoy sunsets. Popular with celebrities. Try the fish specials, veal scallopini, shrimp Provencal, prime rib, and New Zealand lamb chops.

❑ **Casanova:** *Carretera Escénica 5256, opposite the Las Brisas, Tel. 446-6237.* Offering spectacular views over Acapulco Bay, this award-winning restaurant serves excellent Italian cuisine. Can dine indoors or outdoors.

❑ **Bellavista:** *Las Brisas Hotel, Tel. 469-6900. Open 8am to 12:30pm and 7pm to 11:30pm.* Dine indoors or alfresco overlooking the shimmering lights of Acapulco Bay in this smart casual restaurant. Offers an expansive menu of excellent international dishes.

❑ **Spicey:** *Carretera Escénica, Tel. 446-6003. Located next door to Kookaburra.* Another great restaurant with a spectacular view of Acapulco Bay. Offers both indoor and outdoor dining options. While not always consistent, you may get lucky with the seafood dishes and spring rolls.

❑ **Le Jardin des Artistes:** *Vicente Yañez Pinzón 11, Tel. 484-8344.* Located next to Acapulco's top gallery, Rudic Art Gallery, this chic outdoor French restaurant with tables interspersed with large bronze sculptures is noted for its excellent dishes. Try the red snapper in mustard sauce.

❑ **Carlos 'n' Charlie's:** *Costera Miguel Alemán, Tel. 484-1285.* This continues to be one of Acapulco's most popular, eclectic, and fun American-style restaurants. Serves excellent ribs, stuffed shrimp, and oysters.

❑ **100% Natural:** *Costera Miguel Alemán, Tel. 485-3982.* More than a vegetarian restaurant, this popular and reasonably priced eatery is open 24 hours a day. Serves hearty breakfasts. Try the soy burger, grilled chicken sandwich, yogurt shakes, and fresh fruit drinks. Excellent service.

Enjoying Your Stay

Acapulco is a non-stop city for things to see and do. Its major attractions include the following.

SIGHTSEEING

❑ **La Quebrada:** *Mirador Hotel, Old Acapulco.* You can't visit Acapulco without seeing its legendary attraction – the cliff divers of La Quebrada. Located just north of the downtown area, La Quebrada attracts hundreds of visitors each day who anxiously wait for the daredevil divers to leap 130 feet into the rushing waters below. Divers go through this diving ritual five times a day: 1:00 in the afternoon and 7:30, 8:30, 9:30, and 10:30 in the evening. In the evening, many visitors stake out an outdoor table at the La Perla restaurant-bar (a 130-peso minimum) in the Mirador Hotel where they can view the divers while enjoying a hearty piña colada.

❑ **Fort San Diego (El Fuerte de San Diego):** *Old Acapulco. Open Tuesday through Sunday, 10am to 5pm.* Located on a hill east of the zócalo and overlooking Acapulco Bay, this fort was originally built by the Spanish in 1617 to protect the city from encroaching pirates infesting the surrounding water. Restored after a devastating earthquake in 1776, the fort now functions as the Acapulco Historical Museum (Museo Histórico de Acapulco) which provides information and several interesting displays on the city's history.

❑ **House of Masks (Casa de Mascaras):** Located down the hill from the entrance to Fort San Diego, this house includes an interesting collection of wood-carved masks from the seven regions of Guerrero state. Includes a resident carver demonstrating the art of mask making.

ACTIVITIES

❑ **Beaches:** Acapulco is justly famous for its many fine beaches. Each has its own particular character. The most popular beaches stretch along Acapulco Bay, running west to east, with many of the most active beaches in front of the major hotels. Playa Caleta (on the western tip of the bay) is especially popular with the locals in the morning. The beautiful Playa Condesa (between Continental Plaza and El Presidente hotels on the Condesa) is the center for lots of activities. Other popular beaches include Playa Los Hornos, Playa Guitarron, and Playa Icacos.

❑ **Water sports:** Many visitors take advantage of the major water sports offerings readily available: water-skiing, scuba diving, snorkeling, windsurfing, jet boating (Shotover Jet), paragliding, and fishing. Kids enjoy the water sports at the CICI Water Park (Tel. 484-8033). Check with your hotel for details on where to go and whom to contact for such activities.

❑ **Golf:** Acapulco offers several spectacular golf courses. The premier one is the 18-hole Tres Vidas Gold Club (Tel. 462-1000). Also check out the two championship golf courses at the Fairmont Acapulco Princess and Pierre Marques hotels, the Mayan Palace Gold Club (Tel. 466-2305), and the municipal golf course (nine holes) at the Club de Golf on the Costera.

❑ **Tennis and spas:** Many of the major hotels (Fairmont Acapulco Princess, Pierre Marques, Hyatt Regency, Mayan Palace, Villa Vera, Las Brisas) have their own tennis courts. You can also play tennis at the Costa Club (Tel. 485-9050). The largest spas are found at Spa Willow Stream (Fairmont Princess Hotel, Tel. 4679-1000) and Villa Vera Spa and Fitness Center (Villa Vera Hotel, Tel. 484-0333).

❑ **Bullfights:** Held every Sunday at 5:30, from early January until Easter, at the Plaza de Toros (Av. Circumvalación, Tel. 482-1181). You can purchase tickets through most major hotels.

ENTERTAINMENT AND NIGHTLIFE

Acapulco rocks at night. Justly famous for its many spectacular discos, nightclubs, and bars with live music, light shows, pyrotechnics, and special activities, the city's evening entertainment starts around 10:30pm and continues until dawn. Most of the major discos are found in the Costera area and farther east along Carretera Escenica near Las Brisas. Some of the most popular places include:

❑ **Alebrije:** *Costera Miguel Alemán 3308, across from the Hyatt Regency, Tel. 484-5902.* This huge operation is famous for its flaming torches, reflecting pools, tropical gardens, and Friday night foaming of the crowd. Considered one of the largest discos in the world, with a seating capacity of nearly 2,000! Dress code is smart-casual to formal.

❑ **Andromedas:** *Costera Miguel Alemán 16, Tel. 484-8815.* Designed as a medieval castle with a subterranean interior. Includes live mermaids in a huge fish tank. Especially popular with young people who like the latest techno-pop tunes.

❑ **Baby'O:** *Costera Miguel Alemán 22, near the Hyatt Regency, Tel. 484-7474.* One of Acapulco's oldest and classiest discos that continues to draw huge crowds to this 650-seat cavernous club. Enforces a dress code requiring anything from casual to formal. Especially popular with celebrities and wealthy locals. Offers a nice range of appealing music for all age groups.

❑ **Disco Beach:** *Costera Miguel Alemán 111, at Playa Condesa, Tel. 484-8230.* This popular open-air disco especially appeals to young people. Reputed to be a good pick-up place.

❑ **Enigma/Siboney:** *Carretera Escenica, near Las Brisas, Tel. 484-7154.* Formerly the Extravaganzza, this beautifully sited two-in-one disco overlooking the bay offers two different entertainment options. Enigma is a large and lively disco famous for its Egyptian theme and light show. Smaller and more intimate Siboney offers salsa, mambo, cumbia, and other Latin music. Also owns the nearby Palladium disco (Tel. 481-0330).

❑ **Hard Rock Café:** *Costera Miguel Alemán 37, Tel. 484-0047.* This branch of a popular international restaurant-bar chain includes live music (after 11pm), a huge bar, and a large dance floor.

❑ **Palladium:** *Carretera Escenica, near Las Brisas, Tel. 481-0330.* Popular with young people, this lively disco has a spectacular view of Acapulco Bay through its huge windows.

❑ **Salon Q:** *Costera Miguel Alemán 23, Tel. 481-0114.* This large disco/dance hall with a live band is especially noted for its salsa, cumbia, and other Latin music. Dubs itself the "Cathedral of Salsa."

❑ **Zucca:** *Carretera Escénica near Las Brisas, Tel. 484-6727.* Designed like a Greco-Roman palace with imposing columns, this disco is especially popular with couples. Noted for playing music from the '70s, '80s, and '90s. Dress is casual to formal.

Most major hotels and resorts have happy hours, piano bars, and live evening entertainment.

Acapulco also is famous for its Acapulco Symphonic Orchestra. Check with your hotel for performance dates.

Mexican fiestas, which include music and dancing, are put on at the Las Brisas Hotel (El Mexicano Restaurant, Tel. 469-6900, Saturdays, December to April) and the Convention Center (Acapulco International Center, Costera Miguel Alemán, Tel. 484-3218, on Wednesdays and Fridays, and also Mondays from December to April.

Not for Everyone

It's easy to hype Acapulco because of all its legendary seaside and nighttime pleasures. If you enjoy beaches, golf courses, water sports, restaurants, nightlife, crowds, and the noise of lively resorts, you'll probably thrive in fun-loving Acapulco. But if this is not your travel style, Acapulco can become an oppressive concrete jungle from which you may want to quickly escape. Keep in mind that there is little traditional culture and sightseeing here. This is not the Mexico you may fall in love with when you visit more traditional Morelia, Guanajuato, Querétaro, Puebla, and Oaxaca.

Acapulco is still a unique playground of the rich and famous who have opened this community to other pleasure-seekers. Simply put, it's a well developed resort that manages to entertain 1.5 million fun-loving visitors each year. People come here to escape from other places and themselves – a kind of glitzy oasis on the Pacific coast. As you will quickly discover, there is much more to Mexico than what is represented in the many decadent pleasures of Acapulco. Go east and northeast for a few miles and you'll quickly encounter a very different Mexico as you leave the Acapulco oasis!

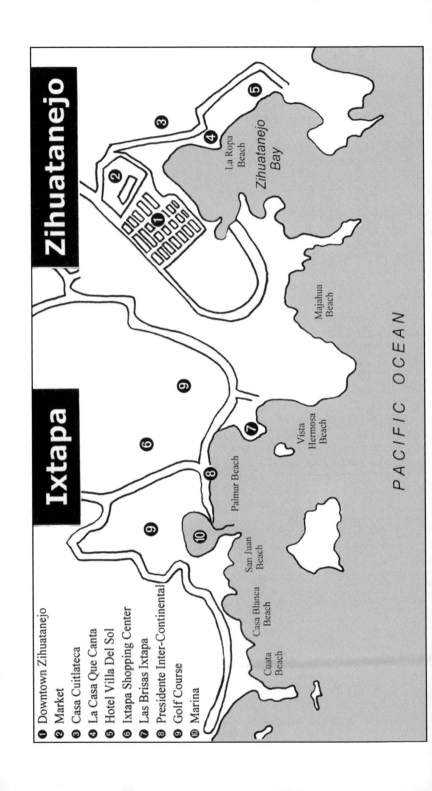

Ixtapa

Zihuatanejo

1. Downtown Zihuatanejo
2. Market
3. Casa Cuitlateca
4. La Casa Que Canta
5. Hotel Villa Del Sol
6. Ixtapa Shopping Center
7. Las Brisas Ixtapa
8. Presidente Inter-Continental
9. Golf Course
10. Marina

Cuata Beach

Casa Blanca Beach

San Juan Beach

Palmar Beach

Vista Hermosa Beach

Majahua Beach

La Ropa Beach

Zihuatanejo Bay

PACIFIC OCEAN

Ixtapa & Zihuatanejo

I F YOU LOVE PURE RELAXATION in a lovely and quiet seaside setting, with all the amenities of five-star resorts juxtaposed with the charming character of a small seaside Mexican town, drive northwest of Acapulco for a few hours. You're about to discover one of Mexico's great destinations – a picturesque seaside town (Zihuatanejo) linked by a short stretch of four-lane highway to a well planned, antiseptic resort (Ixtapa).They are two vacation styles in one.

A Small Town and Resort

Located nearly 150 miles northwest of Acapulco along the Pacific coast, with the Sierra Madre mountains in the background, the small but twin coastal towns of Ixtapa and Zihuatanejo (nicknamed "Zihua") are Pacific coast gems. With a combined population of nearly 40,000, these are two of Mexico's most popular beach destinations for couples and adults (children are not encouraged in many places). Blessed with excellent weather, gorgeous beaches and sunsets, a first-rate tourist infrastructure, great meeting facilities, a connecting four-lane super highway, and direct international flights, Ixtapa and Zihuatanejo are ideal destinations for discerning travelers and business groups in search of quality travel.

From the high-rise hotels and condominiums, nicely manicured lawns, shopping plazas, a convention center, and golf courses of well planned Ixtapa to the unique boutique hotels, fine restaurants, gorgeous views, wonderful beaches, and tempting artisan market and small shops of more chaotic and spontaneous Zihuatanejo, these two complementary communities may well become your favorite Mexican destinations for rest and relaxation. Indeed, they are a big change from the glitzy mega-resort of noisy Acapulco. Many visitors to this area, who tend to be upscale travelers, meeting groups, noted artists, writers, and actors, much prefer Ixtapa and Zihuatanejo to more crowded, hectic, and ostensibly fun-loving Acapulco. As many visitors to this area quickly discover, these twin beachside towns have a lot to offer travelers.

❏ These are two of Mexico's most popular destinations for couples and adults.

❏ Located only four miles from each other, these two communities offer very different yet complimentary vacation styles.

❏ Ixtapa is a government-planned resort community that appeals to upscale travelers, meeting groups, and condo and time-share owners.

❏ Zihuatanejo is a real functioning community where over 90 percent of the local population are permanent residents.

❏ Ixtapa and Zihuatanejo offer complementary travel experiences.

Getting to Know You

Connected to each other by one of Mexico's most envious superhighways, Ixtapa and Zihuatanejo are only four miles from one another – a quick 10-minute drive. Despite their close proximity, these two communities offer very different travel styles. Ixtapa, for example, is a small and tightly planned community originally designed from scratch in the 1970s by the National Fund for Tourism Development, which also helped develop the planned resorts of Cancún, Huatulco, and Los Cabos. It attracts meeting and incentive groups as well as real estate investors. As such, these two communities are still young and developing tourist centers.

Ixtapa especially appeals to well-heeled visitors who stay in its many high-rise hotels or invest in its numerous condominiums and timeshare units. The large hotels in this area also cater to meeting and incentive groups, offering a full range of business facilities and catering services. These include the Riviera Beach Resort Ixtapa (has its own convention center), the all-inclusive Meliá Azul Ixtapa and Presidente Inter-Continental, Las Brisas Ixtapa, Krystal Ixtapa, Hotel Continental Plaza, Radisson Resort Ixtapa, and Dorado Pacífica. Beautifully landscaped, Ixtapa is a well maintained and manicured community that lacks the spontaneous and low maintenance looks of most Mexican communities.

As a government-planned resort community, Ixtapa is a sanitized version of Mexico that makes many visitors feel more comfortable and reassured about their Mexican surroundings. While

it may not represent the "real" Mexico, it presents a new version of Mexico that is most appealing to visitors in search of quality, predictability, and security. From beaches and sports to dining, shopping, and entertainment, Ixtapa is a self-contained community where you need not venture far from your hotel or condominium. Everything is here – restaurants, shops, golf courses, tennis courts, beaches, swimming pools, water sports, and more. A  few all-inclusive hotels even dissuade guests from leaving their premises for a restaurant beyond their doors.

Zihuatanejo, on the other hand, has more local character and color. It's a real functioning community where over 90 percent of the area's population resides. It's a great place for people who want to explore the community, from discovering great beaches to uncovering unique markets, shops, and restaurants. Upscale independent travelers fall in love with this place. Once an old fishing village, today this picturesque town is noted for its beautiful beaches, a scenic diamond-shaped bay, and a sheltered harbor with yachts and fishermen. It's a relatively laid-back community offering a good range of accommodations, many excellent restaurants, and varied shopping and dining experiences. Just drive through its chaotic streets or visit its crowded artisan market (Mercado de Artesanias) on Cinco de Mayo, and you know you're still in Mexico. This is the much less sanitized and more spontaneous version of the country – the "real Mexico" – that many visitors enjoy.

Taken together, Ixtapa and Zihuatanejo offer complementary travel experiences. If you enjoy staying in small intimate boutique hotels with gorgeous views of a bay and exploring communities on your own, plan to stay in charming Zihuatanejo. If you prefer large resort-type hotels, complete with a full range of resort activities and group functions, set your sights on well organized Ixtapa. Whatever your choice, make sure you visit both communities.

Communities on the Web

As part of your pre-trip planning, you may want to visit these websites for information on Ixtapa and Zihuatanejo, including hotel reservations:

- **Ixtapa-Zihuatanejo**   www.ixtapa-zihuatanejo.com
- **Ixtapa**   www.ixtapa.net
- **Zihua-Ixtapa**   www.zihua-ixtapa.com
- **Go2Ixtapa**   www.go2ixtapa.com
- **Zihuatanejo-Ixtapa.net** www.zihuatanejo.net
- **Zihua.net**   www.zihua.net
- **Ixtapa-Zihuatanejo**   www.ixtapa-zihuatanejo.org

Several other websites specialize in hotel reservations, property rentals, and real estate investments.

The Streets of Ixtapa and Zihuatanejo

Being small resort communities, both Ixtapa and Zihuatanejo are relatively easy to get around in because of the convenient roads and signs. The hotel sections – Zona Hotelera – are well marked. However, it's not always easy to get a map of the area. Many hotels do not have maps, or they give you a copy of "Turistero," the local advertising brochure that includes maps of both communities. In reference to the superhighway that links the two, signage is very good. Once in Ixtapa, the four-lane boulevards that lace this attractive community are clearly marked with signs for the major hotels and shopping areas.

You will need transportation to navigate both communities since they are relatively spread out and thus not easy to cover on foot. Having your own car is the most convenient way to get around and parking is relatively easy. Renting a car once you arrive in Ixtapa or Zihuatanejo can be very expensive – over US$100 a day. It's much cheaper to arrange for a rental car through one of the major car rental firms (Alamo, Avis, Hertz, Budget) prior to arriving in Mexico. Getting around by taxi is relatively inexpensive with rides between Ixtapa and Zihuatanejo costing around US$4 per trip.

Most major hotels and restaurants will be found in the Zona Hotelera section of both communities. Shopping will be focused on the "Zona Comercial" in Ixtapa and "Centro" in Zihuatanejo. Within Zihuatanejo, the adjacent shopping streets, located between Juan N. Alvarez and Av. José Ma. Moreles, are of most interest to visitors: Av. Cinco de Mayo, Cuauhtemoc, and Nicolás Bravo. Here you'll find several handicraft and jewelry shops.

Shopping Ixtapa and Zihuatanejo

Most people come to Ixtapa and Zihuatanejo for relatively laid-back resort-style relaxation, which includes beaches, golf, water sports, and dining. Shopping is one of those nice add-on activities that can result in some surprisingly good shopping – from handicraft stalls and art galleries to upscale designer boutiques – in places that ordinarily would not be considered significant shopping areas. You'll find good selections of folk art, leather goods, hammocks, Guerrero ceramics, hand-embroidered clothing, jewelry, art, and handicrafts in both communities.

Most shops are open Monday through Saturday from 9am or 10am to 2pm and from 4pm to 8pm.

Shopping is surprisingly varied in these two towns. Both Ixtapa and Zihuatanejo offer colorful handicraft markets called **Mercado Tursítico de Artesanás**. These markets were created by the local governments in 1990 to discourage roaming street and beach salespeople from pestering tourists (a few still do). The market in Zihuatanejo (on the western side of town along Cinco de Mayo) is much larger (nearly 250 stalls) than the one in Ixtapa (around 80 stalls), but both offer similar handicrafts, souvenirs, silver jewelry (often "alpaca" or silver with a high nickel content), and decorative items. The attractive hardwood fish sculptures and handmade leather sandals (*huaraches*) are especially good market buys. Several hotels also include a few quality shops.

Except in the markets, don't expect to do much bargaining here since most shops consider their prices to be fixed. However, some places that normally accept credit cards will give a discount for making cash rather than credit card purchases. Always ask about a cash discount, which can be 10 to 15 percent, before making a purchase.

Ixtapa includes small shopping plazas which are clustered together in the central shopping area ("Zona Comercial") across the street from the major high-rise hotels along Paseo Ixtapa. While you will find a few good shops and restaurants here, the area fell on hard times immediately after 9/11 as few visitors came to this area even during the high season, and many shops closed. This area should bounce back once tourism rebounds. A few of Ixtapa's top shops remain open for business. The major shopping plazas include:

❑ **Plaza Las Fuentes:** This small but modern two-level shopping center includes clothing stores (**Nautica**, **Peer**, and **Bye-Bye**) and a silver jewelry shop (**Sterling Silver**).

❑ **Plaza Ixpamar:** While many shops in this outdoor shopping center closed after 9/11, two of the survivors represented excellent Mexican folk art, handicrafts, and souvenirs: **El Amanecer** (Tel. 553-1902) and **Mexico Lindo** (Tel. 553-0546).

❑ **Plaza La Puerta:** Located behind the market, this shopping center includes several small shops and restaurants, including **Mic-Mac** (Tel. 553-1733) for numerous handmade items, from clothes and metal figures to handbags, jewelry, painted napkin rings, and wind chimes and **Alberto's** (Tel. 554-2161) for attractive gold and silver jewelry, with precious and semiprecious stones, and pearls.

❑ **Plaza Los Patios:** Offers a good selection of clothes, sportswear, art, and handicrafts. Look for **Galeria San Angel** and **La Fuente** for art, ceramics, and decorative items, and **D'Leon**, **Sergio Tacchini**, and **Tanga** for leather goods, sportswear, and beachwear.

Best of the Best

ZIHUATANEJO

❑ **La Galeria Que Canta:** *Camino Escénica a Playa La Ropa, Zihuatanejo, Tel. 555-7030 or Fax 554-7040.* Located at the exclusive boutique hotel La Casa Que Canta, this small shop offers an excellent selection of top quality ceramics, copper pots, painted bowls and trays, and art books. Several of the large ceramics and pots spill into the lobby area of the hotel – all are for sale. This shop also is responsible for decorating the lovely rooms of this fine boutique hotel.

❑   **Arte Mexicano Nopal:** *Av. 5 de Mayo 56, Centro, Zihuatanejo, Tel./Fax 554-7530.* Located directly across the street from the artisan market, this colorful shop is jam-packed, from floor to ceiling, with lights, lanterns, picture frames, painted boxes, carved wood masks, pots, woven bags, boxes, tin mirrors, and ceramic figures from all over Mexico. Offers good quality and selections of Mexican folk art with special emphasis on copies of pre-Columbian art. You are bound to find something of interest in this inviting, although visually disorienting, shop.

❑ **Coco Cabaña:** *Vincente Guerrero Street 5-A, behind Coconuts Restaurant, Tel. 554-2518. Website: www.zihua.net/cococabana.* Offers an attractive selection of top quality Mexican handicrafts and folk art from around the country. Look for tin mirrors and lamps, candlesticks, hand-carved and painted wood animals and boxes, ceramics, and tableware from some of the best artisans in Oaxaca, Puebla, Guanajuato, and San Miguel de Allende. Is the exclusive representative for Guerrero's leading artist, Nicolas de Jesus, who produces distinctive "skeleton" paintings. Also owns the popular Coconuts Restaurant.

❑ **Lupita's:** *Juan N. Alvarez 5, Tel. 554-2238.* Offers beautiful hand-embroidered women's clothes from Chiapas, Oaxaca, Yucatán, and Guatemala. Will take special orders and ship.

❑ **Galeria Maya:** *Nicolás Bravo 31, Zihuatanejo, Tel. 554-4606. Website: www.zihrena.com (website operates as a virtual gallery only).* Specializes in colorful Mexican folk art. Offers an interesting collection of masks, jewelry, painted figures, and clothes. Also operates a second gallery, **Galeria Ixchel Maya** at Nicolas Bravo 33, which offers life-size wooden sculptures.

❑ **Galart:** *Hotel Villa del Sol, Playa Le Ropa, Zihuatanejo, Tel. 554-7774. E-mail: galart@cdnet.com.mx.* This small boutique shop includes numerous oil paintings and bronze sculptures and a nice collection of jewelry and crafts. Includes both silver jewelry and necklaces made from semi-precious stones. Very nice designs. Often changes exhibits of artists and jewelers.

❑ **Mueblart:** *On Cinco de Mayo.* Offers a nice selection of handcrafted furniture, woven baskets, black clay pottery from Oaxaca, carved wood masks, and unusual handicrafts.

❑ **Alberto's:** *Cuauhtémoc 12-15, Tel. 554-2161, Zihuatanejo.* Located near the artisan market, this entrepreneurial shop specializes in offering a wide selection of good quality silver jewelry. Includes their own workshop. Offers free drinks and friendly service. Also has a smaller but very nice branch shop on La Puerta in Ixtapa.

❑ **Casa Marina:** *Paseo del Pescador 9, Tel. 554-2373.* Located next to the square and basketball court, this building includes three shops offering a wide range of handcrafted items (embroidered clothing, wool rugs, serapes, masks, woven bags) from Guerrero, Oaxaca, and Guatemala: **El Embarcadero**, **La Zapoteca**, and **El Jumil**.

IXTAPA

❑ **Astrid:** *Las Brisas Hotel, Playa Vista Hermosa, Ixtapa, Tel. 553-0109.* If you're looking for quality jewelry, Astrid is the place to visit. Found in several major hotels throughout Mexico, this reputable shop is known for its quality silver, white and black pearls, and coral jewelry. Offers nice designs. Also includes a line of silver figures – ducks, elephants, and Aztec heads.

❑ **El Amanecer:** *Plaza Ixpamar 29, Ixtapa, Tel. 553-1902.* This small shop includes a very nice collection of excellent quality Mexican folk art. Look for ceramic chickens, pots, and painted trays, bowls, and fish.

❑ **Mexico Lindo:** *Plaza Ixpamar 30, Ixtapa, Tel. 553-0546.* Specializes in offering handicrafts from Oaxaca and other areas of Mexico. Includes a nice selection of black clay pottery, Alebrijes, terracotta, hand-blown glass, wood puzzles, rainbow clay, candle holders, picture frames, and ponchos.

❑ **Mic-Mac:** *Shopping Center La Puerta, Tel. 553-1733, Ixtapa.* This colorful shop specializes in handmade folk art and handicrafts. Includes an interesting collection of metal figures (cats and owls), clothes, pillows, handbags, painted napkin rings, coasters, jewelry, papier mache, wind chimes, and napkins. Also owns a nearby (Shopping Center Los Patios) arts and crafts shop, **La Fuente**.

❑ **Galeria San Angel:** *Los Patios, Ixtapa.* Offers an interesting collection of mirrors, sculptures, enamel work, and brass boxes. Includes a Sergio Bustamante section displaying his colorful and whimsical sculptures. See our descriptions of his galleries in Mexico City, Acapulco, and Guadalajara.

❑ **Alberto's:** *La Puerta, opposite Hotel Dorado Pacifico, Ixtapa, Tel. 554-2161.* This attractive shop includes a nice selection of gold and silver jewelry using precious and semi-precious stones – rings, necklaces, and bracelets. Also includes jewelry made from fresh-water and cultured pearls. Will do custom work. Also has an attractive shop in Zihuatanejo (Cuauhtémoc 12-15).

Accommodations

Ixtapa and Zihautanejo are not equal when it comes to selecting accommodations. Ixtapa is the place to stay if you prefer large hotels that offer amenities expected of large properties – restaurants, health/fitness club, lots of recreation choices, perhaps a hairdressing salon, bars, and discos. Several properties also offer "romance packages," which include everything from a destination wedding to a honeymoon. Ixtapa has a small "town center" with clusters of commercial plazas housing shops, which include a grocery store from which you can re-stock your mini bar; small art galleries, pharmacies, banks, travel agencies, car rental agencies, and restaurants. But this area definitely has the feel of tourists on vacation. In fact, in addition to the numerous large hotels in Ixtapa, there are several timeshare properties, many of which are owned by U.S. and Canadian residents who come here during the winter months.

Zihautanejo is more laid back and exudes a more Mexican character than Ixtapa. It's also home to some of the most lovely boutique hotels in Mexico, attracting guests who prefer the intimacy of a smaller property in a secluded setting to the large high-rise hotels that line the beach of Ixtapa. Some of these properties, such as the exclusive Casa Cuitlateca and Villa del Sol, offer wedding packages.

IXTAPA

❑ **Las Brisas Ixtapa:** *Playa Vista Hermosa s/n, 40880 Ixtapa-Zihuatanejo, Gro. Mexico, Tel. (52-755) 553-2121, Fax (52-755) 553-1091. Toll-free from the US & Canada 888-559-4329. E-mail:* ixtapa@brisas.com.mx. *Website:* www.brisas.com.mx. Touted as an example of modern architecture with a prehistoric style, Las Brisas Hotel rises like a great pyramid and slopes down the hillside to its own secluded beach. Grounds are lush with tropical vegetation. Each of the 423 guestrooms has a private balcony (with hammock), an ocean view, and a table for in-room dining. Guestroom decor is somewhat minimalist, but includes Mexican handicrafts. Although expected amenities are provided, guestrooms are not as luxurious as one might expect. Four restaurants offer a variety of cuisines from Mexican at *El Mexicano* to Italian at *Portofino*. Also try *La Brisa*, *Bellavista*, or *Solarium*. A small shopping arcade offers a variety of items. Las Brisas has four freshwater pools connected by waterfalls and a secluded beach. Tennis courts, aerobics, beach volleyball, a nearby golf course,and deep sea and sport fishing provide a variety of recreation choices. Conference/Banquet Facilities.

❑ **Presidente Inter-Continental Ixtapa:** *Blvd. Ixtapa s/n, 40880 Ixtapa, Gro. Mexico, Tel. (52-755) 553-0018, Fax (52-755) 553-2312. Toll-free from the US & Canada 800-327-0200. Website:* www.interconti.com. The 420 guestrooms and suites are decorated in shades of pastel cream and white. There are four restaurants, and the room rates include meals. Presidente Inter-Continental has two pools. Exercise Facilities and Sports Activities; Meeting Rooms.

ZIHUATANEJO

❑ **La Casa Que Canta:** *Camino Escénico a Playa La Ropa, Zihuatanejo, Gro. Mexico, Tel. (52-755) 555-7030, Fax: (52-755) 554-7040. Toll-Free from U.S. & Canada: 888-523-5050. E-mail: lacasaquecanta@pro digy.net.mx. Website: www.lacasaquecanta.com.* Translated as "The House that Sings," this gem is a member of the exclusive group of Small Luxury Hotels of the World. La Casa Que Canta is located on a hilly promontory, surrounded by water, and guests enjoy gorgeous views of Zihuatanejo Bay. The dramatic multi-tiered architecture is fashioned entirely from natural materials – no glass or metal here. Adobe walls, thatched roofs, and wooden louvered doors and windows surround guests with the feel of tropical Mexico. Twenty-four suites, each one different from the others, are located in three cliff-side buildings. Each suite, ranging from 800 to 1,600 square feet, includes a sitting area, bedroom, bath, and a spacious private terrace. All suites have two views of the bay. There are ten private pool suites, eleven grand suites, and three terrace rooms. Bathrooms are spacious and feature double sinks, separate enclosures for toilet and bidet, and an oversized walk-in shower. The infinity pool terrace provides a picture-perfect setting for breakfast and guests select from such specialties such as lime pancakes or eggs Mexican style. Mexican specialties, salads, and grilled seafood are served at the pool terrace throughout the afternoon. By dinner time, flickering lanterns cast their glow upon the waters of the pools and the bay as guests dine on such dishes as grilled red snapper fillet with pico de gallo and green mole, baby chicken with lemon butter, or jumbo shrimps breaded in coconut campeche style. From December through April, the bar offers an additional lighter dining option – a selection of Mexican tapas. A wonderful gift shop on the entrance level offers a variety of quality Mexican art and crafts. Fitness Center; Water Sports; Freshwater Infinity Pool and Free Form Saltwater Pools. Golf Course and Tennis Courts nearby.

❑ **Hotel Villa Del Sol:** *Playa la Ropa S/N, P.O. Box 84, Zihuatanejo, Gro. 40880 Mexico, Tel. (52-755) 554-2239, Fax (52-755) 554-2758. Toll-free from U.S. and Canada: 888-389-2645. E-mail: hotel@villasol.com.mx. Website: www.hotelvilladelsol.net.* A member of The Small Luxury Hotels of the World and winner of several prestigious awards, Villa del Sol's 56 individually designed rooms and suites are tucked away in several two-story casitas amidst luxuriant tropical gardens with an abundance of coconut trees, tall bamboo, brilliantly hued bougainvillea, and colorful hibiscus. A small stream runs though the entire property splashing as waterfalls or fountains into several pools. All guestrooms and suites are tastefully and colorfully decorated with Mexican art and handicrafts. *The Restaurant at Villa del Sol* features Mexican and international cuisine with an emphasis on local ingredients and fresh seafood. *La Cantina Bar & Grill* serves Mediterranean foods in a casual setting. A small art gallery and gift shop are worth looking at. Four swimming pools including one 60-ft. lap pool and an infinity pool right on the beach; a large variety of water sports; tennis courts; golf nearby; Fitness Center; Meeting Facilities.

❏ **Casa Cuitlateca:** *Playa la Ropa, Apdo. 124, Zihuatanejo, Gro. 40880 Mexico, Tel. (52-755) 554-2448, Fax (52-755) 554-7394. Website: www.casacuitlateca.com.* A very small boutique hotel – at night the feel is magical and the view breathtaking. By day you will think you have arrived at a castaway's tree house. Four guestrooms: 1 suite, 1 magnificent room with a large private deck, and 2 executive rooms. There is a large open-air great room and above this a tower penthouse with a private tanning area and a Jacuzzi tub available to guests. The decor of each of the four rooms is unique and reflects the quality of Mexican art and crafts. The art selections are beautifully presented – especially at night when the lighting shows them off to advantage. Each room includes a king-sized bed and a private deck or garden. An intimate restaurant on premises serves a variety of food. Art works may be for sale.

Restaurants

Both Ixtapa and Zihuatanejo offer a good range of restaurants, with many having lovely settings that overlook the ocean. Several restaurants are popular for viewing sunsets. Be sure to make reservations for all major restaurants. Some of the area's best restaurants include:

IXTAPA

❏ **Beccofino:** *Veleros 7 and 8 at Plaza Marina Ixtapa, Tel. 553-1770. Open 10am to midnight.* Situated on the waterfront, this elegant and romantic northern Italian restaurant continues as one of the most popular restaurants in the area. Offers outstanding selections of seafood dishes and pastas. Try the chicken cacciatore, salmon ravioli, or fish fillet in black butter and rosemary.

❑ **Villa de la Selva:** *Paseo de la Roca, just beyond the Las Brisas Hotel, Tel. 553-0362. Open 6pm to 1am.* Take in the lovely view and spectacular sunsets from this romantic terraced hilltop restaurant that once served as the villa of a former Mexican president. Serves excellent international dishes, especially seafood.

❑ **El Galeón:** *Plaza Marina Ixtapa, Tel. 553-2150. Open 9am to midnight.* Offers excellent Mexican-style seafood dishes in an interesting nautical and outdoor setting along the waterfront.

ZIHUATANEJO

❑ **Coconuts:** *Agustín Ramírez 1, Tel. 554-2518. Open 12noon to 4pm and 6pm to 11pm.* Closed mid-July to mid-October. Housed in one of the town's oldest buildings, this garden restaurant offers a wide range of excellent dishes with an emphasis on inventive seafood dishes. Consistently one of the area's top restaurants. If you plan on dinner, come early to first check out the owner's attractive Coco Cabaña folk art and handicraft shop behind the restaurant.

❑ **Kau Kan:** *Carretera Escénica, Playa la Ropa Lote 7, Tel. 554-8446.* Boasting a wonderful view of Zihuatanejo Bay, this is one of the area's most elegant restaurants. Chef Ricardo Rodriquez, formerly with Casa Que Canta, offers a very inventive menu of seafood dishes. Try the stingray in black butter, lobster patata, or mahi-mahi carpaccio, although everything here tends to be good.

❑ **Villa Del Sol:** *Village del Sol Hotel, Playa la Ropa, Tel. 554-2239. Open 8:30am to 10:30pm.* Serves excellent dishes in a charming setting with a view of the beach. Try the fettuccine with seafood, smoked tuna, or duck. End your dinner with an excellent citrus creme brulee with coconut ice cream.

❑ **La Casa Que Canta:** *La Casa Que Canta Hotel, between La Playa la Ropa and Playa La Madera, Tel. 555-7030. Open 7am to 10:30pm.* Somewhat hard to find because of the lack of signs, this terraced restaurant has a lovely view of the bay and beaches. While the dishes here are normally excellent, especially the recommended seafood specialties, a busy night can result in a disappointing dining experience, from poor service to cold dishes. Come early to avoid the crowds and to shop in the small but lovely hotel boutique with its fine selection of ceramics.

❑ **Chez Paul's:** *Avenida Benito Juárez, Tel. 554-6528. Open 2pm to midnight.* The delightful Swiss owner-chef produces excellent seafood dishes for discriminating diners. Especially popular with locals and some visitors in the know. Famous for its fresh artichokes and shrimp in dill sauce.

Enjoying Your Stay

Ixtapa and Zihuatanejo are all about beaches and resort-related activities. Their rather subdued nightlife pales in comparison to Acapulco. Most activities tend to be centered in Ixtapa.

BEACHES

Ixtapa and Zihuatanejo are blessed with many fine beaches. The most popular ones are:

ZIHUATANEJO

❑ **Playa La Ropa:** Located on the east side of Zihuatanejo Bay, this beach serves three major hotels: Hotel Paraiso Real, Villa Del Sol, and Villa Mexicana Zihuatanejo. Considered by some beach lovers to be one of the most beautiful beaches in Mexico.

❑ **Playa La Madera:** On the north side of Zihuatanejo Bay, it serves the following hotels: Brisas de Mar, Bungalows Pacificos, Irma, and Villas Miramar.

❑ **Playa Principal:** *West of Playa la Madera and in front of the town square.* This is where you can see fisherman depart for sea at night and return early in the morning with their catches.

❑ **Playa Las Gatas:** Located on the south side of Zihuatanejo Bay and southwest of Playa La Ropa. Popular for sunbathing, swimming, snorkeling, and diving.

IXTAPA

❑ **Playa Del Palmar:** This is Ixtapa's two-mile long beach that services all the major hotels, from Posada Real Ixtapa in the west to Bárcelo Ixtapa Beach in the east.

❑ **Playa Vista Hermosa:** Located south of Playa Del Palmar on a cove between two tall rock formations, this beach is primarily accessible from the Las Brisas Ixtapa Hotel.

❑ **Playa Linda and Playa Quieta:** Located about five miles northwest of Ixtapa's"hotel zone," these two beaches face Ixtapa Island. Playa Linda, known as the "Beautiful Beach" of white sand located in a jungle and coconut plantation, is the jumping-off point for taking a water taxi to Ixtapa Island. Both Playa Linda and Playa Quieta serve the Club Med, El Capricho, Meliá Azul, and Qualton Club hotels.

❑ **Ixtapa Island:** Located less than a mile offshore of Playa Linda, water taxis depart for this lovely island every 10 minutes between 11:30am and 5pm (roundtrip fare is US$2). The island is popular for swimming, snorkeling, and diving. The most popular beaches here are Playa Cuachalalate, Playa Varadero, Playa Coral, and Playa Carey.

SPORTS

As a major resort destination, Ixtapa and Zihuatanejo offer a full range of sports opportunities. These include:

❑ **Golf courses:** The area has 18-hole championship golf courses: Club de Golf Marina Ixtapa (Tel. 553-1410) and Palma Real Golf Club (Tel. 553-1062). Expect to spend $65 to $85 for greens fees, cart, and caddie.

❑ **Tennis:** All major hotels and golf clubs in Ixtapa have tennis courts. Court fees run $10-12.

❑ **Scuba diving:** The area has numerous dive sites. Equipment rentals, guided dives, and instruction are readily available. Contact the **Zihuatanejo Scuba Center** at the Centro Comercial Ixtapa (Tel. 554-3873; Fax 554-2147; website: www.divemexico .com) for more information.

❑ **Water sports:** Most beaches have vendors offering a variety of water sports options, from parasailing, windsurfing, and waterskiing to Hobie Cats and banana-boat rides.

❑ **Sportfishing:** Several companies offer shallow and deep sea sportfishing opportunities. For more information, contact **Whisky Water World** (Tel. 554-0147; website: www.ixtapa-sportfishing.com), **Cooperative de Pescadores** (Tel. 554-2056), Cooperative Benito Juárez (Tel. 554-3758), or your hotel. **Aeromexico Vacations** (800-245-8585) and U.S.-owned **Ixtapa Sportfishing Charters** (Tel. 570-688-9466; website: www.ixtapa sportfishing.com) offer sportfishing packages.

❑ **Horseback riding:** Playa Linda (**Rancho Playa Linda**, Tel. 554-3085) and the tour company **VIPSA** (Tel. 553-2214) offer horseback riding opportunities.

NIGHTLIFE

Nightlife in this area is somewhat subdued, with most bars and discos found at the major hotels in Ixtapa. Zihuatanejo is relatively quiet,, with evening activities ending by midnight. Since the area especially appeals to couples, a night on the town often involves finding an excellent restaurant with a romantic view of the bay. However, the towns do have a few discos for the dance crowds:

❑ **Christine:** *Krystal Hotel, Ixtapa, Tel. 553-0333. 10pm to 4am.* This is the area's biggest, best, and most expensive disco.

❑ **Carlos 'n' Charlie's:** *Located on Playa el Palmar, next to the Posada Real Hotel, Ixtapa, Tel. 553-0085.* A popular restaurant that has a raised platform for disco dancing at the beach.

❑ **D'Latino:** *Corner of Nicolas Bravo and Guerrero. Open from 10pm.* This is Zihuatanejo's only disco that is more like an inexpensive bar. Popular with locals who liven up the place with the latest salsa and Latin rhythms.

❑ **Señor Frog's:** *Plaza La Puerta, Ixtapa, Tel. 553-0272. Open from 3pm.* Part of a popular international chain of restaurant-bars, this somewhat rowdy place is known for its heavy drinking and dancing crowd.

❑ **Los Mandiles:** *Located behind Señor Frog's in the Centro Comercial, Ixtapa, Tel. 553-0379.* This combination restaurant, bar, and disco has an open-air dance floor on the upper level.

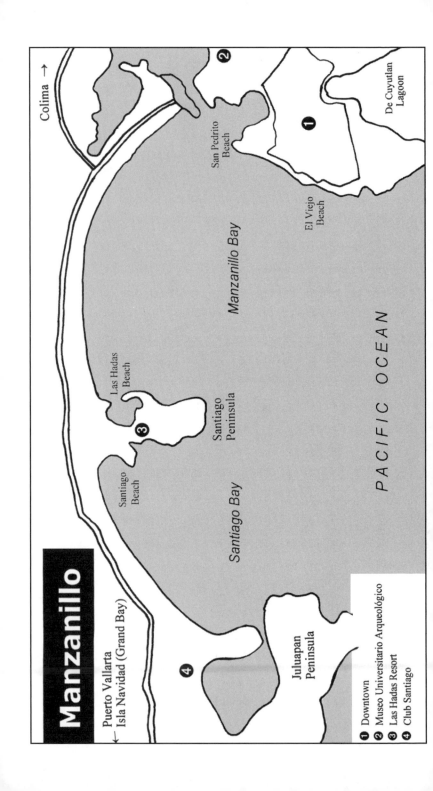

8

Manzanillo

I F YOU ARE DRIVING FROM Ixtapa-Zihuatanejo to
Puerto Vallarta, Manzanillo is a good place to overnight
or spend a couple of leisurely days enjoying this area's
many outdoor pleasures. Between Ixtapa-Zihuatanejo and
Manzanillo it's a long and tiring seven- to eight-hour
drive along a meandering two-lane coastal road. But once you
arrive, you're rewarded with a very quiet and laid-back resort
community that's home to many expatriate retirees who own
condos and timeshare units and who seem preoccupied with
the city's many beaches, golf courses, and water sports activities.

Laid-Back and Lonely

As you will quickly discover, this community of over 100,000
people is rather subdued in comparison to other more exuberant west coast resorts. Located along Mexico's Golden Riviera
and boasting lovely bays, beaches, and lagoons, Manzanillo is a
popular destination for sports enthusiasts, beach lovers, and
honeymooners. It's especially important to the regional economy
because of its industrial port facilities, which are linked by rail

to the area's agricultural hinterland. It's also famous for its naval base, international fishing tournaments, and the early 1980s Bo Derek and Dudley Moore movie 10.

Manzanillo can be a pleasant surprise for many visitors who are expecting a typical glitzy west coast resort community on the par of Acapulco or Puerto Vallarta. You won't find it here. Nor will you find many jet-setters heading to this area. Manzanillo especially appeals to individuals interested in beach and sports activities.

An Arrested and Fading Star

Manzanillo is justly famous for its crescent-shaped bay, long wide beaches, and excellent diving sites, sailfishing, and golf courses. It's known as the "Sailfish Capital of the World" because of its popular national and international fishing competition which takes place in November and February. However, this community has been in a state of arrested tourism development, even decline, for nearly a decade as more and more people bypass Manzanillo for the more entertaining and modern resort of Puerto Vallarta to the northwest. With fewer direct flights coming into Manzanillo from the United States and Canada, not many tourists arrive here by air, especially compared to a decade ago. Those who do come are primarily interested in the beaches, golf, and sailfishing. As a result, you don't feel you're in a big tourist center.

❑ This laid-back resort community is home to many expatriate retirees who own condos and play golf.

❑ Manzanillo is especially important to the regional economy because of its industrial port facilities.

❑ Manzanillo is known as the "Sailfish Capital of the World." It hosts annual international fishing competitions.

❑ Visitors primarily come here for the beaches, golf, and sailfishing.

❑ Many resorts now offer all-inclusive deals which hurt many local restaurants.

Within the past few years, more and more budget travelers have arrived on charter flights – especially Canadians on special all-inclusive package deals. In fact, some locals dependent on the tourist trade complain about such groups – they spend little money once they arrive in Manzanillo. Since many hotels now offer all-inclusive deals, many local restaurants understandably suffer from the lack of tourists who would normally venture outside their hotels for dining. Consequently, don't expect to find many great local restaurants inside or outside the hotels.

Getting to Know You

Manzanillo is primarily a quiet resort community, industrial center, and major port. The immediate area of this community consists of two towns with two bays – Manzanillo on the east and Santiago on the west – separated by the Santiago Peninsula, which is primarily the property of the distinctive white and pink Las Hadas resort. The whole beachfront

area, much of which is known as the Zona Hotelera (Resort Zone), runs for about 10 miles, from central Manzanillo to the southern tip of Santiago (Peninsula de Juluapan). The major hotels and restaurants begin just north of the town center (La Posada Hotel), circle Manzanillo Bay, and continue to the center of Santiago Bay (Fiesta Mexicana). Most resort activities are centered in the Manzanillo Bay area. The Santiago area is much less developed, with only a couple of major resorts.

Manzanillo's busy downtown area, centered around the Jardin, or town square, has very little of interest to visitors beyond encountering a few souvenir street vendors, seeing its working seaport, and visiting the nearby **Museo Universitario Arqueológico.** The museum displays more than 5,000 artifacts from the area.

For many visitors, Manzanillo is the perfect place to just relax and get away from everything. The community is so laid back that shops often close early and you may have difficulty finding someone working at the front desk of your hotel. For others, this is a boring place best driven through on the way to nearby Colima (60 miles northeast) or Puerta Vallarta (160 miles northwest).

One of the major developments taking place in this area is the huge Isla Navidad resort complex (www.islaresort.com.mx/history.htm) located about 50 miles north of Manzanillo or 20 miles north of the Manzanillo international airport. This gorgeous 1,230-acre resort seems to spring out of nowhere with its carefully manicured lawns, 27-hole golf course, marina, Grand Bay Hotel, and other amenities associated with five-star resorts. It's definitely one of Mexico's top five properties, and it ranks high on most lists of the best resorts in the world. Upscale travelers in search of a unique resort experience – completely self-contained with nothing nearby – increasingly shift their attention to this resort complex rather than stay at the aging hotels and less upscale resorts in Manzanillo. In fact, if you decide to stay in the Manzanillo area, you may want to select the unique Isla Navidad Resort/Grand Bay Hotel rather than a place in the city of Manzanillo.

Resources on the Web

In preparation for your visit to the Manzanillo area, check out these websites for useful information on the area:

- **Go Manzanillo**   www.gomanzanillo.com
- **Manzanillo Mexico**   http://manzanillomexico.com
- **Go2 Manzanillo**   www.go2manzanillo.com

Once you arrive in Manzanillo, or even before, you may want to get a copy of Susan Dearing's 150-page tourist guide, *Manzanillo and the State of Colima: Facts, Tips, and Day Trips*. Information on this book can be found on the Go Manzanillo website: www.gomanzanillo.com/guidebook/index.htm.

Shopping Manzanillo

Manzanillo offers very little interesting shopping for visitors. Most shops are open Monday through Saturday from 10am to 2pm and 4pm to 8pm; many are open on Sunday from 10am to 2pm. One of the best shops in Manzanillo is **Galeria Siles** (Tel. 32000, ext. 606) at the Hotel Sierra Manzanillo (Av. de la Audiencia 1, Playa La Audiencia). Operated by long-time resident Carmen Siles Grifing, the shop includes good quality jewelry and some bronze art pieces. The big bright blue two-level **Las Primaveras** (Juárez 40 in Santiago) includes a large collection of varying quality ceramic tiles, figures, and pots along with glassware and papier-mâché figures. The **Plaza Manzanillo**, the largest mall in the Hotel Zone, includes several handicraft, beachwear, and shoe and accessory shops.

Accommodations

Manzanillo offers a good range of resort accommodations. Most major hotels and resorts are found along the beach fronting Manzanillo Bay and a few others are located along Santiago Bay. The very best resorts for the Manzanillo area include these two properties:

❑ **Grand Bay:** *Puerto De La Navidad, Isla Navidad, Jalisco 48987, Mexico, Tel. (52-315) 355-5050, Fax (52-315) 355-6071. Toll-free from the US & Canada, 888-472-6229. Website: www.grandbay.com.* Technically located in Puerto De La Navidad, which you may not find on many maps, Grand Bay is a short drive from Manzanillo – about 30 minutes north of the Manzanillo airport – and worth every minute of the drive. Without a doubt, Grand Bay provides the most luxurious accommodations in or close by Manzanillo. Drive onto the property and at once you feel you are entering a grand tropical estate. Grand Bay is actually a golf, marina, and beach resort – the centerpiece of the most exclusive community on Mexico's Pacific Gold Coast. The gated community embraces multimillion-dollar estates, a shopping village, and protected natural areas. Fountain-filled plazas and colonnaded terraces reflect the heritage of colonial Mexico. Thirty-three elegant suites include three hillside retreats which share a private pool and garden. The 158 oversized guestrooms each have a sitting area, balcony, marble bath, and dramatic water views. Three casual and formal restaurants combine classic culinary techniques with bold local flavors. Fitness Center; Recreational Facilities include three Swimming Pools and Ocean Beaches; Tennis; Championship Golf Course; Yachting/Fishing from the Marina.

❑ **Las Hadas Golf Resort & Marina:** *Av. Vista Hermosa s/n, Peninsula de Santiago, Manzanillo, Colima 28867, Mexico, Tel. (52-314) 331-0101, Fax (52-314) 331-0121. Toll-free from U.S. or Canada, 888-559-4329. E-mail: lashadas@brisas.com.mx. Website: www.brisas.com.mx.* A setting out of the Arabian Nights, the Moorish inspired architecture of Las Hadas provides a fairytale setting located about 28 miles from the international airport and 30 minutes from downtown Manzanillo. The 234 guestrooms and suites, each with a private terrace or balcony, are relatively spacious and attractive. However, throughout the property, both in public spaces and in the guestrooms there were empty areas, such as niches, that yearned to be filled with pottery or something decorative. *Legazpi* serves Italian and Mediterranean style dishes. *Los Delfines* offers seafood and steaks in a spacious seaside "palapa" with a spectacular view of Las Hadas Bay. *El Terral* offers Mexican and international cuisine, and *El Palmar*, situated poolside, offers casual dining from a Mexican and Continental menu. Recreational Facilities include Beach and Pools; Tennis & Golf; and Marina; Conference/Banquet Facilities.

Also worth considering are these two large all-inclusive resorts:

❑ **Karmina Palace:** *Av. Vista Hermosa 13, Fracc. Peninsula de Santiago, Santiago, Colima 28200, Mexico, Tel. (52-314) 334-1313, Fax (52-314) 334-1915.*

❑ **Hotel Sierra Manzanillo:** *Av. de la Audiencia 1, Playa La Audiencia, Manzanillo 28200, Tel. (52-314) 333-2000 or 800-448-5028 or Fax (52-314) 333-2272.*

For a very special resort experience, drive northeast toward Colima and stay at the fabulous all-inclusive Amanresort – **Mahakua: Hacienda de San Antonio** – a restored 19th century hacienda (Municipio de Comal, CP 28450, Colima, Tel. (52-312) 313-4411 or Fax (52-312) 314-3727, E-mail: hacienda@mahakua. com.mx). But expect to pay from US$900 to US$1,600 per night for this unique experience.

Restaurants

Most visitors who stay at the all-inclusive resorts do not go out to eat. That's unfortunate since Manzanillo has several good restaurants. Many are patronized by local expatriates who know where to go for both a great view and excellent food. Some of the area's best restaurants include:

❑ **L'Recif:** *Cerro del Cenicero s/n, El Naranjo, Condominio Vida del Mar, Peninsula de Juluapan, Tel. 335-0900. Open noon to midnight. Closed May to October.* Nicely located on a cliff overlooking the ocean, this is a great place to have drinks or dine alfresco as the sun sets. But get here early, around 6:30pm, if you want to catch the lovely sunset. Try the mahi-mahi with dill and pepper sauce, fish in blackened butter, or the beef carpaccio.

❑ **Legazpi:** *Las Hadas, Av. de los Riscos, Zona Hotelera, Santiago Peninsula, Tel. 334-0101. Open daily, 7pm to 11:30pm, during high season; open Tuesday, Thursday, and Saturday during low season.* This is the city's most elegant restaurant. Serves excellent Continental cuisine with a nice view of the city and bay. Try the grilled salmon or roast duck.

❑ **Toscana:** *Blvd. Miguel de la Madrid 3177, Zona Hotelera, Tel. 333-2515.* Very popular with the local expatriate community (represents the remnants of the popular but now defunct Willy's), this oceanfront Italian restaurant turns out lots of good fish dishes. Try the grouper or mahi-mahi.

Enjoying Your Stay

This is a laid-back resort community where everyone seems to be at the beaches, on the golf courses, or engaged in some type of water sports, from windsurfing and snorkeling to scuba diving and sportfishing. Information on the full range of activities is available through the major hotels and tour companies.

BEACHES

The area's most popular beaches are located around Manzanillo Bay and Santiago Bay. They include:

- Playa las Brisas
- Playa Azul
- Playa Santiago
- Playa la Audiencia
- Playa Miramar

DIVING

Divers should check out this website for information on the many excellent diving opportunities in the area:

- Dive Manzanillo   www.divemanzanillo.com

SPORTFISHING

Manzanillo is a great place for sportfishing, with sailfish, marlin, dorado, rooster fish, and tuna being the major catches. It also hosts the international sailfishing competition in November. Contact **Ocean Pacific Adventures** for deep sea fishing charters and tours: Tel./Fax (52-314) 335-0605 or 357-0717 (cell); E-mail: fish@bay.net.mx.

GOLFING

Golfers will find excellent golf courses at **La Mantarraya Golf Course** at the Las Hadas resort (18 holes – Tel. 331-0101), **Isla Navidad** (27 holes – Tel. 335-6439), and **Club Santiago** (9 holes – Tel. 335-0410).

NIGHTLIFE AND ENTERTAINMENT

While Manzanillo's nightlife is relatively tame compared to other major Pacific resort communities, you will find many places for live music and dancing. Check with your hotel for the current "in" spots. Some of the popular night spots include:

- **Colima Bay Café:** *Av. Audiencia Pacifico Blvd. Costero 921, Zona Hotelera, Tel. 333-1150.*

- **Carlos 'n' Charlie's:** *Av. Audiencia Cocoteros s/n, Tel. 334-0555.*

- **Tropigala:** *Blvd. Miguel de la Madrid Km 14, Zona Hotelera, Tel. 333-2474.*

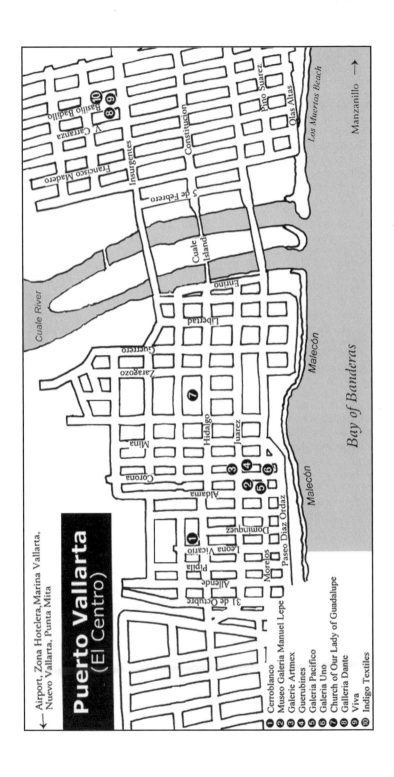

← Airport, Zona Hotelera, Marina Vallarta,
Nuevo Vallarta, Punta Mita

Puerto Vallarta
(El Centro)

Cuale River

Cuale Island

Bay of Banderas

Malecón

Los Muertos Beach

Manzanillo →

❶ Cerroblanco
❷ Museo Galeria Manuel Lepe
❸ Galerie Artmex
❹ Guerubines
❺ Galeria Pacifico
❻ Galeria Uno
❼ Church of Our Lady of Guadalupe
❽ Galleria Dante
❾ Viva
❿ Indigo Textiles

9

Puerto Vallarta

P UERTO VALLARTA IS ONE of Mexico's real jewels. Selected by *Condé Nast Traveler* in 2001 as one of the world's top 10 destinations, Puerto Vallarta enjoys a delightful climate, beautiful beaches, a wonderful bay, a picturesque setting, and a terrific tourist infrastructure that attracts millions of visitors each year. From great hotels and restaurants to tempting shopping, outdoor sports, ecotourism, and evening entertainment, Puerto Vallarta seems to have it all. Whatever you do, don't miss this delightful place!

A Fabulous Destination

Puerto Vallarta has a very special place in our hearts. Indeed, we chose it as our honeymoon destination more than 25 years ago. Driving through narrow, winding roads and dodging goat herds on the roads, we encountered a somewhat sleepy but gorgeous beachside resort on a palm-lined Pacific coast. Made internationally famous by John Huston's 1964 movie *Night of the Iguana* starring Richard Burton, who was accompanied by Elizabeth Taylor, Puerto Vallarta has rightfully developed an enticing reputation for beauty, charm, and romance. While Mexicana Airlines first built an airport and inaugurated air service to the sleepy town in 1954, a paved highway first reached Puerto Vallarta in 1969, putting it within four hours driving distance from Guadalajara. In many respects, today's Puerto Vallarta is to Guadalajara what Acapulco is to Mexico City – its beachfront playground. On weekends Puerto Vallarta can get very crowded as visitors from Mexico's second largest city descend on Puerto Vallarta's many hotels, restaurants, and nightclubs. Puerto Vallarta of the mid-1970s was one of Mexico's up-and-coming destinations, similar to Acapulco in the 1950s.

❏ Puerto Vallarta has rightfully developed an enticing reputation for beauty, charm, and romance.

❏ Puerto Vallarta is to Guadalajara what Acapulco is to Mexico City – its beachfront playground.

❏ This community of 250,000 residents attracts over 2 million visitors a year.

❏ Hotels, condos, time-share units, and multi-million-dollar villas abound along a sprawling coastline that runs for more than 70 miles from south to north.

❏ Puerto Vallarta is reputed to be Mexico's second largest art market.

How times and the tourist infrastructure have changed! Today Puerto Vallarta is a community of 250,000 residents that attracts more than 2 million visitors a year. It's also home to hundreds of U.S. and Canadian expatriates who have settled here permanently or return seasonally to reclaim their choice properties. The city still remains friendly and charming, but it's also a bustling and sophisticated resort community offering a full range of holiday pleasures. It remains a very special place blessed by great weather, wonderful activities, romantic settings, intriguing art, and many upscale travelers and expatriates who spend a great deal of money on the many treasures and pleasures of this community. Hotels, condos, timeshare units, and multi-million-dollar villas abound along a sprawling coastline that runs from south of the city to Punta de Mita in the north – an area stretching for more than 70 miles. Beautiful white sand beaches, secluded coves, towering cliffs, and swaying palm trees set within both an old colonial town of white stucco buildings and cobblestone streets and a modern urban resort community make Puerto Vallarta one of Mexico's most attractive destinations. If you are like many others who have discovered this delightful place, Puerto Vallarta will most likely become one of your favorite destinations. While the tabloids covering Richard Burton's and Elizabeth Taylor's sizzling affair may have initially put Puerto Vallarta on the international tourist map, today this city offers a full range of attractions that keep visitors coming back to this seductive resort community.

Getting to Know You

Located 175 northwest of Manzanillo, 260 miles west of Guadalajara, and 720 northwest of Mexico City, Puerto Vallarta lies along Mexico's largest natural bay, Bahia de Banderas, which stretches for nearly 100 miles. It's a very pretty setting which still has a friendly small town atmosphere. The city is ringed by lush mountains and lovely beaches, paved with cobblestone streets, and accented with colorful bougainvillea, a landmark cathedral, and attractive whitewashed buildings with red tile roofs. While traffic and crowds can be heavy, especially during the high season, the city is relatively easy to navigate.

Puerto Vallarta is divided into several sections. The center of the city (**El Centro**), or downtown area, consists of two adjacent north-south neighborhoods (Playa los Muertos area) bisected by a river, the Cuale River (Río Cuale). Each has its own character – the north is more commercial while the south is more laid back. Often congested, this whole area is best covered on foot. The neighborhood immediately to the north of the river, which runs about 12 blocks northeast and five blocks east, is known as **Old Town Vallarta** (Viego Vallarta). You can't miss this area since it is noted for its cobblestone one-way streets; the popular ocean boardwalk, or *malecón*, lined with tall palm trees

and unexpectedly accented with a fascinating collection of famous bronze statues (by noted artists Ramiz Barquet, Alejandro Colunga, and Sergio Bustamante); Guadalupe Church with its photogenic crown top that symbolizes the city; "Gringo Gulch" which was a popular residential area for U.S. expatriates in the 1950s and 1960s; Casa Kimberly (Calle Zaragonza 445) where Liz Taylor and Richard Burton carried on their steamy affair; and numerous galleries, shops, restaurants, and a large handicraft market. It's best to start covering this area at the northern end – intersection of Diaz Ordáz and 31 de Octubre streets. If you're driving, you may be able to find parking on one of the side streets around this area. From here, walk southwest along the *malecón* until it merges into Calle Morelos which soon leads to the main town square, Plaza de Armas. Immediately to the east of the square is the Palacio Municipal (City Hall) and the famous church of Our Lady of Guadalupe (La Iglesia de Nuestra Señora de Guadalupe). The two main parallel streets that run northeast from the river, Calle Morelos and Juárez, as well as several east-west streets linked to these main streets, include many shops of interest to visitors.

The El Centro area immediately to the south of the Cuale River is known as the **Zona Romántica** (also referred to as Olas Altas and the South Side). Extending approximately eight blocks southwest, this is the city's bohemian neighborhood which boasts the area's most popular beach, Playa los Muertos (Beach of the Dead). Adjacent to Playa Olas Altas, this wide beach is

lined with sunbathers, water sports enthusiasts, eateries, strolling vendors, and thatched-roof *palapas*. This also is a popular center for budget travelers who come here to find inexpensive accommodations and restaurants, lively bars and cafes, and lots of fun beach action. This area also includes several excellent shops. The main streets are Insurgentes, Ignacio Vallarta, and Olas Altas. The best shops and restaurants tend to be concentrated along Basilio Badillo Street.

Lying between these two neighborhoods is the long and narrow **Cuale River Island**, which is in the middle of the Río Cuale. This five-acre island includes lovely botanical gardens, the Río Cuale Museum of Anthropology, the Cultural Center, and several market stalls and small restaurants, including three of Puerto Vallarta's most popular restaurants – Le Bistro, Oscar's, and The River Cafe.

Once you leave the downtown area, you also leave much of the charm and beauty of old Puerto Vallarta. North of Old Town Vallarta is the **Hotel Zone** (Zona Hotelera), which encompasses several beaches and major four- and five-star hotels (Krystal Vallarta, Fiesta Americana, La Jolla de Mismaloya, Continental Plaza Beach and Tennis Club) and extends to the marina and cruise ship terminal.

Marina Vallarta is at the north end of the Hotel Zone and just south of the airport. Self-contained and brimming with resort services, this lovely well-planned community includes an 18-hole golf course, a water park, a well-protected 555-slip marina filled with pricey yachts, two shopping centers, art galleries, condominiums, timeshare units, a cruise terminal, restaurants, a park, and several luxury hotels and resorts, including the Marriott Casa Magna, Westin Regina, and the Meliá Puerto Vallarta.

Farther north of Marina Vallarta and the airport (eight miles north of the downtown area), but still along the expansive Banderas Bay, is **Nuevo Vallarta**. This is a well planned upscale resort community of oceanfront homes and condominiums on canals that connect to the bay. It also includes several all-inclusive resorts. However, there is very little here in terms of shopping or restaurants.

Farther north is an even more exclusive resort development, **Punta de Mita**. Lying at the northern end of Bandera Bay, this area includes a golf course, the luxurious Four Seasons Resort, and numerous private villas. This area is expected to attract even more luxury resorts and golf courses in the near future.

Several hotels, resorts, exclusive residential communities, including villas of the "rich and famous," and beaches also are found to the south of the city around Conchas Chinas and Playa Mismaloya. However, most of Puerto Vallarta's new resort developments are to the north of the city.

As many visitors quickly discover, there's a different Puerto Vallarta for different types of travelers. If you love golf and self-contained resort-style accommodations, you may want to confine your stay to the many properties and supporting services and activities found in the Hotel Zone, Marina Vallarta, Nuevo Vallarta, and Punta de Mita areas – all located north of the downtown area. These are Puerto Vallarta's planned resort communities, similar in concept and outcome to Ixtapa, Huatulco, and Cancun. But if you are looking for more local character, including charming chaos, plan to spend some time in the downtown areas of Old Town Vallarta and the Zona Romantica. You'll find many lively shops, restaurants, cafes, bars, beaches, and sites in this delightful section of the city. In fact, many of the city's best shops and restaurants are now found in these two adjacent neighborhoods.

Puerto Vallarta on the Web

Several websites focus on the many treasures and pleasures of Puerto Vallarta. For starters, visit these sites:

- **Virtual Vallarta**   www.virtualvallarta.com
- **Puerto Vallarta**   www.puertovallarta.net
- **Vallarta Online**   www.vallartaonline.com
- **All About Puerto Vallarta**   www.allaboutpuerto
                                            vallarta.com

- **Go to Vallarta**   www.go2vallarta.com
- **Puerto Vallarta**   www.puerto-vallarta.com
- **Inside Vallarta Magazine** www.hypermex.com
- **Insider's Guide to Vallarta** http://vallartainfo.com
- **Gay Guide to PV**   www.discoveryvallarta.com

Shopping Puerto Vallarta

Puerto Vallarta offers the best resort shopping in all of Mexico – far surpassing Acapulco and Cancun. Reflecting the type of visitors and residents who enjoy this attractive community, Puerto Vallarta abounds with quality shops offering everything from fine jewelry, clothes, textiles, and leather goods to art, handicrafts, home decorative items, and T-shirts. In fact, it's one of the best places in Mexico to engage in lifestyle shopping – great beaches, hotels, restaurants, and shops complement each other. If you love to shop in a resort setting which also has lots of local character, Puerto Vallarta will certainly become one of your favorite destinations in Mexico.

SERIOUS ART

While many products come from outside Puerto Vallarta, many others are produced locally. Indeed, Puerto Vallarta has a very active local art community – both Mexican and expatriate – that produces top quality paintings, sculptures, glassware, and crafts that are showcased in more than 20 local art galleries. Many galleries host monthly exhibitions and special events. Galleries are especially active during "Art Season" which runs from November to April. During this time galleries in the downtown area and at Marina Vallarta sponsor "Art Walks," which include cocktail exhibitions and outdoor entertainment. Be sure to pick up a map at the various Old Town galleries with "Art Walk" dates for the downtown area – usually every other Wednesday, from 6pm to 10pm, beginning October 31st and ending in late April. Marina Vallarta's "Marina Art Night" is usually held every third Friday of the month from 6pm to 10pm beginning in November and lasting until April. In fact, Puerto Vallarta is reputed to be Mexico's second largest art market. While one of Mexico's largest fine art communities is found in nearby Guadalajara, Puerto Vallarta is a much more important commercial center for artists than Guadalajara. Serious art buyers who have the means to buy top quality art, especially wealthy owners of villas and condominiums, are more likely to be found in Puerto Vallarta than in Guadalajara.

The **Huichol Indians**, who live in the hills north and east of Puerto Vallarta, produce distinctive yarn paintings and colorful beaded folk art (animal figures, masks, prayer bowls, plants) that are found in several area shops.

SHOPPING BASICS

Much of Puerto Vallarta's quality shopping is found in several shops along the major streets of El Centro, both the Old Town Vallarta and the Zona Romantica neighborhoods, and along the *malecón* in Marina Vallarta. You'll also find local handicraft markets and beach vendors offering varying quality handicrafts and souvenirs. Major hotels also will have a few quality shops offering jewelry, clothes, handicrafts, and gift items. But serious shoppers head for the many quality shops found in the downtown area and Marina Vallarta.

Most shops are open Monday through Saturday from 9am to 2pm and again from 4pm to 9pm. Several shops also are open on Sunday. Like elsewhere in Mexico, most shop prices are fixed, although many will offer a discount for cash. Be sure to bargain in the markets and with beach vendors – offer 40 to 50 percent of the initial asking price but expect to settle somewhere around 70 to 80 percent of that price.

OLD TOWN VALLARTA

We recommend starting near the northern end of this neighborhood and walk south along the main streets and side streets. Along the way you'll find many nice jewelry, handicraft, and fine art shops. You'll find the best shops along seven streets in this neighborhood – Leona Vicario, Juarez, Morelos, Aldama, Corona, Guerrero, and Libertad.

Leona Vicario is becoming the area's upscale shopping street. Look for **Cerroblanco** (Leona Vicario 226, Tel. 223-3546) for uniquely designed silver jewelry by San Miguel de Allende designer Pepe Cerroblanco; **Jades Maya** (Leona Vicario 226a, Tel. 222-0371, website: www.centramerica.com/jades) for beautiful jade jewelry, carved figures, and replicas of museum pieces; **Galerie des Artistes** (Leona Vicario 248, Tel. 223-0006) for an excellent collection of paintings, sculptures, and glasswork by several contemporary artists; and **Galeria Omar Alonso** (Leona Vicario 249) for photos. One of Puerto Vallarta's best restaurants is found at the eastern end of this street – **Café des Artistes** (Guadalupe Sanchez 740, Tel. 222-3228).

Juarez, which runs north and south, is one of this area's major thoroughfares. At the intersection of Leona Vicario, walk south along Juarez for several blocks. If you take some of the side streets east toward the *malecón*, you'll cross Morelos and encounter several interesting shops along the way. Along Juarez you'll find many intriguing shops. In particular, look for

Indigera (Juarez 628, Tel. 223-0800), a large arts and crafts shop; **Museo Galeria Manuel Lepe** (Juarez 533, Tel. 222-0515, website: www.manuellepe.com) for the colorful primitive paintings, posters, and folk art of beloved local artist Manuel Lepe; **Galeria Artmex** (Juarez 528, Tel. 222-7620), a huge ceramics shop which also includes rugs, mirrors, glass, and paintings; **Galeria Rosas Blancas** (Juarez 523, Tel. 222-1168) for an interesting collection of fine art and folk art; **Querubines** (Juarez 501-A, Tel. 222-2988) for an attractive collection of ceramics (big pieces), rugs, glassware, candles, textiles, dolls, and home decorative items; **Galeria Terranova** (Juarez 449) for a nice collection of antiques, including religious icons and paintings; and **Instituto de la Artesania Jalisciense** (Juarez 284, Tel. 331-3201, website: http://mexplaza. com.mx/artesania) for lots of arts and crafts from the state of Jalisco.

Morelos parallels Juarez one block to the west. Here you'll find several interesting art galleries. Also, be sure to explore several side streets that connect to Juarez, especially Josefa Ortiz de Dominguez, Aldama, Corona, Galeana, and Mina. Look for **Galeria Arte Latinoamericano** (Josefa Ortiz de Dominguez 155, Tel. 222-4406) for two floors of paintings and sculptures by 10 artists; **Galeria Pacifico** (Aldama 174, Tel. 222-1982, website: www.ArtMexico.com) for one of the finest selections of contemporary paintings and bronze sculptures in Puerto Vallarta, including the fabulous works of Ramiz Barquet (see his life-size bronze sculptures along the nearby *malecón*; **Galeria Uno** (Morelos 561, Tel. 222-0908, website: www.mexonline.com/ galeriauno.htm) for a delightful collection of paintings and bronze sculptures by 35 artists displayed in an inviting white stucco open gallery; **Majolica** (191 Corona) includes two rooms of nicely designed colorful ceramics; **Arte Magico Huichol** (Corona 179, Tel. 222-3077) includes an interesting collection of beaded art work produced by the Huichol Indians; **Hecho a Mano** (Zoragoza 160, Tel. 223-1455, website: www.hecho-amano.com) on the main plaza (En La Plaza Principal) includes a nice collection of interior design and home decorative items; and **Galeria de Olas** (Morelos 101-3B, Tel. 223-1045) for a nice collection of pottery from the Mata Ortiz community. At the southern tip of Old Town Vallarta is the **Mercado D'Artesanias** (at Libertad and Rodriguez, daily from 9am to 7pm), which includes many small stalls selling handicrafts, clothes, and accessories.

One block west of Morelos is the *malecón* which runs along Diaz Ordaz street. Look for **Sergio Bustamante** art gallery (Diaz Ordaz 542, Tel. 222-5480, website: http://sergiobustamante.com .mx), which includes the master artist's ceramic and papier-mâché figures, bronzes, and jewelry. But best of all, look across the street along the beach where you'll see Sergio Bustamante's fabulous life-size bronze sculpture, three men on a ladder, looking out to the ocean (photos on pages 73 and 205).

ZONA ROMANTICA

Located immediately south of Old Town Vallarta, across the Cuale River, this trendy area includes lots of good shopping for fine arts, crafts, clothing, jewelry, and home decorative items. The main shopping street here is **Basilio Badillo**. Some of the best shopping along this street include the following galleries and shops: **Galleria Dante** (Basilio Badillo 269, Tel. 222-2477, website: www.galeriadante.com), which features one of the area's largest collections of paintings and sculptures; **Patti Gallardo Eclectic Art** (Basilio Badillo 250, Tel. 222-5712) for a colorful and whimsical collection of paintings, rugs, furniture, jewelry, clothing, and metal sculptures; **Galeria Piramide** (Basilio Badillo 272, Tel. 222-3161) for an interested collection of Huichol handicrafts, masks, paintings, posters, pre-Columbian reproductions, and gift items; **Viva** (Basilio Badillo 274, Tel. 222-4078, website: www.vivacollection.com) for a terrific collection of jewelry, handbags, and accessories from 350 designers from all over the world; **Alba** (Basilio Badillo 276, Tel. 222-7494) for handmade bed linens, including many hand-painted items; and **Indigo Textiles** (Basilio Badillo 278, Tel. 223-0107, website: www.indigotextiles.com) for handmade pillows, bedspreads, and shawls from Guatamala, Mexico, India, and Indonesia.

Several other shops, restaurants, cafes, and bars are found along Ignacio Vallarta and Olas Altas streets. Look for **Azul Azul** (Ignacio L. Vallarta 228, Tel. 223-0060) for lanterns, ceramics, jewelry, paintings, and painted animals; **Nomada** (Ignacio L. Vallarta 176, Tel. 223-3710) for baskets, jewelry, and handbags; **San Miguel** (Ignacio L. Vallarta 236, Tel. 223-2345) for glass and art items; **Safari Accents** (224 Olas Altas, Tel. 233-2660) for attractive home furnishings; and **La Tienda** (122 Rodolfo Gomez, Tel. 222-1535) for furniture, antiques, and home accessories.

MARINA VALLARTA

This self-contained upscale resort community offers lifestyle shopping in a delightful setting. The area boasts two small shopping centers, **Plaza Neptuno** and **Plaza Marina**, that primarily service the local residents who occupy the many condominiums and timeshare units in Marina Vallarta. Open from 10am to 8pm (closed Sundays), they include a supermarket, banks, dry cleaners, florist, medical center, decorator shop, and several specialty stores. In **Plaza Neptuno**, look for **Andrea's Silver and Art** (Tel. 221-1761) for sterling silver jewelry; **Caprichoso** (Tel. 221-3067) for unique clothes and gift items; **Colleccion La Bohemia** (Tel. 221-2160) for local fashion items, including hand-painted Artwear, produced by Toody Walton; **Rodo Padilla** (Tel. 221-2246) for amusing ceramic sculptures, including Rodo Padilla's trademark and collectable laughing fat cowboys; and Tonatiuh (Tel. 221-2230) for attractive contemporary jewelry and handicrafts. **Plaza Marina** includes the attractive hand-crocheted lace and white dresses of designer Delia Cortez at **Vogue Vallarta** (Tel. 221-0557).

Several art galleries and craft shops are found along the *malecón* at **Marina Las Palmas II**. During the winter season several art galleries in this area sponsor festive monthly outdoor art events, such as the popular **"Marina Art Night"** (third Friday of the month), to showcase various exhibits. A few shops, such as **Galeria EM**, are open seven days a week. Some of the most interesting shops here include **Terracota** (Edificio Marina Sol 3, Malecón, Tel. 209-0453) for an attractive collection of ceramic plates, pots, and bowls as well as glassware and black pottery; **Galeria EM** (Marina La Palmas II, local 17, Tel. 221-1728, website: www.galeriaem. com) for beautiful stained-glass decorative art pieces by Estela Herrera and Mario Perez; **Art de las Americas** (Marina las Palmas II, Tel. 221-1985) for paintings and bronze sculptures by noted international and local artists as well as several emerging artists; and **Puerco Azul** (Marina Las Palmas II, Tel. 221-0594) for a nice collection of folk art, paintings, and tableware.

Best of the Best

FINE ART

❑ **Galeria Pacificio:** *Aldama 174, Old Town (Centro), Tel. 222-1982 or Fax 222-5502. E-mail: gary@pvnet.com.mx. Website: www.art mexico.com. Open Monday through Saturday, 10am to 2pm, 4pm to 8pm, and by appointment.* This is Puerto Vallarta's second oldest gallery (opened in 1987) and one of its best for top quality bronze sculptures and paintings. Owned and operated by seasoned art dealer Gary Thompson, the gallery currently represents five sculptors and 10 painters. The two-level gallery showcases many leading and promising artists. Includes the bronzes of local sculptor Ramiz Barquet as well as the works of several other noted local artists – Rogelio Diaz, Patrick Denoun, Gabriel Colunga, Brewster Brockman, and Meredy Volz. From November to April, the gallery sponsors well attended exhibitions every two weeks. During January, February, and March, the gallery sponsors walking art tours every Tuesday from 10am to 12noon. Led by Gary Thompson, the groups usually visit three to five local artist's studios as well as discuss Mexican art history and the current local art scene.

❑ **Galleria Dante:** *Basilio Badilla 269, Zona Romantica (Centro), Tel. 222-2477 or Fax 222-6284. E-mail: info@galleriadante.com. Website: www.galleriadante.com. Open Monday through Friday, 10am to 2pm and 3pm to 5pm and by appointment.* This 6,000-square foot gallery and sculpture garden represents nearly 60 artists each year. It regularly sponsors shows. Includes a nice selection of contemporary sculptures, reproductions of classical bronze sculptures, and abstract paintings.

❑ **Sergio Bustamante:** *Diaz Ordaz 542, Old Town (Centro), Tel. 222-5480. Website: http://sergiobustamante.com.mx.* This is a smaller version of the larger Sergio Bustamante galleries found in Mexico City and Guadalajara. Located across the street from the life-size beachfront bronze sculpture of three figures ascending a ladder – entitled *In Search of the Reason* (miniature versions less than 5 feet in height available for US$4,240) – this gallery showcases several of famed artist Sergio Bustamante's trademark pieces – ceramic and papier-mâché figures, bronzes, and jewelry. For a good overview of what to expect in this and other Bustamante galleries, be sure to visit his website, which includes a catalog of his many fascinating collections.

❑ **Galeria Uno:** *Morelos 561, Old Town (Centro), Tel. 222-0908. E-mail: galeriauno@pvnet.com.mx. Website: www.mexonline.com/galeriauno.htm. Open Monday through Saturday, 10am to 9pm.* This is Vallarta's oldest gallery. Representing nearly 35 artists, this inviting white stucco gallery showcases a nice collection of bronze sculptures as well as many contemporary paintings. The mobile animals by Daniel Palma are especially intriguing. Hosts frequent exhibitions and features different artists each week during the November to April Old Town Art Walk. **Arte de las Americas** is its sister art gallery on the Marina Vallarta Promenade.

❑ **Galeria EM:** *Marina La Palmas II (Marina Vallarta), local 17, Tel. 221-1728. E-mail: info@galeriaem.com. Website: www.galeriaem.com. Open daily, 10am to 9pm.* Workshop located nearby at Av. Fco. Medina Ascencio 2758. The talented husband-wife team of Estela Herrera and Mariano Pérez produces beautiful custom-made, stained-glass windows, doors, mirrors, bowls, and art pieces.

❑ **Galeria Arte Latinoamericano:** *Josefa Ortiz Dominguez 155, Old Town (Centro), Tel. 222-4407. Open Monday through Saturday,*

10am to 9pm. Specializes in Mexican contemporary paintings, sculptures, posters, etchings, and lithographs. Features the works of such noted local artists as Marta Gilbert, Fernando Sanchez, Maria Fernanda Matos, and Edith Palombi, as well as many artists from elsewhere in Mexico.

❑ **Galeria Rosas Blancas:** *523 Juarez, Old Town (Centro), Tel. 222-1168. Open Monday through Saturday, 9am to 9pm, and Sunday, 10am to 6pm.* This combination contemporary art gallery and art supply shop, with a large central courtyard, features several Mexican and local artists. Also operates the popular folk art shop next door, **Querubines**.

❑ **Galeria Artmex:** *Juarez 528, Old Town (Centro), Tel. 222-7620 or Fax 222-3007. E-mail: indigena@jal1.prodigy.net.mx. Open 10am to 3pm and 6pm to 9pm.* This combination art gallery, ceramics shop, and home decorative and handicraft emporium includes a wide selection of Huichol Indian art (yarn and bead works), ceremonial masks, Talavera ceramics, pre-Columbian replicas, religious figures, rugs, mirrors, and glassware. The upstairs area exhibits paintings of 10 permanent artists as well as presents changing exhibits of other artists.

❑ **Museo Galeria Manuel Lepe:** *Juarez 533, Old Town (Centro), Tel. 222-5515. E-mail: macella@manuellepe.com. Website: www.manuellepe.com.* Showcases the famous works ("naif" paintings) of talented local artist Manuel Lepe who died in 1984 at the age of 46. His joyful paintings, which are now primarily available in poster and print forms, are colorful, imaginative, and playful "primitive" scenes of Puerto Vallarta depicting smiling angels, children, buildings, boats, and the ocean. One of his most famous paintings is a fun mural of Puerto Vallarta on the second floor of the Palacio Municipal (City Hall). Operated by his daughter Marcella Lepe, the gallery offers Vallartan "naif" art, ceramics, jewelry, and other souvenirs.

ARTS, CRAFTS, AND HOME DECORATIVE

❑ **Galeria San Jacinto:** *Av. Mexico 1320, Loc 8 Esq. Nicaragua, Col. 5 de Diciembre, Tel. 222-2658 or Fax 222-0745. E-mail: sitex@hotmail.com. Website: www.galeriasanjacinto.com.mx.* This expansive two-level international gallery is jam-packed with arts, crafts, antiques, furniture, and home decorative items from Mexico, South America, Africa, and Asia. Everything here is nicely displaced and inviting to anyone interested in home decor. Look for doors, chests, and columns from India, ceramics and rugs from Morocco, and candlesticks and mirrors from Mexico. Also includes shops in the San Angel and Santa Fe sections of Mexico City.

❑ **Querubines:** *Juarez 501-A, Old Town (Centro), Tel/Fax 222-2988. Open Monday through Sunday, 10am to 9pm.* This delightful corner shop (at Galeana) is filled with quality arts, crafts, silver jewelry, rustic furniture, embroidered clothes, wool rugs, and decorative items from all over Mexico. Look for tin mirrors and lamps, hand-blown glass, Talavera pottery, Panama hats, straw bags, carved wooden masks, and Indian crafts.

❑ **Hecho a Mano:** *Zaragoza 160, Old Town (Centro), Tel. 223-1455 or Fax 222-2895. E-mail: hechoamanopv@pvnet.com.mx. Website: www.hecho-amano.com.* Located adjacent to the town square, this spacious and inviting shop includes a nice collection of home furnishings and accessory items – sofas, wicker furniture, candles and candlestick holders, metal art pieces (chickens, cacti, lamps, bird cages, pots, fish), wrought iron, placemats, baskets, and bowls as well as a large assortment of wood, clay, leather, straw, tin, and terracotta items.

❑ **Safari Accents:** *Olas Altas 224, Zona Romantica (Centro), Tel. 223-2660. Open daily from 10am to 11pm.* Offers an attractive collection of home furnishings, glassware, and reproduction paintings.

❑ **Galeria Artmex** (see description on page 214)

❑ **Arte Magico Huichol:** *Corona 179, Old Town (Centro), Tel. 222-3077.* If you're interested in the unique yarn and bead art work of the Huichol Indians, this shop includes a good selection of such items. Most items depict various animal figures.

ANTIQUES

❑ **Galeria Terranova:** *Juarez 449, Old Town (Centro).* This corner antique shop includes an interesting and eclectic collection of religious icons and figures, crucifixes, paintings, furniture, candlesticks, picture frames, Indian chests, and Balinese carvings.

JEWELRY

❑ **Cerroblanco:** *Leona Vicario 226, Old Town (Centro), Tel. 223-3546. E-mail: pepecerroblanco@hotmail.com.* If you're tired of seeing similar looking silver jewelry designs in Mexico, this shop may surprise you. Showcases the many unique modern silver jewelry designs of Pepe Cerrablanco (based in San Miguel de Allende). Includes many attractive necklaces, bracelets, rings, and earrings that incorporate semi-precious stones.

❑ **Viva:** *Basilio Badillo 274, Zona Romantica (Centro), Tel. 222-4078 or Fax 222-4850. E-mail: marysue@vivacollection.com. Website: www.vivacollection.com. Open daily, 10am to 10pm.* Operated by 15 women who search the world for beautiful jewelry, shoes, ballet slippers, espadrilles, handbags, sarongs, hats, and accessories, this stunning shop with beautiful displays includes a wonderful section of fashionable items in a very inviting setting. Primarily an international jewelry shop which features the creations of leading jewelry designers, such as Francesca Roman of Brazil and Van der Straeten of Paris. Offers many one-of-a-kind jewelry designs by young up-and-coming designers. Includes the works of 350 designers from around the globe. Offers many items from France and Spain as well as Majorca pearls.

❑ **Jades Maya:** *Leona Vicario 226a, Old Town (Centro), Tel. 222-0371 or Fax 222-0326. E-mail: jadesmaya@pvnet.com.mx. Website: www.centramerica.com/jades.* This attractive shop specializes in jade jewelry and carved figures. Includes replicas of jade carved museum pieces. The jade comes from a jade factory in Antiqua, Guatamala.

FABRICS AND LINENS

❑ **Alba:** *Basilio Badillo 276, Zona Romantica (Centro), Tel. 222-7494. E-mail: albastore@usa.net.* This small but attractive shop includes handmade and hand-painted bed linens, from sheets to pillow covers. Can purchase complete sets as well as order from available designs.

❑ **Indigo:** *Basilio Badillo 278, Zona Romantica (Centro), Tel. 223-0107. E-mail: indigopv@usa.net. Website: www.indigotextiles.com.* Offers handwoven and embroidered bedspreads, pillows, mosquito nets, and books from Mexico, Guatemala, India, and Indonesia.

Accommodations

Puerto Vallarta abounds with a good range of accommodations. Budget travelers like the Zona Romantica area. Most of the major four- and five-star hotels and resorts are found north of the downtown area in the Hotel Zone and Marina Vallarta. Some of Puerto Vallarta's very best properties include:

❑ **Marriott Casa Magna:** *Paseo De La Marina No. 5, Marina Vallarta, C.P. 48354, Puerto Vallarta, Jalisco, Mexico, Tel. (52-322) 221-0004, Fax (52-322) 221-0760. Toll-free from U.S. & Canada, 800-223-6388. Website: www.offshoreresorts.com.* Located in the Marina Vallarta complex, on the Bay of Banderas with the Sierra Madre Mountains as a backdrop, Marriott Casa Magna is one of Vallarta's largest and most glamorous hotels. The large, plant-filled lobby is hung with wrought iron chandeliers. The 433 spacious guestrooms, including 29 suites, feature private balconies and all the expected amenities. Guestrooms are decorated like those at most beach resorts, with floral bedspreads, tile floors, and a colorful print on the wall. A variety of restaurants offer a selection of cuisines and ambience. *Las Casitas* is a poolside and oceanfront grill that serves snacks and beverages in a casual atmosphere. *La Estancia*, overlooking the pool and ocean, serves a Mexican menu with a different dinner buffet every night. *Mikado*, a Japanese steakhouse, features Teppan-yaki cooking, sushi and other Japanese selections. *Champions Sports Bar*, an American sports theme restaurant/bar, combines casual dining, sports viewing, and dancing. Fitness Center; Full range of Resort Beach Activities; Golf Course; Marina; Conference/Banquet Facilities.

❑ **Camino Real Puerto Vallarta:** *Carretera Barra de Navidad km. 3.5, Playa Las Estacas S/N, 48300 Puerto Vallarta, Jal., Mexico, Tel. (52-322) 221-5000, Fax (52-322) 221-5400. Toll-free from the U.S. & Canada 800-996-7325. E-mail: reservaciones@pvr-caminoreal.com. Website: www.pvr-caminoreal.com.* Located 5 minutes south of town in a secluded cove, Camino Real is in a lovely setting between its own private beach and a green mountain backdrop. The main tower, opened in 1969 and completely remodeled in 1998, offers 250 spacious guestrooms and suites overlooking the Pacific. *The Club Tower*, the newer of the two buildings, offers 87 luxurious guestrooms – 41 feature a Jacuzzi sunken into the terrace or balcony – and the same gorgeous views of the Pacific. VIP service in the Club Tower includes complimentary American breakfast and afternoon cocktails and hors d'oeuvres. *Azulejos* is a casual restaurant serving Mexican and international dishes. *La Perla* is an award-winning gourmet restaurant featuring fine international and Mexican cuisine. *Finestra* is an Italian restaurant, and *La Brisa*, an open-air oceanside restaurant features fish caught fresh from the bay. Fitness Center; Open-Air and Beach Activities; Conference/Banquet Facilities.

❑ **Four Seasons Resort Punta Mita:** *Punta Mita, Bahía de Banderas, Nayarit 63734, Mexico, Tel. (52-322) 291-6000, Fax (52-322) 291-6060. Toll-free from the U.S. 800-332-3442 and from Canada 800-*

268-6282. Website: *www.fourseasons.com/puntamita*.Located 45 minutes northwest of Puerto Vallarta International Airport, Four Seasons Resort Punta Mita features 114 guestrooms, called casita rooms, and 26 suites. Guestrooms and suites provide more amenities than the guest ever thought he/she needed. The rooms are spacious; the beds are heavenly with comforters/down duvets that you snuggle into as you drift to sleep; oversized bathrooms with a deep soaking tub, separate glass-enclosed shower, double vanity with twin basins, and toilet in a separate enclosed area with telephone; and everything is plush and luxurious. All casitas and suites have an ocean view with a spacious terrace or balcony ideal for a romantic dinner. All suites have private plunge pools. *Aramara Restaurant*, the main restaurant, with an outdoor terrace, offers fine Nuevo Latino cuisine, plus a range of seafood and international dishes. *Ketsi Pool Restaurant and Bar*, an open-air restaurant with a traditional thatched roof, offers a wide variety of dishes in a casual setting. Fitness Center as well as a full range of resort/water activities including a private 18-hole Jack Nicklaus designed championship golf course with eight oceanside holes. Freeform pool with whirlpool in one of the most beautiful settings imaginable. The Apuane Spa utilizes the unique talents of the experienced Mexican massage staff, and the abundant local healing plants and minerals. An innovative menu of choices was created to convey a sense of place in this special setting. Tequila, used for some of the spa treatments, is said to be better outside the body than inside! Even though there is a professional overnight laundry service, a nice touch are laundry rooms provided for guests' use. A Cultural Center, located off the main lobby, offers books, videos, computers, Internet access, lectures and tours. A professionally supervised program called "Kids for All Seasons" is offered in the Spa with indoor and outdoor activities. A separate children's pool and play area is available. Guests interested in conservation can feel good knowing that The Four Seasons was designed with careful concern for the environment and constructed with several systems in place to conserve the resources of the area. Meeting/Banquet Facilities.

Restaurants

It doesn't get much better than dining in Puerto Vallarta, especially for lifestyle shoppers who enjoy combining great shopping with great restaurants! Boasting more than 250 restaurants, Puerto Vallarta is a wonderful place for excellent quality food, inventive dishes, and gorgeous restaurant views of the city, ocean, and sunsets. While seafood, or "Mariscos," tops the list for diners, the city offers an excellent range of local and international cuisines, including Italian, French, Greek, German, Japanese, and Chinese restaurants. Many experienced and award-winning international chefs can be found in several of Puerto Vallarta's fine kitchens. Some of Puerto Vallarta's best restaurants include:

❑ **Café des Artistes:** *Guadalupe Sanchez 740, Old Town (Centro), Tel. 222-3228. Website: www.cafedesartistes.com. Open 6pm to 10:30pm. Reservations are essential.* Truly a great restaurant that has received rave international reviews as one of the finest restaurants in all of Mexico. Award-winning owner-chef Thierry Blouet has turned dining into an artistic experience with his many signature dishes. Try the cream of prawn and pumpkin soup; filet of red snapper wrapped in black olives; grilled lamb chops with rosemary and Mexican spices; or roasted duck glazed with honey, soy, and ginger. Nicely located at the end of Puerto Vallarta's most upscale shopping street with a beautiful ocean view.

❑ **Trio:** *Guerrero 264, Old Town (Centro), Tel. 222-2196. Open 12noon to 4pm and 6pm to 12am.* Operated by popular German chef Bernhard Güth, who came to Puerto Vallarta in 1994 after working in some of the best restaurants in Milan, New York, and London. This attractive multi-level eatery in a colonial townhouse serves outstanding Mediterranean cuisine with a Mexican flair. Try the shrimp from San Blas on broiled Nopal cactus and fennel tomato vinaigrette; chile-roasted red snapper fillet over ratatouille and lime cilantro sauce; or veal scallops with gnocchi, sage, broccoli, almonds, and marsala sauce.

❑ **Café Maximillian:** *Olas Altas 380-B, Zona Romantica (Centro), Tel. 223-0760. Open 6pm to 11pm. Closed Sundays.* Located in the popular Los Muertos Beach area, this charming restaurant features traditional Austrian and European dishes with Mexican influences. Try the braised baby lamb strips with rosemary and chile poblano; sauteed squid and San Blas shrimp; Zwiebelrostbraten; or Rahmschnitzel.

❑ **Daiquiri Dick's:** *Olas Altas 314, Zona Romantica (Centro), Tel. 222-0566. Website: www.ddpv.com. Open 12noon to 10:30pm.* Located along Los Muertos Beach, this sophisticated contemporary restaurant includes an eclectic menu of Mexican, American, Thai, Indian, and Japanese dishes. Try the fillet of Huachinango in "Santa Fe Rubdown"; lobster tacos; "Yellow Bowl" of pistachio chicken and polenta; or BBQ spareribs. Top it all off with the house specialty dessert – key lime pie!

❑ **The River Café:** *Isla Rio Cuale Local 4, Tel. 223-0788. Open 9am to 11:30pm.* Located in a lovely setting on Cuale Island, this elegant and romantic restaurant offers great food, atmosphere, and service. Try the rainbow shrimp; mahi mahi; rack of lamb; or mignon supreme. If you're not in a romantic mood, try the bar.

❑ **de Santos:** *Morelos 771, Old Town (Centro), Tel. 223-3052. Open 5pm to 1am.* This trendy contemporary bar, lounge, and restaurant serves excellent Mediterranean cuisine in an attractive white chapel setting. Try the pizza, lobster ravioli, roasted ginger chicken breast, or de Santos rib eye.

❑ **Porto Bello:** *On the malecón at Marina Vallarta. Marina Sol, Local 7, Tel. 221-0003. Open 12noon to 11pm.* This elegant Italian restaurant offers both indoor and outdoor dining options (dine outdoors for a nice view of Marina Vallarta). Try the excellent lasagna, cannelloni, Fusilli Porto Bello with artichokes, black olives, and basil; Vitello Porto Bello in a white cream sauce; or Pollo Francés.

❑ **Don Pedro's:** *Marlin 2, Sayulita, Nayarit, Tel. 275-0229. Open 11am to 11pm.* This popular Mediterranean-style restaurant, located along the ocean 30 minutes north of Puerto Vallarta and under a giant thatched palapa, serves excellent cuisine with a Mexican flair. Chef and co-owner Nicholas Parrillo serves many unique dishes. Try the Italian thin-crust pizza; frutti di mare pasta; spring chicken; Pesce Portofino; or live Pacific lobster.

Enjoying Your Stay

From beaches, whale watching, and hiking in the Sierra Madre Mountains to diving, sportfishing, golfing, and bar hopping, Puerto Vallarta has lots of things to see and do even for the most jaded traveler. Indeed, this is Mexico's most varied community for travelers who want anything from pure relaxation to very active outdoor adventures.

SIGHTSEEING

Puerto Vallarta has a few interesting places for tourists in search of local history, architecture, and sights:

❑ **Malecón:** Puerto Vallarta has two interesting oceanfront boardwalks. The *malecón* in downtown Puerto Vallarta (parallels Diaz Ordaz Street for nearly 15 blocks) is a great place to stroll along the lively beach, view the bronze statues of several leading Mexican sculptors, enjoy beautiful sunsets, and browse the many shops, restaurants, and cafes lining Diaz Ordaz. The *malecón* at Marina Vallarta is lined with shops, art galleries, cafes, and restaurants facing a beautiful marina, another good place to catch lovely sunsets.

❑ **Gringo Gulch:** Located immediately north of the Cuale River, this was the residential center for U.S. expatriates in Puerto Vallarta during the 1950s and 1960s. It's the site of **Casa Kimberly** (Calle Zaragoza 445, Old Town, Tel. 222-1336), Elizabeth Taylor's home, which was connected by an overhead bridge to Richard Burton's home. The house includes Elizabeth Taylor's possessions which were sold with the house during the late 1980s. You can tour both Casa Kimberly and Richard Burton's home daily from 9am to 6pm. Admission $6.

❑ **Our Lady of Guadalupe (La Iglesia de Nuestra Señora de Guadalupe):** Located one block east of the zócalo on Calle Hidalgo in the Old Town, this is the city's famous landmark and symbol – the church with the crown on top, a replica of the crown worn by the empress of Mexico, Carlota, in the 1860s.

❑ **Cuale River Island (Isla Rio Cuale):** Located in the middle of the Cuale River, this long and narrow five-acre island includes the popular Rio Cuale Museum of Anthropology (open daily from 9am to 6pm), the Cultural Center, botanical gardens, market stalls, cafes, and fine restaurants. A delightful place to relax and enjoy the island ambience.

❑ **City Hall (Palacio Municipal):** Located on the northwest corner of the zócalo at Juarez and Independencia in the Old Town, this building houses the Municipal Tourism Office (open Monday through Friday from 9am to 8pm, Tel. 223-2500, ext. 230) and the tourist police. Look for the colorful mural of Puerto Vallarta by Manuel Lepe in 1981 which is in the stairwell on the second floor.

BEACHES

Puerto Vallarta is famous for several beaches along the Bay of Banderas. The most popular beaches include:

❑ **Playa los Muertos and Playa Olas Altas:** adjacent to each other in the Zona Romantica.

❑ **Playa Mismaloya:** Located eight miles south of the city center. Made famous as the site for the filming of *The Night of the Iguana*.

❏ **Playa La Animas, Yelapa, Majahuitas, and Quimixto:** Secluded beaches and fishing villages accessible only by boat.

❏ **Nueva Vallarta and Nayarit:** Popular with locals, these beach areas are located north of Puerto Vallarta, at the upper end of the Bay of Banderas.

WATER SPORTS

Puerto Vallarta offers excellent opportunities for scuba diving and snorkeling. Contact your hotel concierge, local travel agency, or the following specialty companies for such opportunities:

❏ **Vallarta Adventures:** *Marina Vallarta (Tel. 221-2111) and Nuevo Vallarta (Tel. 297-1212). Website: www.vallarta-adventures.com.*

❏ **Chico's Dive Shop:** *Diaz Ordaz 770-5, Old Town (Centro), Tel. 222-1895.*

ECOTOURS

Within recent years Puerto Vallarta has justly earned a reputation for ecotourism. Several tour companies offer opportunities for humpback whale-watching in the Bay of Banderas (from mid-December to mid-March), bird watching, boat trips to the Marietas Islands, swimming with the dolphins, hiking in the Sierra Madre Mountains, sea kayaking, and visiting turtle breeding camps:

❏ **Ecotours of Mexico (Ecotours de Mexico):** *243 Ignacio Vallarta (Zona Romantica), Tel. 222-6606.*

❏ **Open Air Expeditions (Expediciones Cielo Abierto):** *Guerrero 339, Old Town, Tel. 222-3310.*

❏ **Vallarta Adventures:** *Marina Vallarta (Tel. 221-2111) and Nuevo Vallarta (Tel. 297-1212). Website: www.vallartaadventures.com.*

FISHING

Anglers have numerous opportunities to go deep sea fishing in the Bay of Banderas as well as freshwater fishing in nearby lakes. November is sailfishing tournament time, which attracts many international enthusiasts. For information on the tournament, contact:

Puerto Vallarta International Sail Fish and
Marlin Tournament
Tel. 223-1665
Website: www.fishvallarta.com

The following companies offer a variety of fishing charters and expeditions:

- ❑ **Charter Fishing in Puerto Vallarta:** *Tel. 221-5402. Website: http://vallartafish.8m.com.*

- ❑ **Puerto Vallarta Sailing/Fishing Unlimited:** *Tel. 221-0920. Website: www.travelvallarta.com.*

- ❑ **The Puerto Vallarta Fishing Company:** *Tel. 222-1863.*

- ❑ **Natura Expeditions:** *Tel. 224-0410.Website: www.vivatours-vallarta.com.*

- ❑ **Fishing With Carolina:** *Tel. 224-7250.*

- ❑ **Fantasia Maritima:** *Tel. 221-0116.*

CRUISES

The following companies offer a variety of day cruises encompassing the Islas Marietas (near Punta Mita), whale-watching, and other types of activities, including sunset cruises:

- ❑ **Vallarta Adventures:** *Tel. 221-0657. Website: www.vallarta-adventures.com.*

- ❑ **Charter Dreams:** *Tel. 221-0690. Website: www.charterdreams.com.*

- ❑ **Sailing/Fishing Unlimited:** *Tel. 221-0920. Website: www.travel vallarta.com.*

- ❑ **Princesa Bay Tours:** *Tel. 224-4777.*

- ❑ **Fiesta Cruise:** *Tel. 985-2237.*

- ❑ **Bloodhound:** *Tel. 225-8657.*

- ❑ **Yellow Submarine:** *Tel. 224-4131.*

GOLF AND TENNIS

Golf and tennis enthusiasts have several opportunities to engage in these sports activities. Major 18-hole golf courses in the resort areas include:

- ❑ **Marina Vallarta Golf Club:** *Tel. 221-0073.* A beautiful Joe Finger-designed course located at Marina Vallarta.

- ❑ **Flamingos Golf and Country Club:** *Tel. 296-5006.* Located 10 miles north of the city at Nuevo Vallarta.

- ❑ **Four Seasons Hotel Golf Course:** *Tel. 291-6000.* This Jack Nicklaus-designed course is located 35 north of downtown Puerto Vallarta at Punta Mita.

Opportunities to play tennis are found at the **Continental Plaza Tennis Club** (Tel. 224-0123), **Iguana Racquet Club** (Tel. 221-0863), and at most large hotels.

HORSEBACK RIDING

Several companies offer opportunities to go horseback riding in the nearby countryside. Most companies include guides and some offer up to five-day trips into remote areas. Contact the following companies for more information: **Rancho el Ojo de Agua** (Tel. 224-8240), **Rancho Charro** (Tel. 224-0114), **Backcountry Tours** (Tel. 222-0386), **Natura Expeditions** (Tel. 224-0410), or **Rancho Manolo** (Tel. 228-0018).

LEARNING HOLIDAYS

If you have time and want to study Spanish and/or take courses in painting, textiles, ceramics, and jewelry making, contact the local branch of the **Instituto Allenda** (Tel./Fax 222-0076) which is located on Cuale River Island. For art classes, contact the Instituto de Art (Tel. 289-9882 or e-mail: artinstitutevallarta@hot mail.com). A local branch of the University of Guadalajara also offers Spanish classes for visitors (Tel. 223-2082).

NIGHTLIFE

Puerto Vallarta can be a fun city at night, especially for those who like to drink and dance. The city starts coming alive around 10pm and stays active until 3am or 4am. Most activities focus on restaurants, sidewalk cafes, sports bars, discos, strolling musicians, and people-watching in the downtown area, Hotel Zone, and Marina Vallarta. One of the city's liveliest night spots is along **Ignacio L. Vallarta**, just south of the Cuale River. Here you'll find numerous restaurants, bars, and a live salsa dance club and blues club. Puerto Vallarta's gay scene tends to be centered along this street and nearby Olas Alta area in the Zona Romantica neighborhood (see www.discoveryvallarta.com for an excellent online guide to gay Puerto Vallarta). The most popular discos and dance clubs are found in these places:

❑ **Christine:** *Krystal Vallarta Hotel, Av. Francisco Medina Ascencio, Tel. 224-0202.*

❑ **J&B Salsa Club:** *Av. Francisco Medina Ascencio, Tel. 224-4616.*

❑ **Emporium by Collage:** *Calle Proa, just south of Plaza Neptuno, Marina Vallarta, Tel. 221-0505.*

❑ **The Zoo:** *Paseo Diaz Ordaz 630, Old Town, Tel. 222-4945.*

❑ **Señor Frogs:** *Ignacio L. Vallarta and Venustiano Carranza, Tel. 222-5171.*

❑ **Cactus:** *Vallarta 399, Tel. 222-0391.*

10

Guadalajara

WELCOME TO MEXICO'S second largest city. Capital of the state of Jalisco, Guadalajara has a population of nearly 5 million. This is a big, friendly, attractive, and cultured city with many things to see and do. Imposing plazas, fountains, churches, colonial architecture, wide boulevards, green parks, and flowers blooming year-round give Guadalajara a very appealing ambience. If you think this is just a large industrial metropolis, which in part it is, think again. This is a very seductive community that constantly unfolds with new surprises.

Lifestyle shoppers, who enjoy a distinctive Mexican flavor to their music, art, dining, sightseeing, and shopping, often fall in love with this lively city and its surrounding area. Guadalajara showcases well many of Mexico's best treasures and pleasures.

A Special Place

Guadalajara is famous for many things. Being one of Mexico's most conservative religious communities, it boasts numerous churches and a rather subdued nightlife. It is especially noted for four of Mexico's major traditions – tequila, rodeos (charreadas),

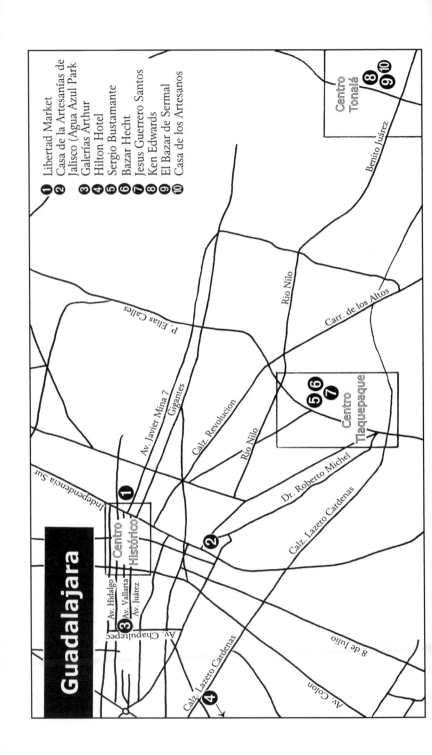

mariachi music, and the Mexican hat dance (jarabe tapatío) – and for its interesting Churriqueresque architecture. Home to a large community of expatriate business people, artists, writers, and retirees, the city is blessed with an idyllic climate, delightful plazas, excellent restaurants, numerous shopping centers, and a good road system connecting the downtown area to outlying suburban communities and beyond.

While Guadalajara is Mexico's major industrial and high-tech center, it's also a shopper's paradise for a wonderful range of arts, crafts, and leather goods that are produced in and around this city. Indeed, Guadalajara's famous artisans and workshops turn out a fascinating collection of ceramics, glassware, furniture, metal work, sculptures, paintings, and home decorative items which are found in shops throughout Mexico as well as exported abroad. From the shops and factories in the southeast satellite communities of Tlaquepaque and Tonalá to the many galleries found in the expat and art community of Ajijic along the beautiful shores of nearby Lake Chapala, Guadalajara is a delightful place to shop for all types of handcrafted items. From top quality jewelry, ceramics, paintings, antiques, and glassware to kitschy painted boxes, figurines, dolls, lamps, and candles, the many shops of Guadalajara have something to offer every level of budget and taste.

❑ This is a very seductive community that constantly unfolds with new surprises.

❑ Guadalajara is one of Mexico's most conservative religious communities with a rather subdued nightlife.

❑ Guadalajara is Mexico's major industrial and high-tech center.

❑ This is a delightful place to shop for all types of handcrafted items – from top quality to kitschy.

❑ Despite its large size, Guadalajara is a relatively easy city to understand and navigate.

❑ Most shopping is centered on two of the city's satellite communities – Tlaquepaque and Tonalá.

Spend a few days in Guadalajara and you will certainly leave with some lovely purchases. Spend longer and you'll discover why so many expatriates from the U.S. and Canada have decided to call Guadalajara their seasonal or permanent home.

Getting to Know You

Guadalajara is conveniently located within a few hours driving distance of several major cities, towns, and resorts. It's only a four-hour drive from Mexico City to Guadalajara via the Guadalajara-Mexico City superhighway. By road, Guadalajara also is located four hours east of Puerto Vallarta and three to six hours west of the delightful colonial towns of Morelia, Patzcuaro, Guanajuato, Querétaro, and San Miguel de Allende, It's also located within 30 miles of the northwest town of Tequila in the central highlands. Another 30 miles south takes you to the shores of lovely Lake Chapala, with a large expatriate community centered in the delightful lakeside town of Ajijic.

Direct flights also service Guadalajara from 20 locations within Mexico as well as from 10 cities in the U.S. and Canada.

Despite its large size, Guadalajara is a relatively easy city to understand and navigate. Much of the downtown section (Centro) is laid out in a grid pattern which, in turn, is connected by expressways to outlying areas.

Guadalajara has four distinct sections and satellite or suburban communities of special interest to shoppers: Centro, Tlaquepaque, Tonalá, and Zapopan. If you have limited shopping time, you may want to spend most of your time in **Tlaquepaque** and **Tonalá**. Lake Chapala especially appeals to travelers interested in exploring the many galleries and shops found in the quaint town of **Ajijic**.

CENTRO

Centro is the relatively compact downtown area known for its four plazas, two-towered cathedral, churches, colonial architecture, government buildings, museums, and theater. Most of the city's historical and architectural sites are found in this pleasant

area which is best covered on foot. The main east-west streets defining this area are Independencia, Hidalgo, Morelos, Moreno, and Juárez. The main north-south street that connects to these streets is Avenida Alcalde which also becomes Avenida 16 de Septiembre.

Most visitors to Centro focus on sightseeing activities centered on the plazas, cathedral, and nearby colonial buildings. However, this area also offers some good shopping opportunities for arts, antiques, and clothes. Most of the quality shopping is found in the city's Zona Minerva area that stretches 21 blocks west, from the cathedral to the north-south Avenida Chapultepec. The best quality shops are found close to Avenida Chapultepec along Avenida Vallarta, which is the western continuation of Avenida Juárez.

TLAQUEPAQUE

Located nearly five miles southeast of Centro, via Calzada Revolución, the satellite town of Tlaquepaque (population nearly 500,000) is Guadalajara's lifestyle shopping center for quality arts and crafts. Consisting of pleasant pedestrian malls and plazas lined with over 300 shops and restaurants, this is a great place to spend a day treasure hunting, people watching, sightseeing, and dining. Encompassing several blocks of renovated old stately summer homes of the city's upper class that have been converted into appealing upscale shops and restaurants – especially the pedestrian-only Avenida Independencia – the area is very popular with local and international visitors. Most of Guadalajara's quality arts, crafts, silver, jewelry, glassware, pottery, leather goods, handwoven clothing, furniture, and home decorative items are nicely displayed in the many shops of Tlaquepaque.

TONALÁ

Located five miles east of Tlaquepaque, via Calzada Revolución, Tonalá is an old pueblo that has become a big and colorful village jam-packed with artisans, workshops, home studios, and shops. Many famous artisan families live and work here. While Tonalá lacks the elegance and upscale ambience of Tlaquepaque, this community has a decided local character and the feel of a village. Its narrow, dusty, and bustling cobblestone streets and lively plaza are lined with colorful stucco buildings that house hundreds of utilitarian studios and shops selling a wide range of varying quality merchandise. Many people come here for bargains since prices are reputed to be better in Tonalá than elsewhere in Guadalajara. While the area is especially noted for its ceramic production, you'll also find a varied selection of glassware, textiles, wrought iron, papier-mâché, lamps, candles, and furniture in the many small shops and workshops that define this area. Expect to find everything from the tasteful to the tacky here. Market days, or Tianguis Artesanal (a market of crafts), in Tonalá are every Thursday and Sunday.

ZAPOPAN

Located nearly five miles northwest of the city center, this suburb of nearly 1 million people is famous for its imposing Basilica of the Virgin of Zapopan (Basilica de Zapopan), one of Mexico's most important religious centers. Indeed, thousands of pilgrims come each year to pay homage to Guadalajara's patroness, the tiny statue (13 inches tall) of the Virgin of Zapopan (Nuestra Señora de Zapopan). On Sundays shoppers head to the 200-year-old Ex-Hacienda La Mora in Zapopan to shop for a nice range of arts, crafts, textiles, furniture, and home decorative items.

Guadalajara on the Web

For English language information on various aspects of travel to Guadalajara, visit the following websites:

- **All About Guadalajara**   www.allaboutguadalajara.com
- **Mexico Connect**   www.mexconnect.com
- **Mexguide.net**   www.mexguide.net/guadalajara
- **Go2Guadalajara**   www.go2guadalajara.com
- **Guadalajara Reporter**   www.guadalajarareporter.com
- **Mex Web**   www.mexweb.com
- **Trip Advisor**   www.tripadvisor.com

Shopping Guadalajara

Guadalajara is reputed to be Mexico's premier shopping destination because of its profusion of shopping centers, markets, galleries, factories, workshops, and specialty shops. This is especially true in certain product areas, such as the arts and crafts. You'll find lots of shopping opportunities in Guadalajara, more so than in most places in Mexico. In fact, you may spend more time shopping in Guadalajara simply because there are fewer other things to do in this city. Given Guadalajara's strong arts, crafts, and home decorative traditions – coupled with its growing middle class that enjoys visiting shopping malls – the city offers many different shopping venues for both locals and visitors.

Most stores are open Monday through Saturday from 10am to 8pm, with many closing between 2pm and 4pm. Several shops also are open on Sunday from 10am to 4pm. Most shopping malls are open daily from 10am to 8pm.

SHOPPING AREAS

Guadalajara has four major shopping areas: Centro, Tlaquepaque, Tonala, and Lake Chapala. You'll also find numerous shopping centers (50+) throughout the city and suburban areas as well as daily street markets (tianguis) that open on different days of the week. Most of these places are of primary interest to local shoppers. The shops we identify for the various shopping areas, as well as our recommended "Best of Best," are of special interest to international visitors in search of unique and quality shopping.

CENTRO

While Centro is especially popular with locals, it does offer some good shopping opportunities for visitors interested in arts, crafts, antiques, and footwear. The huge covered **Libertad Market**

(Mercado Libertad), near the intersection of Calzada Independencia and Avenida Javier Mina, offers a wide selection of food, produce, and merchandise for local residents and bargain hunters – more a cultural experience than an adventure in quality shopping. **Casa de las Artesanías de Jalisco** at Agua Azul Park, just south of the city center (intersection of Calzadas Independencia and Gonzalez Gallo 20), includes an outstanding collection of arts and crafts produced by top artisans throughout the state of Jalisco – a "must visit" place for anyone interested in good quality local arts and crafts. For a large selection of locally produced footwear, visit the **Shoe Forum** (Forum del Calzado) and the **Shoe Gallery** (Galeria del Calzado) on Avenida Mexico as well as the many shoe and leather shops that line Calle Esteban Alatorre (just north of Avenida Hidalgo and east of Calzada Independencia). For high-end arts and antiques, head west of the Centro Historico for more than a dozen blocks along Avenida Juárez, which becomes Avenida Vallarta. Look for **Galerias Arther** (Avenida Vallarta 1214, Tel. 3825-3100) for a fine collection of Mexican, French, and Italian antiques, and **Jesus Guerrero** Santos (Avenida Vallarta 1222, Tel. 3825-9527, website: www.jps.com.mx) for beautifully crafted vases, lamps, mirrors, icons, and other religious items in silver and ceramics. The **Fiesta Americana**, **Presidente Inter-Continental**, and **Camino Real hotels** (all west of Centro Historico in Zona Minerva) have small but excellent quality shopping arcades (look for branches of the noted **Tane** and **Aplijsa** jewelry shops).

TLAQUEPAQUE

Welcome to Mexico's premier shopping district. It simply doesn't get much better than this! Tlaquepaque is everyone's favorite lifestyle shopping area. Located five miles southeast of Centro, this upscale shopping district con-sists of a central pedestrian mall (Independencia) lined with fine shops and restaurants; a parallel street (Juárez) with arts, crafts, antiques, and boutique shops; and pleasant plazas boasting numerous shops and restaurants. Plan to spend at least a day here since Tlaquepaque's many shops and restaurants will command your attention like no other place in Mexico. In fact, you may well need to return here for a second day of intensive shopping.

When you visit Tlaquepaque, you experience the "best of the best" in Mexican shopping, especially for arts, antiques, and home decorative items. So plan to do some serious – and very rewarding – shopping in this delightful suburban area of Guadalajara. You won't be disappointed!

Especially active on weekends (Saturday being the best day since several shops are closed on Sunday), Tlaquepaque draws a large crowd of local and international visitors in search of quality shopping and dining. Discerning shoppers discover some of Mexico's best arts and crafts here. Look for fine ceramics, glassware, furniture, candles, papier-mâché figures, metal art, lanterns, fountains, silver, jewelry, paintings, baskets, and home decorative items in Tlaquepaque. Many of the old and architecturally interesting summer homes of Guadalajara's rich and famous have been converted to shops and restaurants that give Tlaquepaque a very special aristocratic and upper class Mexican character. It exudes a feeling of quality lifestyle shopping.

You can easily spend a day here browsing the many shops and enjoying the cafes and restaurants. This is also the center for several of Mexico's most famous artists: **Sergio Bustamante**, **Rodolfo Padilla**, **Alex Mata Taylor**, and **Agustin Parra**. Shops of special interest to visitors include **Sergio Bustamante** (Independencia 236, Tel. 3639-5519, website: http://sergiobusta mante.com.mx) for exquisitely crafted bronze and copper sculptures, silver and gold jewelry, ceramic and papier-mâché figures, paintings, and furniture with the unique Sergio Bustamante style; **Agustin Parra Diseño** (Independencia 154-158, Tel. 3657-8530, website: www.agustinparra.com.mx) for a unique collection of wood carved and ceramic baroque-style religious figures, furniture, and accessory pieces – definitely an acquired taste; **Rodo Padilla** (Independencia 139, Tel. 3657-3712) for an amusing and whimsical collection of ceramic sculptures of Mexican charros (cheerful fat men in sombreros and on bicycles), angels, and sports figures – with a restaurant-bar attached; **Bazar Hecht** (Juarez 162, Tel/Fax 3659-0205) for furniture, ceramics, pots, antiques, candles, dolls, and masks; **La Casa Canela** (Independencia 258, Tel. 3635-3717) for elaborate furniture, statues, mirrors, paintings, and decorative pieces; **Color y Tierra** (Independencia 225, Tel/Fax 3635-3505) for an attractive collection of home decorative items (furniture, candles, pots, lamps, paintings) displayed in an old house; **Bazar Barrera** (Independencia 205, Tel/Fax 3635-1961) for a large collection of colorful papier-mâché figures, lanterns, ceramics displayed in three rooms of an old house; **Jesus Guerrero Santos** (Independencia 155, Tel/Fax 3659-7373, website: www.jgs.com.mx) for a wonderful collection of unique silver and ceramic pieces, from pots to religious art; **Hans Gallery** (Independencia 182, Tel. 3124-8181) for an attractive collection of candles, slate and copper fountains, bells, and Indian doors; **Alexis David** (Independencia 186B) for attractive leather handbags, woven bags, coats, slippers, and luggage; **El Dorado** (Independencia 145, Tel. 3635-1690) for furniture, ceramics, lanterns, wrought iron, doors, chests, pottery, rugs, candles, jewelry – the list goes on in this attractive old house displaying several rooms of decorative arts; **La Luna Descalza** (Juárez 120, Tel. 3639-3300, website: www.lalunadescalza.com) for a delight-

ful collection of folk art, pots, clothes, metal art, and papier-mâché products; **TeTé Arte y Diseño** (Juárez 173, Tel. 3635-7347) for an attractive selection of wrought iron decorative works, furniture, chandeliers, religious figures, pots, bells, and handicrafts from Mexico, Guatemala, and Peru; **Adobe Diseño** (Independencia 195, Tel. 3657-2405) for a unique collection of decorative items (glassware, metal art, pot-

tery, furniture, candles, baskets) as well as an excellent attached restaurant and bar (Adobe) for "lifestyle shopping"; **Ken Edwards/Los Civios** (Madero 70, Tel. 3635-2426, website: www.loscirios.com.mx) for a combination of ceramics produced by the Ken Edwards factory in Tonalá (go there for a much larger selection) and a unique selection of candles with multiple holders, which is the main emphasis of this shop; **Collecion Herlindo Palacios** (Independencia 227-B, Tel/Fax 3639-1454) for pottery, ceramic bowls, reproduction ceramics, wood carvings (great double-headed celestial carvings), and many other unique decorative pieces; **La Rose de Cristal** (Independencia 234, Tel/Fax 3639-7180) for large hand-blown glass, decorative balls, handbags, candles, ceramics, picture frames, and furniture; and **Antique de Mexico** (Independencia 255, Tel. 3639-2997) for antiques, furniture, paintings, jars, and home decorative items nicely displayed in a beautiful old house; and **Conceptos** (Independencia 281, Tel. 3639-4103) for wrought iron furniture and accessory pieces.

TONALÁ

If you shop in Tlaquepaque before arriving in Tonalá – which we recommend doing – charming Tonalá may be disappointing. It's a very different setting and shopping experience. Indeed, this is a big but somewhat dusty and chaotic village of factories, workshops, and shops offering a wide range of varying quality products – from the acceptable to the truly tacky. Let's be frank – although higher priced, the really good stuff is in Tlaquepaque. Indeed, many of the workshops in Tonalá showcase their products in Tlaquepaque. For example, the Ken Edwards factory shop in Tonalá displays its famous stoneware at Los Civios in Tlaquepaque. Tonalá is for bargain hunters and those who like a festive market and pueblo atmosphere. It's also a major center for buying ceramics and hand-blown glass, including discounted seconds, directly from factory shops. If you're looking for distinctive ceramics and glassware, good buys can be found in the many factory shops of Tonalá. But beyond these items, don't approach Tonalá with high expectations of discovering quality shops.

Most of the major shops are found around the plaza and along Morelos, Constitución, Hidalgo, and Madero streets, which are located east of the main thoroughfare of Tonaltecas. The festive plaza includes many shops, restaurants, and roving mariachi singers. Crowded craft market (Tianguis Artesanal) days in Tonalá are Thursdays and Saturdays when vendors line the plaza and main streets, especially Tonaltecas, with stalls selling a combination of both memorable and forgettable handicrafts and household goods.

If you are driving a car, we recommend parking along the street near the **Ken Edwards** (Morelos 184, Tel. 3683-0313, website: www.kenedwards.com.mx) stoneware factory and showroom and then explore the main streets and plaza on foot. On-street parking can be a problem along the narrow and crowded streets of Tonalá. The Ken Edwards factory includes nicely designed one-of-a-kind blue, brown, and green ceramics at bargain prices, especially in the red dot seconds room. Other shops to look for in Tonalá include **Los Caporales** (Morelos 155-B, Tel. 3683-0312) for brown and blue ceramics and stoneware; **Cocotzin** (Constitución 70-A, Tel. 3683-0524) for nicely designed ceramics and stoneware; **El Bazar de Sermal** (Hidelgo 67, Tel. 3684-0010) for a large and colorful selection of papier-mâché animals and figures produced in this factory shop; **Mexicania** (Hidalgo 13, on the plaza, Tel. 3683-0152) for a mixed collection of ceramics, icons, painted boxes, candles, lamps, and folk art; **Antiqua Santiago** (Madero 42, Tel. 3683-0641) for red, green, orange, and yellow handmade glass bowls, vases, and plates; **La Garto** (Madero 52, Tel. 3683-3845) for glass items and rustic clay pots; and **Galeria Bernabe** (Hidalgo 83, Tel. 3683-0040) for distinctive blue ceramics and tiles. **Casa de los Artesanos** (Tonaltecas 140, Tel. 3683-0590) displays the works of master artisans in its museum as well as offers some ceramics, glass, wood carvings, and other craft items for sale; dealers may want to contact this center in order to make direct contact with the area's major artisans.

Unlike Tlaquepaque, you may be able to shop Tonalá within a couple of hours, especially if you avoid the crowded market days. You'll most likely be able to quickly sort the treasures from the trash!

LAKE CHAPALA

Located nearly 30 miles south of Guadalajara, beautiful but polluted and receding Lake Chapala is home to one of the largest expatriate communities in Mexico. If you travel around the lake, you'll find workshops producing crafts for export. However, the greatest concentration of shopping is found in the main town on the lake. The picturesque lakeshore town of Ajijic is noted for its many talented artists and craftspeople as well as for its numerous galleries, shops, and restaurants. Most of the shops are centered along the main street of Colon, which changes it name to Morelos near the waterfront. The following galleries and shops are well worth visiting: **CABA** (Colon 43, Tel. 3766-1920), a fine arts center selling works of local artists as well as offering cultural tours of the area; **Mi Mexico** (Morelos 8, Tel. 3766-0133) for an interesting collection of fabrics, carpets, clothes, jewelry, and gift items; **Cugini's Boutique and Gallery** (Morelos 15) for designer clothes, jewelry, and folk art; **La Flor de la Laguna** (Morelos 17) for embroidered clothes and handicrafts; **Enrique Velasquez** (16 de Septiembre 7, Tel. 3766-0162) for attractive paintings with local themes; **Galeria Daniel Palma** (Ocampo 30, Tel. 3766-1688) for unique stone and iron sculptures (you may have seen his work in galleries in Puerto Vallarta); **Ferriolo** (Ocampo 33, Tel. 3766-1860) for beautiful handmade textiles, bedding, and gift items; and **La Colección Bárbara** (Independencia 7A-9A, Tel. 3766-1824) for an excellent collection of antiques, jewelry, folk art, and furniture. **Galeria Moon** (Rio Zula 4, Tel. 3766-1000) offers attractive home decorative items by noted designer Billy Moon. Mexican arts and crafts are well represented at the state-operated **Casa de Las Artesanias** (Ajijic-Chapala highway, Tel. 3766-0548) in La Floresta.

MARKETS

If you enjoy shopping in markets, Guadalajara has several daily and weekend markets for bargain hunters. The major markets include:

❑ **Mercado Libertad:** *Located near the intersection of Calzada Independencia and Avenida Javier Mina, just a couple of blocks east of Avenida Juarez in Centro. Open daily from 7am to 8pm, but don't* *come before 10am.* Reputed to be the largest covered market in Latin America, this busy complex has hundreds of vendors offering a full range of goods for local shoppers – clothing, household goods, food, produce, and crafts. You name it, this market probably has it.

❑ **El Baratillo:** *Calle Esteban Loera, 15 blocks east of Mercado Libertad, in Centro. Open Sundays only from 7am to 5pm.* Covering nearly 30 blocks, this huge outdoor flea market offers all kinds of new and used goods, including many antiques for weekend treasure hunters.

❑ **Shoe and leather market/center:** *Calle Esteban Alatorre, in Centro. Located four blocks north of Avenida Hidalgo and east of Calzada Independencia.* While this is not officially a "market," the many shoe and leather shops that line this popular street for nearly four blocks have turned it into a bargain center for such products.

❑ **Tianguis Artesanal:** *Along Avenida Tonaltecas and the plaza in Tonalá. Operates only on Thursdays and Saturdays.* This is Tonalá's popular craft market that includes hundreds of vendors who line the streets and plazas with a varied collection of arts, crafts, and household goods.

SHOPPING CENTERS AND ARCADES

The Guadalajara area boasts more than 50 shopping centers. Most primarily appeal to local shoppers. However, a few of the major shopping malls include shops of interest to visitors. The major shopping centers include:

❑ **La Gran Plaza:** *Avenida Vallarta 3959, Zona Minerva. Open daily from 10am to 9:30pm.* This three-level shopping mall includes over 300 shops and restaurants. Look for **El Charro** for leather goods, **L.A. Cano** for Colombian-style jewelry; **Macame Joyas** for uniquely designed jewelry; **Takasami** for stylish designer clothing; and **Unique** for a good range of gift items.

❑ **Plaza del Sol:** *On Lopez Mateos in the southwest section of the city, Zona Minerva. Open Monday through Friday, 10am to 8pm, Saturday from 10am to 9 pm, and Sunday from 10am to 7pm.* Includes nearly 300 shops and restaurants. Look for **D'Gracia**, **Macame Joyas**, and **Joyeros Martinez Sandoval** for uniquely designed jewelry; **El Charro** for leather goods; and **Elja Joyeria** for rugs and jewelry,

❑ **Presidente Inter-Continental Hotel:** *Across from Plaza del Sol.* Includes an upscale shopping center. Includes branches of the **Tane** and **Aplijsa** jewelry stores.

❑ **Centro Comercial Fiesta:** *Shopping complex attached to the Fiesta Americana Hotel.* Includes branches of the **Tane** and **Aplijsa** jewelry stores.

Best of the Best

Selecting the "best of the best" in Guadalajara is no easy task! More so than most cities in Mexico, Guadalajara, or more specifically the upscale southeastern satellite community of Tlaquepaque, has a disproportionate number of quality shops and workshops with decided arts, crafts, and home decorative themes. All you need to do is just show up on the pedestrian mall – Independencia – and go from one shop to another to immerse yourself in the best of shopping in Guadalajara. The products and displays here tend to be first-class. Indeed, you won't find much of the tacky tourist arts and crafts that dominate so many markets and shops throughout Mexico. Shops in Tlaquepaque represent the very best arts, crafts, and related products that Mexico's many talented artists and craftspeople have to offer discerning shoppers. While our following selections by no means represent a definitive list of the "best of the best," they are a good starting point for discovering Guadalajara's many unique treasures.

Arts, Crafts, and Decorative Items

❑ **Casa de las Artesanias de Jalisco:** *At Agua Azul Park, intersection of Calzadas Independencia and Gonzalez Gallo 20, just south of the city center and on the street opposite to the entrance to the park. Centro. Tel. 3619-1407. Open daily at 10am and closes Monday through Friday at 6pm, Saturday at 5pm, and Sunday at 3pm.* Somewhat difficult to reach because of the one-way streets, long blocks, and turn lanes around Agua Azul Park but seeking out this arts and crafts emporium is well worth the street challenge. Also known as the Instituto de la Artesania Jalisciense, this is one of the best state-sponsored arts and crafts centers in Mexico. Indeed, it's our favorite. The right side of the building houses a museum of ceramics and pottery which is organized by states – a good place to see different styles, patterns, colors, and designs produced throughout the country. The left side of the building consists of two expansive floors of gallery space devoted to nicely showcasing the arts and crafts of Jalisco's best arts, artisans, and craftspeople. It's jam-packed with top quality ceramics, paintings, clothes, candles, glassware, and papier-mâchê items. Everything here is for sale at fixed prices (look for prices on the bottom of each piece). Since the whole gallery is organized by artist or artisan, you can quickly familiarize yourself with the individual behind each work. If you've already visited many shops in Tlaquepaque and Tonalá, you'll recognize several of pieces, such as the whimsical ceramic figures of Rodo Padilla and the papier-mâché animals and figures found at El Bazar de Sermal in Tonalá.

❑ **La Casa Canela:** *Independencia 258, Tlaquepaque, Tel. 3635-3717. Open Monday through Friday, 10am to 2pm and 3 to 7pm; until 6pm on Saturday; and until 3pm on Sunday.* This huge and well appointed shop showcases room by room an attractive collection of elaborate furniture and decorative pieces. Includes many arts, crafts, and home decorative items such as mirrors, paintings, statues, fountain bases, ceramics, glassware, wood carved items, papier-mâché figures, and textiles. Each room is decorated around a particular theme and thus demonstrates how items can be put together for decorating purposes. Its workshop will do made-to-order work.

❑ **Bazar Hecht:** *Juárez 162, Tlaquepaque, Tel/Fax 3659-0205. Open Monday through Saturday from 10am to 7pm and Sunday from 10am to 2:30pm.* Offers a good selection of furniture, religious icons, ceramics, pots, antiques, candles, dolls, masks, and related handicrafts. Manufactures its own line of furniture.

❑ **El Dorado:** *Independencia 145, Tlaquepaque, Tel. 3635-1690.* Similar in concept to La Casa Canela, this attractive old house showcases furniture, ceramics, lanterns, wrought iron, doors, chests, pottery, candles, and rugs in several decorated rooms. Also includes a jewelry section.

❑ **El Bazar de Sermal:** *Hidalgo 67, Tonalá, Tel. 3684-0010.* This combination store and workshop showcases a large and colorful collection of papier-mâché animals and figures, from small hatching cockatoo eggs, butterflies, cats, and pigs to deer, elephants, tigers, hippos, unicorns, giraffes, and clowns – a virtual zoo displayed in several interesting rooms. Visitors can observe artisans painting the friendly creations. Experienced in packing and shipping worldwide.

❑ **La Luna Descalza:** *Juárez 120, Tlaquepaque, Tel. 3639-3300. Website: www.lalunadescalza.com. Open Monday through Saturday from 10:30am to 7pm and Sunday from 11am to 3pm.* You can watch master artisans at the rear of this shop producing intriguing metal art. Includes an interesting collection of folk art (colorful animals and buses), pots, clothes, metal art, and papier-mâché items.

❑ **TeTé Arte y Diseño:** *Juárez 173, Tlaquepaque, Tel. 3635-7347. Open Monday through Saturday from 10am to 7pm.* Offers an attractive selection of furniture, chandeliers, religious figures, pots, bells, stone pieces, and handicrafts from Mexico, Guatemala, and Peru. Includes many wrought iron decorative works and some old furniture.

❑ **Adobe Diseño:** *Independencia 195, Tlaquepaque, Tel. 3657-2405.* Similar to its sister shop in Mexico City (San Ángel), Adobe Diseño includes an attractive collection of furniture, decorative metal chickens and cacti, bird cages, candlesticks, baskets, and other decorative items. Includes many works by noted designers David Luna and Martha Figueroa. The attached restaurant and bar – Adobe – is one of the best in Tlaquepaque.

❑ **La Rose de Cristal:** *Independencia 234, Tlaquepaque, Tel/Fax 3639-7180.* While this shop primarily produces large colorful hand-blown decorative glass balls and figures (you can visit their factory daily between 9am to 2pm, which is located 32 blocks away), the shop also offers handbags, candles, ceramics, picture frames, and furniture.

❑ **Antique de Mexico:** *Independencia 255, Tlaquepaque, Tel. 3639-2997.* Housed in a beautiful old house, this attractive shop includes a combination of old and new furniture from Mexico, India, China, and the Philippines. However, the shop makes most of its own furniture. Also includes antiques, paintings, jars, and home decorative items. The workshop is located within two blocks of this shop.

❑ **Agustin Parra:** *Independencia 154-158, Tlaquepaque, Tel. 3657-8530. Website: www.agustinparra.com.mx. Open Monday through Saturday from 10am to 2pm and from 3 to 7pm, and Sunday from 10am to 5pm.* This is not your typical home decorative shop! This famous shop produces a unique collection of large wood-carved and ceramic baroque-style religious figures, furniture, altars, mirrors, sculptures, and accessory pieces. Creates own designs and manufactures everything in its local factory. You'll need a special place, ideally a church or chapel, to carry these unusual pieces. Includes a model chair produced for the pope. Regularly ships to the U.S. and Canada.

❑ **Casa de los Artesanos:** *Tonaltecas 140, Tonalá, Tel. 3683-0590.* This is a community center for several master artisans. Includes a museum as well as a photo gallery of the masters. Although selections are limited, you can make purchases here as well as contact artisans for custom work. Not much English spoken.

CERAMICS AND STONEWARE

❑ **Ken Edwards:** *Morelos 184, Tonalá, Tel. 3683-0313. Website: www.kenedwards.com.mx. Also represented at Los Civios at Madero 70 in Tlaquepaque, Tel. 3635-2426.* For more than 30 years Ken Edwards, who came from Kansas City, has produced several attractive lines of fired lead-free decorative and utilitarian ceramics and stoneware. This popular factory and shop includes nicely designed blue, brown, and green ceramics and stoneware in the shape of fish, birds, cats, pigs, vases, bowls, and plates. Can purchase a complete set of table service. An attractive alternative to Mexico's popular Puebla-based Talavera ceramics. Includes a seconds room with discounted red dot items.

❑ **Los Caporales:** *Morelos 155-B, Tonalá, Tel. 3683-0312.* Located across the street from the Ken Edwards factory and showroom, this ceramics factory and shop produces brown and blue ceramics and stoneware in the form of pots, plates, and ducks. Also includes clay figures.

❑ **Cocotzin:** *Constitución 70-A, Tonalá, Tel. 3683-0524.* This small but very nice ceramics and stoneware shop includes many attractive designs and appealing colors. Look for plates and bowls as well as some collectible art pieces.

❑ **Collecion Herlindo Palacios:** *Independencia 227-B, Tlaquepaque, Tel/Fax 3639-1454.* Pottery, ceramic bowls, reproduction ceramics, wood carvings (great double-headed celestial carvings), and many other unique decorative pieces;

ART

❑ **Sergio Bustamante:** *Independencia 236, Tlaquepaque, Tel. 3639-5519. Website: http://sergiobustamante.com.mx.* This is the headquarters shop for one of Mexico's most celebrated and innovative international artists, Sergio Bustamante. If you've visited his shops in Mexico City, Acapulco, and Puerta Vallarta, you know the fascinating product line – colorful and whimsical papier-mâché and ceramic figures, bronze and copper sculptures, silver and gold jewelry, and furniture. Visit his website for a good overview of his offerings. It's all displayed in this inviting gallery that includes jewelry showcases, an open fountain area with peacocks and flamingos, and two rooms of sculptures and unique furniture detailed with anatomic features. While

Sergio Bustamante's works may be an acquired taste, especially suited for those who appreciate whimsical and surrealistic art, he is indisputably one of Mexico's most inventive artists and designers. This is his most captivating gallery in Mexico. After much resistance, we succumbed to one of his masterpieces – a nearly 6' bronze sculpture entitled "The Heart of Time" that now commands the entry to our home (see the photo on page i)!

❑ **Rodo Padilla:** *Independencia 139, Tlaquepaque, Tel. 3658-3712. Open Monday through Saturday, 10am to 7pm, and Sunday from 11am to 3pm.* Welcome to the gallery shop of the famous creative ceramic artist and sculptor Rodo Padilla who produces distinctive rotund figures of Mexican charros (cheerful fat men in sombreros and on bicycles), angels, and sports figures that are collectible pieces. This old house nicely displays his appealing works. The workshop includes 22 workers who produce 800 pieces per month. Includes an attached restaurant-bar.

❑ **Jesus Guerrero Santos:** *Avenida Vallarta 1222, Zona Minerva, Tel. 3825-9527; and Independencia 227-A, Tlaquepaque, Tel/Fax 3659-7373. Website: www.jgs.com.mx.* This is one of our favorite shops, a very unique one that is often hard to describe to visitors. It produces beautiful one-of-a-kind ceramic, wrought iron, and silver (German alpaca) pieces in blue, white, and green as well as special Talavera ceramics. Includes many traditional silver religious pieces (crosses and icons). Look for intriguing alpaca and ceramic plates, vases, and mirror frames. Includes a new collection of modern ceramics produced in the form of crackled white, green, and blue celadon. If you're looking for some very special and unique art and home decorative items, be sure to visit these two shops. For more than 15 years this shop has produced some truly distinctive art pieces. Each has some historical significance.

❑ **Galeria Daniel Palma:** *Ocampo 30, Ajijic (Lake Chapala), Tel. 3766-1688. Open Tuesday through Sunday from 10am to 6pm.* This talented artist produces wonderfully inviting animal sculptures, especially birds and kangaroos, crafted in stone, iron, and wood. You'll also find his work represented at the Gallery Uno in Puerto Vallarta.

ANTIQUES

❑ **Galerias Arther:** *Avenida Vallarta 1214, Zona Minerva, Tel. 3825-3100. Website: www.arther.com.* This high-end antique and home decorative shop, housed in a large and stately old home in one of Guadalajara's most upscale neighborhoods, showcases a fine collection of Mexican, Italian, and French antiques and objets d'art. Includes large paintings, ceramics, statuary, mirrors, tapestries, bronzes, lamps, and decorative items. Also produces excellent quality reproduction Mexican furniture and accessory pieces. A true collector's shop operated by a very knowledgeable and personable father-son team.

❑ **La Colección Bárbara:** *Independencia 7A-9A, Ajijic (Lake Chapala), Tel. 3766-1824.* Offers an excellent collection of antiques, jewelry, folk art, and furniture.

JEWELRY

❑ **Sergio Bustamante:** *Independencia 236, Tlaquepaque, Tel. 3639-5519. Website: http://sergiobustamante.com.mx.* This fascinating art gallery includes an excellent collection of Sergio Bustamante's signature gold and silver jewelry creations – necklaces, bracelets, earrings, and pendants – which are a form of wearable art.

❑ **Tane:** *Presidente Inter-Continental, Fiesta Americana, and Camino Real hotels.* These are branch shops of Mexico's premier sterling silver jeweler and designer. Offers exquisite one-of-a-kind jewelry designs as well as produces antique reproduction pieces. Includes some contemporary sculptures.

❑ **Aplijsa:** *Fiesta Americana and Presidente Inter-Continental hotels; Guadalajara Airport; and World Trade Center. Website: www.aplijsa.com.mx.* If you've visited the main Aplijsa shop in Mexico City, you know what these branch shops are all about – beautifully designed jewelry using diamonds, pearls, opals, and other precious stones.

❑ **Macame Joyas:** *Plaza del Sol, La Gran Plaza, and the Presidente Inter-Continental Hotel.* Offers a beautiful line of well designed jewelry using precious and semiprecious stones. Represents Cartier in Guadalajara.

Accommodations

Guadalajara offers an excellent range of accommodations for all budgets. The city's many top hotels are located to the west (Zona Minerva) and southwest (Zona Cruz del Sur) of the city center. A few of the major hotels, such as the Presidente Inter-Continental and the Fiesta Americana, also include shopping centers or are located in close proximity to major shopping malls as Plaza del Sol and La Gran Plaza. Guadalajara's best hotels include the following properties.

❑ **Hilton Guadalajara:** *Avenida de las Rosas No. 2933, C.P. 44540 Col. Rinconada del Bosque, Guadalajara, Jalisco, Mexico. Tel. (52-33) 3678-0523, Fax (52-33) 3678-0521. Toll-free from the U.S. 800-445-8667. E-mail: reservas@hiltonguadalajara.com.mx. Website: www.guadalarahilton.com.mx.* A recent winner of AAA's Four Diamond Award, the Hilton Guadalajara is located 20 minutes from the International Airport and situated directly across the street from ExpoGuadalajara. The downtown historical center and financial center are minutes away by taxi. The 460 guestrooms and suites offer guests the expected amenities. There is a work-sized marble topped desk and acceptable lighting. The bathroom is small. There is nothing in the lobby or guestrooms to suggest one is in Mexico. Once inside, this Hilton could be anywhere in the world. The Executive Floor offers additional amenities which include continental breakfast and canapés and cocktails in the afternoon. The *Belvedere* is a specialty restaurant serving Mexican and international cuisines. *Los Vitrales Restaurant-Café* has an extensive variety of buffets and an a la carte menu. Try the café for breakfast and French pastries. Spa and Fitness Center; Business Center; Convention/Banquet Facilities.

❑ **Quinta Real:** *Avenida México 2727, Zona Minerva 44680, at Av. López Mateos Norte, Guadalajara, Jal., México. Tel. (52-33) 3669-0600, Fax (52-33) 3669-0601. Toll-free from U.S. or Canada 800-457-4000. E-mail: reservaciones@quintareal.com. Website: www.quintareal.com.* An elegant hacienda-style hotel featuring stone and brick walls, graceful colonial arches, and art adorning the public areas, Quinta Real offers 76 plush guest suites on five floors. Decorated with neoclassical furnishings, suites include glass-topped writing desks with stone pedestals and fireplaces with marble mantles. Tile bathrooms have marble sinks. Some of the larger suites have a Jacuzzi. *Quinta Real Restaurant* with a garden view features regional and international cuisines. Pool; Business Center; Conference/Banquet Facilities.

❑ **Presidente Inter-Continental:** *Avenida López Mateos Sur and Moctezuma, 45050 Guadalajara, Jal., Mexico, Tel. (52-33) 3678-1234, Fax (52-33) 3678-1222. Website: www.interconti.com.* The Presidente Inter-Continental's facade is a sleek 14-story modern glass pyramid-looking structure. The 12-story atrium lobby features glass walled elevators, and off the main lobby entrance is a separate check-in area for guests staying in the club rooms. The 411 guestrooms and suites are furnished with comfortable, modern styled furniture which includes a desk, and a small table with two chairs. Club rooms offer additional amenities which include continental breakfast, newspaper, and evening cocktails. Three restaurants offer a choice of international, Mexican or café food. Fitness Center (perhaps the best in the city); Business Center; Conference/ Banquet Facilities.

❑ **Fiesta Americana:** *Aurelio Aceves 225, Zona Minerva, 44100 Guadalajara, Jal., Mexico, Tel. (52-33) 3825-3434, Fax (52-33) 3630-3725, Website: www.fiestamericana.com.* A 22-story hotel with a dramatic glass facade and a 14-story atrium lobby with glass-walled elevators, the 390 guestrooms and suites are some of the largest in the city. Modern furnishings, marble bathrooms, panoramic views, one of the best-equipped business centers in the city, and pricing slightly below many of Guadalajara's luxury hotels make this a favorite with businesspeople. Club floors offer upgraded amenities which include separate check-in, continental breakfast, and afternoon wine and hors d'oeuvres. Two restaurants offer a variety of dining choices. Fitness room; Business Center; Meeting/Banquet Facilities.

❑ **Camino Real:** *Avenida Vallarta 5005, Zona Minerva, 45040 Guadalajara, Jal., Mexico, Tel. (55-33) 3134-2424, Fax (52-33) 3134-2404. Website: www.caminoreal.com/guadalajara.* As the first of Guadalajara's luxury hotels, it is also the city's oldest. The 205 guestrooms and suites are large and well decorated. Many guestrooms surround the pool or garden, while those in the back face the sometimes noisy street. Three restaurants offer a variety of cuisines, and there is an excellent Sunday morning buffet brunch with live musicians serenading the diners. Swimming pools, tennis courts, and putting green.

Restaurants

Guadalajara offers many fine restaurants that serve excellent local and international cuisines in both romantic and festive settings. Many of the best restaurants are found in the downtown area, in or near the major hotels in Zona Minerva, and in Tlaquepaque. Good restaurants for lunch are disproportionately found in Tlaquepaque – where you should be shopping! Some of the city's best dining spots include the following:

❑ **Santo Coyote:** *Lerdo de Tejada 2379, Zona Minerva, Tel. 3616-6978. Open 2pm to 2am.* This is one of our favorite restaurants in Mexico. Once the former residence of the U.S. Consulate, it now serves as one of Guadalajara's best addresses for dining. It's very special at night. Offering a gorgeous outdoor garden setting with lots of lanterns and great service, this unique restaurant and bar serves outstanding nuevo Mexican cuisine. Try the traditional tortilla soup and the queso al epasata (melted chichuahua and mozzarella) for an appetizer. For main courses, select the Santa Fe salmon, charbroiled baby goat, delicia de maria, el capricho chicken, or filete "El Patron" (cactus in cilantra, beef medallion with grilled panela cheese, bathed in freshly made sauce and decorated with guero chili and onion). On a cold evening, the restaurant will supply patrons with wool ponchos – all part of the excellent and attentive service at this very special restaurant!

❑ **El Sacromonte:** *Pedro Moreno 1398, west of Centro, Tel. 3825-5447. Open Monday through Saturday, 1:30pm to midnight.* This romantic restaurant, with hanging lanterns and mariachi singers, serves excellent nuevo Mexican cuisine with special emphasis on fish and meat dishes. Excellent presentations and service.

❑ **Mariscos Progreso:** *Progreso 80, Tlaquepaque, Tel. 3567-4995. Open daily from 10am to 8pm (live music from 3 to 7pm).* This popular seafood restaurant serves excellent Mexican dishes on a shaded outdoor patio. Try the filete especial and parrillada for two.

❑ **La Destileria:** *Mexico 2915, Centro, Tel. 3640-3110. Open Monday through Saturday from 1pm to midnight and Sunday from 1pm to 6pm.* This intriguing combination restaurant and tequila museum includes 230 different varieties of tequila in its upstairs bar. Serves many excellent Mexican specialties. Try the fried cheese with salsa verde, fish in parsley sauce, or molcajete de la casa.

❑ **La Fonda de San Miguel:** *Donato Guerra 25, Centro, Tel. 3613-0809. Open Sunday to Tuesday from 8:30am to 6pm and Wednesday to Saturday from 8:30 to midnight.* This old restored convent (Santa Teresa de Jesús) now includes a courtyard restaurant, art gallery, and shops. Offers many traditional Mexican dishes (try the chile en nogada) including numerous moles.

❑ **Aquellos Tiempos:** *Camino Real Hotel, Avenue Vallarta 5005, Zona Minerva, Tel. 3134-2424.* Open Monday through Friday, 7-11am, 2-5pm, and 7pm to midnight. This award-winning restaurant serves a good range of Mexican and international dishes in an elegant setting. Excellent service.

❑ **Fonda Adobe:** *Independencia and Francisco de Maranda, Tlaquepaque, Tel. 3657-2405. Open 12noon to 7pm.* Attached to the attractive Adobe Diseño arts and home decorative shop, this is a very popular restaurant for lunch. Serves a good range of excellent Mexican specialties, including delicious mole.

❑ **Restaurant With No Name:** *Madero 80, Tlaquepaque, Tel. 3635-4520. Open daily from 8:30am to 10pm.* If you're looking for a unique restaurant while shopping in Tlaquepaque, this is a good choice. Located near Los Civios/Ken Edwards. Somewhat laid back with outdoor dining in an overgrown courtyard complete with roaming peacocks that visit your table, this is a very pleasant place to dine. The old building has lots of local character. Try the no name chicken or chicken fajitas.

❑ **Casa Bariachi:** *Avenida Vallarta 2221, Zona Minerva, Tel. 3615-0029. Open Monday through Saturday until 3am.* Popular with locals, this large and festive mariachi restaurant and bar is a good place to see some of the area's best mariachi bands on stage.

Enjoying Your Stay

Aside from shopping and dining, Guadalajara offers many other things to see and do. From traditional sightseeing to sports and entertainment, charming Guadalajara is a traveler's delight.

DOWNTOWN SIGHTSEEING

If you are into history, museums, and sightseeing, head for the center of the city, the Centro Histórico. Within this 12-square-block area you will find several plazas (Tapatia, Guadalajara, Armas, Liberacion, and Rotonda), fountains, sculptures, buildings, and interesting architecture and historical sites. The city's major sightseeing attractions are interesting but by no means exceptional compared to many other older and more historically significant places in Mexico. Some of the city's top attractions include:

❑ **Cathedral:** *Avenida Alcalde. Open daily from 8am to 7pm.* Dating from the 16th century, this twin tower cathedral is one of the symbols of Guadalajara. Incorporating several architectural styles – Gothic, Moorish, Tuscan, Corinthian, Mudejar, and Byzantine – and boasting 11 altars, this is a very special place in Guadalajara. Located on four converging plazas that form a cross, it includes many interesting old paintings, altar pieces, and a 19th century organ.

❑ **Museo Regional de Guadalajara:** *Liceo 60, Centro, Tel. 3614-9958. Open Tuesday (free) through Sunday from 9am to 5:45pm.* Includes an interesting collection of artifacts, art, and crafts depicting the history and culture of western Mexico. Includes an interesting collection of paintings and old carriages.

❑ **Teatro Degollado:** *Avenida Degollado, Centro, between Hidalgo and Morelos, Tel. 3614-4773. Open Monday through Friday from 10am to 2pm.* This is one of the city's real architectural and cultural showpieces. Constructed nearly 150 years ago as a replica of Milan's grand La Scala, this beautiful theater hosts many theatrical and musical performances throughout the year. The popular Ballet Folklórico is performed here on Sundays at 10am.

❑ **Basilica de la Virgin de Zapopan:** *Avenida Hidalgo at Morelos, Zona Zapopan Norte, Tel. 3633-0141.* Located nearly five miles northwest of the Centro area, this is one of the most venerated churches in Latin America. The tiny Virgin of Zapopan (Nuestra Señora de Zapopan) is supposed to have special powers. Each year millions of people visit this special church.

❑ **Palacio de Gobierno (Government Palace):** *Avenida Corona (between Morelos and Moreno), Centro. Open daily from 9am to 8:45 pm.* This is one of the city's most important historical sites. Initially constructed in 1643, it is here where Father Miguel Hidalgo decreed the end of slavery in 1810 and where President Benito Juarez escaped assassination in 1858. The building, which now serves as a center for state government offices, is noted for its 18th century architecture and large murals by famous artist José Clemente Orozco.

SPORTS

Sports enthusiasts will find many opportunities to play golf and tennis. While most golf courses are part of private clubs, you may be able to get in by paying nonmember greens fees which range from US$40 to US$100. Check with your hotel before venturing to these clubs. Many of these clubs also offer a variety of other sports opportunities as well as spas. The major golf courses include:

❑ **Guadalajara Country Club:** *Mar Caribe 2615, Tel. 3817-2858.* Guadalajara's oldest 18-hole golf course designed by Joe Finger. Can only play with members.

❑ **Club de Golf Santa Anita:** *Carretera a Morelia, Km. 6.5, Tel. 3686-0321.*

❑ **Atlas Country Club:** *Km. 6.5 Carretera Guadalajara - Chapala, Tel. 3689-0240.* Designed by Joe Finger. Offers a tourist package for US$50 which includes greens fees, caddy, and light lunch.

❑ **Club De Golf Santa Anita S.A. de C.V.:** *Carretera Guadalajara – Morelia, Km 6.5, Tel. 3686-0321.*

❑ **El Palomar Country Club:** *Paseo de la Cima 437, Tel. 3684-4434.*

❑ **Las Cañadas Country Club:** *Avenida Bosques San Isidro 7877, Tel. 3685-0285.*

Most major hotels and country clubs have tennis courts. The following places are open, for a fee, to nonguests: **Camino Real Hotel** (Avenida Vallarta 5005, Zona Minerva, Tel. 3134-2424); **Crowne Plaza Guadalajara** (Avenida López Mateos Sur 2500, Zona Minerva, Tel. 3634-1034); and **Club de Tenis Royal** (San Ignacio 316, Zona Minerva, Tel. 3647-5348).

Evening Entertainment

While conservative Guadalajara lacks the nightclubs, discos, and bars commonly associated with Mexico's lively resorts, it does offer its own brand of evening entertainment. Since it's the source for Mexico's mariachis, try these places for mariachi music:

❑ **Casa Bariachi:** *Avenida Vallarta 2221, Tel. 3615-0029.* See above under "Restaurants."

❑ **La Feria:** *Corona 291, Tel. 3613-7150.* This restaurant-bar offers two mariachi band performances each day – at 3:30pm and 10pm.

Much of Guadalajara's evening entertainment is found in the bars of major hotels. Popular bars with live evening entertainment, ranging from salsa to jazz, include:

❑ **Caballo Negro:** *Fiesta Americana Hotel. Open Monday through Saturday from 9pm to 1am, Tel. 3825-3434.*

❑ **El Cubilete:** *Gral. Rio Seco 9. Open Monday through Saturday from 2pm to 1am, Tel. 3658-0406*

❑ **El Manglar:** *Crowne Plaza. Open daily from 11pm to 2am, Tel. 3634-1034.*

❑ **Hard Rock Cafe:** *Avenida Vallarta 2125, Centro Magno, Tel. 3616-4560.*

❑ **La Diligencia:** *Camino Real Hotel, Open Monday through Saturday from 6pm to 2am, Tel. 3134-2424.*

❑ **La Fiesta:** *Crowne Plaza Hotel. Open Thursday to Saturday from 7pm to 1am, Tel. 3634-1034.*

❑ **La Rondalla:** *Hilton Hotel, open daily from 1pm to midnight, Tel. 3678-0505.*

❑ **Lobby Bar:** *Fiesta Americana. Open daily from 6pm to 1am, Tel. 3825-3434.*

❑ **Lobby Bar:** *Presidente Inter-Continental. Open daily from 4pm to 1am, Tel. 3678-1234.*

❑ **Memories:** *El Tapatio Hotel. Open daily from 8pm to 2am, Tel. 3635-6050.*

❑ **Maxim's:** *Hotel Frances, Calle Maestranza 35, Zona Centro, Tel. 3613-1190.*

❑ **Quinta Real:** *Quinta Real Hotel. Open daily from 12noon to midnight, Tel. 3615-0000.*

❑ **Undicci:** *Las Americas 1462, Tel. 3817-4410*

Guadalajara's performing arts are well and alive in the following locations:

❑ **Ballet of the University of Guadalajara:** *Teatro Degollado. Performances every Sunday at 10am, Tel. 3614-4773.*

❑ **Instituto Cultural Cabañas:** *Calle Cabañas 8, Centro Histórico, Plaza Tapitia, Tel. 3617-4377.*

❑ **Orquesta Filarmónica de Jalisco:** *Performances on Sunday at 12:30pm and Friday at 8:30pm at the Teatro Degollado, Tel. 3658-3812.*

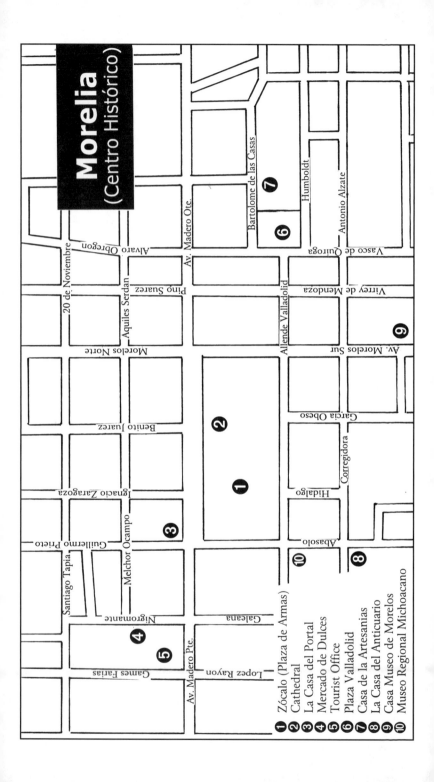

Morelia
(Centro Histórico)

❶ Zócalo (Plaza de Armas)
❷ Cathedral
❸ La Casa del Portal
❹ Mercado de Dulces
❺ Tourist Office
❻ Plaza Valladolid
❼ Casa de la Artesanías
❽ La Casa del Anticuario
❾ Casa Museo de Morelos
❿ Museo Regional Michoacano

11

Morelia, Pátzcuaro, and the State of Michoacán

T
HE STATE OF MICHOACÁN offers one of the most interesting opportunities to shop for arts and crafts directly from artisans as well as explore several Spanish colonial architectural gems. From the delightful old palaces, churches, squares, gardens, and streets of Morelia to the charming squares and picture-postcard streets of Pátzcuaro, Santa Clara del Cobre, Tzintzuntzan, Capula, Tócuaro, and nearby villages, Michoacán has a great deal to offer adventuresome travel-shoppers in search of quality arts and crafts and those interested in meeting talented artisans at work.

Our advice: Plan to spend a few days exploring the area's many towns and villages that specialize in producing arts and crafts. You'll discover many wonderful products, from hand-crafted copper pots, ceramics, and wood-carved masks to intriguing painted furniture, sculptures, Catrinas (ceramic and papier mâché skeleton figures), textiles, and folk art. You'll have a chance to meet many of Mexico's top artisans in their homes, workshops, and factories producing the items you may want to purchase directly from them. In so doing, you'll leave this state with a much better understanding of the people and culture behind the many products you find in Mexico.

Getting to Know You

The villages and towns in Michoacán have a long history and tradition of producing handcrafted items. Indeed, in the 16th century a bishop persuaded Indian villages around Lake Pátzcuaro to produce various arts and crafts. The state subsequently organized communities in the production of arts and crafts. As a consequence, today many villages specialize in one product and village fairs sponsor competition for the best designs. For example, Santa Clara del Cobre is known for its copper artisans. Tzintzuntzan is famous for its straw crafts, ceramics, and wood carvings. Morelia and Pátzcuaro have shops that pull together many of the arts and crafts produced throughout the state's many specialty towns and villages.

If you are interested in spending a day or two exploring the many arts and crafts villages in Michoacán, we recommend contacting a local expert who specializes in personalized arts and crafts tours: **David Ortega**, Ayangupani, Tel. 334-5040, Fax 334-5026, Cell 311-4888, or E-mail: dso7@prodigy.net.mx. He also can be contacted through the shop and front desk of the Villa Montaña (see the section on "Accommodations") in Morelia. David has an intimate knowledge of the area's best artisans and craftspeople, including many promising ones he helps promote. While you can cover the highlights of the area in one long day, we recommend at least two days to tour and shop the area properly. David will serve as both your driver and guide. We recommend using his service because of his expertise. Doing this on your own will be very difficult since many of the artisans and workshops are not well marked and addresses are often nonexistent. David also conducts other types of tours.

❏ Plan to spend a few days exploring the area's many towns and villages that specialize in producing arts and crafts.

❏ If you approach this place properly, you'll have an opportunity to meet many local artisans and purchase directly from them.

❏ Today many villages continue the nearly 600-year tradition of specializing in a particular product.

❏ Pátzcuaro hosts a popular pottery market each Friday.

Morelia is much more than just another interesting city in central Mexico. Capital of the state of Michoacán, it's noted for its wide tree-lined boulevards, beautiful old Spanish colonial architecture, sweets market, and annual music festivals. Designated by UNESCO in 1991 as a World Cultural Heritage site, the city is rich in history and culture. It abounds with old churches, museums, and other historical sites to keep you busy sightseeing for at least a day or two. Nearby historical towns and villages – complete with intriguing churches, picturesque plazas, charming cobblestone streets, timeless village scenes, and bustling shops and markets – encourage visitors to spend several days exploring the state of Michoacán.

For travel-shoppers, Morelia is an important center from which to explore one of Mexico's richest states for arts and crafts. Indeed, hundreds of villages throughout this state produce a dazzling array of products. Just browse through the museum and shop at the Casa de la Artesanias del Estado de Michoacán, housed in the imposing two-story Ex-Convent de San Francisco on Plaza Valladolid in downtown Morelia, and you will get a quick overview of what lies ahead in this state. From the coppersmiths of Santa Clara del Cobre to the mask makers of Tócuaro, this is a state rich in talented artisans who produce a wide range of products in copper, ceramics, wood, straw, papier-mâchê, and cotton. Take a quick day tour of the state's many artisan villages and workshops and you'll come away with several unique treasures.

Morelia

Located approximately 230 miles southeast of Guadalajara and 195 miles northeast of Mexico City, this charming city of nearly 500,000 people was founded in 1541 as Valladolid and subsequently renamed in 1828 after its most famous local hero, José María Morelos, who was executed in 1811 during the independence movement. Today Morelia is especially noted for its beautiful colonial architecture, music festivals, candy production, and seven universities, including the second oldest in the Western Hemisphere, Colegio de San Nicolas.

Situated at an altitude of 1,950 meters (6,400 feet) and surrounded by hills, Morelia tends to have a pleasant climate year round which averages 23°C (73°F). Cool mornings and evenings during the months of November to February require a light sweater or jacket for comfort. March and April tend to be the warmest months.

MAJOR ATTRACTIONS

Morelia is both a traditional and modern city. An architecturally harmonious area, the Historical Center (Centro) includes narrow one-way streets and attractive tree-lined plazas surrounded by numerous old churches and aging two- and three-story government offices, banks, hotels, and commercial buildings constructed of rose-colored stone. Here you will find the city's major sightseeing and historical attractions. At the center is the inviting Plaza de Armas and adjacent pink stone cathedral with its 200-foot high twin towers – located at the intersections of Avenida Madero, Calle Allende, and Calle Abasolo. Other major

attractions include: Temple of Mercy, Public Library, Clavijero Palace, Las Rosas Church and Las Rosas Conservatory of Music, State Museum, Municipal Palace, Michoacán Regional Museum, Morelos' Birthplace, Morelos' House, Museum of Colonial Art, Church of Carmen, Government Palace, Church of San Jose, Federal Palace, Aqueduct, Las Tarascas Fountain, Alfredo Zalce Contemporary Art Museum, and Cuauhtemoc Park. You can easily spend a day or two exploring the major attractions in this expansive downtown section.

Outside Centro, Morelia sprawls both east and south with most of the city lying to the southeast. Here the city takes on a more modern and commercial look with its wide tree-lined boulevards, shopping centers, supermarkets, fast-food restaurants, and high-rise buildings. Just drive along its southern ring road, Periferico Nueva España, and you'll pass by a heavily commercialized area, complete with a popular Wal-Mart, Costco, and Sam's Club.

At least from surface appearances, Morelia appears to be a relatively prosperous city despite its lack of an industrial base. Its economy is largely based on government, education, tourism, and distribution. The city is a magnet for students with its seven universities and numerous other educational institutions. Tourism, with a heavy emphasis on shopping for local arts and crafts, is the lifeblood for supporting thousands of artisans and shopkeepers throughout the state of Michoacán.

While Morelia offers numerous attractions, many of the most interesting things to see and do are found outside this city.

SHOPPING

For the capital of a state so rich in the production of arts and crafts, the city of Morelia is surprisingly short on places to shop. Indeed, much of the city is of little interest to travel-shoppers. The crowded streets of the central commercial area is of greatest interest to history and cultural buffs who come here to marvel at the city's beautiful colonial architecture and visit churches and museums, and to local residents doing their daily shopping. The shops in this area are relatively boring, with a disproportionate number of fabric, clothing, and accessory shops, especially along Allende Valladolid, primarily appealing to local tastes. One senses the fabric and sewing supply shops are in competition with ready-made clothing shops. This is not a place you need to spend much time shopping. In fact, there is basically one shop you should set your sights on for shopping in downtown Morelia – **Casa de la Artesanias del Estado de Michoacán** (Calle Fray Juan de San Miguel 129, Tel. 312-0848). Located in the Ex-Convent de San Francisco on Plaza Valladolid, this is a state-sponsored museum, shop, and artisan center. Built in the 1500s, the imposing two-story stone building is a delightful setting for showcasing the state's many different arts and crafts. The museum on the first floor includes a nice collection of copper pots and ceramics. But it's the state craft shop on the ground floor that showcases the largest range of products, from decorative ceramic plates and copper pots to furniture, guitars, pottery, jewelry, masks, and clothes.

You will find a market and a few shops worth visiting in Morelia. Shoppers are especially drawn to the popular sweets, candy, or sugar market – **Mercado de Dulces** – at Avenida Madero Pte. and Valentin Gómez Farías (behind the tourist office and Palacio Clavijero). **La Casa del Anticuario** (Corregidora 311, Tel. 317-3294) includes an unusual and chaotic collection of antiques and collectibles – a real treasure hunter's paradise. **Itzcoatl** (Aldama 45, Tel. 317-4584), which has its own factory 10 miles outside the city, offers an attractive collection of hand-painted ceramics (plates, bowls, cups) in both traditional and contemporary designs that  also are microwave-proof. **La Casa del Portal** (Guillermo Prieto 30, Centro Histórico, Tel. 317-4217, website: www.lacasadelportal.com), the city's most unusual restaurant, includes several rooms of arts, crafts, and painted furniture – everything here is for sale, including the tables, chairs, and table service you're sitting at and using in the second floor dining area of the restaurant!

Outside the city center, in the hills near the Villa Montaña and Villa San Jose hotels (Calle Patzimba), are a few excellent quality arts and crafts shops. As you drive up the hill toward the hotels, you'll see **Galeria Alcatraz** (Rey Tanganxoán 166, Col. Vista Bella, Tel. 315-7694) on your right. This is Morelia's equivalent of "Pier 1" – a three-level home decorative shop with lots of glass balls, ceramic dishes, metal art, wrought iron furniture, beds, chests, and glassware. Just around the corner from Villa Montaña is one of our favorite arts, crafts, and home decorative shops in Morelia – **Galeria La Bola Santa** (corner of Calle Patzimba and Tanganxoán, Avenida Tanganxoán 575, Tel./Fax 314-0573, open 11am to 8:30pm). Just three doors away is **El Perro Que Fuma** (Tanganxoán 549, Tel. 324-5874, website: www.geocities.com/ el_perro_que_fuma), a small shop with paintings, folk art, jewelry, and tie-dyed T-shirts. Villa Montaña has an arts, crafts, and gift shop that offers some of the best quality handcrafted products in the state.

Pátzcuaro

Located 43 miles southwest of Morelia, Pátzcuaro (population nearly 100,000) is one of the most delightful towns in Mexico. Situated at 7,250 feet in the Sierra Madre mountains (pack a sweater or jacket) and home to the Purépecha Indians, the city is located along the southeast shore of lovely Lake Pátzcuaro. The body of water is famous for its butterfly net fishermen, Janitzio

Island (especially great place to visit for the Day of the Dead festival on November 1-2), and craft villages. Picturesque and exuding lots of local charm, this quaint town of cobblestone streets, white stucco buildings, lovely plazas, and lots of shops and restaurants is a delightful place to visit. It's an extremely inviting town that has the look and feel of old Mexico.

The town has three plazas, located within a few blocks of each other, that variously function as commercial centers: Plaza Vasco de Quiroga (Plaza Grande or Plaza Principal), Plaza Gertrudis Bocanegra (Plaza Chica or Plaza de San Agustín), and Plaza San Francisco. **Plaza Vasco de Quiroga** is a very large and beautiful square surrounded by shops, hotels, and restaurants. During the Day of the Dead celebrations, this plaza becomes the center for vendors and celebrations. The much smaller **Plaza Gertrudis Bocanegra**, located one block north of

Plaza Vasco de Quiroga, is adjacent to the city market (Mercado) and functions as the city's commercial center. **Plaza San Francisco** is located one block west of Plaza Vasco de Quiroga and functions as the site for the popular **pottery market** that takes place here every Friday.

Most visitors focus on the shops and restaurants on the west and southwest side of Plaza Vasco de Quiroga and within one or two blocks of this plaza. Be sure to visit the **Casa de los Once Patios** (House of the Eleven Patios, one block southeast of Plaza Vasco de Quiroga on Calle Madrigal de las Altas Torres s/n) which has a few arts, crafts, textile, clothes, and silver jewelry shops and an excellent restaurant. Each shop specializes in a regional craft, such as copperware from Santa Clara del Cobre and straw products from Tzintzuntzan. One of the most interesting shops in this complex is **Seshashi** (Tel. 342-4753) for hand-painted plates, bowls, and gourds using a special pre-Hispanic Indian maque painting technique (looks like lacquer but the coating is a mixture of insects and herbs).

On the west side of the main plaza, look for **Casa Del Naranjo** (Plaza Vasco de Quiroga 29-2), a building that houses several arts and crafts shops as well as an excellent restaurant – El Primer Piso – overlooking the plaza. We especially like **Artesanias La Mojiganga** (Plaza Vasco de Quiroga 29-2, Tel. 342-4695) for a collection of attractively designed ceramics, masks, and Day of the Dead skeleton figures. Just across the street on the southwest corner of the plaza is **Herrajas Artisticos** (Plaza Vasco de Quiroga 36, Tel. 342-0674) for nice embroidered dresses, blouses, children's clothes, pillows, and tablecloths.

The city **market** (across from northwest corner of Plaza Gertrudis Bocanegra), which is especially crowded on Sunday, Monday, and Friday, includes some crafts as well as shawls, sarapes, and local textiles.

You also may want to visit a few villages along the lakeshore where you can buy directly from artisans. Many of the villages in this area continue to specialize in one particular craft – a tradition dating from the 16th century, when Bishop Vasco de Quiroga attempted to improve the welfare of the poor and exploited Indians by establishing specialty craft villages.

Santa Clara del Cobre

Located nearly 13 miles northeast of Pátzcuaro, the quaint town of Santa Clara is Mexico's famous copper town. Here you'll find numerous artisans producing copper pots, plates, trays, napkin rings, candlesticks, jewelry, and other objects. You can visit some of the artisans, such as **Margarito Garcia Nuñez** (Ignacio Allende 90, Tel. 343-0670), who still makes copper objects the old-fashioned way – firing scrap copper and pounding it into fascinating art objects which are for sale in his home shop. **Taller Pérez e Hijos** (Lázaro Cárdenas 311, Tel. 343-0144) is the factory and

home of master artisan Felipe Pérez Ornelas who works in both silver and copper and produces distinctively designed 12-headed copper pots.

Most of Santa Clara's retail copper shops are found around the small plaza along Portal Juárez. The best shop here is **Galeria Carmelita** (Portal Juárez 171, Tel. 343-0103) which represents the works of major artisans throughout the state of Michoacán who produce copper and silver pots, ceramics, textiles, pottery, and masks. This shop also is owned by David Ortega who conducts arts and crafts tours of the area and operates a shop at the Villa Montaña in Morelia (see page 252). Next door you'll find another copper shop run by David's relatives – **El Arco** (Portal Juárez 170, Tel. 343-0103) – which offers less expensive items produced primarily for the mass market.

If you're in the area during August 11th and 12th, you may want to attend the **National Copper Fair**. It also coincides with a couple of other local festivals and includes hammered copper work competition, parades, dancing, bands, and outdoor activities.

A word of caution when buying copper pots supposedly produced and signed by master artisans. Some famous artisans are known for acquiring unsigned pieces and then putting their own names on the pots, which then results in doubling or tripling the prices. Be very suspicious of any pricey signed pots that seem to proliferate in shops. The nature of this copper work is such that it can take weeks to complete a single piece, from forging and hammering to finishing a design. After comparing the quality work found at Galeria Carmelita and produced in the home workshops of masters Margarito Garcia Nuñez and Felipe Pérez Ornelas, you'll begin seeing the difference between the real artistic work and the many imitations that can easily fool the uneducated eye.

Nearby Towns and Villages

You can easily spend a week visiting the many towns and villages throughout the state that specialize in producing and selling a wide variety of arts and crafts. Here's a sampling of what lies ahead. Most of these towns and villages are located either between Morelia and Pátzcuaro or around Lake Pátzcuaro and can be visited as part of a day trip from either Morelia or Pátzcuaro:

❑ **Capula:** Located 10 miles west of Morelia, this town is famous for its hand-painted red-clay pottery. It includes the beautiful home and workshop of one of Mexico's most famous sculptors and painters, **Juan Torres** (La Candelaria, Belia Canals Henriquez, Tel. 320-5637). It's also home of noted potter **Pedro Ruiz Martinez** (Calle Jose Maria) who produces special dot pottery and only sells from his home workshop.

❑ **Tzintzuntzan:** Located 10 miles north of Pátzcuaro, this village is noted for ancient Tarascan tombs and crafts. Specializes in wood carvings, straw crafts, and ceramics. Look for one of Mexico's best ceramicists here – **Luis Manuel Morales Gámez** (Ceramica Tzintzuntzan Plaza Principal s/n, Tel. 354-0938) who produces top quality pottery with distinctive blue and brown pre-Hispanic designs.

❑ **Tócuaro:** This small village specializes in masks and wood carvings. It's home to one of Mexico's master mask makers, **Juan Horta Castillo**, and his family (sign on door to family compound says Juan Orta Mascaras, Calle Hildago 4, Col. Ibarra, Tel. 318-9493).

❑ **Econgarícuraro:** Located near the southwestern shore of Lake Pátzcuaro, this village is home to a large furniture factory that turns out a wide variety of brightly painted furniture – **Mfa Eronga, Inc.** (Avenida Urueta Carrillo S/N, Tel. 344-0207. Website for warehouse in the U.S.: www.mfaeronga. com.)

❑ **Quiroga:** Located five miles northeast of Tzintzuntzan, this town is famous for what the locals call "cha-cha shopping" – lots of tacky arts and crafts, including baskets, guitars, and shoes. For shoppers with little or no taste!

Best of the Best

MORELIA

❑ **Casa de las Artesanias del Estado de Michoacán:** *Ex-Convento de San Francisco, Calle Fray Juan de San Miguel 129, Centro, Tel. 312-0848. Open Monday through Saturday, from 10am to 3pm and 5-8pm, and Sunday from 10am to 4:30pm.* Located four blocks east of the city's famous cathedral, this interesting old stone building was once a convent. It now houses both a museum (primarily copper pots from Santa Clara del Cobre in glass cases on the ground floor) and several arts and crafts shops on the ground and first floor. This is a good place to get an

overview of products and talent in the state of Michoacán. The best shop here is the state-operated arts and crafts emporium (Casa de las Artesanias) which is found immediately to the right of the main entrance to the building. The first room of this shop displays many beautiful ceramics, some of which are award-winning pieces that are for sale. The other rooms include nice displays of furniture, musical instruments (guitars, violins, harps), pottery, masks, jewelry, blouses, jackets, dresses, table-cloths, and linen placemats. The upstairs workshops and shops offer a mixed (often disappointing) assortment of handicrafts and souvenirs that really don't represent the best local talent. The good stuff is downstairs and in the various towns and villages we discussed earlier.

❑ **La Casa del Anticuario:** *Corregidora 311, Centro, Tel. 317-3294.* This place initially looks like a hole-in-the-wall, but it quickly unfolds with many surprises the higher you climb! If you like antiques, collectibles, or just rummaging through interesting old stuff, this could become one of your favorite shops. Climb a stairway narrowed by collectibles and junk on both sides, and you'll enter the first of several rooms that define this four-level house-turned-antique emporium. You'll immediately know you're in a very special place that has lots of age. Eclectic, interesting, and occasionally appealing to the pocket-book, this shop includes several rooms jam-packed with photos, old trays (Pepsi), glasses, chests, tin boxes, large cruci-fixes, old chairs, trunks, books, furniture, religious paintings, lanterns, cash registers, pharmacy items, and ceramics. It's an unusual and chaotic collection of antiques and collectibles that begs to find the right buyers. Be sure to climb to the roof where you will be treated to a nice view of the cathedral. Also, don't miss the surprising working chapel on the third floor with its many interesting old religious figures.

❑ **La Casa del Portal:** *Guillermo Prieto 30, Centro Historico, Tel. 317-4217, website: www.lacasadelportal.com.* Located just off the main square and behind Burger King and across from the American Express office, here's a great shopping and dining concept. This combination restaurant and shop is a real dining and shopping treat. In addition to serving excellent food, the restaurant-shop showcases several rooms of quality arts, crafts, and painted furniture. Look for candles, jewelry, T-shirts, lanterns, pots, ceramic tableware, painted furniture, drawings, watercolors, oil paintings, and religious figures. They even offer the whimsical ceramic sculptures of Rodo Padilla (fat cowboy and sports figures). Everything here is for sale, including the tables, chairs, and table service that may be in use. If you like what you see, regardless if someone is dining at your favorite table, buy it!

❑ **Galeria La Bola Santa:** *Corner of Calle Patzimba and Tanganxoán (near Villa Montaña, Avenida Rey Tanganxoan 575 Vista Bella-Santa Maria, Tel./Fax 314-0573. Open 11am to 8:30pm.* Previously known as the Galeria Santa Sirenita, this shop is filled with a tasteful collection of top quality arts, crafts, and home decorative items. Look for contemporary furniture, paintings, ceramics, copper pots, lamps, candle holders, alabaster bowls, and tableware. Includes many unusual pieces not found in the typical local arts and crafts shop. This is the type of shop that would show and do well in the upscale Polanco area of Mexico City.

❑ **Villa Montaña Shop:** *Patzimba 201, Col. Vista Bella C.P., Tel. 314-0231.* Offers a fine collection of quality arts and crafts from the state of Michoacán – copper pots, glassware, Catrina figures, porcelain, jewelry, candles, and masks. Organized and operated by local arts and crafts specialist David Ortega, who works directly with many of the artisans represented in this shop and who takes visitors on artisan tours of the state.

PÁTZCUARO

❑ **Arteanias La Mojiganga:** *Located in Casa Del Naranjo, Plaza Vasco de Quiroga 29-2, Tel. 342-4695.* One of the area's best quality shops. A good source for acquiring uniquely designed ceramics. Also includes masks and Day of the Dead skeleton figures.

❑ **Herrajas Artisticos:** *Located just across the street from the southwest corner of the plaza, Plaza Vasco de Quiroga 36, Tel. 342-0674.* Offers a nice collection of embroidered dresses, blouses, pillows, children's clothes, and tablecloths that represents the work of local craftspeople.

❑ **Seshashi:** *House of the Eleven Patios (La Casa de los Once Patios Local 2), one block southeast of Plaza Vasco de Quiroga on Calle Madrigal de las Altas Torres s/n, Tel. 342-4753.* Artisan Mario Agustin Gasper produces uniquely designed painted plates, bowls, and gourds that look like lacquer but actually use a special Indian and pre-Hispanic painting technique (*maque*) involving insects and herbs.

SANTA CLARA DEL COBRE

❑ **Galeria Carmelita:** *Portal Juárez 171, Tel. 343-0103.* If you're looking for a one-stop shop that represents some of the area's top artisans, be sure to visit here. Owned and operated by

David Ortega and his family, this shop specializes in silver and hammered copper pots, ceramics, furniture, candles, textiles, and masks. Once you visit here, you'll recognize the difference between quality arts and crafts versus the many made-for-tourist handicrafts and souvenirs found in markets and many other shops. The shop next door, El Arco Artesanias en Cobre (Portal Juárez 170, Tel. 343-0103), includes a less expensive line of attractive copperware suitable for display. Galeria Carmelita is the perfect place for collectors of fine arts and crafts.

❑ **Taller Pérez e Hijos:** *Lázaro Cárdenas 311, Tel. 343-0144.* This is the workshop and shop of one of Mexico's master artisans, Felipe Pérez Ornelas, who works in copper and silver. He's especially famous for his hammered internal and external incising of copper pots and 12-headed copper pot figures.

❑ **Margarito Garcia Nuñez:** *Ignacio Allende 90, Tel. 343-0670.* This small home-based workshop and shop produces beautiful artistic copper pots. Using traditional forging and hammering techniques, the very talented Margarito starts with scrap copper and forges it into finished art pieces. While much of his work is available at Galeria Carmelita, you can also buy directly from him here.

CAPULA

❑ **La Candelaria:** *Belia Canals Henriquz, Tel. 4320-5637.* Welcome to the expansive home compound, workshop, and chapel of famous sculptor and painter Juan Torres. Surrounded by adobe walls, this compound is a real treat for art lovers. The uniquely designed and colorful separate chapel building is filled with paintings by the artist. The large workshop produces his distinctive and popular Catrina figures – elegantly

dressed skeleton women. Here Juan Torres both produces and teaches other artisans how to make these compelling figures.

TZINTZUNTZAN

❑ **Ceramica Tzintzuntzan:** *Plaza Principal s/n., Tel. 40938.* Located adjacent to the Ex-Convento de San Francisco, this is the workshop of one of Mexico's finest ceramicists – Luis Manuel Morales Gámez. He produces lovely blue and brown pottery with unique pre-Hispanic figures and primitive designs, many of which came from his father. The best time to come here is when Manuel fires his furnace and opens his oven, which is once every two to three months. In fact, many dealers come here on the day of the firing so they can have the first pick of his new products. If you arrive just before a firing, you may find very little inventory remaining, or perhaps only be able to buy his seconds or rejects and watch Manuel  work the wheel in shaping new pots. Arriving here on the day he opens his oven or shortly thereafter will allow you to acquire some terrific ceramics that are best described as art or collectible pieces.

TÓCUARO

❑ **Juan Horta Castillo:** *Sign on door to family compound says Juan Orta Mascaras, Calle Hildago 4, Col. Ibarra, Tel. 318-9493.* Meet talented mask maker Juan Horta Castillo and his family at this small home workshop. One of Mexico's master  traditional mask makers, who carves masks from wood and paints and lacquers the finished product. Has won national awards and exhibited abroad.

ECONGARICURARO

❑ **mfa/Eronga, Inc.:** *Avenida Urueta Carrillo S/N, Tel. 344-0207. Website for their warehouse in Tucson, Arizona: www.mfa eronga.com.* Established in 1981 by an American couple, Maureen and Steve Rosenthal, who headed up a state-sponsored craft project for promoting rural development, mfa/

Eronga is now one of the premier hand-crafted painted furniture factories in Mexico. Few people are neutral about this furniture – you either love it or hate it. This is definitely an  acquired taste for someone who has special design needs and a place that can carry such whimsically designed and colorful items. Producing brightly painted carved tables, chairs, chests, screens, armoires, beds, consoles, office furniture, and accessory pieces, this factory creates its own unique designs as well as does custom work. Much of this brightly colored work is fascinating as is the process of watching local villagers cut, carve, assemble, and paint this unusual furniture. The carved and painted products, such as a Venetian bridge, expressionist floral, or underwater headboard and a dalmation dog or Day of the Dead chair, require very special places where colorful design tastes are welcome. Indeed, we can see some of this furniture being popular in parts of Arizona, New Mexico, or Florida or in a bar or sun room. You'll find this furniture in a few restaurants in Mexico (check out La Casa del Portal in Morelia). Given the labor-intensive nature of this work, as well as the nature of the factory labor, much of this work is expensive by local standards – painted chairs, for example, run from US$400 to US$600 each, and a small table and four-chair set can run from US$2,000 to US$4,000. The factory has catalogs with pictures of their various products. Nearly 50 percent of the everything produced here is exported to the United States. Given the problems of shipping from Mexico, you may want to consider purchasing items from their warehouse in Tucson, Arizona. The company website (www.mfaeronga.com) primarily showcases items available from that warehouse. For a good overview of what you are likely to encounter in the factory, do visit this website where you will find numerous photos of their creations. A visit to the factory in the village of Econgarícuraro is an interesting experience in local design, craftsmanship, and entrepreneurship. Tour the factory, view the products, and examine the catalogs. You may just find something you fall in love with and have a place for!

Accommodations

Many visitors to this area stay in either Morelia or Pátzcuaro. However, we prefer being based in Morelia since there is more to do here at night and the best hotels and restaurants are found in Morelia. Pátzcuaro is more for budget travelers, with modest hotels and few good restaurants. The following properties in Morelia represent the best in accommodations:

❑ **Villa Montaña:** *Patzimba 201, Col. Vista Bella C.P., 58090 Morelia, Michoacán, Mexico, Tel. (52-443) 314-0231, Fax (52-443) 315-1423. Toll-free from U.S. & Canada, 800-525-4800. Website: www.villamontana.com.mx.* Nestled in the Santa María hills overlooking the picturesque city, Villa Montaña is secluded, yet readily accessible to the city center within ten minutes by car. Enter the reception area and you feel you have entered an upscale European home. The stone fireplace, rich paintings, ceramic jars, and selected pieces of antique furniture provide a peaceful setting to converse with friends or simply relax. Each of the cottage-like guest suites has its own setting amid luxuriant gardens, patios, and terraces with panoramic views. Thirty-six spacious units include a presidential suite, 4 master suites with 2 bedrooms and baths, 5 one-bedroom master suites, 13 junior suites, and 13 standard rooms. Each guestroom is unique and decorated with antique pieces mixed with regional handcrafts and folk art. Spacious baths are tiled and some have decorative stone columns from tub surround to ceiling. All guestrooms and suites have one or more fireplaces as well as amenities expected of a luxury hotel. (There is no mini-bar.) *The Terrace Restaurant* offers excellent regional and international cuisine in a lovely setting. Personal tailored and guided tours are offered to nearby craft towns or to the Monarch Butterfly Sanctuary (see reference on pages 268-269). The view from the swimming pool is spectacular. Tennis Court; Exercise Room; Spa; Golf nearby; Business Center; Meeting/Banquet Facilities.

❑ **Hotel Los Juaninos:** *Morelos Sur 39 Col. Centro, C.P. 58000, Morelia, Michoacán, México, Tel. (52-443) 312-0036, E-mail: juaninos@mich.1.telmex.net.mx. Website: www.hoteljuaninos.com.mx.* Located in the heart of the city, right on the town square, Hotel Los Juaninos, through its eclectic-romantic design, is a masterful blend of revival styles including Mexican colonial, neoclassic, romantic, gothic, and even elements of native Indian design. It retains the best of its heritage while providing all the comfort, luxury, and services expected by today's guests. Entry to the lobby is by way of a spacious hall lined with arches that frame original 19th century stained glass panels from the Art Nouveau period. The hall contains French-style furniture that recalls the luxury of the former palace. Thirty-three guestrooms, each decorated in a distinctive style, are set around two courtyards. Modern tiled bathrooms retain the European-styled bathtubs. *La Azotea Restaurant* offers diners the flavor of Mexican haute cuisine, influenced by international trends, and created using local ingredients. Business Center; Conference/Banquet Facilities.

Restaurants

MORELIA

❑ **Casa de la Calzada:** *Calzada Fray Antonio de San Miguel 344, Tel. 313-5319. Website: www.casadelacalzada.com*. Located near the aqueducts, the popular restaurant serves excellent contemporary Mexican dishes in the elegant setting of one of Morelia's historic homes. Try the pollo del jardin de los naranjos, filete sor tequila, salmon de la gloria, or pasta citrus. Check out their inventive menu, with delectable photos, by visiting their informative website.

❑ **Terrace Restaurant:** *Patzimba 201, Col. Vista Bella C.P., Tel. 314-0231*. This well appointed and romantic restaurant with live music was one of our best dining experiences in Mexico. Offers excellent regional and international cuisine and outstanding service. Try the salmon trout or shrimp stuffed chicken.

❑ **La Casa del Portal:** *Guillermo Prieto 30, Tel. 317-4217. Website: www.lacasadelportal.com*. This colorful second floor restaurant overlooks the Plaza de Armas. Part arts and crafts gallery and painted furniture shop with four dining rooms, this place has lots of great character. It also serves excellent dishes. Try the arrachera Valladolid.

❑ **San Miguelito:** *Avenida Camelinas Contraesquina del Centro de Convenciones, Tel. 324-4411. Website: www.sanmiguelito.com.mx*. This combination restaurant, bar, and gallery offers one of the area's most interesting dining experiences. The ambience is borderline tacky but nonetheless fascinating. Includes 180 upside-down statues of St. Anthony. Everything in this unique restaurant, including the statues, is for sale. The bar is set up as an in-your-face black and red bull ring! One of those unforgettable restaurants that also serves some decent dishes. Try the tortilla soup.

PÁTZCUARO

❑ **El Primer Piso:** *Vasco de Quiroga 29, Tel. 342-0122. Open Wednesday through Monday, 1-10pm; Sunday 1-8pm*. Located on the second floor overlooking Plaza Vasco de Quiroga, this airy restaurant also functions as an art gallery – all paintings on the walls are for sale. Includes a surprisingly inventive and eclectic menu for Pátzcuaro. Try the Gloria Chicken or Chicken Nogada, two really excellent dishes.

❑ **El Patio:** *Plaza Vasco de Quiroga 19, Tel. 342-0484. Open 8am to 10pm.* This popular restaurant is especially noted for its many delicious fish dishes (try the local whitefish), pollo en mole, sopa tarasca (a regional bean soup), enchiladas, and quesadillas.

Enjoying Your Stay

Being a rich historical and cultural area, the state of Michoacán has a great deal to offer visitors. From the impressive colonial architecture, museums, churches, and plazas of Morelia to the charming white stucco buildings, narrow cobblestone streets, and lakeside setting of Pátzcuaro and many other towns and villages, this is a beautiful area to explore for history, culture, and sightseeing. If you visit this area during the Day of the Dead festival period (November 1-2), you'll be treated to one of the most impressive celebrations found anywhere in Mexico. This is not a particularly attractive area for sports enthusiasts or individuals interested in a late night bar and disco scene, although opportunities do exist for such activities.

Except in Morelia, there's not a great deal to do at night in most towns and villages in Michoacán. Most places are relatively quiet by 10pm.

Being a state capital and a university city, Morelia is a lively city for evening dining, shopping, and strolling. It has a few folkclubs, nightclubs, and theaters. Popular clubs with folk and Latin music include **La Porfiriana** (Calle Corregidora 694, Tel. 312-2663), **Peña Colibri** (Galeana 36, Tel. 312-2261), and **La Casa de los Espiritus** (Galeana 70, Tel. 334-3118). The city offers some evening cultural activities, such as musical and dance performances, films, and art exhibitions. Check with the local **tourist office** (Secretaría Estatal de Turismo, Palacio Clavijero, Calle Nigromante 79, Tel. 317-2371) or the **Casa de la Cultura** (Avenida Morelos Nte. 485) for information on current and upcoming events. For example, the world-famous **Boy's Choir of Morelia** occasionally performs in Morelia. The city hosts three international musical festivals: **International Guitar Festival** (May); **International Organ Festival** (May); and the **International Festival of Music** (June).

For history and cultural buffs, sightseeing highlights in the state of Michoacán near Morelia and Pátzcuaro include the following:

Morelia

❑ **Casa Museo de Morelos:** *Avenida Morelos Sur 323, Tel. 313-2651. Open daily from 9am to 7pm. Free on Sunday.* This attractive two-story museum chronicles the history of several independence leaders with paintings, photos, and artifacts.

❑ **Catedral:** *Avenida Madero and Plaza de Armas.* Built between 1640 and 1744, this towering cathedral (twin 200-foot towers) is one of the city's major symbols. Inside the cathedral you'll find an awesome 4,600-pipe organ which plays a major role in the international organ festival held in Morelia each May.

❑ **Museo Regional Michoacano:** *Calle Allende 305, Tel. 312-0407. Open Tuesday through Saturday from 9am to 7pm and on Sunday from 9am to 4pm.* Covers the history of Mexico from pre-Hispanic times until 1940, the year President Lázaro Cárdenas of Michoacán ended his presidency. Includes a unique collection of paintings and artifacts.

PÁTZCUARO

❑ **La Basilica de Nuestra Señora de la Salud (Basilica of Our Lady of Health):** *Ensañanza Arciga, near Calle Benigno Serrato.* One of the oldest and most important churches (dating from 1554 and elevated to the status of a basilica in 1924) in the area. Constructed by Michoacán's famous first bishop, Don Vasco de Quiroga, who is entombed just to the left of the entrance. Includes the much revered figure of Our Lady of Health, the patron saint of the region, which was constructed of maize paste in the 16th century.

❑ **Museo de Artes Populares:** *Enseñanza Arciga, Tel. 342-1029. Open Tuesday to Saturday from 9am to 7pm and Sunday from 9am to 2:30pm.* Houses an interesting collection of colonial and contemporary arts and crafts from the state of Michoacán – paintings, copperware, shawls, ceramics, masks, and lacquerware.

❑ **Biblioteca Pública Gertrudis Bocanegra:** *North end of Plaza Bocanegra. Open Sunday through Friday from 9am to 7pm and on Saturday from 10am to 2pm.* This building is noted for its famous mural of the area painted by Juan O'Gorman in 1942.

❑ **Isla de Janitzio (Janitzio Island):** Located in the center of Lake Pátzcuaro, this somewhat touristy island of the Purépecha Indians takes about 20 minutes to reach by boat. The ride along the picturesque lake, where you see fisherman using the famous butterfly nets, alone is worth the trip. The island is basically a fishing village which is noted for its towering (130-foot) statue of hero Don José Morelos y Pavón. The island also is the scene of the popular candle-lit "Night of the Dead" ceremony on November 1st of each year, which attracts many international visitors.

ELSEWHERE IN MICHOACÁN

❑ **El Rosario Monarch Butterfly Sanctuary (Santuario de Mariposas el Rosario):** *70 miles east of Morelia via Highway 15 to*

Zitácuaro. Open daily from 10am to 5pm. Each year, in late October and early November more than 100 million monarch butterflies fly over 2,500 miles from south central Canada and northern United States to hibernate and reproduce in eastern Michoacán. They leave for a return trip in mid-March. This fascinating phenomenon attracts thousands of visitors to the state each year. Organized tours to this area take about 10 hours. For information on monarch butterflies, visit www.mon archwatch.org.

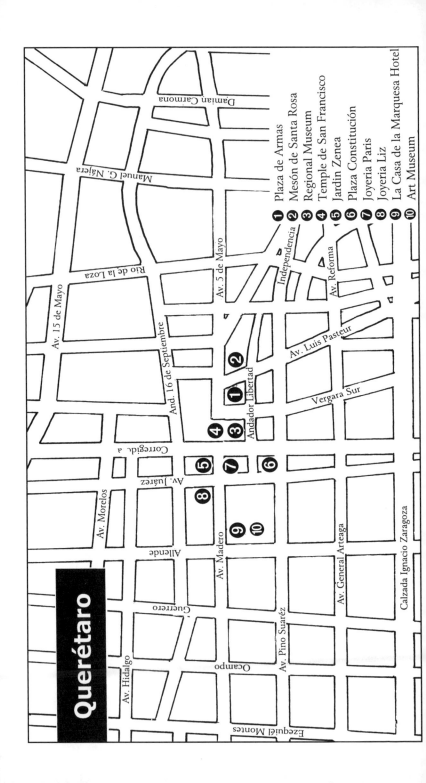

Querétaro

1. Plaza de Armas
2. Mesón de Santa Rosa
3. Regional Museum
4. Temple de San Francisco
5. Jardin Zenea
6. Plaza Constitución
7. Joyeria Paris
8. Joyeria Liz
9. La Casa de la Marquesa Hotel
10. Art Museum

12

Querétaro

R ICH IN HISTORY AND CULTURE, picturesque
Querétaro is one of Mexico's real colonial gems. If
you are exploring the Morelia, San Miguel de Allende,
and Guanajuato areas, be sure to include surprising
Querétaro in your travel plans. It may well become one of your
favorite places in Mexico. A large city with a small-town atmosphere, it's a great place to just relax among lovely plazas, outdoor restaurants, and architectural masterpieces.

An Important Center

Centrally located and only 130 miles northwest of Mexico City
and 50 miles southeast of San Miguel Allende, Querétaro played
many important roles in the Mexican independence movement.
In fact, the movement began here in 1810; the treaty of Guadalupe
Hidalgo ending the Mexican-American War was signed here in
1848; the Emperor Maximilian was defeated and executed here
in 1867; and the Mexican Constitution was signed here in 1917.

Querétaro, a beautiful old colonial city of over 850,000 residents, is especially noted for its delightful baroque architecture,
churches, temples, mansions, museums, and plazas. While this

□ Centrally located, this is one of Mexico's most charming cities – and possibly its neatest and cleanest.

□ The city is noted for its delightful baroque architecture, churches, temples, mansions, museums, and plazas.

□ Querétaro is the center for Mexico's opal production. Look for fiery red and rock opals, amethysts, and other semi-precious stones and jewelry in the city and surrounding area.

city has little to offer travel-shoppers, it does boast one unique product that distinguishes it from other cities in Mexico – fiery red and rock opals, amethysts, and other semi-precious stones and jewelry. Querétaro is the center for Mexico's opal production. If you are familiar with opals elsewhere in the world, and especially the famous Australian opal, you will find Mexican opals to be a fascinating variation of the opal family.

Getting to Know You

Querétaro is the capital of one of Mexico's smallest states, Querétaro, with a population of 1.4 million. It's a scenic state rich in history, intriguing architecture, gems, and appealing thermal waters for hot springs and spa enthusiasts. Visitors are especially attracted to the city of Querétaro as well as the charming towns of San Juan del Rio and Tequisquiapan, which offer some interesting shopping opportunities for gems, jewelry, arts, and crafts.

There's something about Querétaro that makes this an especially appealing city for many visitors. It's one of the cleanest and neatest cities in Mexico due to the extraordinary efforts of local authorities to keep it that way. Indeed, the downtown area is very pedestrian-friendly. Most street vendors have been relocated to one neat and tidy pedestrian-only street, Andador Libertad, which connects Corregidora and Pasteur streets.

An extremely charming city with lots of character, Querétaro boasts many ornate baroque buildings, monuments, fountains, plazas, and a five-mile long aqueduct with 74 arches. The downtown area is relatively compact and thus easy to cover on foot. The city center is located around Jardin Zenea, the main plaza, which is located between Avenida Juárez on the west, Avenida

Corregidora on the east, 16 de Septiembre on the north, and Madero on the south. Here you'll find the city's main museums, churches, and shops all within a relatively compact 10-block area. If you stay at either of the city's two top hotels – **La Casa de la Marquesa** (Madero 41) or **Mesón de Santa Rosa** (Pasteur Sur 17, Plaza de Armas) – you'll be at either the west or east side of the downtown area.

The Streets of Querétaro

Being a relatively small central city with three major plazas in close proximity to one another, this is an easy place to understand and navigate on foot. Most major sites and shops are found within a short five-minute walk. If you orient yourself to the city's three major plazas – Plaza de Armas, Plaza Constitución, and Jardin Zenea – and its two major intersecting streets – Independencia and Corregidora – and focus your shopping along the pedestrian-only walkway of Andador Libertad as well as Madero and Corregidora, you can quickly find your way around the heart of this delightful city. If you drive into the city, let a hotel park your car (underground) since parking within the downtown area is nearly impossible.

The tourist office (Pasteur Norte 4, Tel. 212-1412, open daily from 8am to 8pm) at Plaza de Armas has maps and brochures on the city and area.

Shopping Querétaro

Most shopping of interest to visitors is found in and around the city's major hotel, La Casa de la Marquesa, and along Andador Libertad, Corregidora, Juárez, and Madero streets. Many small shops, push carts, and kiosks line the pedestrian-only street of **Andador Libertad**, which runs immediately west of Hotel Mesón de Santa Rosa and along the south side of Plaza de Armas and connects to Avenida Corregidora. The quality and selections here are quite mixed, with a disproportionate amount of kitschy jewelry and handicraft offerings. It can be a fun place to shop for souvenirs and T-shirts.

One of the best shops in Querétaro is found at the **La Casa de la Marquesa Hotel** (Madero 41, on the corner of Madero and Allende, Tel. 212-0092). This is truly an international shop filled with tasteful arts, crafts, furniture, and home decorative items from Mexico, India, Indonesia, Morocco, and elsewhere. Across the street, but also on the corner of Madero and Allende, is **Agustin Parra**, an extension of the hotel shop. This place includes a nice selection of interesting furniture, chests, ceramics, linens, and candles.

A few interesting gem and jewelry shops are found around the main plaza, Jardin Zenea. Look for **Joyeria Liz** (Juárez 4, Tel. 214-0244) for opals in a wide range of colors and designs – especially rock and fiery opals made into rings, pendants, and earrings and stone slices – as well as a large selection of watches. On the south side of Jardin Zenea look for **Joyeria Paris** (Avenida Brasil 273, Tel. 213-1558), which is both a gemologist and jewelry designer with another shop in San Miguel de Allende. This shop offers beautiful rock opals set as pendants. Its other jewelry is set in silver, gold, and diamonds.

The imposing and popular **Regional Museum** (Corregidora Sur 3 and the corner of Andador Libertad, Tel. 214-2069) also includes a nice shop offering a good selection of pottery, stone carvings, costumes, masks, folk and religious art, and furniture. The La Casa Blanca commercial center includes a couple of interesting shops: **el Rehilette** (Jazmines 11 San Angel, Tel. 263-5361), a small art shop offering interesting paintings and picture frames, and **Sol y Luna** (Tel. 212-0366) for all metal mirrors, lights, and picture frames.

Since the state of Querétaro is especially famous for the production of semi-precious stones, many travel-shoppers enjoy making a trip to the nearby town of **San Juan del Rio**, which is located 32 miles southeast of Querétaro. This is one of the major production and shopping centers for semi-precious stones – opal, amethyst, turquoise, and topaz – and jewelry.

Best of the Best

❑ **La Casa de la Marquesa Hotel Shop:** *Madero 41, on the corner of Madero and Allende, Tel. 212-0092.* This well-appointed shop, housed in the city's famous 18th century baroque boutique hotel, includes an excellent collection of arts, crafts, furniture, and home decorative items from Mexico, Morocco, India, and Indonesia. Look for nicely designed ceramics, jewelry, paintings, textiles, glassware, and boxes. Also operates the shop across the street – **Agustin Parra** – which includes paintings, furniture, chests, ceramics, linens, and candles.

❑ **Joyeria Liz:** *Juárez 4, Tel. 214-0244.* This small shop just west of the central plaza (Jardin Zenea) offers a good selection of rock and fire opals made into rings, pendants, and earrings. Also includes synthetic opals and a large selection of watches. A good place to survey local opals for different colors and designs. Prices appear reasonable.

❑ **Joyeria Paris:** *Avenida Brasil 273, Tel. 213-1558.* Located across the street from the south side of Jardin Zenea, this combination gem and jewelry shop offers a good selection of loose stones and jewelry using beautiful rock opals. Designs own jewelry using gold, silver, and precious and semi-precious stones. Includes all the necessary "tools of the trade" for examining the quality of gemstones. Also has a similar jewelry shop in San Miguel de Allende.

Accommodations

Most major accommodations can be found in the downtown area near the major plazas. Some of the best properties include:

❑ **Mesón de Santa Rosa:** *Pasteur Sur 17, 76000, Querétaro, Mexico, Tel. (52-422) 224-2623, Fax (52-422) 212-5522.* Located on the Plaza de la Independencia, this wonderfully renovated 18th century hotel feels larger than it actually is. The open courtyards give a spacious feel to the grounds, and each of the 21 guestrooms and suites seem spacious as well. Tile bathrooms are roomy and provide expected amenities. Some guestrooms overlook the central courtyard with its fountain while others overlook the courtyard with the heated pool. The patio restaurant serves a variety of food.

❑ **La Casa de la Marquesa:** *Madero 41, 76000, Querétaro, Mexico, Tel. (52-422) 212-0092, Fax (52-422) 212-0098.* A member of the Small Luxury Hotels of the World, La Casa de la Marquesa fills a baroque, 18th century mansion that has been converted into a 25-room hotel. Fourteen of the guestrooms are housed in the main mansion; eleven guestrooms are housed in an adjoining building. Each room is individually decorated and furnished with antiques or antique-styled furnishings and equipped with all expected luxury and modern conveniences. The award winning restaurant, *Comedor de la Marquesa,* serves excellent food and is elegant, although the wait staff seem to be trained not to smile. The service is efficient, but taciturn.

❑ **Doña Urraca:** *5 de Mayo 117, Querétaro, Mexico, Tel. (52-422) 238-5400. Website: www.donurraca.com.mx.* This combination hotel and spa, with a panoramic view of the downtown area, is a great place to get pampered in style. Includes 24 suites in a charming colonial setting with all the amenities of a luxury hotel. Includes well equipped facilities, an excellent restaurant, and hotel/spa packages. Check out their website for detailed information and photos of the property.

Restaurants

Querétaro abounds with good restaurants. Some of the city's best restaurants are found in the major hotels and around the aqueduct and plazas.

❑ **La Casa de la Marquesa Restaurant:** *Madero 41, Tel. 212-0092.* Hands down, this is the best restaurant in Querétaro. As part of the famous baroque mansion turned luxury hotel La Casa de la Marquesa, the restaurant tends to be a bit formal and service is perhaps best described as extremely sullen and reserved. Waitresses wear uniforms reminiscent of the Flying Nun and provide robotic service. But the food here often tends to be outstanding. Try the duck in blackberry sauce, chicken breast stuffed with lobster, or red snapper Veracruz style.

❑ **La Nueva Fonda del Rufgio:** *Jardin de la Corregidora 25, Tel. 212-0755.* Serves excellent Mexican and regional dishes in both indoor and outdoor dining areas. Try the filete de huitlacoche.

❑ **1810:** *Andador Libertad 62, Tel. 212-3324.* Located on Plaza de Independencia, this indoor/outdoor restaurant serves excellent Mexican and regional specialties. Try the enchiladas Queretanas.

Enjoying Your Stay

The city offers several interesting sightseeing opportunities relating to local history, art, and culture. If time permits, include the following on your "must do" list:

❑ **Regional Museum (Museo Regional):** *Corregidora and Jardin Zenea, Tel. 212-2031. Open Tuesday to Sunday from 10am to 7pm.* This attractive museum, housed in the beautiful old Convent of San Francisco, showcases important collections from pre-Hispanic to the republican period. Nice displays of pottery, stone carvings, costumes, masks, folk art, furniture, and religious art. The largest and most significant museum in the city. Includes a nice gift shop with books, pottery, jewelry, masks, and unique bookmarks – all proceeds go to supporting the museum.

❑ **Art Museum (Museo de Arte):** *Allende Sur 14, Tel. 212-2357. Open Tuesday to Sunday from 11am to 7pm.* Housed in the former San Agustin Monastery, this museum includes a fine collection of paintings from the 16th to the 20th centuries. Displays European and Mexican art, including several Querétaro artists and photographic exhibits.

❑ **Convento de la Santa Cruz:** *Corner of Acuña and Independencia, Tel. 212-0335. Open Tuesday to Friday from 9am to 2pm and Saturday from 9am to 4:30pm.* Rich with history, including Emperor Maximilian's headquarters prior to his execution in 1867, the building includes many interesting artifacts, displays, and stories.

❑ **La Casa de la Corregidora:** *Plaza de la Independencia (northwest corner). Open Monday to Friday from 8am to 9pm and Saturday from 8am to 3pm.* Also known as the Palacio de Gobierno, this building currently houses state government offices. In 1810 its famous occupant, Doña Josefa Ortiz, warned revolutionaries Ignacio Allende and Father Miguel Hidalgo of their impending arrest. They subsequently rang the bell (a replica is now perched on top of the building) that signaled the beginning of the independence movement.

❑ **Plaza de Armas:** *At the convergence of Av. 5 de Mayo, Av. Libertad Orients, Luis Pasteur, and Vergara Sur.* Also known as Plaza de la Independencia, this lovely square is noted for its fountain and surrounding buildings.

❑ **Hot springs and health spas:** The town of Tequisquiapan, 45 miles west of Querétaro, is famous for its hot springs. It also includes opportunities to shop for arts and crafts. During the end of May (or early June), the town sponsors a national food festival.

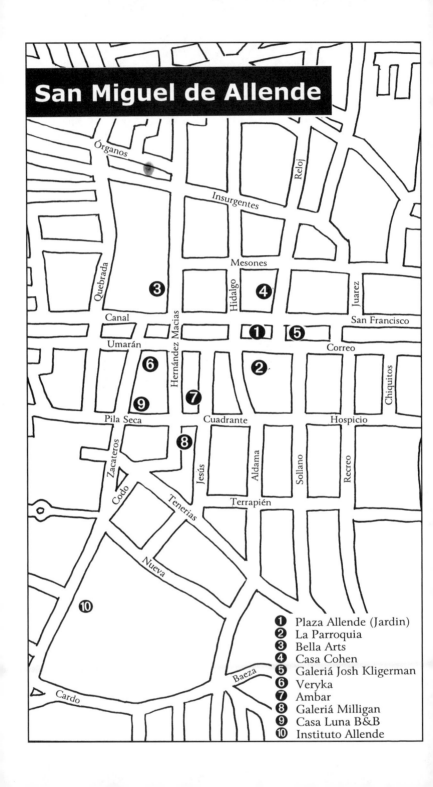

San Miguel de Allende

Órganos

Reloj

Insurgentes

Mesones

Quebrada

Hidalgo

❸

❹

Juarez

Canal

Hernández Macías

❶

❺

San Francisco

Umarán

Correo

❻

❷

Chiquitos

❾

❼

Pila Seca

Cuadrante

Hospicio

❽

Zacateros

Jesús

Aldama

Sollano

Recreo

Codo

Tenerias

Terrapién

Nueva

❿

Baeza

Cardo

13

San Miguel de Allende

WELCOME TO ONE OF Mexico's most delightful colonial cities and the ultimate destination for lifestyle shopping. Deservingly ranked by *Condé Nast Traveler* in 2000 as one of the world's 10 top cities outside the United States, San Miguel de Allende continues to exhibit all the signs of maintaining its world-class reputation. This town is to Mexico what Santa Fe is to the United States – an idyllic and compelling community where art, culture, money, and talent come together in producing a very stimulating visual and intellectual setting.

Embracing Praise

Located 180 miles northwest of Mexico City and 40 miles north of Queretaro at an altitude of 6,300 feet in the Sierra Madre Occidental mountains, this popular town of 80,000 residents is noted for its wonderful climate, beautiful flowers, lovely gardens, charming architecture, colorful buildings, colonial mansions, cobblestone streets, intriguing churches, resident artists, expatriate community, students, festivals, cultural activities, arts and crafts, studios and galleries, factories and workshops, boutique hotels, and excellent restaurants. For many travel-shoppers, San Miguel is a great place to pursue their lifestyle passions.

The list of San Miguel's positives goes on and on. But make no mistake about it – this is a "gringo" town where talent, class, style, and ambience take center stage. Unlike many other places in Mexico, this town has a real sense of community, which is partly a function of its very active community-oriented expatriates. One of Mexico's premier artist colonies and educational centers, San Miguel is a friendly and laid back community where one of the most pleasurable activities is to just stroll its many cobblestone streets in search of local treasures. In many respects, it's the ideal place to visit if you enjoy the ambience of a quaint Mexican city that also has a great deal to offer visitors who enjoy fine hotels and B&Bs, charming and entertaining restaurants, quality shopping, and numerous stimulating intellectual and cultural activities. Whether it is day or night, the town always seems to yield exciting new treasures and pleasures. It's also a very safe place to visit.

> ❑ This is a gringo town where talent, class, style and ambience take center stage.
>
> ❑ San Miguel is one of Mexico's premier artist colonies, educational centers, and expatriate communities.
>
> ❑ This is a community that likes its lifestyle to be centered around quality art, education, relaxation, dinner parties, and charitable activities.
>
> ❑ San Miguel de Allende is to Mexico what Santa Fe is to the United States – an idyllic and compelling community of art, culture, money, and talent.

A Truly Seductive Place

But be careful here. You're about to be seduced without even knowing it! San Miguel is one of those wonderfully seductive places that has changed the lives of thousands of Americans and Canadians who first came here as simple tourists but then decided to make this their permanent (3,000) or seasonal (thousands more) home as expatriates. Others decide to settle here short-term as students, attending the community's many art, language, and cultural classes and workshops. And still others are drawn to the community's intellectual climate that is entertaining, educational, and enlightening.

Declared a national historic monument in 1926, and lovingly restored during the past 30 years, laid back yet vibrant San Miguel is a very special place. As you may quickly discover, it's very easy to fall in love with such an exotic, magical, entertaining, cultured, and beautiful place that exudes a friendly and safe small-town atmosphere. Spend two or three days here and you'll understand why so many people continue to sing the praises of San Miguel and why so many talented and active foreigners have settled here as contented expatriates. Once you leave this city, many of your fondest memories of Mexico may be centered on this community.

Getting to Know You

Charming San Miguel is not what many visitors expect, especially if they arrive with visions of discovering an upscale Santa Fe, New Mexico or Carmel, California in the midst of Mexico's Sierra Madre Occidental mountains. Visually appealing with strong architectural character and color, San Miguel is still well-worn Mexico noted for its crumbling elegance in the midst of a relatively affluent community of artists, expatriates, retirees, and tourists. Compared to most other places in Mexico,  this town has a much softer edge and greater color, character, and artistic expression because of its unique residents, clientele, and historical setting that have shaped this place in so many ways.

Despite its somewhat exaggerated international reputation, San Miguel is a charming Third World city best appreciated by seasoned travelers who are well adjusted to the bumps and bruises of navigating places noted for their limited tourist infrastructure. This is not a resort city with grand hotels, swimming pools, nearby beaches, haute cuisine, and chic boutiques. Nor is it an inexpensive destination. It's an exceptionally picturesque city with bumpy streets – often laid with the crudest of stone paving – that are sometimes dusty, in disrepair, and difficult to walk.

But it's the particular community of artists, artisans, students, and expat entrepreneurs and retirees who have shaped San Miguel like no other town in Mexico. It's a community that likes its lifestyle to be centered around quality art, culture, education, relaxation, dinner parties, and charitable activities. It's a place perhaps best appreciated on the Sunday house and garden tour (see page 294) that allows visitors to peek beyond the adobe walls and stately wooden doors and into the many wonderful homes and idyllic lifestyles of local residents. Indeed, many expats have settled here to escape the stresses of life elsewhere, become part of a unique community, and enjoy a new quality of life. The longer you stay here, the more apparent these values become in a town that seems obsessed with enjoying the simple pleasures of small-town life.

Useful Print and Online Resources

Compared with most cities in Mexico, San Miguel has a great deal of useful English-language visitor information. Several hotels and shops carry the latest edition of Archie Dean's guide-book to living in and navigating the town – *The Insider's Guide to San Miguel* (US$17.00). If you wish to acquire a copy of this book prior to arriving in Mexico, visit the author's website for order information: http://insidersma.tripod.com. Primarily a directory to the town, the book includes maps and listings of everything from art galleries, schools, and restaurants to night-clubs, dentists, gyms, hospitals, shipping, tortilla factories, and supermarkets. The shopping listings are very reliable. We highly recommend getting a copy of this book for detailed informa-tion on the who, what, and where of life and commerce in San Miguel. For a beautiful pictorial treatment of the town, see the new *Visions of San Miguel: The Heartland of Mexico* by Dianne Kushner and Archie Dean (US$33.00). This book also can be ordered through the above website. Also, look for a copy of *The Best Map of San Miguel de Allende*, which is available in vari-ous outlets in San Miguel for US$2.50.

More so than most communities in Mexico, San Miguel is well represented with English-language websites. Several of these sites should prove useful in preparing for your travel-shopping adventure to this charming city:

- **Portal San Miguel**   http://portalsanmiguel.com
- **Mexico Online**   www.mexonline.com/sma.htm
- **INFO San Miguel**   www.infosma.com
- **Internet San Miguel**   www.internetsanmiguel.com
- **San Miguel Guide**   www.sanmiguelguide.com
- **San Miguel Artists**   www.sanmiguelartists.com

A Shopper's Delight

For travel-shoppers, San Miguel offers more lifestyle shopping opportunities for international visitors than most cities in Mexico. Given the city's long tradition as a center for expat artists, crafts-men, and entrepreneurs, numerous shops and galleries offer a wide range of products from Mexico and abroad. The major emphasis here is on arts, crafts, and home decorative items. Local painters and sculptors showcase their talents in several art galleries, studios, and shops throughout the town. A few quality folk art galleries represent the works of Mexico's top artisans. The town also offers a few exciting jewelry surprises not found elsewhere in Mexico. From fine art to souvenirs, there's always something of interest to shop for in San Miguel. Not surprisingly, whether you're a dedicated shopper or not, you'll often find yourself making repeated trips along the major streets to discover more treasures in the town's many tempting shops. If you leave San Miguel empty handed, chances are you ended up on the wrong streets!

The Streets of San Miguel

San Miguel is basically a walking town. Indeed, it seems to be designed for walking. Its inviting narrow and rough cobblestone streets and alleys favor individuals on foot rather than motorized vehicles, although cars and buses often make walking a hazardous exercise. If you arrive by car, find a good place to park it and then plan to see the town on foot. Be sure to select a hotel near the **Plaza Allende** (Jardin) or town center – **Casa Luna**, **Casa de Sierra Nevada**, and **Villa Jacaranda** are excellent choices – so you can easily walk to the town's major shops, restaurants, and sites. Staying in this area will conveniently put you within a five- to 15-minute walk of most everything of interest in San Miguel.

The central focus in the town is **Plaza Allende**, which is also called the **Jardin**. Located at the intersection of Hidalgo, Canal, San Francisco, Umarán, and Correo streets, this plaza is accented by the imposing larger-than-life gothic-style structure, La Parroquia, the parish church of San Miguel Arcángel. You'll most likely find yourself visiting this pleasant plaza several times during your stay, both day and night. Locals often give directions in reference to the "Jardin" as well as in reference to the inclines of streets – up hill or down hill. With a basic map of the town and focusing on the Jardin as the center of the town, you can easily find your way around the many narrow streets. Be sure to watch where you walk since token sidewalks are at best fit for a single occupant, cars park along the narrow streets, and speeding cars, taxis, and buses often make navigating the streets on foot a hazardous exercise.

Shopping San Miguel

San Miguel is well organized for travel-shoppers in search of unique treasures and pleasures. You can easily spend a couple of days shopping this city. Most shops are open Monday through Saturday, from 9 or 10am to 2pm and from 4pm to 8 or 9pm. Some shops are open on Sunday.

SHOPPING TOUR

If you're interested in taking a shopping tour of the city, contact **Gaby Hernandez** at Arte Mestizo (Umarán 25, Tel. 152-1073). Trustworthy and reliable, she offers customized shopping tours that take clients into various factories and workshops where they can buy directly from manufacturers and artisans. She also can arrange trouble-free shipping, which alone is well worth using her services!

USEFUL RESOURCES

In addition to referring to the extensive shopping section in Archie Dean's *The Insider's Guide to San Miguel* and getting a good map of the city (see page 282), several art galleries distribute free copies of the following publications which disproportionately emphasize shopping for art:

❑ **Art Gallery Guide:** A five-panel glossy advertising brochure that plots 20 participating art galleries on a map.

❑ **Inside San Miguel:** A 130-page bilingual guide to the town, including art galleries, restaurants, hotels, and cultural activities. Also visit their websites: www.insidedentro.com and www.PortalSanMiguel.com.

The weekly (published on Sunday) English-language newspaper, *Atención San Miguel*, includes information on the latest art shows, musical performances, and theatrical productions.

WHAT TO BUY

You can find just about everything you want in San Miguel. This is a city with a high concentration of quality shops specializing in fine arts (paintings and sculptures), folk art, handicrafts, jewelry, textiles, clothes, and home decorative items. Many shops feature the works of local artists while others acquire products, especially folk art, from all over Mexico. Art lovers should visit the city's many galleries as well as check on special exhibitions, many of which take place in restaurants, banks, and artists' studios. Since San Miguel is a major production center, you also can visit several artisan workshops and factories during your stay here.

WHERE TO SHOP

San Miguel's major shopping and sightseeing streets are found within a one-kilometer radius of Centro, with the Jardin at the center:

- Zacateros/Ancha de San Antonio
- Hernández Macias
- Jesús
- Umarán/Correo
- Canal/San Francisco
- Reloj
- Hidalgo
- Mesones
- Balderas

Over 90 percent of the town's major shops can be found along these streets, many of which radiate from the Jardin. In fact, you are well advised to start your shopping and sightseeing adventures at the Jardin, or along a street that leads into the Jardin, and then follow the various streets that lead to and from the plaza. The largest number of shops are concentrated to the south and west of the Jardin.

Located southwest of the Jardin is **Calle Hernández Macias**. This long north-south street houses several interesting galleries and shops. **Bazar El Nuevo Oeste** (Hernández Macias 126, Tel. 152-7571) offers an interest-

ing collection of antiques, from brown sugar molds and furniture to religious art and pots. Be sure to visit the "Please do touch" gallery/studio of Sharon Adams Milligan, **Galería Milligan** (Hernández Macias 104, Tel. 152-6923, website: www.sanmiguel artists.com/milligan), a very talented sculptor who works in bronze and ceramics. Nearby is **Zócalo** (Hernández Macias 110, Tel. 152-0663) for ceramic Catrinas and pineapples, folk art, candles, pottery, and copper candlesticks. **Rigen** (Hernández Macias 92, Tel. 154-8387) offers decorative furniture and textiles. **Bazar Unicornio** (Hernández Macias 80, Tel. 152-1306) showcases an eclectic, bordering on weird, collection of arts, crafts, antiques, and collectibles. **Casa de la Hoja Seco** (Hernández Macias 85, Tel. 152-2643), similar to a Pier 1, presents a colorful collection of ceramics, glassware, flowers, painted figures, mirrors, paintings, jewelry, and candlesticks. The popular **Belles Arts** cultural center (Hernández Macias 75, Tel. 152-0289) includes galleries and exhibitions. Across the street is **Plaza Colonial** with several small art, lamp, jewelry, crafts, and clothing shops. One of the best places here is **Cerroblanco** (Plaza Colonial, Canal 21 Int. 109, Tel. 154-4888) for contemporary silver and gold jewelry.

Parallel to the east of Hernández Macias is cobblestoned **Jesús**. This relatively quiet street is home to several of the city's

best shops. One of our very favorites here is the relatively new **Ambar** (Jesús 21-B, Tel. 154-4058) which showcases a dazzling array of wonderful amber jewelry and carved figures from the state of Chiapas. **SaVia** (Jesús 12, Tel. 154-4866) offers good quality folk art, prints, and paintings of both established and unknown artisans. **Galeria Atenea** (Jesús 2, Tel. 152-5965) showcases the works of several contemporary Mexican artists as well as the unique sculptures and jewelry of Sergio Bustamante (see our descriptions of his work for his shops in Mexico City, Puerto Vallarta, and Guadalajara).

Near the **Jardin**, look for **Casa Cohen** (Reloj 12, Tel. 152-1434) for an extensive collection of wrought iron furniture, benches, copper sinks, brass hardware, fireplace accessories, wine racks, lanterns, and silver trays. **La Antiqua Casa Canela** (Umaran 20, Tel. 152-1880) includes several rooms of home decorative items, including stone sculptures, furniture, ceramics, and religious art. **Casa Maxwell** (Canal 14, Tel. 152-0247) includes an impressive collection of folk art, furniture, and home decorative items. **Casa Maria Luisa** (Canal 40, Tel. 152-0130), a large home decorative shop, includes a modern and somewhat funky collection of ceramics, candles, furniture, light fixtures, and folk art. **Galería Josh Kligerman** (San Francisco 11, Tel. 152-0951) offers colorful contemporary Mexican and international art. The shop at the rear of this gallery – **Girasol Boutique Willa Mina** (Tel. 152-2734) – includes nicely designed clothes under its own label. **Galería San Miguel** (Plaza Principal 14, Tel. 152-0454) includes the works of several regional, national, and international artists. **Galería Goded** (Plaza Prinicipal 20-A, Tel. 152-1366) exhibits the works of Jaime Goded as well as colorful textiles from Mexico and Guatemala. **Arte Studio Daniel Rueffert** (Cuna de Allende

11, Local 6 and 7, Tel. 152-0437 x103), located across from the west side of La Parroquia and La Capilla Restaurant, showcases the paintings of local artist Daniel Rueffert as well as the works of other international artists.

Zacateros Street, which runs south from the Belles Arts complex, includes many interesting shops. For silver jewelry, visit the two adjacent shops of **Joyeria David** (Zacateros 13, Tel. 452-3100) as well as two other related shops along this street. One of the city's best folk art shops is **Veryka** (Zacateros 6-A, Tel. 152-2114). **CLAN Destino** (Zacateros 19, Tel./Fax 152-1623) is jampacked with arts, crafts, jewelry, and furniture from Mexico, Africa, and India. **Arte en Cobre** (Zacateros 55, Tel. 152-0056) offers a good collection of copper pots, trays, and plates. **Studio/ Galeria Frank Gardner** (Zacateros 75, Tel. 152-2926, www.frank gardner.com) exhibits a wonderful collection of paintings of local street scenes and landscapes. **Lisa Simms** (Zacateros 46, Tel. 152-6459) includes jewelry, puppets, masks, drawings, paintings, and sculpture, with special emphasis on large paintings and wearable sculpture. **Galeria Dos Culturas** (Zacateros 83-A, Tel. 154-7962) includes many nice paintings.

The parallel east-west streets of **Umarán/Correo** and **Pila Seca** include several interesting shops and galleries. **Arte Mestizo** (Umarán 26, Tel. 152-1073) includes a small collection of folk art, paintings, and Moroccan rugs. Be sure to ask for Gaby who specializes in organizing shopping tours and arranging shipping (see page 284). **Antigüa Casa Canela** (Umarán 20, Tel. 152-1880) offers several rooms of home decorative items, including stone sculptures, furniture, ceramics, and religious art. **Antigüedades Dávila** (Correo 22, Tel. 152-1689) is known for its collection of bronzes, furniture, and tapestries. **Galería Duo Duo** (Pila Seca 3, Tel. 152-6211) offers many home decorative items, including an eclectic mix of folk art, pillows, bags, picture frames, and an art gallery showcasing the paintings of **Mary Breneman** (www. marybreneman.com).

If you enjoy shopping in local markets, be sure to visit the **Artesanos of San Miguel** (Plaza Lanaton, Tel. 152-2844) which includes several vendors offering arts, crafts, and silver jewelry. Two to three times a year on Saturdays the **Instituto Allende** (south of Zacateros on Ancha de San Antonio) hosts an interesting market in the court area. Here you can shop among several vendor stalls offering everything from jewelry, paintings, and textiles to music CDs and handmade shawls and bags. This special market tends to attract many talented expatriate artists and artisans who display their unique works. In our most recent visit, we acquired a wonderful CD of specially recorded piano music from local musician Elsmarie Norby.

Best of the Best

ART GALLERIES

❑ **Galería Milligan:** *Hernández Macias 104, Tel. 152-6923. Website:* *www.sanmiguelartists.com/milligan*. Meet the very talented artist Sharon Adams Milligan who showcases her wonderful ceramic and bronze sculptures in this delightful gallery/studio. Her special attention to surfaces and her "Please do touch" sign invite visitors to appreciate her many intriguing and fun contemporary sculptures.

❑ **Galería Frank Gardner:** *Zacateros 75, Tel. 152-2926; and Hidalgo 4, Tel. 152-6290. Website: www.frankgardner.com*. This small studio/gallery (Zacateros 75) includes the very appealing oil paintings of gifted artist Frank Gardner. Known for his unique use of light and color, he depicts many local street scenes, marketplaces, and landscapes. This could well become your favorite gallery for local art.

❑ **Galería Atenea:** *Jesús 2, El Centro, Tel. 152-0785*. Exhibits the works of both local and international artists, including the intriguing sculptures and jewelry of Sergio Bustamante. Includes oil paintings, watercolors, prints, sculptures, and jewelry.

❑ **Galería Josh Kligerman:** *Calle San Francisco 11, Tel. 152-0951*. This popular and colorful gallery includes an interesting collection of contemporary Mexican and American art. Represents many major Mexican artists such as Carlos Orozco Romero, Leonardo Nierman, and David Leonardo. Also includes a popular clothing and jewelry boutique (Girasol) at the rear of the shop.

❑ **Galería San Miguel:** *Plaza Principal 14, Tel. 152-0454*. Facing the Jardín, this long-established (since 1962) and reputable gallery showcases an excellent collection of contemporary Mexican art – paintings, sculptures, and graphics. Operated by the very knowledgeable Sylvia Samuelson and Maria Mendoza.

❑ **Galería Duo Duo:** *Pila Seca 3, Tel. 152-6211*. This whimsical gallery offers an eclectic mix of home decorative items (bags, pillows, picture frames, folk art) displayed in several rooms. Look for the appealing contemporary paintings of local artist Mary Breneman, which are located in the art gallery room near the rear of this building. The gallery also displays the works of Jon Schooler.

❏ **Arte Studio Daniel Rueffert:** Cuna de Allende 11, Tel. 152-0437, ext. 103. Website: http://portalsanmiguel.com/danru effert. Working here since 1969, Daniel Rueffert displays his many contemporary paints with local themes – village and street scenes, children, and women. The gallery also displays the works of a few other artists.

ANTIQUES

❏ **Bazar El Nuevo Oeste:** *Hernández Macias 126, Tel. 152-7571.* Consisting of two shops across the street from one another, Bazar El Nuevo Oeste is filled with an interesting collection of antiques and collectibles. Look for brown sugar molds, wood benches, pottery, masks, furniture, doors, wood saddles, large carriages, religious figures, and irons.

FOLK ART

❏ **Veryka:** *Zacateros 6A, Tel. 152-2114.* It doesn't get much better in Mexico for top quality folk art than at this shop. Two rooms of this small gallery offer the works of Mexico's master folk artists. Look for the wonderful wire and papier-mâché animals of Saulo Moreno (but prices for his work are higher here than in Mexico City). Includes colorful ceramic Catrinas and painted wood carvings. Also has a wonderful sister shop in Oaxaca – Indigo.

❏ **SaVia:** *Jesús 12, Tel. 154-4866.* Offers excellent quality folk art, prints, paintings, masks, wood carvings, and Catrinas. Includes both established (has a few Saulo Moreno pieces) and unknown artisans. Attempts to represent Mexico's most "authentic" folk artists. Includes a nice collection of unique bamboo decorative bark panels using pre-Hispanic production and artistic techniques.

❏ **Casa Maxwell:** *Calle Canal 14 and Umarán 3, Tel. 152-0247.* Filled with numerous rooms and small shops offering a wide selection of arts, crafts, and home decorative items – glass, ceramics, folk art, wrought iron furniture, candles, beds, and lacquerware. The building seems to go on and on. Be sure to probe the back rooms that eventually lead to another entrance.

❏ **Artes de Mexico:** *Calzada Aurora 47, Tel. 152-0764.* This well established shop offers a good selection of handicrafts, ceramics, furniture, lamps, and tin work. Manufactures many gift items, furniture, and tin work. Much of the nice folk art – lizards, birds, monkeys – comes from Oaxaca.

❑ **La Calaca:** *Calle Mesones 93, Tel. 152-3954.* Emphasizes Latin American folk and ceremonial art. Includes both antique and contemporary masks, carvings, textiles, pottery, folk furniture, and ethnic jewelry and represents noted artisans.

DECORATIVE ITEMS

❑ **Cantadora:** *Recreo 8, Tel. 152-6444.* E-mail: <u>cantadora8@ hotmail.com</u>. Popular with architects, designers, and home decorators, this shop specializes in paintings, furniture, baptismal fonts, fireplace fronts, columns, altarpieces, and doors.

❑ **CLAN Destino:** *Zacateros 19, Tel./Fax 152-1623.* This is San Miguel's version of an international Pier 1! A large and interesting shop, it includes a very eclectic mix of furniture, ceramics, folk art, handicrafts, textiles, and jewelry. Look for Indian furniture, pots, stools, African masks, textiles, jewelry, and folk art. At the rear of the shop, look for an outdoor shopping area as well as a room displaying art. One of the more interesting shops in the city. Excellent displays and service.

JEWELRY

❑ **Ambar:** *Jesus 21-B, Tel. 154-4058.* This small shop, operated by local jewelry designer Thomas le Noir, offers a breath-taking collection of yellow, green, and red amber stones, carvings, and jewelry. The amber is mined in the southern state of Chiapas where Thomas acquires all of the product and then fashions it into necklaces and rings. The intricate amber carvings are produced in Ubud, Bali, where Thomas spends three months each year.

❑ **Cerroblanco:** *Calle Canal 17, Tel. 152-0502.* Produces some of Mexico's most attractive contemporary silver and gold jewelry incorporating semi-precious stones. Offers many unique contemporary designs that set its work apart from many other jewelry shops in Mexico.

❑ **Joyeria David:** *Calle Zacateros 53, Tel. 152-0056.* Offers a good selection of silver, gold, copper, and brass jewelry in four shops along Calle Zacateros. Also includes some jewelry using semi-precious stones.

❑ **7th Heaven:** *Sollano 31, Tel. 154-4677.* Specializes in producing silver and gold jewelry as well as amber carvings.

FASHION

❑ **Girasol:** *San Francisco 11, Tel. 152-2734.* Located in the rear of the popular Kligerman Galeria, Girasol offers many nicely designed clothes manufactured under its own label.

Accommodations

San Miguel offers a wide range of accommodations, from budget hotels and upscale B&Bs to all-suite boutique hotels. Be sure to book early if you plan to visit during the high season. Two of the best places to stay here are:

❑ **Casa Luna Bed & Breakfast:** *Pila Seca #11, San Miguel de Allende, Gto, 37700 Mexico, Tel./Fax (52-415) 152-1117 E-mail: casaluna@ unisono.net.mx. Website: www.casaluna.com.* Casa Luna is located in the historic Centro district just a short walk from the town square with its beautiful cathedral, jardin, and shops galore. The 300-year-old Spanish colonial home has been lovingly restored by its owner. With 2-foot thick walls and 20-foot high ceilings, Casa Luna blends many of the best features of a small boutique hotel with those of a bed and breakfast. The central courtyard is filled with plants and flowers and is graced by an elegant fountain and a large bougainvillea tree. Guestrooms are spacious and luxurious and each has at least one fireplace and ceiling fans. Fluffy comforters and specially designed and made-to-order headboards make the beds inviting for an afternoon siesta – if you can tear yourself away from the charming streets, squares, and shops of San Miguel. Guestrooms and public spaces are decorated with folk art from Mexico as well as other countries such as Morocco and India. Each of the nine rooms, one of which is a suite, is decorated with a theme such as the Santos Suite which is filled with memorabilia of the saints or the Frida Kahlo Blue Room. Each guestroom has its own private ensuite bath with tub and/or shower.

The indoor living room/library as well as the outdoor patio (with honor bar) made comfortable by a fireplace for cool winter evenings are spots where guests may read or gather together to compare notes on great finds for shopping or dining. Several patios with fountains provide peaceful respites for a break from daily activities. A full breakfast with fresh fruit and juice, breads, and a different hot dish each day is included. Children under 12 are welcome when the entire house is rented to one party. Casa Luna staff will make up picnic baskets for an early morning departure or day trip beyond the city. Cooking classes are frequently offered on Friday afternoon. In-room massage treatments are available, but must be booked in advance. Small gift shop. The proprietor, Dianne Kushner, and her staff provide a wealth of information on the area.

❏ **Casa de Sierra Nevada:** *Hospicio 35, San Miguel de Allende, Guanajuato, 37700 Mexico, Tel. (52-415) 152-7040, Fax (52-415) 152-2337.* Located a few blocks from the town's central square, this small luxury hotel, originally built in the 16th century, features ten colonial mansions with 37 finely appointed suites. Arches, wide windows, patios, fountains, colorful potted flowers, brick or stone floors, and antique pieces alternate with contemporary Mexican-style decor. Each guest suite is decorated with Mexican accents, but each is different from the others. Casa Sierra Nevada's two restaurants are listed with the top hotel dining establishments in Mexico. The Equestrian Center, located in Rancho La Loma, offers horseback riding and instruction as well as dressage exhibitions. Swimming Pool and Spa; Tennis and Golf available; Meeting Facilities for small groups.

Restaurants

San Miguel boasts many fine local and international restaurants that cater to its many expatriates and tourists. Many restaurants have live music, lively bars, and great ambience. Some of our favorite restaurants include:

❏ **La Capilla:** *Cuna de Allenda 10, Tel. 154-4944. Open Wednesday to Monday from 1pm to 3am. Serves Sunday brunch from 11am to 3pm.* Located adjacent to the city's famous parish church, La Parroquia, this combination art gallery and restaurant is located on the upper level of a beautifully old restored building filled with antiques. Includes both indoor and outdoor dining areas with a nice view of the street below that leads into the nearby plaza. Wonderful ambience and excellent service. Serves both regional and international dishes. Try the stuffed chicken breast, red snapper, shrimp and mushroom, or duck. For dessert, the sugar-domed creme brulee is a real treat. Live music. Arrive after sunset and be wowed by the candlelight ambience as you enter the building.

❏ **El Market Bistro:** *Hernandez Macias 95, Tel. 152-3229. Open daily from 1pm to 11pm and weekends until midnight.* This charming French bistro is a good choice for lunch or dinner. Everything here tends to be excellent, although we found the crepes and the chicken and pasta with walnuts and basil to be outstanding. Nice setting with a very tempting menu.

❑ **Tio Lucas:** *Mesones 103, Tel. 152-4996. Open daily from 12noon to midnight.* This popular restaurant and bar, with both indoor and outdoor dining, offers nightly entertainment (jazz/blues band) and many fine dishes. Famous for its Caesar salad and beef and chicken dishes. Try the chateaubriand and filete Chemita.

❑ **Bugambilia:** *Hidalgo 42, Tel. 152-0127. Open daily 12noon to 11pm.* Newly remodeled, this long-established restaurant (since 1945) serves excellent Mexican dishes. Specialties include pollo en mole poblano, chiles en nogada, and sopa azteca. Excellent service and friendly atmosphere. Offers a 20% discount when paying with cash on Tuesday, Wednesday, and Thursday. Live guitar music nightly starting at 8pm.

❑ **Harry Bissett's New Orleans Café and Oyster Bar:** *Hidalgo 12, Tel. 152-2645. Open daily from 12noon to midnight.* This lively bar and restaurant attempts to recreate the tastes of New Orleans. Serves spicy cajun jambalaya, seafood gumbo, and calamari. Try the blackened tuna, salmon, duck, and certified Angus beef. Serves a New Orleans jazz brunch on Saturday and Sunday, from 11am to 3pm. While the kitchen gets mixed reviews and the service can be spotty, the atmosphere here is always lively and friendly.

Enjoying Your Stay

In addition to shopping and dining, San Miguel has a very active cultural scene and lots of good entertainment. Some of the major highlights of the city include:

❑ **La Parroquia:** *South side of the Jardin.* This impressive 17th century spiraled pink sandstone neo-gothic parish church is one of the great symbols of San Miguel de Allende. Especially beautiful when lit at night.

❑ **Bellas Artes:** *Hernández Macias 75, Tel. 152-0289, Open Monday to Saturday, 9am to 8pm and Sunday, 10am to 2pm.* Once the old Convento da la Concepción, this building now houses the Centro Cultural Ignacio Ramírez. Includes galleries and art exhibits along with several famous murals. Check out the bulletin board at the entrance that includes postings of local art and cultural activities.

❑ **Instituto Allende:** *Ancha de la San Antonio 20. Open Monday to Friday, 8am to 6pm.* This famous institute draws hundreds of students from the United States and Canada who come here each year to study language and arts. If time permits, you may want to study here.

❑ **Biblioteca Pública:** *Insurgentes 25, between Reloj and Hidalgo.* This local library has a good selection of English-language newspapers and books, a café, and informative bulletin board with information on current community activities. The popular house and garden tour departs from here each Sunday.

❑ **House and Garden Tour:** *Tel. 152-4987.* Every Sunday at 12noon a house and garden tour departs from the **Biblioteca Pública** (Insurgentes 25, between Reloj and Hidalgo). This is good opportunity to see several outstanding homes and gardens in the city. The cost is US$15 and proceeds go to the Biblioteca Pública.

❑ **Golf and Tennis:** Try the **Club de Golf Malanquin** at Celaya Highway, Km 3, Tel. 152-0516. Open Tuesday through Sunday. Includes a 9-hole golf course, tennis courts, pool, and steam baths open to the public.

❑ **Ballooning:** A great way to see this lovely area is by hot air balloon. Contact **Gone With the Wind Balloon Adventures** at Calle Secreo 68, Tel. 152-6735. Departs early morning (6 or 7am) when in season. Includes flights over the city and surrounding area.

❑ **Entertainment:** Much of San Miguel's entertainment centers around its cultural life. Check out what's going on at the Bellas Artes, Instituto Allende, public library, and the weekly (published on Sunday) English-language newspaper *Atención San Miguel* in terms of art shows, musical performances, and theatrical productions. During August San Miguel de Allende hosts the popular Festival de Musica de Camara. At the end of November the city hosts the Jazz Festival International.

On the Road to Dolores Hidalgo and Guanajuato

If you're going to or from Guanajuato, which lies just 62 miles west of San Miguel via Highway 35, you'll pass through the town of Dolores Hidalgo. Located only 27 miles northwest of San Miguel, Dolores Hidalgo is famous historically for its role as the birthplace of the Mexican independence movement. Today it's also famous for its many ceramics, pottery, and Talavara tile factories and shops as well as for a few antique and furniture shops. If you're looking for inexpensive, mass produced ceramics, this is the place to shop. However, the really good stuff is found closer to Guanajuato, where you will discover the works of some of Mexico's master ceramicists, such as Gorky González and Javier de Jesús Hernández (see the "Best of the Best" section in the next chapter on Guanajuato).

As you approach Dolores Hidalgo, you'll pass by numerous factories and shops that line the highway and city streets. Displaying their wares along the road, these places offer colorful painted and glazed pottery, tiles, sinks, vases, tableware, and fountains. If you get carried away here, you may have a real packing and shipping problem! Most of the shops and factories only accept cash – no credit cards – and few offer shipping services. Some of our favorite factories and shops in this area include:

❏ **Talavera San Gabriel:** *San Miguel Allende Km. 14, Tel. 182-0100.* Located two miles south of Dolores Hidalgo, this factory boasts a huge showroom of ceramic tiles, sinks, mirrors, pots, vases, cups, table service, mugs, tables, garden stools, and fountains. Nice quality and excellent prices. Strictly cash and carry.

❏ **La Diligencia:** *Carretera Dolores-San Miguel de Allende (Entrada Rancho Santa Clara), Tel. 814-5524.* This antique shop includes an interesting collection of furniture, pots, bowls, old keys, phonographs, religious figures, masks, icons, guns, copper pots, saddles, and wagon wheels.

❏ **Chulavista:** *San Miguel de Allende Km. 2, Tel. 183-0700.* This very unusual and fascinating roadside shop is filled with religious folk art from San Luis Potosi. Look for painted crosses, chests, cabinets, and icons. Also includes some ceramics. Much of this art looks old but is actually newly created.

❏ **Juan F. Guerrero Vajillas:** *Galzada de los Heroes, Tel. 182-0305.* Offers excellent quality ceramic dishes produced in its adjacent workshop.

❑ **Azulejos Talavera Cortés:** *Calle Distrito Federal 8, Tel. 182-0900.* Offers one of the largest selections of good quality ceramics in Dolores Hidalgo.

❑ **Muebles y Decoraciones:** *Calzada de los Héroes Km. 3.5, Tel. 182-2195.* This large antique and decorative shop offers everything from old carts to new furniture, ceramics, paintings, and carvings. Does made-to-order cedar and pine furniture. Will ship to the border.

❑ **Garper Express:** *Cerretera San Miguel Km. 5. Tel. 187-6873.* This small ceramics shop includes many attractive and inexpensive items. It's surrounded by three other ceramics shops that offer a good selection of pots, plates, picture frames, and serving pieces.

14

Guanajuato

W ELCOME TO ONE OF Mexico's most fascinating, intriguing, and seductive colonial cities. Once Mexico's most important silver producer, today Guanajuato ("the hilly place of the frogs") is known as a city of hills, tunnels, mummies, winding cobblestone streets and lanes (callejones), students, music, art, culture, festivals, muralists Diego Rivera and José Chávez Morado, and Cervantes.

Not a Gringo City

Since you won't find many expatriates and tourists in Guanajuato, don't expect to discover many great restaurants, fine hotels, or entertainment establishments normally associated with major international tourist destinations in Mexico. Less trendy than the nearby expat center of San Miguel de Allende and yet to be discovered by many international tourists, Guanajuato exudes a certain Mexican character that is charming, colorful, and magical. It's the closest you'll get to a Mexican medieval and Spanish city. Indeed, you'll often feel you are walking the streets of Spain or Italy! It's definitely a walking city where cars are un-

❶ El Pipila
❷ Jardin de la Union
❸ Teatro Juarez
❹ Basilica
❺ University
❻ Plaza de la Paz
❼ Museo del Pueblo
❽ Museo Diego Rivera
❾ Mercado Hidalgo

Guanajuato

welcome sights and public nuisances. Stroll this city's web of winding and hilly streets, visit its popular Jardin, follow the singing and guitar strumming troubadours through the callejones, get lost in its labyrinth of tunnels and lanes, or view its more than 100 well preserved mummies, and you'll know you are in a very special place, unlike any other in Mexico.

If you are like many visitors to Guanajuato, you'll fall in love with this city of rich architecture, art, culture, and character. Best of all for travel-shoppers, you'll discover some lovely ceramics produced by two of the country's leading ceramicists.

❑ Less trendy than the nearby expat center of San Miguel de Allende, Guanajuato exudes a certain Mexican character that is simultaneously charming, colorful, and magical.

❑ This is the closest you'll get to a Mexican medieval and Spanish city. Indeed, you'll often feel like you're walking the streets of Spain or Italy!

❑ This subterranean city offers intriguing architecture, art, and culture.

❑ Travel-shoppers discover some lovely ceramics produced by two of Mexico's leading ceramic artists.

Getting to Know You

Located 220 miles northwest of Mexico City and 58 miles west of San Miguel de Allende, Guanajuato has a population of nearly 80,000, of which 20,000 are students. Nestled in a valley surrounded by hills and flanked by the Sierra Madre mountains and laced with underground tunnels that serve as roadways, it's Mexico's only subterranean city. A very disorienting city, Guanajuato is especially famous for confusing even the best drivers and road navigators. A map-maker's nightmare, Guanajuato is one of those delightful cities where getting lost and found by car and on foot is half the fun of visiting this charming and challenging place. From the moment you arrive until the day you leave, you'll be delighted with having chosen to visit this intriguing city.

Once one of the richest cities in the Americas because of its silver production, today Guanajuato serves as a state capital and education center. Old stately mansions, elaborate baroque churches, intriguing museums, and neo-Moorish architecture testify to the fact that this city was once a center of great wealth. Indeed, from the 16th to the 18th centuries, Guanajuato produced much of the silver wealth that fueled the Spanish empire in the Americas and Southeast Asia.

The Streets of Guanajuato

Given Guanajuato's confusing tunnels, narrow streets, and limited parking, it's best to approach this city by taxi and on foot. If you're driving, park your car at your hotel and take a taxi to the city center, the Jardin, from where you can easily navigate the city on foot. You'll want to use your car later for exploring sev-

eral ceramic studios and shops outside the city.

The total length of this relatively small and compact city center can be covered on foot within 15 minutes. One of the best ways to approach this city is to take a taxi to the hill overlooking the city – El Pipila – and then take the funicular (incline rail car) to the bottom of the hill where you can walk to the Jardin within three minutes. This small triangular plaza with neatly trimmed trees is surrounded by outdoor cafes and restaurants, strolling mariachi singers, and the imposing six-pillar Teatro Juárez. Evening is a good time to visit, when it becomes a very festive area crowded with many young people from nearby schools and universities. From the Jardin, walk northwest along Av. Juarez past Plaza de La Paz and down the hill. This is the heart of the commercial area. While you'll pass numerous small shops, restaurants, and cafes, don't expect to do much shopping here. Except for T-shirt shops and clothing stores, there's not much of interest here for travel-shoppers. We recommend visiting this area primarily to see the local sights, experience the festive atmosphere, enjoy the mariachi singers and occasional minstrels (estudiantinas – singing university students dressed in 17th century costumes). This whole area may remind you of a Spanish and Italian town with a medieval flavor.

Shopping Guanajuato and Beyond

The most rewarding streets in Guanajuato for travel-shoppers are found outside the city center as well as beyond the city. Essentially ceramic workshops and showrooms, these places are well worth visiting. You can cover the major places within a half day. Start in town by visiting the somewhat difficult to find workshop and showroom of famous ceramicist **Gorky González Quiñones** (Alfarería Tradicional, Ex Huerta de Montenegro s/n,

Col. Pastita 45, Tel. 731-0462)
and then head out of town
toward Dolores Hidalgo.
First drive to the small
mountain village of Santa
Rosa which is 13 kilometers
from Guanajuato. One of
the best places to visit in this
village for colorful and inexpensive hand painted ceramics is **Mayolica Santa
Rosa** (road to Dolores
Hidalgo, km 13, Tel. 739-
0572). On the way back to
Guanajuato, stop in the

small village of Valenciana to visit the ceramic studio of **Capelo**
(road to Dolores Hidalgo, km. 5, Tel. 732-8964). For a real treat,
stop for lunch at the delightful restaurant/gallery **Casa del Conde
de la Valenciana** (across from the church on the main road to
Dolores Hidalgo, km. 5, Tel. 732-2550). This place is filled with
excellent quality arts, crafts, furniture, ceramics, pottery, and
home decorative items.

Shopping in and around Guanajuato is all about unique local
ceramics. This is an especially interesting area to shop for ceramics because the clays and colors found in Guanajuato are different from elsewhere in Mexico and thus result in a different ceramic look.

Best of the Best

❑ **Alfarería Tradicional (Gorky González Quiñones):** *Pastita ex
Huerta de Montenegro s/n, Pastita 45, Tel./Fax 731-0462. E-mail:
gorkyono@redes.int.com.mx. Website:
www.gorkypottery.com (if and when
it works!).* This is the studio and
shop of Gorky González, one of
Mexico's leading potters, who produces beautiful but simple and un-
pretentious ceramics that are
sought by decorators and collectors worldwide. Producing the traditional Spanish-inspired white-
glazed majolica ceramics and
Talavera ceramics, Gorky has established himself as one of

Mexico's premier artisans. Influenced by his famous ceramist
father, Rodolfo González, as well as by studying ceramics

techniques in Japan, his work is both subtle and elegant and merges pre-Hispanic and Spanish colonial influences. A visit to his pottery studio will introduce you to Gorky's playful style of ceramics, which comes in numerous forms – dinnerware, lamps, vases, and platters. Unlike the many heavy, brightly colored, and amateur designs found in the roadside ceramic factories of Dolores Hildalgo, Gorky's designs exude a sense of true artistic talent and quality. His son, Gorky Jr., speaks excellent English and operates a restaurant-bar across the street, La Casona del Cielo.

❑ **Capelo:** *Mineral de Valenciana, Cerro de la Cruz s/n, Tel. 732-8964. E-mail: ceramicapelo@prodigy.net.mx.* A little hard to find if you miss the sign on the main road that leads to the hilltop studio of one of Mexico's very famous ceramists, Javier de Jesús Hernández. Specializing in majolica-style ceramics influenced by Spanish colonial forms and designs, his studio produces some of the finest ceramics in Mexico. A former teacher of architecture and design at Guanajuato's university and influenced by his studies of majolica techniques in Italy, Spain, and Portugal, Capelo blends 13th century design elements with the talents of both a painter and architect. From his expansive hilltop home and studio, you get a panoramic view of the city below. Depending on when you visit, the inventory here may be very thin. Indeed, most of his product gets quickly shipped as soon as it comes out of production. Be sure to visit his brother's workshop (**Ceramica La Cruz**), which is located nearby in a small brick dimly lit building overlooking the valley. This shop offers an interesting collection of brown, gray, blue, and rose glazed pots, many exhibiting very subtle Asian design elements.

❑ **Mayólica Santa Rosa:** *Road to Dolores Hidalgo, km. 13, Santa Rosa, Tel./Fax 739-0572. E-mail: maystaros@yahoo.com.* Turn off the main road (look for Restaurante de la Sierra) and drive up the hill and into the little rustic village of Santa Rosa. At the top you'll find this factory shop (look for the building with arches), which is a real bargain hunter's paradise for majolica-designed ceramics. The small showroom is jam-packed with colorful green, yellow, and blue vases, pots, plates, serving dishes, and bowls. The bold and attractive designs depict inviting fruits, chickens, butterflies, fish, and people. Compared to many

other ceramic factories and shops, the prices here are very reasonable, indeed downright cheap! But be careful. You may get carried away buying numerous pieces for yourself, family, and friends. The shop only takes cash. It will ship DHL, although such shipments can become very expensive since ceramics tend to be heavy. It's probably best to make this a cash-and-carry stop.

❑ **Casa del Conde de la Valenciana:** *On the main road to Dolores Hidalgo (across the road from the big red church, La Iglesia de San Cayetano), km. 5, Valenciana, Tel./Fax 732-2550.* Many visitors find this combination restaurant and gallery to be their favorite shopping destination in the Guanajuato area – the ultimate lifestyle shopping destination for tasteful selections and displays – after getting lost in medieval Guanajuato and trying to locate hard-to-find ceramic factories. While more pricey (for example, expect to pay three times more for the nicely displayed and polished Gorky, Capalo, and Santa Rosa ceramics), it's all here under one roof in Casa del Conde. Where else can you find an excellent indoor and patio restaurant that also offers good quality shopping for arts, crafts, furniture, ceramics, pottery, and home decorative items? The gallery consists of four different rooms located on both the upper and lower levels. Each room has a different mix of nicely displayed decorative items. The upstairs rooms include folk art, ceramics, pots, lacquer trays, black pottery from Oaxaca, ceramic birds from Chiapas, pots from Chiwawa, jewelry, glass plates, lamps, candle holders, wrought iron furniture, metal birds, and copper lanterns. The shop outside and down the stairs to the lower level includes folk art, large pots, metal animals, ceramics by Gorky, painted chests, leather furniture, lamps, lanterns, patio furniture, metal fish, mirrors, other home decorative items, and a fascinating outdoor fountain made of pots. Be careful here. Your lunch stop could well become a very lengthy and expensive shopping adventure! Whatever you do, be sure to stop at this restaurant and gallery.

❑ **Mercado Hidalgo:** *Avenida Juárez.* This is the city's main market. Built like an aircraft hanger but modeled after a French train station, this aging 100-year-old building houses the usual mix of colorful local arts and crafts, including folk art, pottery, baskets, jewelry, embroidered clothes, T-shirts, toys, and other products of some passing interest to visitors who enjoy the local market experience.

❑ **Casa de las Artesanías:** *Route 110, 12 miles southwest of Guanajuato.* Housed on the grounds of the Ex-Hacienda San Gabriel de Barrera. This is the government-operated arts and crafts center. Offers a limited selection of copper lanterns, glasses, ceramics, and jewelry. Interesting for glassware but may not be worth a special trip.

Accommodations

With La Casa de Espiritus Alegres now closed, sadly, there are fewer upscale choices for Guanajuato lodging.

❑ **Quinta Las Acacias:** *Paseo de la Presa 168, Guanajuato, Guanajuato 36000, Mexico, Tel./Fax (52-473) 731-1517.* This French-style residence was built in the 19th century and is located in one of Guanajuato's finest neighborhoods. Quinta Las Acacias's nine elegant suites are spacious. Each one is uniquely decorated to reflect the historical influences of the area's heritage. Some are European in style while others reflect Mexican decor. The personalized attention bestowed on each guest reflects both the intimate nature of this boutique property and the hospitality for which Guanajuato is known. Hydro-massage pool on the grand terrace.

❑ **Parador San Javier:** *Plaza Aldama 92, El Centro 36000 Guanajuato, Mexico, Tel. (52-473) 732-0626, Fax (52-473) 732-3114.* Located about 1.5 miles from the downtown area. An old safe from the Hacienda San Javier and old wood trunks decorate the spacious, plant-filled lobby. This former mining hacienda with 115 guestrooms and suites has lovely grounds and a friendly atmosphere. Guestrooms have blue and white tile baths. A few of the guestrooms have fireplaces. Two Restaurants; Pool.

Restaurants

Guanajuato has many small cafes and restaurants that primarily cater to local residents. Some of the best places for dining include:

❑ **Casa del Conde de la Valenciana:** *On the main road to Dolores Hidalgo (across the road from the big red church, La Iglesia de San Cayetano), km. 5, Valenciana, Tel./Fax 732-2550. Open from 12:30pm to 6pm.* You have to get out of town for this one, but it's well worth the trip. This combination restaurant and gallery is one of the most delightful places to dine for lunch in the Guanajuato area. Offering both indoor and outdoor dining options (we prefer outdoors), the kitchen serves excellent Mexican dishes in a charming setting. Try the Crema Tarator (cold yogurt and nut soup), pork loin, and pollo con flor de calabaza. The chicken mole and enchilada dishes are excellent as are the deserts (carrot cake and ice creams). For more information on what is one of our favorite lifestyle shopping destinations, see our entry above under "Best of the Best" for shopping.

❑ **La Hacienda de Marfil:** *Arcos de Guadalup 3, Marfil, Tel. 733-1148, open Tuesday to Sunday, from 1:30pm to 6pm.* Covered by a large awning, this charming French-style restaurant overlooks a lovely lawn and garden. Combines Mexican and French cuisine. Try the filet a la pimienta flameado en cognac.

❑ **El Gallo Pitagórico:** *Centro, located on a hillside under the Pipila, Tel. 732-9489.* Open Tuesday through Sunday from 12noon to 11pm. This relatively new restaurant serves Italian food and has a wonderful view of city.

❑ **La Tasca de Los Santos:** *Plaza de la Paz, Tel. 732-2320.* This outdoor restaurant features several Spanish dishes. Try the chicken in white wine.

❑ **Truco 7**: *Truco 7, on the right side of the Basilica.* This very inexpensive café and restaurant offers many good dishes. Try the comida corrida (three-course meal with beverage).

❑ **Posada Santa Fe:** *Jardin, Tel. 732-0084.* Located on the Jardin, this is a good place to people watch and enjoy the music of loud strolling mariachis who invariably look for the ostensibly rich gringos dining at this popular outdoor restaurant. If you wait long enough, the gringos at some other table – hopefully farther away where the music is less noisy and oppressive (these mariachis sound better from a distance!) – will probably pay for a performance! The food is okay and forgettable, but the ambience is excellent and most memorable – this may well become one of the highlights of visiting Guanajuato, especially in the evening.

Enjoying Your Stay

Guanajuato offers several interesting attractions that can easily occupy a full day of sightseeing. Among its many attractions are:

❑ **El Pípila:** *Carretera Panorámica.* This is a good place to start exploring the city of Guanajuato. Located on a hill overlooking the city (south of the Jardin), this war memorial to Juan José de los Reyes Matinez, hero of the War of Independence of 1810, offers a panoramic view of the city below. Take a taxi here, spend 20 minutes enjoying the breathtaking view of this quaint city (sunset is a great time to visit), and then walk down or take the funicular (open 9:30am to 10pm) to the lower level, which deposits you within a five-minute walk of the Jardin.

❑ **Museo de las Momias (Mummy Museum):** *Panteón Municipal, Tel. 732-0639. Open daily from 9am to 6pm.* Includes more than 100 glass-enclosed corpses, the city's most gruesome attractions. The philosophy of the old municipal cemetery was "If you can't pay, you can't stay." Bodies were disinterred from crypts when families couldn't keep up with the burial rent payments. Bodies were mummified because of the dry climate and chemical composition of the soil. A rather gross and redundant museum.

❑ **Museum Gene Byron:** *Ex-Hacienda Santa Ana, Domicilio Conocido, Marfil, Tel. 733-1029. Open Tuesday through Sunday from 10am to 3pm.* This beautiful combination museum, art gallery, and shop/workshop is found on the lovely grounds of the late Canadian artist Gene Byron's old hacienda. Includes many of her intriguing ceramics and paintings as well as a permanent collection of art. The expansive gallery area is used for concerts and shows. A shop, located next to the workshop, offers brass lamps and fixtures (made in the workshop), jewelry, clothes, and textiles.

❑ **Alhóndiga:** *Calle 28 de Septiembre 6, Tel. 732-1112. Open Tuesday through Saturday from 10am to 1:30pm and 4-5:30pm and Sunday from 10am to 2:30pm.* Once a granary and fortress, this impressive stone building now serves as a state museum showcasing important aspects of local history, archaeology, and crafts. Famous as the place where the first battle of the 1810 revolution took place, where El Pípila burned down the fortress door, and where the Spanish hung the heads of the Mexican revolutionaries Father Hildalgo, Ignacio Allende, and others.

❑ **Diego Rivera Museum:** *Calle Pocitos 46, Tel. 732-1197. Open Tuesday through Saturday, 10am to 6:30pm, and Sunday from 10am to 2:30pm.* Guanajuato is the birthplace of famous muralist Diego Rivera. This is the house where he was born in 1886. The ground floor includes furniture and antiques. The next three floors exhibit several works of the artist along with paintings of several local artists.

❑ **The Plaza:** *Jardín de la Unión.* Enjoy a touch of Paris with outdoor cafes, handicraft vendors, and strolling mariachis. This small neatly landscaped triangular plaza with a central gazabo/ bandstand is a center for evening musical performances and people watching. Located adjacent to the Teatro Juárez and the pink stone facaded Iglesia de San Diego.

❏ **Festival Internacional Cervantino:** Taking place during three weeks in October, this popular festival attracts performing artists from around the world. Includes the performance of extremeses, 16th-century one-act plays written by Cervantes. Also includes symphony orchestras, soloists, opera, jazz and rock groups, dance troupe, theater groups. Performances take place nightly at the Teatro Juárez and other places in the city. For information on the festival, Tel. 731-1161 or Fax 732-6775.

Excursion Beyond Guanajuato

Given Guanajuato's close proximity to Dolores Hidalgo and San Miguel de Allende, you can easily visit these places on a day trip. See the previous chapter on San Miguel de Allende for information on visiting these two places.

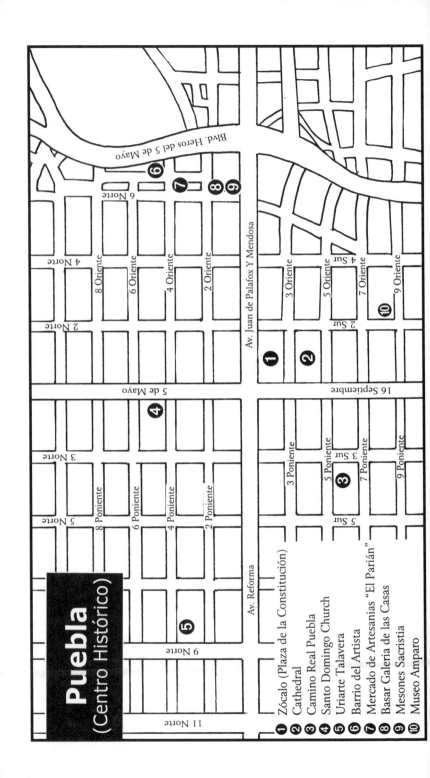

Puebla
(Centro Histórico)

❶ Zócalo (Plaza de la Constitución)
❷ Cathedral
❸ Camino Real Puebla
❹ Santo Domingo Church
❺ Uriarte Talavera
❻ Barrio del Artista
❼ Mercado de Artesanías "El Parián"
❽ Basar Galeria de las Casas
❾ Mesones Sacristia
❿ Museo Amparo

15

Puebla

D ESIGNATED AS A UNESCO World Heritage Site, Puebla is Mexico's fourth largest city. It's also the country's most Spanish-style city with great colonial architecture and numerous elaborate mansions, churches, and convents – the largest concentration in all of Mexico. Puebla also is a major center for Mexican cuisine – noted for its mole, chiles en nogada, and sweets – and for shopping. For travel-shoppers, Puebla, the "City of Tiles," is the country's center for admiring and acquiring the hand-painted Talavera tiles and dishes.

Getting to Know You

Boasting a population of nearly 2 million and situated at an altitude of 7,000 feet, Puebla has an ideal climate year round. Given its close proximity to Mexico City, Puebla should definitely be on your "must visit" list.

Located only 80 miles east of Mexico City, Puebla can be easily reached by car within two hours as part of a day trip, which might also include visits to nearby towns of Tlaxcala and Cholula and the archaeological sites of Cantona, Cacaxtla, and Xochitécatl.

Puebla has a very interesting history which it showcases well in its attractive architecture and numerous museums and churches. This is the city where Spanish artisans first introduced the production of Talavera tiles in the 16th century and where ceramic production continues today. Indeed, Puebla is famous throughout Mexico for its unique pottery. Puebla also is responsible for one of Mexico's most celebrated holidays and street names – Cinco de Mayo. In the Battle of Puebla on May 5, 1862, which has become a symbol of national pride, nearly 2,000 Mexican troops defeated an invading French army of 6,000 soldiers.

❑ Puebla is Mexico's most Spanish-style city with great colonial architecture and numerous elaborate mansions, churches, and convents – the largest concentration in all of Mexico.

❑ Puebla is famous for its unique pottery and Talavera ceramics.

❑ The main plaza, the zócalo or Plaza de la Constitucion, is a good place to start your adventure.

❑ The city's major shopping areas flow for several blocks north and northeast of the main plaza.

A relatively prosperous community, today Puebla is noted for its textiles, arts, and crafts. Famous for producing the world's classic Volkswagen Beetle car, Puebla's auto production facilities were finally closed in 2003. This brought to an end the last existing such industry in the world. It also raised questions about Puebla's continuing prosperity.

The Streets of Puebla

While Puebla is a large city, it's relatively easy to get around on foot. The center of the city, or Centro Histórico, is where the sightseeing and shopping action is found. The main plaza, the zocalo or Plaza de la Constitución, is a good place to start your adventure. Located at the intersection of Av. 16 de Septiembre/Av. 5 de Mayo and Av. Reforma/Av. Juan de Palafox, this large tree-lined plaza is surrounded by the Cathedral, arcades, restaurants, and a McDonald's. It's a great place to enjoy a cup of coffee, people-watch, and admire the attractive architecture surrounding the plaza before heading off into the side streets. The city's major shopping areas flow for several blocks north and northeast of the plaza.

If you drive into the city, it's best to leave your car at your hotel or park along a side street near the main plaza. This is not a car-friendly city when it comes to finding parking spaces. While you may do a great deal of walking, most everything of interest to visitors is within a half mile radius of the plaza. Once you get your initial bearings in reference to the plaza, Puebla will become one of the easiest cities to navigate on foot.

Shopping Puebla

Despite its size and location, Puebla is not a great shopping city. You can probably shop it within four hours, maybe even in less time, depending on your interests and good luck. You'll find a few shops and markets primarily offering Talavera pottery, ceramics, antiques, collectibles, bric-a-brac, furniture, souvenirs, gift items, and sweets. But it's the Talavera pottery for which Puebla is justly famous. This pottery was first introduced into Mexico via Puebla by artisans from the Spanish town of Talavera. It originally consisted of hand-painted tiles from the Moors who introduced it into Spain during the 8th century. Today Puebla boasts numerous factories and shops that produce and sell a large range of the popular Talavera pottery, from truly fine quality to the tacky market variety. Indeed, shopping in Puebla is all about discovering some of the best and the worst Talavera pottery in Mexico.

Puebla is a city of small shops, artisan workshops, galleries, markets, and factories. Starting at the plaza, turn north and walk along Av. 5 de Mayo which becomes a pedestrian mall lined with shops that primarily appeal to local shoppers. Within three blocks you'll see a huge metal structure that looks like an old Victorian train station – **La Victoria** or **Suburbia**. It houses several shops and restaurants which are relatively nondescript but worth browsing nonetheless. From here, turn onto 4 Poniente, which runs in front of La Victoria and the beautiful old **Santo Domingo Church** (Iglesia de Santo Domingo). Be sure to visit this church, where you will encounter huge paintings and elaborately carved walls, ceilings, and altars – probably the most elaborate you will encounter in all of Mexico! The area to the left of the front altar is the most impressive section of the church. If you walk four blocks west along 4 Poniente, you'll come to Pueblo's oldest and most famous Talavera factory and showroom – **Uriarte Talavera** (4 Poniente 911, Tel. 232-1598). You can join tours of the factory which take place three times a day (11am, 12noon, and 1pm),

Monday through Friday. On the way to this shop, as well as along neighboring streets, you'll pass by several candy shops for which Puebla is famous. However, the largest number of **sweets shops** are found east of 5 de Mayo along 6 Oriente. Most of the sweets are an acquired local taste rather than of great international appeal.

Several shops and markets appealing to visitors are clustered together with a four-square-block area northeast of the plaza (four blocks east of 5 de Mayo). If you walk east along 6 Oriente, you'll first come to a large Talavera ceramics workshop and showroom – **Centro de Talavera Poblana** (6 Oriente 11, Tel. 232-9331). Here you can watch women painting ceramics in yellow, blue, green, and rose colors while listening to their favorite music through headphones attached to CD players. Nearly three blocks farther east, and on your right, you'll come

to the unique artist complex called **Barrio del Artista** (intersection of 5 Oriente and 6 Norte, open daily from 10am to 6pm). Consisting of over 40 small artist studios primarily offering paintings and sculptures, with names of some artists displayed next to the studio number, you may have a chance to meet

several artists here and purchase directly from them. However, don't expect many artists to remain in their studios all the time. Many are frequently closed, the artists ostensibly attending to other business. If you want to see a particular painting, go to the front office and ask the person in charge to open the studio for your inspection. Across the street (4 Oriente) is the city's major shopping area for arts, crafts, and antiques. Look for **Mercado de Artesanías "El Parián"** (open daily from 10am to 7:30pm), a large arts and crafts market with numerous stalls offering typical market products, especially ceramics, textiles, onyx, and handicrafts. Long stone benches run down the middle of the outdoor market area.

Around the southern corner and three blocks south of the arts and crafts market is the charming cobblestone street called the **Alley of the Toads** (Callejón de los Sapos). An up and coming trendy area of shops and restaurants, here you may need to kiss a few toads to find some nice stuff! But there are a few decent shops along this street, although you don't need to linger long if this is not your shopping style. The shops along this one-block street primarily specialize in antiques, collectibles, rustic furniture, gift items, and bric-a-brac. On Sundays the street becomes an open-air antiques, collectibles, and flea market. One of the best antique shops here is part of the small boutique hotel and restaurant, **Mesones Sacristia** (6 Sur No. 304, Callejón de los Sapos, Tel. 242-3554). Other shops along this street worth exploring include **Bazar Galeria de Las Casas** (6 Sur No. 310, Callejón de los Sapos, Tel. 242-0702), **Antigüedades "La Casa de la Abuela"** (6 Sur No. 312, Tel. 242-1155), and **Galerie de Arte "San Miguel."** If you turn right at the end of this street, you'll be on Oriente 5. This street also includes a few antique and collectible shops. Look for **La Laba** (5 Oriente 210, Tel. 232-5595) for an interesting and eclectic mix of antiques and collectibles, including religious carvings.

Calle 8 Norte includes many small shops and vendors selling Talavera pottery and handicrafts.

Best of the Best

❑ **Uriarte Talavera:** *Av. 4 Pte. 911, between Avs. 9 and 11 Nte. (or calle 4 Pte. 911).* This is one of Mexico's top Talavera pottery factories which has been in operation since 1824. It uses only five natural colors in its hand-painted designs – blue, black, yellow, green, and pink. It offers daily tours of the factory (11am, 12noon, and 1pm, Monday through Friday). The small showroom includes plates, bowls, dishes, and tiles in the distinctive Talavera colors as well as in attractive blue and white. Look for a few special designs for a complete set of tableware. Service tends to be slow. They will pack and ship, but we question their shipping competence (see our critical comments about their problematic shipping in reference to the Mexico City shop). Very expensive. The showroom in Mexico City is much more interesting than this headquarters factory and shop. If you find something you love, we recommend buying it immediately and taking it with you in order to avoid any disappointments.

❑ **Bazar Galeria de Las Casas:** *6 Sur No. 310, Callejón de los Sapos, Tel. 242-0702.* This well appointed gift shop is filled with four rooms of showcases and wall displays that include an eclectic mix of attractive paintings, amber jewelry, sculptures, ceramics, papier-mâché dolls, folk art, religious art, mobile wood figures, masks, and bric-a-brac.

❑ **Mesón Sacristia:** *6 Sur No. 304, Callejón de los Sapos, Tel. 242-3554. Website (in Spanish): www.mesones-sacristia.com. Open 11am to 10pm.* Located in a small boutique hotel by the same name, this antique shop offers nice quality furniture, bronzes, ceramics, and baskets. The rooms in the hotel and restaurant include several antiques which also are for sale.

❑ **Antigüedades "La Casa de la Abuela":** *6 Sur No. 312, Tel. 242-1155*. Offers two floors of furniture, old dolls, religious figures, candle holders, jewelry, pots, toys, ceramics, and animals (pigs, reindeer, horses). The second floor primarily displays furniture. Look for nice rustic chests and doors. The shop will fabricate copies of old furniture.

❑ **Centro de la Talavera Poblana:** *6 Oriente 11 (between 2 Norte and 5 de Mayo), Tel. 232-9331*. This large workshop and showroom offers brightly colored Talavera ceramics, especially cups, saucers, and plates. The production workshop is located at the rear of the shop where you can observe women painting designs on the ceramics. A food shop with candies, **Dulcerias La Colonial**, is located at the front of the showroom.

❑ **Barrio del Artista:** *Intersection of 5 Oriente and 6 Norte (across the street from the northern end of Mercado de Artesanías "El Parián." Open daily from 10am to 6pm*. This is a center for more than 40 painters and sculptors who display their works from small studios and galleries. You can observe several of the artists at work as well as buy directly from them. Some will want to paint your portrait (agree on a price before he starts his "commission"). Not all of the studios/galleries are open all of the time. If you see something you like but no one is around, go to the front office to get someone  to unlock the gallery. A rather laid-back area of artists ostensibly "at work."

❑ **Mercado de Artesanías "El Parián":** *Intersection of 6 Norte and 4 Oriente. Open 10am to 7:30pm*. This large handicraft market includes several shops and stalls offering ceramics, clothing, textiles, onyx, leather, jewelry, silverware, candles, sweets, and papier-mâché items. Like many other artisan markets in Mexico, this one is an interesting place to browse, but you may not find much worth buying. Be sure to bargain here.

Accommodations

❑ **Camino Real Puebla:** *7 Poniente 105 Centro Histórico, Puebla, Puebla 72000 Mexico, Tel. (52-222) 229-0909, Fax (52-222) 232-*

9251, Toll-free from the U.S. & Canada 800-722-6466. Centrally located downtown, Camino Real Puebla, a former convent, was named a World Heritage Site by UNESCO in 1987. The reception area is across an open courtyard from the front street entrance. There are 84 spacious guestrooms with ochre-painted ceilings and umber-colored walls. Guestrooms and suites are adorned with original frescoes and furnishings from the Vice Regal period. A red armoire wardrobe with a gold-colored carved front catches one's attention. There is no re-frigerated mini bar, but some items normally found in a mini bar are available. Cream-colored tile bathrooms provide the expected amenities. Some baths have a shower, but no tub. The signature restaurant, **El Convento**, specializes in nouvelle Mexican cuisine; **Azulejos**, with tables on the outdoor patio, serves breakfast and provides a choice of venue for other meals served in a more casual setting. Live music accompanies refreshments at **Las Novicias** Bar. Meeting/Banquet Facilities for up to 400 people in La Concepción meeting room surrounded by fanciful frescoes and stately chandeliers.

❑ **Mesón Sacristía de la Compañia:** *6 Sur 304, Callejón de los Sapos, Tel. 242-3554. Website (in Spanish):* <u>www.mesones-sacristia.com</u>. Located in a beautiful refurbished 18th century mansion, this is a very special boutique property with eight spacious rooms, each with its own distinct character. The rooms include many antiques and works of art which are for sale.

❑ **Mesón Sacristía de Capuchinas:** *9 Oriente 16, Tel. 232-8088. Website (in Spanish):* <u>www.mesones-sacristia.com</u>. This centrally located all-suite boutique hotel, with seven rooms, is the contemporary luxury and quieter counterpart to its sister property, **Mesón Sacristía de la Compañia**. Also well appointed with lots of antiques and paintings.

Restaurants

Puebla is justly famous for its mole, chiles en nogada, and sweets. If you enjoy mole, Puebla is the place to experience some of the best in the country. Some of the city's stand-out restaurants include:

❑ **Fonda de Santa Clara:** *3 Poniente 307 (Tel. 242-2659) and 3 Poniente 920 (Tel. 246-1952). Open 9am to 10pm.* This cosy restaurant offers excellent regional poblano cuisine, including many seasonal specials. Try the mole (it's very spicy – recommend cutting it with the tortillas) and chiles en nogada.

❑ **Restaurant Sacristía:** *6 Sur 304, Callejón de los Sapos, Tel. 242-3554.* Attached to the wonderful Mesón Sacristía de la

Compañia boutique hotel and antique shop, this popular restaurant serves traditional poblano cuisine in a very attractive dining room and patio setting of an old colonial mansion. Like the antiques in the hotel rooms, most of the antiques in the restaurant are for sale. Try the mole Sacristia. Live music in the courtyard until late at night.

❑ **Las Bodegas del Molino:** *Molino de San Jose del Puente, Tel. 249-0399.* Located near the outskirts of town, approximately 15 minutes by car from the main plaza, this romantic restaurant is part of a lovingly restored 16th century mansion and hacienda. Offers excellent Mexican nouvelle cuisine as well as many international specialties. Try the popular mole. If time permits, ask to take a tour of the charming property.

Enjoying Your Stay

Just walking through the center of this city is a treat unto itself. The pleasant main plaza, colorful old buildings, distinctive colonial architecture, churches, fountains, old hotels, and Talavera tiles on buildings give this city a very unique character.

Pueblo is especially noted for its many churches and museums. Five major highlights for sightseers include:

❑ **Museo Amparo:** *2 Sur 708, Tel. 246-4210. Open Wednesday to Monday from 10am to 6pm.* One of Mexico's showcase museums. Housed in two beautiful old colonial buildings, this museum nicely displays and explains pre-Hispanic artifacts and colonial art. Friendly to visitors, the museum's explanations are in both Spanish and English. An excellent audiovisual system, with rented headsets, provides information in Spanish, English, French, German, Portuguese, and Japanese. Includes a library, cafeteria, and bookstore.

❑ **Museo de Artes Populares and Ex-Convento de Santa Rosa:** *14 Poniente (between 3 and 5 Norte), Tel. 232-9240. Open Tuesday to Sunday from 10am to 5pm.* Includes a large collection of handicrafts from the state of Puebla – pottery, glass, metal work, onyx, costumes, and leather. One of the highlights of the required 20-minute tour (departs hourly) is the large tiled kitchen where supposedly the famous mole poblano was first created. Includes a small handicraft shop.

❑ **Museo Bello:** *3 Poniente 302, Tel. 232-9475. Open Tuesday to Sunday from 10am to 5pm.* Showcases the private art collection of 19th-century industrialist José Luis Bello y González and his family. Includes a fascinating collection of art, antiques, furniture, porcelain (French, English, Japanese, and Chinese), and

Puebla Talavera. Includes guided tours in both Spanish and English.

❑ **Santo Domingo Church (Iglesia de Santo Domingo):** *Intersection of 5 de Mayo and 4 Poniente. Open daily from 10am to 6pm.* This is one of Mexico's most elaborately carved baroque churches. Its Rosary Chapel is simply over-the-top with intricately carved and gilded altar, walls, and ceilings. Simply an unforgettable church interior of artistic excess.

❑ **Cathedral:** *2 Sur (southern side of the main plaza).* Open daily from 10am to 6pm. Known for its impressive twin towers, the second tallest in Mexico, the cathedral was built in 1649. Includes an impressive altar made of marble, onyx, and gold. You may already recognize the facade of the cathedral and its towers – they grace the 500-peso bill.

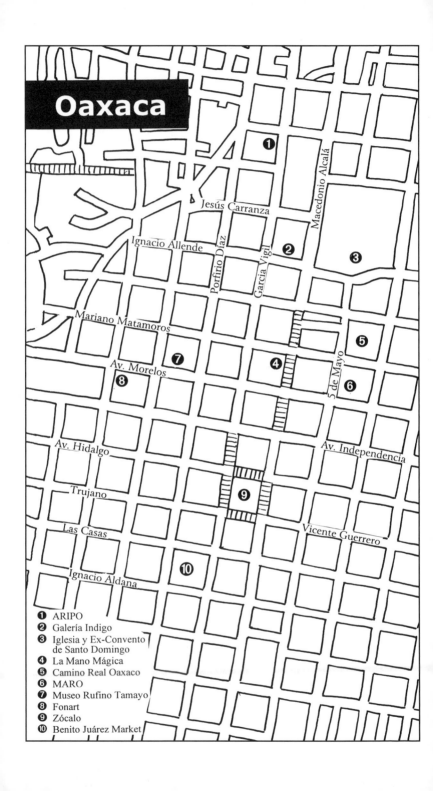

Oaxaca

❶ ARIPO
❷ Galería Indigo
❸ Iglesia y Ex-Convento
  de Santo Domingo
❹ La Mano Mágica
❺ Camino Real Oaxaco
❻ MARO
❼ Museo Rufino Tamayo
❽ Fonart
❾ Zócalo
❿ Benito Juárez Market

16

Oaxaca

MOST VISITORS TO OAXACA take an instant liking to this festive city and its nearby towns, villages, and historical sites. It's a charming and romantic place that may well become your favorite destination in all of Mexico. Offering a unique combination of Indian, Spanish colonial, and Mexican cultures, Oaxaca simply looks and feels good. Perhaps it's the weather, architecture, people, shops, markets, street theater, restaurants, or all of these pleasures combined that are so appealing.

An Imaginative Local Culture

Representing Mexico's largest Indian population, Oaxaca is an exceptionally inviting place to visit. It's cultured, laid-back, friendly, and simply fun to visit. Best of all for travel-shoppers, this is rich shopping country for folk art, pottery, textiles, paintings, leather goods, and even jewelry. As you will quickly discover, the arts and crafts play a central role in both the culture and economy of Oaxaca. Colorful and intriguing folk art adds a dash of mystery to what appears to be a highly imaginative local culture.

Spend a few days in Oaxaca and you will discover a very delightful artistic community. You'll have many opportunities to visit workshops, meet talented artists and craftspeople, and acquire some of Mexico's best arts and crafts at very reasonable prices. Spend time around the vibrant zócalo, dine in the city's many fine restaurants, or just leisurely walk its inviting streets, and you'll discover this is a very special place that probably deserves more time to explore and savor than you initially planned. This is definitely a lifestyle destination unlike any other in Mexico. If you are like many other visitors to Oaxaca, you'll plan to return to explore its many treasures and pleasures.

❑ Oaxaca offers a unique combination of Indian, Spanish colonial, and Mexican cultures.

❑ This is rich shopping country for folk art, pottery, textiles, paintings, leather goods, and even jewelry.

❑ One of Mexico's poorest states, Oaxaca offers visitors a rich travel and shopping experience.

❑ The city and nearby towns and villages offer a dazzling array of quality arts and crafts with a special emphasis on folk art.

A Very Special Place

Located 340 miles southeast of Mexico City, Oaxaca is the capital of Mexico's largest Indian state and a gateway city to the country's lush southern region. While it is also one of Mexico's poorest states economically, Oaxaca offers visitors one of the richest travel and shopping experiences in all of Mexico. Indeed, this is a place of great beauty, talent, and intrigue. It boasts a charming urban setting amid gorgeous mountain scenery, an exceptionally talented arts and crafts community, friendly people, and many fine restaurants, hotels, and shops. The center of the city, with its delightful colonial architecture, is very pedestrian-friendly with lovely plazas and vehicle-free zones. Walking the cobblestone streets of this inviting section of the city both day and night is one of the highlights of visiting Oaxaca. As you pass by expansive and entertaining plazas, elegant crumbling buildings, ornate churches, and intriguing stone archways and appealing balconies, you know you are in a very special place where the treasures and pleasures are likely to be exceptionally rewarding.

For travel-shoppers, Oaxaca may be the closest they get to a Mexican shopper's paradise. The city and nearby towns and villages offer a dazzling array of quality arts and crafts with special emphasis on local folk art and related products: woodcarvings, rugs, pottery, terracotta figurines, ceramics, paintings, sculptures, baskets, embroidered clothing, fajas (woven belts), rebozos (shawls), huipiles (brocaded blouses woven from rough cotton), and chocolate. The local population of 3 million reputedly includes nearly 400,000 artisans who produce a wealth of arts and crafts to supply shops throughout Mexico as well as abroad. Living in a poor area, many people work in folk art to support themselves and their families. The folk art tradition here is very strong. Oaxaca is where art, culture, and shopping form a very special relationship that makes for a great travel-shopping adventure. Our advice: Plan to spend at least three days here absorbing the area's many unique treasures and pleasures. This will certainly become one of the highlight destinations of your stay in Mexico. In the end, you may revisit Mexico the way many others return to this country: they bypass all other places and go straight to their favorite destination, Oaxaca.

Getting to Know You

Oaxaca can be easily reached from Mexico City by air or road. The direct flight from Mexico City to Oaxaca takes about one hour. The trip by road takes nearly five hours, if you go by way of the toll road. The winding old road can take from 9 to 12 hours to complete the trip.

Few areas in Mexico are so rich with arts, crafts, and history and offer such varied attractions for visitors as Oaxaca. The city, nearby towns and villages, and the pre-Hispanic sites of Monte Alban and Mitla draw thousands of visitors to this area each year. They primarily come here to explore the ancient ruins, visit the many churches and museums, enjoy the ambience, and shop the numerous stores, galleries, and artisan homes that house Oaxaca's many treasures.

Any visit to Oaxaca should focus on both the city and its outlying areas. Plan to spend at least two days exploring the city and another day or two in the towns, villages, and ancient sites. Having a car at your disposal – either a self-drive rental or a car and driver – makes good sense for exploring this intriguing area.

Useful Resources

Oaxaca offers several useful services to help visitors enjoy their stay. The Tourism Office is located just off the zócalo at Independencia 607. This is one of the most helpful such offices we encountered in Mexico. It offers maps, a booklet, and helpful personnel who can answer your questions. The Tourist Police, consisting of both men and women, constitute a relatively new service. The men provide security services, while the women (currently 10) provide information. They all speak English, although their proficiency varies. Nonetheless, they can be useful resources, especially around the zócalo, if you have any questions or need assistance with anything.

Given Oaxaca's rich arts and crafts tradition and its interesting history, you'll find numerous books about various aspects of Oaxaca in several bookstores in the city. Folk art lovers should look for these books:

Crafting Tradition: The Making and Marketing of Oaxacan Woodcarvings (Michael Chibnik)
Mexican Folk Art From Oaxacan Artist Families (Arden and Anya Rathstein)
Oaxacan Ceramics: Traditional Folk Art by Oaxacan Women (Lois Wasserspring)
Oaxacan Woodcarving: The Magic in the Trees (Shepard Barbash)

For art books on Oaxaca, visit the **Amate Bookstore** (Macadonio Alcala 307-2, Tel. 516-6960) and the **Tamayo Museum Shop** (Morelos 503). Your hotel and the Tourism Office should have a good map of the city and valley. You also can find a useful 280-page shopping book on Oaxaca which is available through a few local bookstores:

Shopping in Oaxaca (Judith Hancock Sandoval)

For a pictorial treatment of shopping in Oaxaca, look for the multilingual (English, Spanish, French, German) *Shopping in Oaxaca*.

As part of your pre-trip planning, you may want to visit these useful websites that focus on travel to Oaxaca:

- **Oaxaca**   http://oaxaca.gob.mx/sedetur
                        (Oaxaca Ministry of Tourism)
- **Visit Mexico**   www.visitmexico.com
                        (Mexican Government
                        Tourism Office)
- **Oaxaca Travel**   www.oaxaca-travel.com
- **Planeta Oaxaca**   www.planeta.com/oaxaca
- **Oaxaca Info**   www.oaxacainfo.com
- **Oaxaca Restaurants** www.oaxaca-restaurants.com
- **All About Oaxaca** www.allaboutoaxaca.com
- **OaxacaOaxaca**   www.oaxacaoaxaca.com
- **Oaxaca Chat**   www.oaxaca.com

Streets and Valleys of Oaxaca

Oaxaca offers great street theater for anyone interested in absorbing the unique character of this city. From exploring its major shopping streets to strolling through its festive zócalo and plazas both day and night, Oaxaca is a visual and auditory delight.

The zócalo at Avenida Hidalgo and Garcia Vigil is where much of the city's street entertainment and commerce takes place. Indian women hawk baskets, serapes, embroidered fabric, placemats, and other handmade goods to passing tourists; numerous balloon vendors disappear beneath the mass of colorful and odd-shaped inflatables which no one seems interested in buying; young entrepreneurs offer freelance shoeshines while their more established adult counterparts elevate their customers to high chairs and foot stools; at night marimba players, dance troupes, and fire eaters entertain large crowds of lo-

cals and tourists who seem to have nothing better to do than to observe what often is marginal entertainment. Add to this diverse scene many young lovers smooching on the wrought iron benches, flower vendors, unassertive beggars, students entertaining themselves, and groups of American, Canadian, English, Spanish, German, and French tourists enjoying the sidewalk cafes and restaurants, and you have a very festive mix of characters and activities to make for colorful street theater.

If you're driving a car, park it somewhere for most of your stay within the city. This is a very compact city that begs to be explored on foot. Most major points can be reached with a quick 5- to 15-minute walk. However, watch your head as you walk the city streets, since many window sills have metal grillwork that protrudes onto the sidewalks at eye-level. If you are tall and not alert to these potentially dangerous structures, you can easily knock yourself out or smash your face as you gingerly walk the city streets!

The major pedestrian-only street, **Macadonio Alcala**, is a good place to begin exploring the city. Start at the corner of Allende and Macadonio Alcala streets, just opposite the plaza with Santo Domingo Church at its center. Most of the city's major shops, galleries, restaurants, cafes, bars, museums, churches, and Internet cafes can be found along this and adjacent north-south streets – García Vigil and Cinco de Mayo – which stretch south to the zócalo. The intersecting east-west side streets of Allende,

Constitucion, Abrasolo, Murguia, Morelos, Independencia, and Hidalgo yield even more great shopping and sightseeing discoveries.

If you're planning to travel outside the city, be sure to get a map of the Oaxaca valley from your hotel front desk. You should plan to spend at least a day visiting several towns and villages that specialize in producing pottery, folk art, and textiles. Most of these places are within one hour driving distance of the city.

Shopping Oaxaca

Shopping in Oaxaca is concentrated in numerous shops and galleries that line the city's major streets as well as is found in a few lively markets. Unlike other large cities in Mexico, Oaxaca lacks

modern shopping centers and malls. In the city of Oaxaca, you go shopping in street shops or markets. If you have limited time, we recommend focusing on the shops that line three major streets: Macadonio Alcala, García Vigil, and Morelos.

Oaxaca is justly famous for its profusion of colorful handicrafts, textiles, folk art, and fine art which are produced throughout this state. The area is especially noted for its distinctive black and green-glazed pottery; woven woolen rugs using natural dyes in red and purple colors; and brightly painted woodcarvings (Alebrijes), which usually come in many imaginative animal figures brightly painted in red, yellow, purple, and green. Oaxaca literally produces a treasure-trove of fascinating arts and crafts which are represented in many shops throughout Mexico as well as in many other countries around the world. Many visitors quickly find they have a shipping problem in Oaxaca – they bought too much to hand-carry home. Indeed, the airport in Oaxaca reputedly boasts the highest excess baggage revenue of any airport in Mexico! Fortunately, many shops in Oaxaca will arrange shipping, and the local DHL office is easy to work with.

Several shops and galleries within the city represent the best of Oaxacan arts and crafts. For example, if you visit **La Mano Magica**, **Galería Indigo**, **Corazon del Pueblo**, or **ARIPO**, you'll quickly discover that the best arts and crafts have found their way into these key shops. Indeed, these four shops work hard at monopolizing the very best arts and crafts produced by family workshops in Oaxaca. While you may be tempted to travel to the production sources in nearby towns and villages where prices are reputed to be lower, the best quality arts and crafts will be found in a few city shops that specialize in representing Oaxaca's top artisans and artists. Visit the towns and villages for the cultural experience – meet working artisans and acquire some interesting products at the production sources – but don't be disappointed to discover the best quality arts and crafts are still found in the key city shops.

Oaxaca also is famous for its local markets (*tianguis*). If you enjoy the hustle and bustle of market shopping, including the accompanying photo opportunities, Oaxaca will not disappoint you. While most markets are open daily, Saturday is usually considered market day in Oaxaca. Drawing many Indian vendors from nearby towns and villages, the markets and adjacent streets become especially crowded and lively on Saturdays. The major markets include:

❏ **Abastos Market:** Open daily, but the crafts section is only open on Saturday. Located in the southwestern section of the city, next to the Periférico, this sprawling open-air market is Oaxaca's largest. It includes everything from baskets, rugs, and green-glazed and black pottery to fruits, vegetables, meats. flowers, bird cages, hammocks, toys, leather goods, clothes, and footwear. A great place to people watch.

❏ **Benito Juárez Market:** Open daily. Located two blocks southwest of the zócalo – encompassed by Las Cases, Aldama, Cabrera, and 20 de Noviembre streets – this is Oaxaca's original and most popular market. The place is jam-packed with stalls offering fresh produce, spices, household goods, textiles, clothes, and flowers. Most of the handicrafts are found in stalls that line the Las Casas and 20 de Noviembre Street section (western) of the market.

❏ **20 de Noviembre Market:** Open daily. Located across the street (Aldama) from the Benito Juárez Market, this market includes the usual assortment of arts, crafts, and foods.

❏ **Mercado de Artesañas:** Open daily, 9am to 8pm. Located four blocks southwest of the zócalo at the corner of Zaragoza and J.P. Garcia. Also known as the Handicrafts Market, this market is noted for its many handcrafted items, including leather goods, pottery, and textiles.

Many nearby towns host weekly markets which are held on different days of the week:

- Sunday   Tlacolula
- Tuesday   Ayoquezco
- Wednesday   Villa de Tela and Zimatlán
- Thursday   Zaashila
- Friday   Ocotlán

The markets in Tlacolula (most authentic market) and Ocotlán (town of the Aguilar sisters) are of special interest to many visitors who schedule their trips to these towns on the respective market days.

Shipping

Most major shops can arrange shipping by either air or ground. If you are buying from several shops, you may want to consolidate your purchases with a single shop. ARIPO (García Vigil 809, Tel. 514-0861), for example, will do such consolidation if you are making purchases through them, which is very easy to do given their huge inventory of folk art. Oaxaca also has a DHL office (Amado Nervo No. 104-D, Esq. Av. Heroes de Chapultepec, Tel. 515-7734) which is conveniently located north of the downtown area. You can take your purchases to this office to have them shipped by air to your destination. We found this office to be especially helpful in shipping light-weight bulky purchases such as art work. However, be sure to pack your treasures well before taking them to this office. It is not a packing office.

Best of the Best

As might be expected of Mexico's folk art center, many of Oaxaca's best shops specialize in folk art produced through the state of Oaxaca. It also has several fine art galleries and a few good jewelry shops. But shopping in the city disproportionately favors colorful folk art.

FOLK ART

❏ **La Mano Magica:** *Alcalá 203, Tel./Fax 516-4275. E-mail: lamanomagica@spersaoaxaca.com.mx.* Located between Morelos and Matamoros, this is Oaxaca's premier folk art gallery. If you want to know what real quality folk art is in comparison to market kitsch, be sure to visit this shop. Its many colorful rooms showcase the best of Oaxacan folk art. Indeed, the shop's manager, Mary Jane Gagnier de Mendoza, primarily works with the top artisans in the state. Most sell their best works directly to her. In fact, you'll quickly discover that this shop has monopolized quality folk art. You can spend a few days traveling to outlying villages and towns in search of similar art, but you won't find it since the artisans sell their best works here. Look for an excellent collection of painted woodcarvings (Alebrijes), masks, Day of the Dead figures, beaded art of the Huichol Indians, tapestries and rugs of Arnulfo Mendosa, ceramics, watercolors, prints, black pottery, and art books. Our recommendation: make this your first folk art stop in Oaxaca to get a good idea of the product range, quality, and pricing of local folk art. Many visitors to Oaxaca really don't

know what good quality folk art is until they see it and feel it in this shop. Chances are you will be back to make some important purchases at this fine shop.

❏ **Galería Indigo:** *Allende 104, Centro Histórico, Tel./Fax 514-3889. E-mail: info@indigo.org.mx. Website: www.indigo.org.mx.* This is one of our very favorite galleries in Mexico. This two-story art gallery showcases top quality arts and crafts of famous artisans from all over Mexico. Look for ceramics, pottery, paintings, Day of the Dead figures, baskets, and other interesting art displayed in several gallery rooms. The gallery even includes carvings from Bali, Indonesia and furniture from India. We're especially drawn to the terrific painted wire papiermâché animal figures by Saulo Moreno, ceramics from Capélo in Pueblo, fascinating metal sculptures of Hugo Tovar, and the unique beige and black pottery molded with tiger figures

of Alberto Bautista. A delightful gallery filled with wonderful folk art and fine art. Also operates Galería Indigo in Guanajuato and Galería Veryka in San Miguel Allende.

❏ **ARIPO (Artesaniase Industrias Populares de Oaxaca):** *García Vigil 809, Col. Centro, Tel. 514-0861. E-mail: aripod@oaxaca.gob.mx.*

Website: www.oaxaca.gob.mx/aripo. Located on top of the southern end of the old stone aqueduct, this somewhat hard-to-find (address numbers across the street are in the 700s rather than corresponding 800s) arts and crafts emporium offers a wide selection of products from all over Oaxaca. Operated by the state government, ARIPO includes several display rooms filled with good quality folk art carvings, tin mirrors and figures, black pottery, tableware, furniture, rugs, leather saddles, terracotta pots and figures, jewelry, knives, fabrics, and clothes. The black pottery here is some of the best we found anywhere. The terracotta pots tend to be huge and created in many unique designs. ARIPO publishes a full-color catalog (100 pesos) which includes everything available though their shop. They are experienced in packing and shipping – both air and ground. They will even consolidate your purchases from other shops. With a copy of their catalog in hand, you can easily order their arts and crafts once you return home, with the expectation that everything will be packed and shipped to your expectations. This is one of the best shops for viewing a good range of products available in Oaxaca. The displays suggest various home decorative uses of Oaxacan arts and crafts – a real plus for many visitors who are uncertain how to integrate such pieces into their homes. You may want to visit this shop early on in your visit to Oaxaca.

❑ **Corazon del Pueblo:** *Alcalá 307-9. Tel. 514-1808. Fax 516-7181. E-mail: corazonoax@prodigy.net.mx.* Located above Amate Bookstore, this small shop offers a good selection and range of Oaxacan folk art. Look for Huichol Indian beaded art, painted woodcarvings, masks, ceramic figures, copper pots, tin mirrors, painted boxes and gourds, green ceramic pottery, jewelry, and textiles.

❑ **Galería Arte Mexicano:** *Alcalá 407. Tel. 514-2815.* This very attractive small gallery, located in a small shopping center, includes several folk art works of major artisans, limited edition prints, jewelry, and gift items. Of particular interest are the playful contemporary metal sculptures of Hugo Tovar incorporating tricycles and other wheeled vehicles. If you're interested in Tovar's wonderful work, be sure to also survey similar pieces at **Galería Indigo**. A real quality gallery.

❑ **Artesanias "Chimalli":** *Garcia Vigil 513A, Tel. 514-2101.* If you're in the market for large variety of folk art, be sure to visit this expansive shop. Jam-packed with woodcarvings, black pottery, terracotta pots and figurines, tin mirrors, ceramic doves, and porcelain skeletons, this shop seems to have a little of everything. The shop also extends to a back courtyard that includes large terracotta pieces.

❏ **Casa de las Artesanias de Oaxaca:** *Matamoros 105 esquina Garcia Virgil, Tel. 516-5062. E-mail: artesaniasdeoaxaca@hotmail.com.* Representing nearly 80 cooperatives and family workshops throughout Oaxaca's seven regions, this pleasant complex of six shops surrounding a courtyard offers black pottery, terracotta figures, pottery, woodcarvings, Day of the Dead figures, rugs, clothes, hammocks, leather goods, jewelry, CDs, tapes, and videos.

❏ **Fonart:** *Crespo 114, Tel./Fax 516-5764.* Located at the intersection of Morales and Crespo, this small government shop offers a nice collection of arts and crafts from all over Mexico. Look for folk art, blue glassware, lacquer trays, painted furniture, copper pots, jewelry, shawls, textiles, and ceramic dinnerware. Similar to other Fonart government shops found elsewhere in Mexico, this one offers good selections, quality, and prices.

❏ **Mujeres Artesanas de las Regiones de Oaxaca, MARO (The Regional Association of Craftswomen of Oaxaca):** *5 de Mayo 204, Tel./Fax 546-0670.* This women's regional crafts cooperative consists of several small shops selling a wide range of arts and crafts: pottery (black, green, regular), masks, terracotta figurines, ceramics, textiles, embroidered clothes, woven handbags, footwear, paintings, jewelry, tin art, toys, large Day of the Dead figures, costumes, and rugs. Housed in a two-story building, the cooperative functions similarly to a handicraft emporium and includes product demonstrations. Members of the cooperative are involved in all phases of production, from acquiring raw materials to marketing and sales. Some of the best quality arts and crafts – especially costumes, rugs, and woodcarvings – are found on the second floor. Offers good quality, selections, and prices.

❏ **Filigrana:** *Morelos 406, Tel. 514-2471.* Located near Fonart, this relatively new and trendy shop is a combination art gallery, crafts shop, and café. Throughout two stories it displays an attractive collection of modern paintings, prints, furniture, glassware, ceramics, boxes, wrought iron, and candle holders. One of the more unusual and refreshing shops that is devoted to contemporary arts and crafts.

FINE ART GALLERIES

❏ **Arte de Oaxaca:** *Murguía, Tel. 514-1532. Fax 514-0910. E-mail: artedeoaxaca@spersaoaxaca.com.mx. Website: www.artedeoax aca.com.mx.* This is one of the Oaxaca's most exciting art galleries. Consisting of two floors, the building showcases the paintings and sculptures of famous Oaxacan artists such as

Rolando Royas, Aberlardo López, Alejandra Villegas, Cecilio Sánchez, Rodolfo Morales, and Hugo Federico. Very knowledgeable and helpful staff. Occasionally has special exhibits.

❑ **Beatriz Russek:** *Garcia Vigil 409-A, Tel. 514-8855. E-mail: berussek@hotmail.com*. This relatively new gallery includes a nice selection of paintings and ceramic sculptures. Showcases Mexican and international artists. Includes separate rooms offering clothes, jewelry, handbags, and pillow covers.

❑ **Galeria Angel Azul:** *Garcia Vigil 406, Tel./Fax 514-8476*. This combination restaurant and gallery includes a collection of large paintings in its courtyard and restaurant. Most are produced by Oaxacan artists. All art in the restaurant section is for sale when the restaurant is open.

ANTIQUES AND COLLECTIBLES

❑ **Monedas de Axaca y Antigüedades:** *Abasolo 107, Tel. 516-3935*. Located across the street from the Camino Real Hotel, this eclectic shop is filled with antiques, collectibles, and jewelry. The front rooms of this shop primarily offer jewelry and beads. Be sure to explore the several interior rooms, which yield a large collection of baskets, ceramics, wood horse heads, paintings, books, masks, folk art, and clothes.

JEWELRY

❑ **Oro de Monte Alban:** *Macadonio Alcalá 307, Int. 5. Tel. 516-1812; Fax 516-5370. Website: www.orodemontealban.com*. You can't miss this shop either on the street or in print. It seems to be everywhere – three shops within close proximity of each other along Macadonio Alcalá (307 and 403) and Constitucion, a display window at the Camino Real Hotel, and in the museum shop at Monte Alban. This jeweler offers pre-Columbian designs in 14k gold and gold plated silver. Many of the designs are copies of Zapotec designs from Monte Alban. Also includes silver jewelry.

BOOKSTORES

❑ **Amate:** *Macadonio Alcalá 307-2, Tel./Fax 516-5960. E-mail: corazon@spersaoaxaca.com.mx*. If you're looking for English language books on local history, culture, politics, and folk art, be sure to visit this well stocked bookstore. Includes a bargain book section. Upstairs is one of Oaxaca's best folk art shops, **Corazon del Pueblo**. If you can't figure out what's being displayed in the shop, just go downstairs and get a good book on folk art and you'll quickly be up to speed on

Oaxacan folk art! The bookstore also includes a bargain book section.

❑ **Proveedora Escolar:** *Independencia 1001, Tel. 516-0489. Fax 514-5655.* Located three blocks from the zócalo, the entrance to this two-story bookstore is actually two doors north of the intersection of Reforma and Independencia – on Reforma. Primarily offers Spanish language books and magazines, although it does have some English titles.

Towns and Villages

A visit to Oaxaca would not be complete without exploring a few nearby artisan towns and villages. With a basic map (check with your hotel or the Tourist Office), you can easily drive to these places on your own or hire a car and driver. The roads testify to the fact that this is a poor state – often in disrepair and punctuated with many potholes.

Many towns and villages specialize in a single product line – woodcarvings, green-glazed and black pottery, rugs, or painted terracotta folk art figures. Artisans produce their wares as usual – unhurried and centered around family – despite the many tourists who visit these places. While prices may be cheaper at these production sources, often they are not. Many artisans know the retail value of their work, especially in the case of rugs, and charge accordingly. In addition, the best quality arts and crafts tend to be sold directly to dealers, such as La Mano Magica in Oaxaca, with whom local artisans and craftspeople have special relationships.

Nonetheless, visiting these towns and villages to see the artisans produce various arts and crafts and to meet the craftspeople is one of the highlights of any visit to Oaxaca. Chances are you will discover a beautiful piece of folk art and buy directly from the artisan who signed the piece. The locals tend to be very friendly and welcome visitors who come to appreciate their work and shop. Be sure to take your camera and plenty of film since visits to these towns and villages afford numerous photo opportunities. Best of all, snap some photos of the artisans holding your new purchases – truly memorable photos that will make your shopping adventure even more meaningful in the years to come!

While Oaxaca includes hundreds of artisan towns and villages, the most popular places to visit near Oaxaca include:

WOODCARVINGS

❑ **San Martin Tilcajete:** This is one of three small woodcarving towns (the other two are **Arrazola** and **La Union Tejalapan**) located 23 kilometers south of Oaxaca, just off of Highway 175 (3/4 mile to the right). The locals here produce whimsical and colorful woodcarved animals (Alebrijes), skeleton figures, boxes, banana trees, and motorcycles. The home workshops are found throughout the town. When you visit the workshops, you can see the artisans at work carving figures and painting them with brushes and hyperdermic needles (for dots). One of the first workshops you'll come to when approaching the town is that of the **Sosa brothers** (**Artesanias de Madera "El Cactus,"** Corregidora No. 1, Tel. 571-5430) who produce woodcarvings and paintings. Look for the

"Sosa" sign and then turn right into the compound. If you go into town, you'll come to several nice shops along Avenida Oriente, including two adjacent family shops at No. 8: **Vicente Hernández Vasquez** (Tel. 571-5339) for large and creative designs (giraffes, lobsters, banana trees, rabbits, porcupines), and **Joaquín Hernández** (Tel. 1-951-57) for several large figures, including motorcyclists. **Familia Calvo** (Tel. 1-54-30) also includes many attractive carved giraffes, crosses, tigers, porcupines, and horses. One of the three Sosa brothers also has a shop in town: **Francisco Sosa Gutierrez** (Tel. 510-7022). Other noted families producing quality woodcarvings include Epifanio Fuentes and his son Zeny Fuentes, Ventura Fabián, Delfino Gutiérrez Melchor, Benito Ramirez Ojeda, Maria Jiménez, Rodrigo Melchor Ojeda, and Jacobo Ángeles Ojeda. You'll need to wander through the town and knock on doors to find many of these artisans.

❑ **Arrazola:** Somewhat difficult to find, this small town is located 10 kilometers southwest of Oaxaca, off the road to Zaachila and near Monte Albán. It includes nearly 100 artisan families who produce colorful Alebrijes in home workshops and shops that are primarily found along the main street and a few side streets. While you can wander along the streets to visit shops, you may want to hire the services of a local guide to take you to the best workshops. We especially recommend visiting master carver **Manuel Jimenez** who only sells from his home shop (Tel. 517-2385); **Artesanias de Madera**

"La Iguana" (Alvaro Obregon No. 15) for creative carvings by two young female artisans, Sara and Rocio; **Jimenez Hernández** (Alvaro Obregon #1) for a small but nice inventory of woodcarvings by a top artizan; **Lucina Lopez Carrillo** (Casade Artesanias, Tel. 510-5420) for a nice selection of woodcarvings from one of the town's most creative and exuberant artisans; and **Pepe Santiago** (Albaro Obregon No. 12, Tel. 517-1394) whose shop on the left initially greets you upon entering the town. Other

noted artisans in this town include Francisco Morales Ojeda, Gerardo Ramírez, Miguel Santiago Sorano, Antonio and Ramiro Aragón, Mario Castellanos, José Hernández, and Manuel Jiménez.

❑ **La Union Tejalapan:** This woodcarving village is located northwest of Oaxaca, off of Highway 190. It produces more primitive style woodcarvings and brightly colored carved picture frames. Some of the most famous carvers here include Aguilino García Reyes, Sergio Santos, Jaime Santiago Morales, and Máximo and Octaviano Santiago.

RUGS AND SERAPES

❑ **Teotitlan del Valle:** Located 27 kilometers east of Oaxaca via Highway 190, this 2,000 year-old Zapotec community is the oldest village in the Valley of Oaxaca. Famous for producing colorful rugs and wool serapes using natural dyes, nearly 300 Zapotec families are involved in the local weaving industry. Most of the shops are located along

Avenida Juárez. Many shops include demonstration areas where you can see artisans weaving rugs. Look for the artisan market – **Artesanías el Centro** (Hidalgo esq. 20 de Noviembre No. 23) – for a good selection of rugs, runners, clothes, and shawls. Other shops of note include: **Felipe Pablo Gutierrez Montano** (Avenida Juárez No. 101 – very large shop with a wide range of products); **El Jaguar** (Avenida Juárez No. 42 – includes four types of designs and copies of famous painters); and **Casa Hermilo Ruiz Gonzalez** (Avenida Juárez No. 61 – produces two different styles of rugs). Also look for such famous weavers as Arnulfo Mendoza (shops at Avenida Juárez No. 39 and Venustiano Carranza No. 2) and Jose Gutierrez.

CERAMICS

❑ **Ocotlan de Morelos:** Located 45 minutes south of Oaxaca along crumbling Highway 175, this is a popular market town that is also famous for its ceramics. It's also the town made famous by Nelson Rockefeller who bought painted terracotta folk art figures from Josefina  Aguilar – one of four Aguilar sisters (others include Concepción, Irene, and Guillermina) – and publicized them to the art world. The most famous sister, Josefina, produces folk art that is generally referred to as "Josefinas." Now taxis, tour buses, and car loads of tourists arrive here every day to purchase their folk art. Each sister has her own workshop and shop along the main highway. You can't miss their signage, which is found along both sides of the road just before you enter the town. Much of this art is an acquired taste. The inventory in their shops is often limited, and the nature of the art – terracotta figures of prostitutes, buxom ladies, mermaids, and animals – may not appeal to your folk art tastes. The nativity scenes at Guillermina Aguilar's shop are especially attractive. On Fridays this town holds one of Oaxaca's best weekend markets – just up the road from the Aguilars, near the center of town, beside the Convento de Santo Domingo (now a museum). The market includes wooden figures, cotton textiles, embroidery, pottery, cutlery, and baskets.

POTTERY

❑ **San Bartolo Coyotepec:** Located 13 kilometers south of Oaxaca (also a few miles south of the airport), along Highway 175, this town is famous for producing Oaxaca's unique black un-glazed polished pottery. You'll see shops along both sides of the main highway that cuts through the town. A few shops also give pottery-making demonstrations. While much of the black pottery found in several of Oaxaca's top shops is attractive, we have difficulty getting excited about the selections in this town. The designs and quality tend to be second-rate. Look for large lip pots (Zapotec style), mermaids, flutes, pitchers, bowls, elephants, lanterns, toys, napkin holders, picture frames, planters, beaded necklaces, animal whistles, owls, rabbits, and angel candle holders. Some shops include green-glazed pottery. The popular **Mercado de Artesanias**, located along the highway, includes 15 small shops offering black pottery in simple designs. Famous local potters with home studios in this town include Juan Galán, José López Aragón, Carlomagno Pedro, and Valente Nieto Real (son of well known Doña Rosa who made this art form famous).

❑ **Santa Maria Atzompa:** Located 10 kilometers west of Oaxaca at the foot of Monte Alban, this town is famous for producing green-glazed pottery, natural clay figures, painted glazed pots, and a variety of other glazed items – crosses, wall plaques, animals, boxes, fish, and suns and moons. As you approach the town, you'll see a well organized cluster of over 15 market stalls on your right – **Mercado de Artesanias "Sr. Del Coro"** – offering all types of green-glazed pottery and crosses. Formed in 1993 by 80 local families, this market will give you an excellent overview of local production as well as access to the studios of individual potters (need to ask). The small town includes several markets and small shops/factories making a full range of local pottery and figures. Look for the **Mercado de Artesanias Atzompa** (Libertad No. 303 – next to El Patio Restaurant) for a large selection of pottery which is displayed under the signs of individual artisans. **Artesanias de Doña Teodora Blanco** (Avenida Libertad No. 502, Tel. 512-7942), a small and dusty shop showcasing the works of Luis Blanco Garcia (son of famous Teodora Blanco, who produced large women's figurines) and his wife María Rojas Garcia, includes a good selection of natural clay pots and figures at excellent prices. Famous local potters who have their own workshops include Irma and Bertha Garcia Blanco, Luis Banco Garcia (Teodora Blanco's daughters), Yolanda Ruiz de Juárez and Concepción Ruiz de López (daughters of famous but deceased potter Adelina Maldonado), Dolores Porras, Angélica Vásquez Cruz, and Ernesto Vásquez Reyes and his wife Delfina Cruz Diaz.

Accommodations

Oaxaca offers a good range of accommodations for all types of budgets and travel styles. The very best places to stay include:

❏ **Camino Real Oaxaca:** *Calle 5 de Mayo 300, Oaxaca, Oax. 68000, Mexico, Tel. (52-951) 516-0611, Fax (52-951) 516-0732. Toll-free from the US & Canada 800-722-6466.* Tucked within the halls of the 16th century Ex-Convent of Santa Catalina, Camino Real Oaxaca evokes history while delivering 21st century comfort and amenities. The 91 guestrooms are each different from one another and include 30 Camino Real Club rooms and 6 junior suites. At the same price level, some guestrooms are larger than others, so you may wish to ask to see more than one – especially if the room you are first taken to seems cramped. Oaxaca's distinctive cuisine can be sampled at *El Refectorio* which offers such traditional favorites as a chocolate-based 'mole' sauce as well as a variety of international dishes. On weekends, the hotel chapel comes alive with a traditional 'Guelaguetza', a colorful spectacle of folk dancing, unique handicrafts, and a buffet. *Bugambilias Bar* provides a courtyard oasis for cocktails before dinner, while *Las Novicias* beckons with drinks by candlelight on a pool-side terrace. The hotel garden is frequently used for civil ceremony weddings and the chapel for the reception. For an unusual venue for special exhibits and meetings, Camino Real Oaxaca can accommodate up to 350 people for banquets and 500 for meetings where only chairs are needed.

❏ **Casa Oaxaca:** *Calle Garcia Vigil 407, C.P. 68000, Oaxaca, Oax., Mexico, Tel. (52-951) 516-9923, Fax (52-951) 516-4412. E-mail: casaoax@prodigy.net.mx. Website: www.haciendaloslaureles.com.mx.* Casa Oaxaca is located in the center of Oaxaca, close to the zócalo, and offers guests the opportunity to experience a genuine 18th century colonial house. Completely remodeled to provide the comfort expected by 21st century guests, Casa Oaxaca has received distinction as an Art Hotel for its interior design. With only seven guestrooms, it provides a peaceful ambience and the staff is always ready to meet guests' needs. Large windows with typical wooden shutters set in whitewashed walls overlook a peaceful patio and an inviting pool. Each guestroom is individually furnished and is different from the others. In cooler weather, guests may wish to sit in front of the fireplace. Whether you stay at Casa Oaxaca or elsewhere, make reservations for dinner. Casa Oaxaca boasts one of the best restaurants in town and serves authentic Oaxacan dishes. Continental breakfast is included for guests. Pool; Golf Course Nearby; Business Center.

Restaurants

Oaxaca boasts many excellent restaurants and sidewalk cafes with lots of local specialties served in settings with a great deal of colonial ambience. It's especially noted for its local 'mole' sauces, Oaxacan chocolate, regional spices, and its week-long annual "Food of the Gods Festival," which takes place in early October. In many respects, food in Oaxaca is just another art form awaiting visitors who constantly discover new treasures and pleasures in this place! For useful online food and restaurant information, including local cuisine, cooking classes, and food tours, visit www.oaxaca-restaurants.com.

Most of the city's top restaurants are located in the central city and near the main plaza. Some of the city's best restaurants include:

❑ **Casa Oaxaca:** *Garcia Vigil 407, Tel. 514-4173 or Fax 516-4412. E-mail: casaoax@prodigy.net.mx. Open 7pm to 11pm.* This wonderful restaurant ended up being one of our finest dining experiences in all of Mexico. Part of the Casa Oaxaca boutique hotel, the kitchen here is under the command of talented chef Alejandro A. Ruiz Olmedo Gerente, who trained in both Italy and Germany and is noted for producing outstanding Mexican nouvelle cuisine. Reservations are essential. Entry to the restaurant is very discreet – ring the doorbell to the hotel. This is a small restaurant with both indoor and outdoor (courtyard) seating areas surrounded by attractive tiles, tapestries, and paintings. The fish dishes are excellent, as are the mole, chiles es nogoda, baked duck, and lasagna. Offers excellent service.

❑ **El Naranjo:** *Valerio Trujano 203, Tel. 514-1878. Website: www.elnaranjo.com.mx.* Located near the main square, this lovely colonial restaurant serves contemporary Oaxacan cuisine. Try the various mole sauces for which Oaxaca is famous, especially with chicken and enchiladas. Each day the restaurant features one of seven moles. The chiles rellenos also are excellent.

❑ **El Sol y La Luna:** *Reforma 502, Tel. 514-8069.* This classy restaurant offers a romantic setting in a colonial-style house. Includes lively Latin American music accompanying its international cuisine.

❑ **El Refectorio:** *Camino Real Hotel, Cinco de Mayo 300, Tel. 516-0611.* This attractive colonial-style hotel restaurant with its massive wall of embedded jar bottoms is famous for its huge buffets, especially on Saturday night accompanied by mariachi music, and for Sunday brunch. Also excellent for breakfast.

❑ **Catedral:** *Calle Garcia Vigil 105, Tel. 516-3285.* Located on the corner of Morelos, this lovely colonial-style restaurant is noted for its Mexican and international cuisine, popular Sunday buffet (2pm to 7pm), and live nightly music. Dancing permitted in the bar on Friday and Saturday nights. Dine in the cosy courtyard. Specialties include chicken in squash blossom sauce, mushroom soup with epazote, walnut pie, and coffee.

❑ **El Asador Vasco:** *Portal de Flores 11, Tel. 514-4755. Open 1pm to midnight.* Located on the west side of the main square, this second-floor restaurant is noted for its excellent location (reserve a table with a view of the square) and fine Basque and Mexican dishes. Try the many mole dishes, chiles rellenos, carne asada, tortilla soup, and snapper.

❑ **La Olla:** *Calle Reforma 402, Tel. 516-6668. Closed Sunday.* This attractive combination restaurant and art gallery offers two floors of dining. Noted for its salads and local dishes, especially mole, coloradito, and tamales Oaxaqueños.

❑ **Los Pacos:** *121 Abasolo. Tel. 516-1704.* Set around an open air patio, this cheery restaurant is noted for its moles, service, and ambience.

❑ **Coffee Beans:** *Cinco de Mayo 400-C.* A very popular coffee house serving Oaxacan Pluma Hidalgo coffee along with cakes and quiches.

Enjoying Your Stay

There's much to see and do in Oaxaca. Despite being one of the poorest states in Mexico, Oaxaca is perhaps the richest place to experience a kaleidoscope of travel attractions. In fact, many visitors to Mexico spend most of their time in Oaxaca. From art, music, culture, and food to ancient temples, museums, churches, architecture, and shopping, seductive Oaxaca seems to have it all.

OAXACA CITY

❑ **Zócalo (Jardín Juárez):** Located at the intersection of pedestrian-only Avenida Hidalgo and Macedonia Alcalá, this is one of Mexico's most interesting and lively plazas. Surrounded by sidewalk cafes, restaurants, and restored colonial buildings, and flanked by the Palacio de Gobierno (Palace of the Governor) on the south and the Catedral de Oaxaca on the north, the zócalo is the place of street vendors, musicians, tourists, diners, and lovers. It especially comes alive at night with colorful mariachi and marimba bands and other street performers. Spend at least one evening exploring the plaza.

Our recommendation: reserve a table overlooking the square at the El Asador Vasco restaurant (Tel. 514-4755) to watch all the interesting street activity below.

❏ **Iglesia y Ex-Convento de Santo Domingo (Santo Domingo Church and Ex-Convent):** Located two blocks north of the Camino Real Hotel on Macedonio Alcala (at Gurrión), this impressive baroque church was initially built in the 1500s by the Dominicans and recently restored (1998). The church (open during daylight hours, except 1-4pm) is filled with interesting art works. The adjoining Ex-Convent of Santo Domingo houses the Regional Museum of Anthropology and History (open Tuesday through Sunday, 10am to 8pm) which is especially noted for its wonderful collection of gold artifacts from Monte Alban. Includes an attractive outdoor courtyard.

❏ **Museo de Arte Contemporaneo de Oaxaca (MACO):** *Alcala 202, Tel. 514-2818. Open Wednesday through Monday, 10:30am to 8pm.* Located in the elegant colonial mansion Casa de Cortés, this popular contemporary art museum includes permanent displays of such famous artists as Rufino Tamayo, Francisco Morales, Francisco Toledo, and Rodolfo Nieto. Includes temporary exhibits and special events as well as a library and courtyard café.

❏ **Rufino Tamayo Museum:** *Morelos 503, Tel. 516-4750. Open Wednesday to Saturday from 10am to 2pm and from 4pm to 7pm; Sunday from 10am to 3pm.* If you are interested in pre-Columbian art – from stone carvings to terracotta pottery and figures – don't miss this museum. It's one of the best such museums in Mexico. Housed in an attractive old house with a courtyard, everything here is nicely displayed. A nice size museum – not too big, not too small. Includes a small bookshop at the ticketing desk.

BEYOND THE CITY

❏ **Monte Alban:** Located only eight kilometers from Oaxaca on a plateau 1,200 feet about the city, it takes about 30 minutes to reach the summit via a winding road. This is the ancient capital of the Zapotecs which functioned for nearly 1,200 years – from 500 B.C. to 750 A.D. The impressive low-rise archaeological ruins consist of an expansive esplanade of stone pyramids, temples, patios, palaces, a ball court, and more than 150 tombs. While visitors are free to climb the stone structures, strange signs prohibit the use of tripods and flashes when taking pictures outdoors! Includes a very informative visitor center explaining the origins and history of the area. On a clear day the site offers excellent views of the valley below, including the city of Oaxaca.

❑ **Mitla:** Located 44 kilometers southeast of Oaxaca and near the town of San Pablo Villa de Mitla, this famous Zapotec and Mixtec archaeological site dates from 200 A.D. It's especially interesting for its geometric stone designs. The name Mitla means "Place of the Dead." The ruins include patios, columns, palaces, tombs, and a church (Church Group). Mitla town includes a very informative museum, the Frissell Museum.

❑ **Santa Maria del Tule:** Located 14 kilometers east of Oaxaca on Highway 190 East, this site is famous for the sabina or ahuehuete cypress (Tule) tree. Known as the world's largest tree – 40 meters tall, 47 meters in diameter, and 509 tons – it is reputed to be nearly 2,000 years old. The town also includes an interesting 17th century church and a crafts market.

Indexes

Great Destinations

ACAPULCO

GUANAJUATO

IXTAPA & ZIHUATANEJO

MEXICO CITY

MORELIA

PUEBLA

PUERTO VALLARTA

QUERÉTARO

TAXCO

The Authors

WINSTON CHURCHILL PUT it best – *"My needs are very simple – I simply want the best of everything."* Indeed, his attitude on life is well and alive among many of today's travelers. With limited time, careful budgeting, and a sense of adventure, many people seek both quality and value as they search for the best of the best.

Ron and Caryl Krannich, Ph.Ds, discovered this fact of travel life over 20 years ago when they were living and working in Thailand as consultants with the Office of the Prime Minister. Former university professors and specialists on Southeast Asia, they discovered what they really loved to do – shop for quality art, antiques, and home decorative items – was not well represented in most travel guides, which primarily focused on sightseeing, hotels, and restaurants. While some guidebooks included a small section on shopping, they only listed types of products and names and addresses of a few shops, many of questionable quality. And budget guides simply avoided quality shopping altogether, as if shopping was a travel sin!

The Krannichs knew there was much more to travel than what was represented in travel guides. Avid collectors of Asian,

African, South Pacific, Middle Eastern, and Latin American arts, antiques, and home decorative items, they learned long ago that one of the best ways to experience another culture and meet its talented artists and craftspeople was by shopping for local products. Not only did they learn a great deal about the culture and society, they also acquired some wonderful products, met many interesting and talented individuals, and helped support the continuing development of local arts and crafts.

But they quickly learned shopping in many countries was very different from shopping in North America and Europe. In the West, merchants nicely display items, identify prices, and periodically run sales. At the same time, shoppers in the West can easily do comparative shopping, watch for sales, and trust quality and delivery; they even have consumer protection! Americans and Europeans in other parts of the world face a shopping culture based on different principles. Like a fish out of water, they make many mistakes: don't know how to bargain, avoid purchasing large items because they don't understand shipping, and are frequent victims of scams and rip-offs, especially in the case of gems and jewelry. To shop a country right, travelers need to know how to find quality products, bargain for the best prices, avoid scams, and ship their purchases with ease. What they most need is a combination travel and how-to book that focuses on the best of the best.

In 1987 the Krannichs inaugurated their first shopping guide to Asia – *Shopping in Exotic Places* – a guide to quality shopping in Hong Kong, South Korea, Thailand, Indonesia, and Singapore. Receiving rave reviews from leading travel publications and professionals, the book quickly found an enthusiastic audience amongst other avid travel-shoppers. It broke new ground as a combination travel and how-to book. No longer would shopping be confined to just naming products and identifying names and addresses of shops. It also included advice on how to pack for a shopping trip (take two suitcases, one filled with bubble-wrap), comparative shopping, bargaining skills, and shopping rules. Shopping was serious stuff requiring serious treatment of the subject by individuals who understood what they were doing. The Krannichs subsequently expanded their work to include a series of travel-shopping guides on Hong Kong, Thailand, Indonesia, Singapore and Malaysia, Australia and Papua New Guinea, the South Pacific, and the Caribbean.

Beginning in 1996, the series took on a new look as well as an expanded focus. Known as the **Impact Guides** and appropriately titled *The Treasures and Pleasures of . . . Best of the Best*, new editions covered Hong Kong, Thailand, Indonesia, Singapore, Malaysia, Paris and the French Riviera, and the Caribbean. In 1997 and 1999 new volumes appeared on Italy, Hong Kong, and China. New volumes for 2000-2004 included India, Australia, Thailand, Hong Kong, Singapore, Bali, Egypt, Brazil (Rio and São Paulo), Vietnam, Cambodia, Turkey, Southern Africa, Morocco, Tunisia, and the United States (Santa Fe, Taos, and Albuquerque).

The Impact Guides now serve as the major content for a travel website appropriately called iShopAroundTheWorld:

www.ishoparoundtheworld.com

While the primary focus remains shopping for quality products, the books and website also include useful information on the best hotels, restaurants, and sightseeing. As the authors note, *"Our users are discerning travelers who seek the best of the best. They are looking for a very special travel experience which is not well represented in other travel guides."*

The Krannichs' passion for traveling and shopping is reflected in their home, which is uniquely designed around their Asian, South Pacific, Middle East, African, and Latin American art collections and which has been featured on CNN and in the New York Times. *"We're fortunate in being able to create a living environment which pulls together so many wonderful travel memories and quality products,"* say the Krannichs. *"We learned long ago to seek out quality products and buy the best we could afford at the time. Quality lasts and is appreciated for years to come. Many of our readers share our passion for quality shopping abroad."* Their books also are popular with designers, antique dealers, and importers who use them to source products and suppliers.

While the Impact Guides keep the Krannichs busy traveling to exotic places, their travel series is an avocation rather than a vocation. The Krannichs also are noted authors of more than 40 career books (see page xiv), some of which deal with how to find international and travel jobs. The Krannichs also operate one of the world's largest career resource centers. Their works are available in most bookstores or through the publisher's online bookstore: www.impactpublications.com.

If you have any questions or comments for the authors, please direct them to:

Ron and Caryl Krannich
IMPACT PUBLICATIONS
9104 Manassas Drive, Suite N
Manassas Park, VA 20111-5211 USA
Fax 703-335-9486
E-mail: krannich@impactpublications.com

Feedback and Recommendations

WE WELCOME FEEDBACK and recommendations from our readers and users. If you have encountered a particular shop or travel experience, either good or bad, that you feel should be included in future editions of this book or on www.ishoparoundtheworld. com, please send your comments by e-mail, fax, or mail to:

Ron and Caryl Krannich
IMPACT PUBLICATIONS
9104 Manassas Drive, Suite N
Manassas Park, VA 20111-5211 USA
Fax 703-335-9486
E-mail: krannich@impactpublications.com

More Treasures and Pleasures

T HE FOLLOWING TRAVEL guides can be ordered directly from the publisher. Complete this form (or list the titles), include your name and address, enclose payment, and send your order to:

IMPACT PUBLICATIONS
9104 Manassas Drive, Suite N
Manassas Park, VA 20111-5211 (USA)
Tel. 1-800-361-1055 (orders only)
703-361-7300 (information) Fax 703-335-9486
E-mail: info@impactpublications.com
Online bookstore: www.impactpublications.com

All prices are in U.S. dollars. Orders from individuals should be prepaid by check, moneyorder, or credit card (Visa, MasterCard, American Express, and Discover). We accept credit card orders by telephone, fax, e-mail, and online. If your order must be shipped outside the United States, please include an additional US$2.00 per title for surface mail or the appropriate air mail rate for books weighing 24 ounces each. Orders usually ship within 48 hours. For more information on the authors, travel resources, and international shopping, visit www.impactpublications.com and www.ishoparoundtheworld.com.

Qty.	TITLES	Price	TOTAL
_____	Air Traveler's Survival Guide	$14.95	_____
_____	Stone Gods, Wooden Elephants (novel)	$14.95	_____
_____	The Plane Truth: Shift Happens at 35,000 Feet	$14.95	_____
_____	The Traveling Woman	$14.95	_____
_____	Travel Planning on the Internet	$19.95	_____
_____	Treasures and Pleasures of Australia	$17.95	_____
_____	Treasures and Pleasures...Caribbean	$16.95	_____
_____	Treasures and Pleasures of China	$14.95	_____
_____	Treasures and Pleasures of Egypt	$16.95	_____
_____	Treasures and Pleasures of Hong Kong	$16.95	_____
_____	Treasures and Pleasures of India	$16.95	_____

_____	Treasures and Pleasures of Indonesia	$14.95	_____
_____	Treasures and Pleasures of Italy	$14.95	_____
_____	Treasures and Pleasures of Mexico	$19.95	_____
_____	Treasures...Morocco and Tunisia	$18.95	_____
_____	Treasures and Pleasures of Paris and the French Riviera	$14.95	_____
_____	Treasures and Pleasures of Rio and São Paulo	$13.95	_____
_____	Treasures and Pleasures of Santa Fe, Taos, and Albuquerque	$18.95	_____
_____	Treasures and Pleasures of Singapore and Bali	$16.95	_____
_____	Treasures and Pleasures of Southern Africa	$18.95	_____
_____	Treasures and Pleasures of Thailand and Myanmar	$19.95	_____
_____	Treasures and Pleasures of Turkey	$16.95	_____
_____	Treasures and Pleasures of Vietnam and Cambodia	$16.95	_____
_____	When Tigers Fly (novel)	$14.95	_____

SUBTOTAL ———— $ _____

❑ Virginia residents add 4.5% sales tax $ _____

❑ Shipping/handling ($5.00 for the first title and $2.00 for each additional book $ _____

❑ Additional amount if shipping outside U.S. $ _____

TOTAL ENCLOSED— $ _____

SHIP TO:

Name_____

Address_____

_____

_____

Phone Number: _____

PAYMENT METHOD:

■ I enclose check/moneyorder for $ _____
made payable to IMPACT PUBLICATIONS.

■ Please charge $_____ to my credit card:

❑ Visa   ❑ MasterCard   ❑ American Express   ❑ Discover

Card # _____ Expiration date:_____/_____

Signature _____

Keep in Touch . . .
On the Web!

www.impactpublications.com
www.ishoparoundtheworld.com
www.travel-smarter.com
www.contentfortravel.com
www.winningthejob.com
www.veteransworld.com
www.contentforcareers.com

Discover the Best
Online Travel Deals!

WWW.TRAVEL-SMARTER.COM

- **Hotels**
- **Airlines**
- **Car Rentals**
- **Cruises**
- **Vacation packages**
- **Golf holidays**
- **Travel insurance**
- **Last minute travel deals**

For the very best deals – up to 70% discounts – click onto **HOT RATES** and **HOT DEALS**. This website also is rich with travel services, content, and tools, including:

- e-cards
- city guides
- currency converter
- flight tracker
- and much more

The same travel deals can by accessed through your one-stop travel-shopping website: